Photograph: PHOTO4

RALLYCOURSE™

THE OFFICIAL YEARBOOK OF THE WORLD RALLY CHAMPIONSHIP

CONTENTS

RALLYCOURSE 2008-2009

is published by:
Crash Media Group Ltd
Number One
The Innovation Centre
Silverstone Circuit
Silverstone
Northants NN12 8GX
Telephone: +44 (0)870 3505044
Fax: +44 (0)870 3505088
Email: info@crash.net
Website: www.crashmediagroup.com

Printed by
Butler Tanner and Dennis Ltd,
Frome, England

ISBN: 978-1905334-33-9

DISTRIBUTORS

Gardners Books
1 Whittle Drive, Eastbourne,
East Sussex BN23 6QH
Telephone: +44 (0)1323 521555
E-mail: sales@gardners.com

Menoshire Ltd
Unit 13
21 Wadsworth Road
Perivale
Middlesex UB6 7LQ
Telephone: +44 (0)20 8566 7344
Fax: +44 (0)20 8991 2439

NORTH AMERICA
Motorbooks International
PO Box 1
729 Prospect Avenue
Osceola
Wisconsin 54020, USA
Telephone: 1 715 294 3345
Fax: 1 715 294 4448

Dust Jacket, main: World Rally
Champion Sébastien Loeb.

Inset (left to right): Production
champion Andreas Aigner, WRC
runner-up Mikko Hirvonen and
Junior title winner Sébastien Ogier.
Photographs: PHOTO4

ACKNOWLEDGMENTS

Rallycourse simply wouldn't be the read it is without stalwart sub-editor Gillian Bell. Nothing gets past GB. Once again, I thank you and salute your exceptional knowledge of the sport and the English language. And once those words have been knocked into shape, they're passed on to Rosanne Marriott who transformed 192 blank pages into 192 works of art. Beyond those two, the book would not have been possible without the unstinting help of the following wordsmiths: Anthony Peacock, Richard Rodgers, John Davenport, Marcus Grönholm, Rob Wilkins and Russell Atkins. Accompanying that fine prose, Rallycourse once again offers the finest collection of photographs from the finest sport in the world, courtesy of PHOTO4, Julian Gonzalez/PHOTO4, Race&motion, SWRT.com, Citroën Communication, Jacob Ebrey, Rally-stardriver.eu, CMWi and Joe Bridge.

And last, but certainly not least, thanks (again) to my wife Sandra and children Georgia-Daisy and Oliver who have endured the highs and lows of a tricky season and an oft-grumpy husband and father. Without your love, support and common sense, none of this would be possible.

Publisher
BRYN WILLIAMS

Editor
DAVID EVANS

Sub-Editor
GILLIAN BELL

Art Editor
ROSANNE MARRIOTT

Results and Statistics
ROB WILKINS
OLLIE BARSTOW

Advertising Sales
SIMON SANDERSON

Chief Photographers
PHOTO4

Office Manager
WENDY SALISBURY

Licensing Manager -
International Sportsworld
Communicators
HELEN SHEPHERD

Illustrations
ADRIAN DEAN
f1artwork@blueyonder.co.uk

www.rallycourse.com

WRC in the sunshine
Cyprus Rally
13th-15th March 2009

2009 CYPRUS RALLY

www.cyprusrally.com.cy

FOREWORD BY SÉBASTIEN LOEB

HELLO AND welcome to another year of Rallycourse.

Sorry if you were hoping to see somebody else's picture on this page, but writing these words is part of being the World Rally Champion!

Seriously, 2008 was a tough year. Everybody told me: "Marcus [Grönholm] is gone, you will win easily..." I never thought this, and it wasn't the case at all. Okay, I won 11 rallies, but look past those wins. Look at the stage times. Look at the times in Finland; it was incredibly close. You know, it was a really big fight last season. I had to work hard for this. But that hard work makes the success for me, Daniel [Elena, co-driver] and the whole Citroën team even more sweet. I was really proud of the way we won the manufacturers' title with Dani [Sordo] and Marc [Martí], who have both done a great job this year.

There are two records in the sport that I'm interested in: the number of wins and the number of titles. Now I have both those records, which is nice. But it's not fair to compare this with other drivers. This is a different generation now. How can I say I would have done the same in the 1990s or even the '80s? I can't. All I can do is drive my rally car, and that's what I'll be doing in the C4 WRC again in 2009. I have five titles, what more can I do but aim for six?

I still have a fantastic feeling from driving this car on the stages of the world championship. And I look forward to doing the same again this year. In the meantime, I'm going to sit down and read Rallycourse. Maybe it's good for you to do the same. See you soon.

Sébastien

From the editor

THERE ARE those who thought Sébastien Loeb had faced down every challenge the World Rally Championship had to offer in his five seasons as a factory driver. I must admit, I was beginning to see their point. Until, that was, the Frenchman arrived in at the Royal Welsh Showground in Builth Wells late on the morning of December 5, 2008. He stepped from his Citroën C4 WRC and slid into the front seat of a warm Citroën van, where a warmer plate of beef bourguignon was waiting for him.

Sometime later, Loeb emerged from the van for an espresso and, maybe, a chat.

Prior to the start of the recce for this year's Rally Great Britain, Loeb and mid-Wales had been unacquainted. The Frenchman, with no disrespect to the inhabitants of that part of the country, would have probably preferred it to remain that way.

"I don't like," was Loeb's opening gambit. No questions were needed. First on the road and used to staying there, Loeb was currently holding a slightly less impressive fifth place and hating the icy conditions that had gripped this part of the world.

Espresso done, the explanation continued. "You go, you go, you go, no problem. Good grip, good grip, good grip. Okay. Then the corner; you touch the brakes, and wham! You are facing the other way. It's terrible. I don't like."

A handful of hours on a bitingly cold Friday morning in the middle of Wales had, for me, confirmed once again that the World Rally Championship truly is the best sport in the world. Here we were, barely able to stand at the side of the road, and there they were taking top gear and crossing their fingers in the hope that they might be able to find some kind of resistance between mother earth and Pirelli tyre.

Records and Rallycourse will reflect that Loeb overcame his issues with the Welsh weather to go on and crack another 'classic' rally to complete his set.

Having won Rally Finland earlier in the season, Loeb made no bones about his desire to add GB to his CV. That success in Cardiff would make him the first man to win 11 rallies in a season mattered not a jot to him. He'd collected his record-breaking fifth world title in Japan a month earlier. The number 11 held little attraction.

"I have the record with 10 rallies," he said prior to the start of the 2008 season finale. "If I get 11, it's nice, but it's my record – so I don't worry about breaking it. But I do want to win the rally..."

And win it he did. Every twist and turn of Loeb's season – from the highs of topping the Jyväskylä podium to the lows of his Swedish roll – are covered in detail in Rallycourse's comprehensive and colourful reports section. Anthony Peacock then takes time out from entertaining readers of The Guardian to turn his attention to Loeb for an intriguing piece later in the book.

Loeb hasn't celebrated alone this season. Alongside him for the year-long trip around the globe was Daniel Elena, the man who has stood firmly in the path of any co-driver with world title aspirations since 2003. The relationship between Loeb and Elena is pivotal to their success, as is their ability to communicate their needs and desires from the Citroën team and its C4 WRC. At the end of 2007, questions were asked about how Loeb would cope with the retirement of then-team principal Guy Fréquelin. For many, Fréquelin was Citroën in the WRC. The man who finished runner-up in the 1981 World Rally Championship had masterminded the Paris-based team's attack to ensure they would go one better than he'd managed with Talbot. Under his guidance, Loeb went four better and Citroën collected three manufacturers' titles.

In Fréquelin's successor Olivier Quesnel, Citroën had a totally different animal. Just as passionate about the sport from a competitive perspective, Quesnel

Race&motion

After two years of glory, Ford's hopes of a hat-trick of manufacturers' crowns were dashed last season. With a brace of youthful Finns installed in its factory Focus RS WRCs, there was never going to be a dull moment on the Ford side of the service park. Mikko Hirvonen stepped up to the plate in fine fashion to lead the team and score points on every round of the season (see, it's not just Loeb who can break records), while Jari-Matti Latvala continued on his WRC learning curve at warp factor 10.

The speed of both Ford men was breathtaking, but what was equally impressive was the astute tactical approach the team took to bag big points. The Turkey one-two result was masterminded from the service park control centre and played out to perfection by two world champions in the making. While it won't make the loss of the title any easier, Ford's future looks to be safe in the hands of these two Scandinavians.

Race&motion

Motorsport News rallies editor Richard Rodgers reveals what makes Latvala tick in a compelling read later in Rallycourse. Talking of success stories, Russell Atkins charts Pirelli's year as the first ever control tyre supplier to the WRC. The philosophy of a single-make tyre supplier may not be to everybody's liking, but the service park was universal in its praise for the way in which Pirelli has provided a high-performance product on the stages, as well as the means to unearth the sport's next superstar through its driver development programme.

Subaru and Suzuki's decision to suspend their respective WRC programmes came as a shock to the sport, particularly given the long heritage of the former. The global financial downturn continues to claim victims on a daily basis and the loss of the Impreza and SX4 WRC from the stages next season is proof that success is a vital ingredient for a continued programme at the highest level.

That brace of decisions, taken last December, has done much to focus the WRC's attentions on delivering value. A renewed determination to cut costs by the teams coupled with strong decision-making from the sport's governing body, the FIA, can only help to strengthen the World Rally Championship in the coming years. The way ahead is charted on page 56.

Integral to that vision for the future is International Sportsworld Communicators, the sport's commercial rights holder. It is through an agreement between the Crash Media Group and ISC that Rallycourse can now call itself the official publication of the World Rally Championship. It's a fitting appellation for a book that offers unrivalled coverage of the sport's highest level.

Loeb's record-breaking season has been a joy to watch and write about. We hope that you in turn enjoy the fruits of our labours. Happy reading.

David Evans
Teddington

Above: As well as serving as the championship's official tyre supplier, Pirelli's investment will fund five young talents to contest six events in 2009 as part of its Star Driver scheme.

Top: Changes to the regulations enabled teams to employ road position tactics, which Ford used to gain a one-two finish in Turkey.

Top right: The Junior World Rally Championship unearthed another young ace in Frenchman Sébastien Ogier.
Photographs: PHOTO4 unless specified

attacked the commercial side too. Months into the job of team principal, he locked down funding from Red Bull and then went on to orchestrate success in three of the four FIA WRC titles on offer. Not content with the drivers' and manufacturers' silverware, Quesnel oversaw a successful Junior World Rally Championship campaign to boot. Not a bad first season then.

Venturing out of the French corner there was, err, another Frenchman called Sébastien. Sébastien Ogier (or petite Seb as he soon became known) will have as equally fond memories of 2008 as Loeb. Ogier clinched the JWRC title at his first attempt – and then had the temerity to lead a round of the WRC on his first ever drive in a World Rally Car in Wales. Not even Loeb managed that. Ogier answers Rob Wilkins' questions inside.

Petter Solberg is one of the most established names in the WRC and his potential loss from the series will be keenly felt by fans around the world.
Photograph: Race&motion

Match m

There are few sterner tests for man and machine than a WRC event, but it's finding what makes the perfect match that separates the men from the boys

The World Rally Championship is one of the harshest motorsport environments in the world. Where else are drivers and machinery pitted against the elements on ever-changing road conditions for three days straight?

Snow, ice, gravel, asphalt and in the case of Wales Rally GB, mud. Lots of it. All WRC events have their own unique challenges, but add plenty of rain, fog and wind into the mix and the season finale is arguably one of the toughest.

BP Ford Abu Dhabi Team driver Mikko Hirvonen explains: "The uncertain weather is the biggest concern. Some stages will be held entirely in the dark and if it rains or is foggy then it will be extremely tricky. A driver has to expect everything."

It's not just the weather either. The pace of modern WRC cars means the pressure is relentless. Reaching speeds of up to 190km/h there is no margin for error. Every corner must be inch perfect and all aspects of the car bullet proof. Ford's technical director Christian Loriaux: "There's such a long chain of people working on the car that if one thing in the chain goes wrong then it can take you months to recover."

Mikko and team-mate Jari-Matti Latvala must have a car they can count on and the Castrol-backed BP Ford Abu Dhabi Team works tirelessly to ensure nothing is left to chance. That means driver, chassis, engine, lubricant and tyres must all work as one and with 100 percent reliability.

Castrol and the BP Ford Abu Dhabi World Rally Team – a match made in heaven.

www.castrol.com

ade

"A DRIVER HAS TO EXPECT EVERYTHING."
MIKKO HIRVONEN

The car's lifeblood

The Focus RS WRC must be capable of withstanding extremes. That's the opinion of BP Ford Abu Dhabi Team technical director Christian Loriaux. Choosing the right lubricant is therefore not a decision to be taken lightly.

"We're lucky to have Castrol because they're the best lubricants partner to have – above and beyond what would be considered a normal sponsor," says Loriaux. "They supply us with a very good range of lubricants, but they also follow that up with very good technical support and a superb research lab in Pangbourne in the UK."

Pushing products to the limit in the World Rally Championship enables Castrol to pour that knowledge into the creation of high performance products such as Castrol EDGE.

"The load on the engine and the transmission of the Focus RS WRC are very high because turbocharged engines have a high torque output," continues Loriaux. "We also manufacture parts as small and as light as possible, which means the stress on all mechanical components is extreme and they can only survive with the best possible lubricant."

High five for Loeb

In the year when the Frenchman became the WRC's only five-time champion, Pirelli won plaudits for its new control tyre and the sport lost two teams to the credit crunch. By David Evans.

Race&motion

SÉBASTIEN LOEB, where and when will the numbers ever end? Not a season goes by without another bevy of records for the doyen of the World Rally Championship. And 2008 was no exception. But was it the walkover everybody predicted? Eleven wins from 15 starts certainly sounds like it, but in reality, no, it wasn't.

The Marseillaise once again provided the sound-track to the season – and in the words of the French national anthem, the children of the fatherland did indeed ensure glory arrived. But it wasn't always as straightforward as the statistics would have you believe. While we can't quite point to 2008 as the beginning of the end of Loeb's reign at the top of the sport, there were some mighty big hints that the axis of power is shifting to the next generation.

Loeb, 34, has been winning rallies since 2002. His nearest rival last season was 28-year-old Ford man Mikko Hirvonen, whose nearest rival in turn was team-mate Jari-Matti Latvala, five years his junior. Both of Ford's Finns gave Loeb a tough time. Certainly there were occasions when the Frenchman's genius shone through – the Acropolis being the obvious example of a man in complete control while those around him lost their heads. Equally there were times last year when Loeb was beaten on pace fair and square – New Zealand being the perfect example. Unfortunately for Ford, just when the champagne was being removed from the fridge, Hirvonen and Latvala let that one-two slip and Loeb elbowed his way to the top. But the Frenchman had been all at sea beside the Tasman early on that last Sunday in August, unable to stem the flow of time going Ford's way.

For Loeb, last year was about the big one, the record he really wanted: title number five. It's this fifth successive crown that elevates him above WRC titans Juha Kankkunen and Tommi Mäkinen and sends him into a sporting stratosphere all of his own. Beyond that Loeb also bagged the two rally victories he was still chasing, namely Rally Finland and Rally GB, and eclipsed his own record number of 10 wins in a season, netting number 11 at the 11th hour in Cardiff. So, all in all, not a bad 2008. Essentially it was the year most people predicted after Marcus Grönholm had announced his retirement from the sport at the end of 2007.

"It was not easy," insisted Loeb, the smell of champagne still fresh on his overalls in Wales. "People told me I would be champion by the middle of the year. I was not. Look at the stage times. Okay, I won stages but all the time it was by a couple of seconds or less than a second. It didn't come to me easily – I had to work for this."

A sixth successive title would take Loeb into previously unchartered territory for an FIA series, moving him past Michael Schumacher's astonishing Formula 1 record of five wins with Ferrari from 2000 to 2004, but Loeb's unmoved by any comparisons between himself and the German racer. The pint-sized Alsation remains a man of simple tastes; he just likes driving cars quickly. And for the last five years, he's driven them faster than anybody else and dominated his field in the same way that Steve Davis ruled the world of snooker through the 1980s or Roger Federer monopolised tennis's number one spot from February 2004 until August this year. He's done it with utter professionalism and ruthless ability.

The time has come, however, for those young

Race&motion

Above: Jordan made a big impact on its first appearance in the WRC. The service park was based beside the Dead Sea.

Right: Rally fans came in all shapes and sizes in Jordan.

Middle right: Loeb claims he never had it easy in 2008, although 11 wins from 15 events might paint a different picture.

Above centre right: Even the introduction of a new car couldn't reverse Subaru's sliding fortunes and the make withdrew at the end of the year.

Race&motion

Right: Ford's failure to hold onto its one-two in New Zealand had a major bearing on both the drivers' and manufacturers' championships.

Far right: François Duval's co-driver Patrick Pivato's (right) near-fatal crash put safety in the spotlight on Rally Japan.
Photographs: Photo4 unless specified

Race&motion

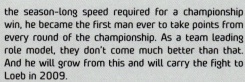

Race&motion

the season-long speed required for a championship win, he became the first man ever to take points from every round of the championship. As a team leading role model, they don't come much better than that. And he will grow from this and will carry the fight to Loeb in 2009.

While Hirvonen toiled away in the engine room of Ford's title tilt, Latvala inspired and infuriated in equal measure. Becoming the youngest ever winner of a WRC round in Sweden last February was the near-perfect start to his works career with Ford, but a mid-year confidence crisis ruined a few Focus RS WRCs as well as Ford's hopes of retaining a third manufacturers' title. That Latvala has massive natural ability is beyond doubt, but it remains to be seen how quickly that speed can be channelled into enough event wins to put together a shot at the world championship. Citroën's Dani Sordo summed up Latvala mid-year when he likened him to a young Colin McRae: desperately quick but not always completely in control.

It's more of that kind of speed and aggression that the sport could do with seeing from Sordo himself. The Spaniard contributed well towards Citroën's points tally in the second half of the season, helping his employer collect its first makes' title since 2005. But he will be only too well aware of the arrival of another Sébastien in the camp – Ogier, the Junior World Rally Champion. Ogier's first event in a C4 WRC on Rally GB was a boom and bust affair – he rolled on the second day, but he will be best remembered for leading for the majority of Friday. Sordo, more than anybody else, will be keen to turn in a win in 2009. In Jordan last year he came mighty close to breaking his duck, but running first on the baking roads of the Hashemite Kingdom he was unable to stave off Hirvonen's attack.

The Jordan Rally was the only all-new event in 2008, although Turkey returned after a year's absence. Jordan was the event that got everybody talking. Finally, the WRC had arrived in the Middle East – and it received an exceptional welcome. The event proved to be as tough as had been hoped with searing temperatures allied to some seriously challenging stages. Jordan added another dimension to the world championship and has done more than enough to cement its place on the bi-annual calendar, which will commence in 2009.

In a year when Toyota – Japan's standard-bearing car manufacturer – made its first operating loss since 1938 and reportedly turned off the hand driers in some of its factory toilets to save money, you begin to realise just how tough this current financial situation is. And the World Rally Championship wasn't immune from that. The WRC lost two manufacturers in as many grim days in December, when both the Suzuki and Subaru World Rally Teams announced that they would not compete in 2009.

Suzuki's decision is a suspension of rally activities,

pretenders to make a play for the crown that has been worn by none other than Loeb since he was handed it by Petter Solberg at the end of 2004.

Hirvonen and Latvala will be at the front of the queue of those ready to take Loeb on. Hirvonen's achievements last season were, in many ways, just as merit-worthy as those of Loeb. Rewind the Jyväskylä-born driver's career to 2005 and you'd find him in limbo. Ditched by Subaru after a wretched season aboard a factory Impreza in '04, Hirvonen was trying to piece together his self-confidence with a programme of events in a private Ford. Three years on and he was starting the season as not only the team leader at Ford, but Loeb's biggest threat to the title. While Hirvonen might have lacked the ability to sustain

New Zealand was a low point for Jari-Matti Latvala who cost Ford valuable manufacturer points when he crashed on the final forest stage.
Photograph: Race&motion

while Subaru has gone – although there is already talk of a return in years to come.

Despite being at either end of the WRC scale in terms of experience, both teams had a lot to offer last season. Suzuki brought the zest and enthusiasm associated with a fledgling outfit at this level, while Subaru was one of the WRC's longest standing manufacturers – and one which, in years gone by, the rest of the service park had measured itself against.

Both teams cited the current global economic downturn and its subsequent negative effect on car sales as the reason for their departure from the sport, but there's no doubt a lack of performance from the SX4 WRC and Impreza WRC2008 forced the hands of those counting the beans. It's now well chronicled that Subaru's last success was more than three years ago and, for a team so readily associated with winning at this level, finishing minutes behind the leader for rally after rally is not going to go down well.

Suzuki's inaugural WRC effort was a tad hamstrung from the outset with the choice of the gangly – in world rally car terms – SX4. Whichever way you cut it, the SX4 was never the most natural of world rally cars. While the Suzuki team didn't win, what it can be collectively proud of is the way it bounced back from some chronic early-season reliability issues. The engine glitches that halted the cars on the first three rounds and the hydraulic gremlins which regularly robbed drivers P-G Andersson and Toni Gardemeister of assisted gear shifts or a workable centre differential were, largely, things of the past once the team introduced its evolution SX4 in Finland.

Low-grip events in Japan and Britain flattered to deceive, masking the car's lack of outright grunt, but on both events Andersson came as close as possible to a podium finish. Would a handful of podiums have made any difference to the outcome of a board meeting in Hamamatsu? Probably not. The big positive to come out of the year – aside from the confirmation of Andersson's ability – is the fact that the Suzuki Motor Corporation remains a very big fan of the WRC.

Sources at the top of the company are already talking in positive terms about returning to the sport and the feeling of unfinished business runs through the firm. And when Suzuki does come back, it will be with a far clearer idea of how to fulfil its desire to add success at the top of the sport to Junior World Rally Championship glory.

Only time will tell if Subaru follows Suzuki back. It's as hard for Subaru employees as it is for the tens of thousands of petrol heads who have flocked to the showrooms to buy the latest incarnation of WRX or STi to imagine a world championship without the presence of this most famous of Anglo-Japanese alliances. Subaru's sales pitch has been so closely tied to rallying for so many years that it's hard to see the factory Imprezas staying away from the WRC for too long.

The declining fortunes of Subaru meant it spent large parts of last season scrapping with the Stobart VK M-Sport Ford World Rally Team. The Cumbrian-based outfit continued to build its reputation at the top of the sport with plenty of strong finishes and a varied squad of drivers, which included the major public relations coup of drafting in multiple MotoGP title winner Valentino Rossi for the final round in Wales.

Unfortunately for Stobart, it was also the focus of the world's attention on the subject of World Rally Car safety after Gigi Galli and François Duval crashed heavily in Germany and Japan respectively. The FIA has to be applauded for the work that has been done and continues to be done to protect crews inside the cockpit of a World Rally Car. It's questionable whether Galli himself and Duval's co-driver Patrick Pivato would have survived their accidents a few years ago.

And while the FIA's patting itself on the back, it should take credit for the introduction of a control tyre to the sport. Most of the recognition should, however, go to Pirelli for carrying out the FIA's wishes to the letter. Prior to the start of last season all manner of scare stories were rattling around the service park about how the field would be decimated by punctures on the super-tough terrain of Greece and Turkey, while the near road-specification tyres would send cars spearing off left, right and centre on asphalt. In the end, none of that happened. Sure, there was the odd puncture, but that's all it was. The tyres worked tremendously well and, while nothing will ever replace mousse-insert technology, the durability and robustness of the Milanese firm's covers drew praise from the very first round, where Pirelli was awarded the Abu Dhabi Spirit of the Rally Award.

Ahead of the season, there was talk of a level playing field tyre-wise opening up Loeb to attack on asphalt. Buoyed by mid-year tar testing, the Ford team was in the mood to put the dampers on Citroën's party – and slotted sealed-surface supremo Duval in alongside Hirvonen to really turn the screws on Loeb. In the end, the ubiquitous Pzero boots beneath them all made little difference. Planet Loeb remained a lonely place with three residents: Seb, co-driver Daniel Elena and the machine of the moment, the Citroën C4 WRC. It was a very French year.

Above: Rallying's new generation continued to shine in 2008, with Mikko Hirvonen and Dani Sordo second and third in the championship standings.

Above left: Pirelli began its stint as the championship's exclusive tyre supplier and was widely praised for its efforts.

Top: MotoGP legend Valentino Rossi's participation on Rally GB created huge interest among fans and media alike.

Opposite top: Suzuki fought back from a troubled start to the year and P-G Andersson impressed. But the manufacturer has suspended its WRC activities due to the economic climate.

Opposite bottom: Citroën's manufacturer success was its first since 2005. The team also attracted high-profile sponsorship from Red Bull during the season.

Photographs: Race&motion

Grönholm's
men of the moment

Who better than a double world champion to pick the top 10 drivers from 2008?

Hello, hello!

I might not have been driving in the World Rally Championship this season, but I have been watching it. I've been keeping an eye on my old rivals, sometimes in front of the computer or TV screen, and sometimes on the rallies as part of my role as an ambassador with Ford. It's been a good year, a little bit of a strange year – but not, I think, such a surprising year for Sébastien...

Anyway, when I was asked to pick my top 10 drivers from the season, it wasn't easy at all. You sit down and think okay, this, this and this driver has to go here, here and here, but then you remember others. In the end, I had 14 drivers – and they won't all fit. My top 10 follows, but the five drivers all at 10.5 or 11 are Sébastien Ogier, Urmo Aava, Mads Østberg, Juho Hänninen and maybe Henning Solberg.

Ogier. Hey, I don't know this guy at all. I didn't hear the name before, but now suddenly everybody is talking about him. He is Junior champion and then in Wales we see some good speed on the first day, but a roll on the second day. It's hard to tell, but he's looking fast for now. Aava had a very good year – he's shown himself to be quite fast and I hope he gets a deal for next season. Østberg is still good, like we know he can be. Hänninen had a good season in the Production class but missed the title, and Henning... Hmm, it was a tough year for him.

Okay, that's enough talking.
Here's what I think...

He was only off the podium for two of the 15 rounds in the championship – and only off the top step for two of those 13 finishes! Even by his standards, this was an exceptional season. He became the first person to claim five drivers' titles (all consecutively) and broke his own record of scoring 10 wins in a season by claiming 11 in 2008. Citroën team principal Olivier Quesnel's view that Loeb could (and in Quesnel's opinion should) have won 14 rallies this year is believable. Loeb's only mistake of any significance was when he rolled in Sweden. He was leading before his road accident in Jordan, was tactically out-manoeuvred in Turkey, and didn't need to go all out for the win in Japan. Could there have been 12, 13 or 14 wins? It doesn't really matter when you end the year as number one.

Marcus says...

It's the same as before for Sébastien. There's no news here. His speed is the same and he won even more rallies and the championship. What more is there to say? Nothing.

SÉBASTIEN LOEB 1

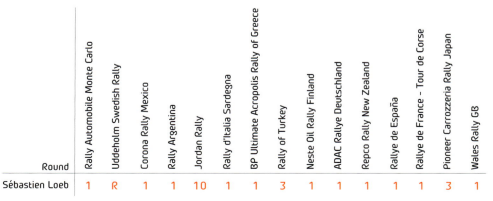

Round	Rally Automobile Monte Carlo	Uddeholm Swedish Rally	Corona Rally Mexico	Rally Argentina	Jordan Rally	Rally d'Italia Sardegna	BP Ultimate Acropolis Rally of Greece	Rally of Turkey	Neste Oil Rally Finland	ADAC Rallye Deutschland	Repco Rally New Zealand	Rallye de España	Rallye de France – Tour de Corse	Pioneer Carrozzeria Rally Japan	Wales Rally GB
Sébastien Loeb	1	R	1	1	10	1	1	3	1	1	1	1	1	3	1

Key: R - retired

It was always asking a lot of Mikko Hirvonen to step up and fill the shoes of double world champion Marcus Grönholm. He managed the job of team leader exceptionally well. Finishing every round not only showed that it wasn't just Loeb who could break records, but it also set the perfect example for his junior team-mate Jari-Matti Latvala. If Latvala had gone anywhere near mirroring Hirvonen's dependable points-scoring approach, Ford would have bagged a third manufacturers' title. What Hirvonen was missing was that devastating turn of pace or the super-quick start that Grönholm had at his disposal. Missing out on a win in Finland hurt Hirvonen; missing out on victory in New Zealand hurt the team even more.

Marcus says...

He had a good season, Mikko. He was consistent, finishing a lot – all – of the rallies. He's been fast sometimes as well. You know the thing we have to remember here is that Mikko is being measured against Loeb, and not many Loebs come along. It's been tough, but sometimes Mikko has got the better of Seb.

2 MIKKO HIRVONEN

Round	Rally Automobile Monte Carlo	Uddeholm Swedish Rally	Corona Rally Mexico	Rally Argentina	Jordan Rally	Rally d'Italia Sardegna	BP Ultimate Acropolis Rally of Greece	Rally of Turkey	Neste Oil Rally Finland	ADAC Rallye Deutschland	Repco Rally New Zealand	Rallye de España	Rallye de France – Tour de Corse	Pioneer Carrozzeria Rally Japan	Wales Rally GB
Mikko Hirvonen	2	2	4	5	1	2	3	1	2	4	3	3	2	1	8

Key: R - retired

Jari-Matti was super-quick, but still prone to making frustrating mistakes. The final round of the season in Wales might have shown a slight change in attitude. He was very, very quick and he made it to the finish, albeit in second place. Latvala definitely has a McRae rather than a Burns approach, and he is always likely to crash rally cars. But when he's not crashing them, he's likely to be spraying them with champagne. His win in Sweden was tremendous, but by his own admission it gave him a false impression of just how tough this job really is. No matter – accidents in Finland, Germany and New Zealand all made him realise that it takes an awful lot more than just a heavy right foot to win at this level.

Marcus says...
He was good to win in Sweden – this was a good start to the season. He's definitely very fast – there is no question. When he was under pressure and the conditions were not so nice or what he was used to, then it was not so good for him.

JARI-MATTI LATVALA 3

Round	Rally Automobile Monte Carlo	Uddeholm Swedish Rally	Corona Rally Mexico	Rally Argentina	Jordan Rally	Rally d'Italia Sardegna	BP Ultimate Acropolis Rally of Greece	Rally of Turkey	Neste Oil Rally Finland	ADAC Rallye Deutschland	Repco Rally New Zealand	Rallye de España	Rallye de France – Tour de Corse	Pioneer Carrozzeria Rally Japan	Wales Rally GB
Jari-Matti Latvala	12	1	3	15	7	3	7	2	39	9	R	6	4	2	2

Key: R - retired

Is it really three years since that Rally Australia victory? Yes, and it's three years since Duval had regular employment in the World Rally Championship. The haughty Belgian started the season well enough in Monte Carlo by finishing fourth, just 1.1 seconds off the podium. But then came seven months of daytime television before he was back for the balance of 2008, courtesy of Gigi Galli's season-ending crash in Germany. And Duval wasn't just part of the Stobart team either – he returned to the official Ford squad for the first time since 2004. He repaid team boss Malcolm Wilson's renewed faith in him by delivering two perfect drives in Latvala's usual works Focus in Catalunya and Corsica. Duval then showed great strength by returning to the car in Wales after a horrible Rally Japan crash, which almost killed his co-driver Patrick Pivato.

Marcus says...

How many rallies for Duval? Not many, hey. And he is straight back – bang – on the pace on asphalt. This shows that he can still drive and make nice times. He's not the easiest driver all the time, but he is very fast. His crash in Japan was tough for him, too.

4 FRANÇOIS DUVAL

Round	Rally Automobile Monte Carlo	Uddeholm Swedish Rally	Corona Rally Mexico	Rally Argentina	Jordan Rally	Rally d'Italia Sardegna	BP Ultimate Acropolis Rally of Greece	Rally of Turkey	Neste Oil Rally Finland	ADAC Rallye Deutschland	Repco Rally New Zealand	Rallye de España	Rallye de France – Tour de Corse	Pioneer Carrozzeria Rally Japan	Wales Rally GB
François Duval	4	-	-	-	-	-	-	-	-	3	R	4	3	R	6

Key: R - retired

After four years and two Junior World Rally Championship titles with the Suzuki team, the Swede finally got his chance to shine on the bigger stage. By mid-season the car was showing admirable reliability, but it wasn't helping P-G to show his pace. Where possible he collected some solid results, such as the two fifth positions he ended his season with. But there was also the odd moment of frustration, such as in Jordan and Finland where he went off the road. If this is the end of Suzuki, it certainly shouldn't be the end of Andersson. He's quick enough to cut it at the sharp end of the field.

Marcus says...

He has gone well from time to time. We don't know too much about the car, but the first thing you have to do in this sport is beat your team-mate, and [P-G] Andersson has done that all through the year.

PER-GUNNAR ANDERSSON 5

Round	Rally Automobile Monte Carlo	Uddeholm Swedish Rally	Corona Rally Mexico	Rally Argentina	Jordan Rally	Rally d'Italia Sardegna	BP Ultimate Acropolis Rally of Greece	Rally of Turkey	Neste Oil Rally Finland	ADAC Rallye Deutschland	Repco Rally New Zealand	Rallye de España	Rallye de France – Tour de Corse	Pioneer Carrozzeria Rally Japan	Wales Rally GB
Per-Gunnar Andersson	8	R	R	24	R	9	11	R	R	15	6	32	17	4	4

Key: R – retired

Really should have won a rally this season. In that respect, this year has to go down as a disappointing one for the Spaniard. On the flip side, he turned in a run of three second-place finishes in the autumn that probably saved Citroën's tilt at the manufacturers' title. It also saved his job. There was a fair amount of frustration when Sordo lost the lead in Greece. A half-minute advantage on a rally like the Acropolis is like a tenth of a second anywhere else, but Sordo knows that was his big chance – and he blew it by not looking after his tyres. He played his 'get out of jail' card with those improved results later in the season and will remain in the car for next year.

Marcus says...

Sometimes he is very quick and sometimes he is not. For many rallies he has not been on the pace of Sébastien and he's in the same car, so this is not so good. There's a little bit missing from the results of Sordo. I don't know, but maybe they [Citroën] didn't let him win rallies this year. This could also be a problem for Dani.

6 DANI SORDO

Round	Rally Automobile Monte Carlo	Uddeholm Swedish Rally	Corona Rally Mexico	Rally Argentina	Jordan Rally	Rally d'Italia Sardegna	BP Ultimate Acropolis Rally of Greece	Rally of Turkey	Neste Oil Rally Finland	ADAC Rallye Deutschland	Repco Rally New Zealand	Rallye de España	Rallye de France – Tour de Corse	Pioneer Carrozzeria Rally Japan	Wales Rally GB
Dani Sordo	11	6	17	3	2	5	5	4	4	2	2	2	R	10	3

Key: R – retired

In terms of raw speed there are few 19 year olds, if any, who can rival Mikkelsen's pace in a World Rally Car. What he missed out on this season was a more regular rally programme. He needed to be competing more often to collect more of the results his talent warrants. His appetite for testing is well known, but that now needs to be channelled between the official timing beams. While his speed is beyond doubt, he has retained some of the recklessness of youth. Time and a works deal will iron out such issues, and could ultimately leave us with another Norwegian world champion.

Marcus says...

He's set some very strong times in the championship this season. His fifth place in Sweden was a really strong finish. It's funny with him – he can be really quick on the first day, with some incredible times, but then there's mistakes or something wrong later in the rally. But hey, don't forget this guy is only 19, so he has a lot of time to come and get the experience.

ANDREAS MIKKELSEN 7

Round	Rally Automobile Monte Carlo	Uddeholm Swedish Rally	Corona Rally Mexico	Rally Argentina	Jordan Rally	Rally d'Italia Sardegna	BP Ultimate Acropolis Rally of Greece	Rally of Turkey	Neste Oil Rally Finland	ADAC Rallye Deutschland	Repco Rally New Zealand	Rallye de España	Rallye de France – Tour de Corse	Pioneer Carrozzeria Rally Japan	Wales Rally GB
Andreas Mikkelsen	-	5	-	-	-	-	-	14	12	11	-	8	11	-	-

Solberg took his eye off the ball mid-season when he fell out with the team – or the team fell out with him. Whatever. The important thing for Petter is to get in the car and drive, and to try and leave the rest of the job to those around him. That he can drive is beyond doubt – you don't luck into world championships. His second place in Greece, on the new car's debut, should have been the high point of the Norwegian's season, but it was spoilt by the kind of internal wranglings that have marked his year.

Marcus says...
Petter has been making the same speed all the time this year. It hasn't really been a good year for him. There's not much more to say, really.

8 PETTER SOLBERG

Round	Rally Automobile Monte Carlo	Uddeholm Swedish Rally	Corona Rally Mexico	Rally Argentina	Jordan Rally	Rally d'Italia Sardegna	BP Ultimate Acropolis Rally of Greece	Rally of Turkey	Neste Oil Rally Finland	ADAC Rallye Deutschland	Repco Rally New Zealand	Rallye de España	Rallye de France – Tour de Corse	Pioneer Carrozzeria Rally Japan	Wales Rally GB
Petter Solberg	5	4	12	R	R	10	8	6	6	5	4	5	5	8	4

Key: R - retired

When the chips are down in a team all you can do is aim to beat your team-mate, and that's just what Atkinson has done. He scored five podium finishes compared with Solberg's one, and finished higher than him in the end-of-season table. Despite all those podiums, Atkinson never truly looked like winning a rally. As the man himself said, second or third place is nice, but it doesn't mean too much if the gap to P1 is three minutes. Chris was probably at his best in Finland where he flew to third, and probably at his worst on Rally GB where he flew to hospital after a terrifying top-gear shunt in Rheola.

Marcus says...
I don't know if it's down to him or the car, but I would say a little bit the same as for Petter: not such a good year.

CHRIS ATKINSON 9

Round	Rally Automobile Monte Carlo	Uddeholm Swedish Rally	Corona Rally Mexico	Rally Argentina	Jordan Rally	Rally d'Italia Sardegna	BP Ultimate Acropolis Rally of Greece	Rally of Turkey	Neste Oil Rally Finland	ADAC Rallye Deutschland	Repco Rally New Zealand	Rallye de España	Rallye de France – Tour de Corse	Pioneer Carrozzeria Rally Japan	Wales Rally GB
Chris Atkinson	3	21	2	2	3	6	R	13	3	6	R	7	6	4	R

Key: R – retired

The Briton scored his first top-10 finish in the championship this season. Once again, Wilson made good strides forward with both his speed and consistency. He was particularly impressive in New Zealand, but retirement cost him points and the chance of a top-four finish. The same happened in Japan when he stopped on day one. Unfortunately for the 21 year old, his rising confidence was hit hard by being first on the scene of François Duval and Patrick Pivato's horrible accident in Japan. All of that will be put behind him by the time he's ready to attack next season. But for Wilson to make the next step, he could certainly do with some more testing time ahead of rallies.

Marcus says...

I have known Matthew for a long time now and he's working hard. This was a good season for him; the results were coming. Okay there is still work for him to do, but hey, don't forget, like Mikkelsen he is still a young guy.

Marcus Grönholm was talking to David Evans

10 MATTHEW WILSON

Round	Rally Automobile Monte Carlo	Uddeholm Swedish Rally	Corona Rally Mexico	Rally Argentina	Jordan Rally	Rally d'Italia Sardegna	BP Ultimate Acropolis Rally of Greece	Rally of Turkey	Neste Oil Rally Finland	ADAC Rallye Deutschland	Repco Rally New Zealand	Rallye de España	Rallye de France – Tour de Corse	Pioneer Carrozzeria Rally Japan	Wales Rally GB
Matthew Wilson	10	R	6	R	5	12	6	7	9	12	17	9	8	7	9

Key: R - retired

Catch him if you can

It may seem hard to believe after a thoroughly dominant run to a fifth WRC title, but Sébastien Loeb does have rivals who are hot on his heels. By Anthony Peacock

Above: Sébastien Loeb flew to 11 victories in 2008. This was win number five in Greece.

Right: Engine failure forced Loeb's retirement in Sweden.

Middle right and below: At his ninth attempt Loeb finally won in Finland – the event regarded as rallying's Holy Grail. The result proved a major setback to his title rival Mikko Hirvonen, who had been expected to win his home event.

Top right: The two men charged with keeping Loeb in check are new Citroen team boss Olivier Quesnel and co-driver Daniel Elena.

Photographs: Race&motion

SÉBASTIEN LOEB is well known for his scrupulous honesty, but on this occasion he may be being slightly disingenuous when he says that the 2008 World Rally Championship battle was as tough as any other. Let's get one thing straight from the start: winning a world title, any world title, is never easy. But there are certainly varying degrees of difficulty.

Also by nature, Loeb is far from arrogant: he's always (quite rightly) quick to make fun of anybody who suffers from that particular malaise. So it's in his nature, as well as his best interests, to talk up his rivals. He tendentiously feels more comfortable discussing the good job that Mikko Hirvonen and Dani Sordo did than talking about his own achievements. "It was close," he says. "I had to fight for every single victory. Maybe people did not expect that at the start of the season, but it was not at all easy for me. Jari-Matti [Latvala], Mikko and Dani all did a really good job."

A lot of that is true of course. Nobody – least of all Jari-Matti himself – really expected Latvala to win in Sweden, on only his second outing with a factory car, for example. Yet this didn't alter the overall complexion of the season. For the best possible reasons, Loeb was forced to keep up the polite pretence that there were other drivers capable of beating him consistently over the course of the season. And whichever way you turn his generous comments of "they were all very quick" and "I had to push very hard", the stark fact is that he was nearly always better than them. Barring a disaster, nobody other than Sébastien Loeb was going to win the 2008 world title. Maybe not even barring a disaster: when Loeb broke his arm and missed four rallies in 2006, he still won it.

This is not to denigrate the opposition in any way.

They pushed Loeb harder than most people thought (probably harder than he himself thought), and the Frenchman has also admitted that Latvala is every bit as quick as he is; maybe even quicker. What Loeb lacked throughout 2008 though was consistent opposition from one person, provided previously by Marcus Grönholm. Press him on the subject and he admits he missed it.

"Marcus is Marcus, and every time I went into a rally [in 2007] I knew it would be a big fight with him," says Loeb. "Really, it was impossible to relax for one moment with Marcus there. OK, maybe [in 2008] it has not always been the same. But Marcus had a lot of experience, so this is normal. In the future, it will be the same again. Already it is tough. These young guys are very good drivers."

Good, but not good enough. In the Rallycourse World Champion feature, it has become customary to talk about the highlights of the new world champion's season, the strengths of his character, his most memorable victories and so forth. In Loeb's case it's probably easier to talk about the rallies he didn't win – all four of them. Of those four, he had two podium places and two retirements. But the truth is that he could have triumphed on at least three of the ones that got away. Equally, as Loeb himself is eager to point out, he was gifted a win in New Zealand. The truth remains though that Loeb could have won his record-breaking fifth world championship title somewhat earlier than Rally Japan and maybe added to his record-breaking 11 wins in one season. Just consider those statistics for a moment. Did anybody really think they were going to beat him?

"Why not? There were times at the start of the season when I thought maybe it would not happen for

me this year," remembers Loeb. "I knew that there was still a long way to go, but Sweden was a big surprise and then Jordan was really bad for me too. In Turkey I lost out because of road position and then I was second in the championship again, so definitely I could see a way where I didn't win it. I thought that, but I tried not to believe it."

After a breathtakingly competent demolition of the Monte Carlo time sheets at the start of the year, Sweden was a low point for Loeb – although what appeared to some to be a seismic shift in the drift of the championship was in fact more readily explained by a random concatenation of circumstances. Loeb went off because he made a mistake on stage four, which was mostly down to the fact that he was first on the road. He would have lived to fight another day had there been a proper service halt rather than a remote service on day one in Sweden, but as it was his C4's broken clutch could not be fixed and he retired in the afternoon. What made things seem worse was the fact that Latvala won, subverting the natural order of age and experience. The events of the Jordan Rally, where Loeb was forced to retire after a low-speed road accident with the similar car of Conrad Rautenbach, were even unluckier.

Yet you don't become the most successful driver in the history of world rallying without some degree of mental strength. Loeb has always refused to blame bad pace notes, bad luck, or Rautenbach for anything that happened in the first half of the season. Then there was the team orders controversy in Turkey, where Ford made sure that Loeb would run first on the road on the final day, meaning that the best he could realistically hope for was third.

While his team boss Olivier Quesnel was making melodramatic declarations about this being alien to sport and claiming (incorrectly, as it turned out) that Citroën would never do such a thing, Loeb accepted his lot stoically – even though it meant he spent the long

summer break three points behind Hirvonen, having won five rallies to his key rival's two.

There would have been enough ammunition there for most people to rail against fate and injustice throughout the hot months of summer, but that's not Loeb's style. He was probably aided and abetted by the knowledge that the three asphalt rounds in the second half of the season would put things back on track.

"We were a bit unlucky in the first half of the season, but then we have also been lucky at other times," he concludes. "There's no point in blaming bad luck or somebody else: these are things that just happen. Sometimes the rules of the sport are hard to understand – I don't see what the problem was with keeping the road position rules as we had them before

A NEW POWER AT CITROËN

WITH THE same car and drivers for 2008, there was only one major change in the Citroën camp: the man in charge. 'Le Grizzly' – Guy Fréquelin – was replaced by an altogether different animal: former publishing boss Olivier Quesnel. In terms of personality and style they could not be more different, but it made no difference to Citroën: statistically 2008 was the rally team's most successful season yet, with first in the drivers' championship, first in the manufacturers' and first in the Juniors, along with 11 overall wins. "In my first year with the team, I have to be happy with that," was how Quesnel summed it up after Rally Great Britain, having returned the manufacturers' title to Satory for the first time in three years.

Fréquelin was like a father figure to Loeb, and it will naturally take more than just a year for Quesnel to build up the same bond. Nonetheless, the foundations are there, and with Quesnel's promotion to the head of Peugeot Sport they are likely to be working even more closely together in future. "The team is much bigger than one person and it has already done a lot of good work, so there is no need for any big changes," says Loeb. "I think Olivier sees that. We have a good relationship, but he is very different from Guy. I have known Guy for many years and Olivier for less time, but I am sure that in the future it could be the same. Olivier is a very sensible person. He has lots of his own opinions, but he listens to those of everybody else too."

For his part, Quesnel fully appreciates what he has in Loeb. While falling short of former Peugeot boss Corrado Provera's florid description of Marcus Grönholm, whom he called "our koh-i-noor", Quesnel realises that Citroën's biggest asset is just as bright a diamond. "Sébastien is just perfect," says Quesnel. "Of course I had very high expectations of him when I started this job, but one thing that has always surprised me is Sébastien's ability to surprise me. If you take the final afternoon of Rally Great Britain, most people would have been affected by being given an incorrect 10-second jump start penalty. Sébastien simply carried on, but made sure that he had enough of a margin to win the rally with the penalty, even though he knew it was false. That's what makes him a champion."

With Citroën poised to continue in the WRC into 2010, despite Quesnel's widely quoted praise of the DTM, the Loeb-Quesnel axis of power looks set to continue some way into the future. And having spent his entire career with Citroën from the very start, who is to say that one day the man sitting behind Quesnel's desk in Paris might not be Loeb himself, presiding over the 2021 methane hybrid World Rally Championship, while reminiscing about the glory days when those old, viciously dangerous, petrol rally cars put out a staggering 300 horsepower?

After crashing out in
Sardinia in 2007 Loeb
was determined to claim
victory on the island event
in '08, which he did albeit
by a scant 10.6 seconds.
Photograph: Race&motion

[top 15 reversed on days two and three] but that was not the fault of Mikko and Ford. Like everybody else, they were just working within the rules. I had a long time to think over the summer and I knew that we had to do as good a job as possible on all the rallies that were left, starting with Rally Finland."

It's only at this point that Loeb allows himself a smile, because he knows full well the significance of the 2008 Rally Finland. In terms of material gain, the result was hardly spectacular: Loeb hauled back just two points from Hirvonen, to lie one point off the lead of the drivers' championship. In terms of psychological gain, beating Hirvonen on his home turf was like dropping a nuclear bomb. As one past master, a multiple winner of Rally Finland, put it: "If I had been beaten there by him, I would have gone home and not spoken to anyone for a week. That's how badly I would have taken it and I would expect Mikko to feel the same."

Loeb himself fully understands the havoc he wreaked on Hirvonen's psyche: what if, for example, Hirvonen had beaten him on the Tour de Corse, or Rallye Deutschland? The Frenchman just smiles weakly and shrugs slightly in response: the thought is too awful to put into words... and he knows it is never going to happen anyway. He won't let it. The weekend in Finland proved once again that Loeb can master the art of guile if he so chooses. Prior to the rally he claimed that chasing a win in Finland (the only event missing off his CV along with Great Britain – two more boxes that were ticked off in 2008) was not on the agenda. Ford's flying Finns were just too quick for him; and what did he know about the roads of Finland compared to them? It was a classic self-denigrating strategy, designed to put the hunted at ease, and used to great effect by luminaries such as Lieutenant Columbo. Every one of Loeb's fastest stage times around Jyväskylä was the equivalent of the man in the dirty mac framing a killer question preceded by: 'just one little thing...'

Loeb watches little daytime TV, so he is probably unfamiliar with the modus operandi of the LAPD Homicide squad. But he certainly gets the picture; still now he is reluctant to admit that he was going all-out to win in Finland. "Of course I loved winning in Finland; maybe it was my favourite win of the year," he says. "But what was more important to me was to do a good job in the championship. If I had not won in Finland my life would not have changed. The same was true on Rally GB: it was another rally I had not won, but the most important thing was to make sure Citroën had the manufacturers' championship. Luckily Dani [Sordo] did a very good job, so it was possible for me to push for the win. I'm happy to have the record for the most wins and the most championships, but the other records don't interest me so much."

Maybe because the opposition is not what it was? "No, I don't think so..." he replies, but that's hardly a vehement denial. He still has the fever of course although even from behind the wheel it's all getting a bit predictable. "There are not so many big surprises anymore," he says, which is why there has been a lot of talk of the 34-year-old retiring soon or even moving full-time into racing. His extra-curricular activities in 2008 included racing in France's Porsche Cup and testing the Red Bull RB4 Formula 1 car, as well as trying out Peugeot's 908 HDi FAP Le Mans contender. He now has an open-ended agreement that

will see him do more testing with Peugeot in 2009, although the Le Mans 24 Hours itself clashes with the Acropolis Rally.

The crunch will come at the end of this year, or more realistically in just a few months' time, when Loeb will have to decide what he plans to do after his current Citroën contract expires. With the news that the next generation of Super 2000-based World Rally Cars will have broadly similar levels of power to the current cars, Loeb may well decide to keep going. Had the decision gone the way of straight Super 2000, he almost certainly would have walked.

"I don't know for sure what I will do next year, but it's likely that I will continue in rallying," says Loeb. "It's possible that I will do other things as well though. With just 12 rallies on the calendar, it becomes a little bit easier."

The fact that Loeb is looking elsewhere is nothing to do with any form of motivational crisis. He loves rallying more than ever: on a rare weekend off he decided to drive a C2 Super 1600 (co-driven by his wife Severine) on the Rallye du Var last year, and he seriously contemplated starting off this year with an unscheduled entry on the Monte Carlo Rally, also in a C2. It's just that he wants to move out of his comfort zone. By his own admission Loeb's recipe for rally wins is quite straightforward: push as hard as you can on day one, then if it's going well keep up the same pace for the morning of day two. Control the advantage in the afternoon of day two, then calm things down to the end on Sunday. Job done.

In racing, he's cooking with raw ingredients. There is no recipe book. "After getting out of the Red Bull Formula 1 car, I knew that there was a lot of speed still to come from me," he concluded. That's certainly not the case in rallying for him. But Loeb looks around the service area and sees plenty of other places, notably underneath the number two Ford tent, where plenty more speed might be coming quite soon. And who knows what the new Super 2000-based regulations will bring in 2010? A Proton on the podium? Stranger things have happened.

As tough – or not – as 2008 has been, one thing is for sure: this year and the year after will be tougher. No wonder that Loeb has more than half an eye on his future outside rallying, which could happen sooner than people think. After such a stunning season in '08, the writing is not on the wall for the record-breaking Frenchman yet: not by a long way. But there are plenty of people eager to take the lid off the pen.

Above: Loeb impressed Red Bull team chiefs during an F1 test at Barcelona last November.

Above middle: Victory on Rally GB completed Loeb's set of hallmark wins.

Top: The combination of Loeb and Elena is the most successful in the WRC.

Left: Loeb has remained undefeated in Germany since the event joined the world championship in 2002.

Photographs: PHOT04 unless specified

Main: Jari-Matti Latvala came of age with his maiden victory in Sweden. The win repaid the loyalty shown in him by the factory Ford team (inset).
Photographs: Race&motion

"There's no question he **will** be world champion"

That's Ford team boss Malcolm Wilson's assessment of his young Finnish charger – and it's high praise indeed. But before Jari-Matti Latvala can rule the world there are some rough edges to be smoothed out. By Richard Rodgers

JARI-MATTI Latvala's maiden victory at world championship level in Sweden last year should have been the catalyst for myriad triumphs. But rather than galvanise the young Finn into the complete performer his potential had suggested there was to be no repeat win, just a season of inconsistency and several costly mistakes.

Amid the frustration, however, there were a number of standout performances and an unwavering demonstration of pace. Proof if it were needed that a glittering career remains in store for the rallying-obsessed 23-year-old.

"A win can never come too soon but it put more pressure on him," says Latvala's team boss Malcolm Wilson of his driver's first place in Sweden. "He'd won the second rally of the season and I think he thought he could go on and challenge for the win on every rally. But he quickly realised that experience, as I've always maintained, counts for so much in the world championship and it's not as straightforward as that."

Latvala's victory on the Karlstad-based event made him the youngest driver to win a World Rally Championship qualifier, surpassing the benchmark set by his idol Henri Toivonen, who was 24 when he won the RAC Rally in 1980.

After an early error on the opening round in Monte Carlo raised doubts that Latvala had the composure to cut it at a global level, his dominant performance in Sweden ended those reservations in an instant and appeared to vindicate Ford's decision to elevate the youngster from the Stobart VK M-Sport squad to the cut and thrust of the main factory line-up.

But Latvala not only failed to emulate his Sweden success, he also began to lose the sparkle that was so evident during that February weekend to the point that in Spain, 10 events later, Latvala described his confidence as "being on the floor".

He threw away second place in Jordan when he broke his Ford's rear suspension by clouting a rock on the final morning. He was leading on the next round in Sardinia only to crash again. He damaged his car's suspension on a rock in Greece, while another mistake in Finland resulted in a high-speed accident on the third stage of the event. He went off the road in Germany and when he crashed out in New Zealand with one stage remaining Ford's patience snapped. As a result Latvala was demoted to the second-string Stobart team for the asphalt events in Spain and Corsica.

The move was designed partly to restore Latvala's flagging confidence but primarily to boost Ford's hopes of claiming a third straight manufacturers' crown, which were hanging by a thread due to Latvala's failure to score consistently.

Looking back, Wilson admits Latvala's promotion came one year too early. But when Marcus Grönholm, formerly the lead Ford driver, announced he would be retiring at the end of the 2007 season, the make was left with few options and Latvala was considered the only real choice for the team's second seat alongside Mikko Hirvonen.

"The original plan was for Jari-Matti to have another 12 months in the Stobart team because we hoped Marcus was going to carry on for one final

Race&motion

Above: Latvala's failure to hold onto the lead in Sardinia when he crashed marked one of several low points in the year.

Right: Ford's European motorsport boss Mark Deans believes Latvala is a future world champion.

Bottom right: The team's technical director Christian Loriaux is keen to help the young Finn improve his knowledge of car set-up.

Middle right: Latvala admitted it took him time to adapt his driving to Pirelli's new control tyre.

Top right: Jari-Matti should have finished second in Jordan, but damaged his rear suspension by hitting a rock.

Far right: The young Finn's win in Sweden propelled him into the international spotlight.
Photographs: PHOTO4 unless specified

season," says Wilson. "When it was obvious things weren't working out for him we were in a fortunate position that we could move him back into the Stobart team and take the pressure off him. It paid big rewards and I know he learned a lot from that experience."

Asphalt expert François Duval replaced Latvala for the Tarmac events, while Latvala switched to the lead Stobart entry before returning to the Ford camp for the final rounds in Japan and Great Britain. It wasn't an easy transition but Latvala responded with two strong performances. He was sixth in Spain and followed that up with a fine fourth in Corsica seven days later.

"My confidence was still not at the highest level but it was getting there after Spain," he says. "We were struggling for two days there with the car set-up. On Friday and Saturday we did a lot of work with the car and finally we found a good set-up. It was on the Sunday that I actually realised how you have to drive with the new Pirelli [control] tyres on asphalt because that was a big issue for me and I struggled."

New tyre regulations for the 2008 season limited drivers to a hard and soft compound. The construction put the onus on durability rather than performance and it took Latvala several months to adjust to their handling characteristics.

"You have to drive the tyres on the edge of the grip limit at the point where the car starts to understeer. But you are not allowed to let the car understeer at all. You have to drive on the edge but not over it, and it took me a long time to work that out. Because I didn't have much testing experience I wasn't always able to give the right information to my engineers and that was also a problem for me."

Christian Loriaux, the Ford team's technical director, admits Latvala's technical input remains a weakness but accepts he doesn't always get the opportunity.

"His input is not massive because he gets into a car when the car is pretty much sorted," says Loriaux. "It's

not like we do loads of development with him but I know he thinks a lot about the car and the set-up, maybe too much sometimes. He's more of a racing driver than a development driver and at the moment I would rather he concentrated on that."

Loriaux admits that Latvala still needs to iron out some of the bad habits he picked up driving a Toyota Corolla WRC during his early career. It utilised fully active differentials while changes to the WRC technical regulations in 2006 forced teams to install mechanical front and rear differentials.

"I never realised he had been driving the Corolla that much until not long ago," says Loriaux. "There's not much difference with an active diff or without but cars are easier to drive in difficult conditions with fully active diffs and that was a problem for Jari-Matti, and maybe caused some of the mistakes."

Latvala's penchant for mistakes was compounded by Hirvonen's ability to remain almost error-free during the 2008 season. Despite his inconsistency, Wilson is convinced Latvala has what it takes to make the grade.

"Every driver is different," he insists. "Jari-Matti is one of these guys who will always end up making two or three mistakes a year because he's a different animal to Mikko. But he learned so much in those last three or four rallies of the season since we took the pressure off him in Spain and Corsica.

"There were mistakes that shouldn't have been made and bringing him into the main team was a big ask of him. But his win in Sweden and the speed he's shown throughout the year mean the positives far outweigh those disappointments."

The task now for Wilson is to make Latvala the solid number two that Hirvonen – and Ford – craves before he's unleashed to challenge for the world title in his own right.

"Jari-Matti has a very hard act to follow in Mikko because he's always so controlled and so consistent,"

Race&motion

Race&motion

Race&motion

THE MAN BEHIND THE MAGIC

WHEN TIMO Jouhki does call time on his glittering career as a renowned talent backer then it will be fitting that Jari-Matti Latvala will be in a prime position to preserve his legacy.

Jouhki not only showed belief in a host of young Finnish drivers – Juha Kankkunen, Tommi Mäkinen, Toni Gardemeister, Mikko Hirvonen and Latvala all owe a huge debt of gratitude to the 58-year-old – but he also showed the gumption to provide vital financial support when nobody else would.

Jouhki stops short of using the word 'retired' but admits that Latvala will be his last 'project'. So there's an enormous sense of pride in his voice when he talks about his youngest charge.

"It's always the best moment of my life when one of my drivers gets their first win," he says. "It's only when they win their first championship that the moment becomes better. With Jari-Matti I wasn't surprised when he won in Sweden because I always believed that he would be a winner, but I have to say I wasn't expecting the win to come so soon.

"When I was asked on the first morning in Sweden who I thought would win I said Jari-Matti straight away because of his previous experience on snow and the fact that his starting position gave him an advantage. But then you think to the mistakes he makes."

Jouhki has watched Latvala make countless errors in his formative years but has always stuck by his man, convinced he would one day secure his breakthrough win.

"Mistakes happen more for the less experienced guys because they haven't got the patience of the older guys," says Jouhki. "It comes with their age. If we look at the statistics it takes a long time for most of the drivers to win an event and then repeat it. Normally you are at least over 25, but Jari-Matti was 22 when he won in Sweden. That was very special."

Jouhki refuses to rank his drivers against one another but points to Latvala's "high expectations" as being one of his key strengths.

"He always wants to do well so any expectations that are put on him from outside I know he can handle them, even though he does make mistakes," he says. "In these situations the main thing you have to tell him is he must drive his own rally, take it calmly and don't take in any pressure.

"The opening round last year in Monte Carlo was an example of him making one of the classic small errors that he does sometimes do, but then on the next event in Sweden he showed just what he could do by concentrating and taking things a little bit easier.

"He can get excited and is not as confident as some of the other drivers. This then causes him to lose some of his concentration but this is mainly because of his age, not because he can't drive in the right way.

"The test for him now is to win again but I know he can do this."

Race&motion

two drivers from the same country," says Deans. "We've always set out to try and win because that's what's expected of us and that's what the followers of the brand want. The way to win is to have two of the finest drivers in the world driving for us. The Ford markets understand that and they know it's better to be world champion, which we've been twice, because that gives you substance and the reason for being involved in the sport.

"From a commercial point of view if we could get a driver of that standard from Britain or Germany, then yes, we would probably look at altering the line-up. If you can find that mix of brilliance and nationality relevant to the market you are in then you've got the optimum. But you've got to be in this to win and nationality has got to come second to the competitive element of the drivers."

Ford has employed two Finnish drivers since 2006. It wasn't such an issue when Grönholm, a double world champion, joined the fold. In doing so he became the Blue Oval's first big-name driver since Colin McRae, who left at the end of the 2002 season. But the problem was exasperated when Grönholm quit, leaving Hirvonen – who had been largely overshadowed by his veteran countryman – at the helm with Latvala being drafted in as a relative unknown.

"Losing Marcus was always going to be a big test because we had to forego his experience but also his stature," says Deans. "Okay, Jari-Matti could have done with another year before he joined the main Ford team, but he's clearly a world champion in the making. And with Mikko we have a driver with tremendous mental strength who has been a great asset to us."

Latvala looks back on his 2008 season with a sense of pride, although he's quick to acknowledge where things didn't quite go to plan.

"Actually I'm very happy with how things have been for me because I have done so much learning and I also understand what winning the world championship really means," he says. "Just because you win a rally it doesn't mean you will be able to keep your rhythm for the next event. When you have a bad rally you lose your rhythm and it's hard to get back to the right level."

Although Latvala is no slouch on Tarmac, he concedes it's not his favoured surface. With only two of the 12 rallies in 2009 run on asphalt, Latvala believes it will boost his chances of adding to his tally of wins.

"Once the set-up is okay I am actually confident with my driving," he says. "I want to get my Tarmac driving better and be close to Sébastien Loeb and Dani Sordo. I also have to improve on gravel because sometimes I am going too sideways. It might be exciting for me and good to watch but to be quick you have to be as precise as possible. It has been a difficult year for me but hopefully I will be stronger for it in 2009. But I have won a rally now and that's more than most people can say."

says Wilson. "It's improving but he's got a long way to go. Jari-Matti's flat-out style and commitment can't change, but a bit more experience from testing will hopefully eliminate some of the little frustrating mistakes that he's made. He's had 12 months to learn, and we know he's definitely learned a lot and taken a lot away from his first year with the team.

"We will be sitting down and having a full debrief for the new season to ensure we've got a plan in place for him. He's still very young and he still wants to win every rally, but he'll mature and start to look at the bigger picture. There is no question he will win a lot of rallies in the future and there's no question he will be world champion. At the moment he wants to do that yesterday and that's probably one of the hardest things we face right now.

"He's so passionate. He doesn't have anything else in his life apart from rallying. He can answer any question about rallying in the 1980s and '90s. He knows it all but that level of enthusiasm needs to be nurtured."

While Ford's Finnish driver pairing wasn't exactly big on experience, it also compromised the team's marketing and promotional efforts. Although both drivers are more than capable of endorsing the virtues of the Ford brand, the company's European motor-sport chief Mark Deans admits that having two drivers from the same country wasn't always an easy sell.

"It's a perennial challenge you face when you have

Above: Despite some of the knocks he had last season, Latvala always managed to raise a smile.

Top: Finishing second on the opening stage pointed to a promising result for Latvala in Argentina until he went off on the very next test.

Right: Latvala was relegated to the semi-works team on the Catalunya Rally, but didn't let this faze him.

Opposite page: It could have been two wins in a row for Latvala in Mexico, only for turbo problems to drop him back to third.
Photographs: Race&motion

International sponsors

ABU DHABI is the largest of the seven emirates which comprise the United Arab Emirates (UAE), forming 80% of the country's land-mass and is home to the capital, Abu Dhabi City. The Abu Dhabi Tourism Authority (ADTA) has embarked on a dynamic campaign to develop a world-class infrastructure as an up-scale sporting, cultural and leisure destination, aimed at discerning visitors. Abu Dhabi is the Official Destination partner of the FIA World Rally Championship.

EASYNET is an international managed networks and hosting company, delivering superbly managed solutions for businesses and enterprises. Easynet sets itself apart through customer service excellence, with operations across Europe and an operation in China. Easynet is part of BSkyB which has a total market capitalisation in excess of £9bn. Easynet is the Official Network and Hosting Company of the FIA World Rally Championship.

MAGNETI MARELLI makes advanced systems and components for motorvehicles. With its 46 production sites, 9 R&D centres and 27 application centres, in 16 countries, the group supplies all leading carmakers. In the motorsport field, Magneti Marelli supplies hi-tech systems such as engine control, data acquisition and telemetry. The company has been involved in motorsports since its birth and has been supporting several world champion teams. Magneti Marelli is the Official Telemetry Sponsor of the FIA World Rally Championship

PIRELLI world leader in ultra high performance tyres, is the official tyre supplier to the FIA World Rally Championship. Pirelli has recently celebrated 100 years of international motorsport victories, the first being the Paris-Peking race of 1907. With a unique record of competing in every year of the WRC since its inception, Pirelli has accumulated 19 world rally championship titles, demonstrating outstanding commitment and success in the sport of rallying .

WRIGLEY'S AIRWAVES ® is the second fastest selling chewing gum brand in the UK worth £33.7m*. The Wrigley company is the world's leading manufacturer of chewing and bubble gum and a major player in the confectionery industry worldwide. Wrigley brands sold in the UK include Wrigley's Spearmint,, Juicy Fruit,, Doublemint,, Extra, (chewing gum and mints), Hubba Bubba,, Orbit Complete,, and Airwaves,. Airwaves® is the Official Chewing Gum Sponsor of the FIA World Rally Championship.

* (ACNielsen MAT 29.12.07 Total Coverage.)

Dark times for Subaru:
economic concerns coupled
with a winless streak have
forced out one of the WRC's
most popular makes.
Photograph: Race&motion

All that's left is the legacy

From title glory and huge popularity to in-fighting and WRC withdrawal,
the Subaru World Rally Team's tale is a cautionary one. By David Evans

THE SUBARU World Rally Team has left the building. Get that? SWRT's gone. Finished. Sayonara. This is a mad world. In the same way that Lehman Brothers filing for bankruptcy sent shockwaves around the world of investment banking, Subaru's departure from the World Rally Championship has rocked our sport. Subaru was blue chip WRC.

From June 1990 until December 2008, the WRC has functioned to the aural backdrop of a flat-four boxer engine. Despite work and testing on the Impreza WRC2009 being already underway, the motor has fallen silent; next year's new car stillborn, the team disbanded. How did it come to this?

The global economic downturn undoubtedly impacted on Subaru's continued participation, but the absence of a real win since March 2005 stands out more than falling car sales and a reddening hue to the balance sheets. The cost of competing in the World Rally Championship has been on the decrease for months following a raft of FIA measures to try and avoid just this scenario, but a 51-event absence from the winners' circle was most likely the straw that broke this particular camel's back.

For years, Subaru was the perfect case study in how to turn sporting success in the WRC to commercial success in the showroom. Sales of the Legacy road car never really felt the full benefit of the WRC programme – hardly surprising given that the model

only completed one full campaign. Even when the Legacy RS came out, the Impreza was in its design phase – waiting in the wings. A car more than capable of usurping its forerunner.

Unleashed on the stage, the Impreza squashed everything in its path. It lifted both the drivers' and manufacturers' crowns in only its second season and Subaru would remain unbeaten in the makes' race for three years. On the street, a new B-road hero was born. Hot-hatches were left trailing in the wake of this devastatingly effective piece of machinery. And as the years rolled by, providing you could come to an understanding with your local insurance broker, near-super-car performance became readily available to Joe Public. The mid-1990s signalled not only the peak of Subaru's domination of rallying, but also the start of a new cult. The Subaru troop had arrived.

Only Ford's Escort and possibly the Mini could claim to rival the following that Subaru developed. But in an age of increasing disposable incomes and a slick, special stage-driven marketing campaign, the Impreza surpassed anything the sport had known in terms of road-going replicas. In Britain, it wasn't all about the car though. A certain Scot played his part too.

Colin McRae's RAC Rally win in 1994 and world championship success the following year had an enormous impact on Subaru's turnover. Everybody wanted what Britain's conquering hero had. McRae, success and the Impreza – usually of the 555 flavour – went hand in hand. Six years after McRae's global success Subaru won again with Richard Burns, but the first ever world title for an Englishman, though popular, couldn't rival the magic conjured by McRae.

And then came the darling of Subaru Tecnica International, Petter Solberg. The charismatic and emotional Norwegian became the blue-eyed boy metaphorically and quite literally around the Mitaka home of STi. Solberg's 2003 world championship was the last season-long success for Subaru. A title defence boasting five wins would, in any other year, have been successful. Unfortunately, Solberg's nemesis had well and truly arrived on the scene. Frenchman Sébastien Loeb claimed the 2004 title and has remained unbeaten ever since.

At the start of 2005, still flush from his world title win in 2003 and near success in '04, Solberg stepped into the spotlight at Subaru's season launch at the

Hotel Columbus, Monaco and talked of winning 10 rounds of the series. Oh dear. There were uncomfortable looks from the rest of the team as their man raised the stakes higher than ever. It's fair to say Solberg was made to regret that statement.

Ten rally wins in a season was indeed possible and it was achieved in 2005. But by Loeb, not Solberg. Solberg and Subaru's demise had started. And the slide wouldn't stop until they'd slipped all the way into world rallying oblivion.

The start to the 2005 campaign wasn't bad. Three rounds in and Solberg was topping the points table with wins in Sweden (the last outing for the

WRC2004) and Mexico (the WRC2005's debut). The team had started Mexico under a cloud, following the death of STi founding president Ryuichiro Kuze. Kuze, a board member of Subaru's Fuji Heavy Industries parent company, was the man who had opened negotiations with David Richards' Prodrive firm in the late '80s to run its WRC effort. Up until his death, Kuze remained the strongest ally anybody within SWRT could have hoped for. Winning the event in Kuze's memory was a fitting tribute, but that success masked a myriad of problems with the new car. It's fair to say that what has happened to the team since March 2005 would have tested the resolve of even the ever-smiling Kuze-san.

It's easy to lay the blame for the current predicament at Richards' door, pointing to his personal diversification into Formula 1 and the commercial world of the WRC, but the loss of Subaru came about via the culmination of numerous factors. Richards' decision not to remain at the helm was probably the catalyst, however. DR's capabilities are well chronicled; embroiled in the BAR F1 team, he reversed the fortunes of the ailing race outfit and catapulted it to the front of the grid and second in the manufacturer standings in 2004. Simultaneously, Subaru lost its mojo.

Above: After Colin McRae became Britain's first world champion aboard an Impreza, rally fans flocked to the showrooms.

Top: Ari Vatanen, seen here finishing second in Finland in 1993, played a crucial role in the early development of the team.

Below left: Piero Liatti was signed for his pace on asphalt and repaid the team by winning the 1997 Monte Carlo Rally, the first victory for a World Rally Car.

Right: Richard Burns, pictured with co-driver Robert Reid, gave Subaru's profile another boost by becoming the first English World Rally Champion in 2001.

Photographs: SWRT.com

Above: The Japanese make struck gold again with Petter Solberg in 2003, before starting its gradual decline.

Top: For years Subaru was a force to be reckoned with in the WRC. This is Burns and Reid en route to victory in Portugal in 2000.

Photographs: SWRT.com

Soon after Richards departed BAR, he began working on Prodrive's own F1 venture. And SWRT's technical guru David Lapworth was a willing accomplice. Lapworth had mastered just about everything there was to master in the mechanical side of rallying. He'd broken new ground in transmission technology and created title-winning machinery year after year. Now he was ready for a change. The loss of two such senior figures within the establishment hit hard. Suddenly the driven, tightly-knit team that had topped the world was beginning to look lost. And soon it would start to list.

With the benefit of hindsight, the 2005 Impreza was floored by the location of key parts beneath the bonnet. The car's handling – formerly one of the Impreza's strongest points – was spoiled. Consistency was a thing of the past and as evolutions of the WRC2005 were rolled out nothing appeared to improve – and certainly in the damping area, things got an awful lot worse. So bad was the suspension in 2008 that it's rumoured the drivers were banned from using the d-word (dampers) when they were interviewed. Subaru was ready to switch supplier to Ohlins for next season, but it was too little too late.

By this time, Richards and Lapworth had both returned in an effort to right the wrongs of years gone by. But again, that was too little too late.

Privately, senior sources within the team were more than happy to lay the blame for the downward spiral on its drivers. With his first title under his belt, Solberg's powerbase within SWRT grew and grew. Richard Burns had been due to re-join Subaru in 2004, but the Englishman's terrible and ultimately terminal medical condition put paid to that. When Burns became

unavailable, Colin McRae was sized up and slotted in. That was until then-team principal Lapworth elected to offset sizeable budget cuts from Japan by taking the cash on offer to run Mikko Hirvonen. This was another key moment in the team's demise.

A strong and tenacious character like McRae would have challenged the direction in which the team was going. Instead Solberg forged his own path, which according to team insiders could change from day to day.

Solberg was joined in 2005 by WRC rookie Chris Atkinson after Hirvonen was given short shrift, having failed to flourish in the famously regimented environment of SWRT. Subaru deemed it to be the continuation of its young driver policy; the reality was one of a genuinely talented – but very well funded – Australian driver. Time has shown Atkinson deserves a place in the WRC on speed alone, but at that time he was not what the team needed. The team needed direction and a joint number one driver with his own thoughts on car set-up. What it got was a completely inexperienced Queenslander who had nothing and nobody to benchmark himself against other than a succession of horrid-handling Imprezas and an increasingly truculent team-mate.

Whether or not another driver – such as Marcus Grönholm who was tipped to join Subaru in 2009, or Markko Märtin who had come close to a brace of asphalt outings in '08 – would have won will never be known. What is known is that the team paid the ultimate price for failing to win.

While redundant SWRT employees are now in turn feeling the price of Subaru's demise, the wider world of rallying will count the cost of losing arguably its most iconic brand for many years to come.

Above: Despite winning five rallies Petter Solberg fell short in his efforts to defend his world title in 2004.

Right: Solberg's agony in 2008 was compounded when he lost out on a certain podium finish in Japan with this time-consuming crash.

Above right: Subaru gave its all-new Impreza WRC its debut on the Acropolis Rally.

Top right: The Impreza WRC2005 scored a debut win in Mexico, but largely failed to live up to that form.

Far right, from top: Subaru's mechanics worked tirelessly but with little reward in recent seasons.

Photographs: SWRT.com

Subaru World Rally Team – the numbers

First event: Acropolis Rally, 1990 Subaru Legacy RS

First win: Rally NZ, 1993 Colin McRae

1 win for Subaru Legacy RS

46 wins for the Subaru Impreza

3 drivers' titles

3 manufacturers' titles

26 official drivers

1,053 fastest stage times

119 podiums

18 successive WRC campaigns

Last win: Rally GB, 2005 Petter Solberg

Last event: Rally GB, 2008, Subaru Impreza WRC2008

After 19 seasons Subaru has turned
its back on the World Rally
Championship. But for how long?
Photograph: SWRT.com

NEWS

FEATURES

RESULTS

COLUMNS

VIDEO

PICTURES

PODCASTS

COMPETITIONS

DOWNLOADS
BABES

COMMUNITY
DIRECTORY

THE WORLD'S BIGGEST MOTORSPORT COMMUNITY

Working from the ground up

Most of 2008's technical challenges were based around the introduction of Pirelli's new control tyre, although the ill-fated Subaru and Suzuki teams both trialled new cars. By Clive Hughes

RALLY ENGINEERS are constantly looking for ways to improve areas like engines, suspension, aerodynamics and weight distribution. In 2008, however, the biggest technical challenge they faced was an unfamiliar one – how best to tune their cars to suit Pirelli's new range of control tyres.

Apart from the tyres there were few technical regulation changes for the season. Instead of radical redesigns the year was all about fine-tuning. Some new safety measures were evident, however, with the mandatory introduction of more elements of the FIA's Advanced Side Impact System. Seats had to be fitted with wrap-around head restraints and a 200mm block of impact-absorbing foam was added to the void between head rests and b-pillars. The factory Subaru Impreza was alone in starting the season with FIA-advised safety netting between driver and co-driver, but this was removed after one rally. Another part of the FIA's safety system, a stronger and more supportive seat, was made available from Rally Japan onwards.

But the biggest change was the tyres. "From a technical point of view it was interesting," says Subaru World Rally Team technical director David Lapworth. "It changed our approach - considerably. In the past we would pressure the tyre manufacturers to keep improving their tyres, and then work around that with the car. But it completely turned it the other way. The only way to work was to get the best out of them. There was no point asking for a better tyre because there wasn't one."

Pirelli's tyres were built differently to those from previous years. With anti-deflation mousse inserts banned, the sidewalls and tread were reinforced to have puncture resistance built in. As a consequence

they were up to double the stiffness. To decrease tread wear the rubber compounds were generally harder too. The additional stiffness was one of the biggest technical problems to overcome. Small bumps previously absorbed by the sidewall were now transmitted straight into the car via the dampers. All this extra energy caused the suspension more work and some cars, particularly in Group N, struggled to keep their dampers cool.

Among the World Rally Cars problems were most noticeable at Ford, where additional stresses on rougher rallies caused suspension failures early in the year. As late as the Acropolis Rally the team suffered broken components on stages – components that had given no cause for concern when Michelin tyres were used the previous year. Experimenting with reduced tyre pressures put more flex in the sidewalls but came at the risk of tyres being pulled off the rim.

The new rubber also had different performance characteristics. On the limit the tyres couldn't carry simultaneous lateral (in cornering) and longitudinal (in a straight line) acceleration as well as the more specialised rubber. They reached their maximum temperature in different ways too, forcing some drivers to adapt their driving styles to optimise performance. But any pre-season hopes that the control tyre would bring more sideways action proved unfounded.

"I would say they affected the style of driving a little bit but not massively," says Lapworth. "The fact is that people like Sébastien Loeb have learned that a spectacular style isn't the fastest – and they can't unlearn that. If you look at any modern motorsport formula it has gone the same way; sideways isn't the best way to go forwards."

Above: Pirelli became the WRC's control tyre supplier and more than rose to the challenge.

Right: David Lapworth oversaw the introduction of Subaru's new Impreza WRC2008.

Middle right: Ford introduced its 2008-specification Focus in Germany, but it couldn't stop Citroën's dominance on asphalt.

Bottom right: A well-drilled operation helped Ford to remain one of the leading contenders.

Far right: Ford's technical chief Christian Loriaux celebrated four wins but not a third straight makes' title.

Top right: The strength of the modern-day rally car saved Gigi Galli's life when he crashed in Germany.
Photographs: PHOTO4

Average speeds this year were generally comparable with 2007 but some stage records were broken when tyre limitations were balanced out by improvements elsewhere on the cars. "In performance terms, when we measured the tyres they were slower than before but we've proved that we've kept on improving the cars because some of the benchmark stage times have been beaten," says Christian Loriaux, technical director at the BP Ford Abu Dhabi team. "In all fairness to Pirelli the tyres worked fantastically well. It could have been chaos but Pirelli delivered something reliable and consistent and still with reasonable performance. They did really well."

When it came to car development, Subaru and Suzuki had the most to do in 2008, while Ford and Citroën did their best to fine-tune their proven rally winning packages. Ford began the season with an evolution of the Focus RS WRC introduced in August 2007. After shock loading problems on Rally Argentina and Greece, many suspension components were reinforced in time for the team's one-two win in Turkey. A 2008 homologation of the Focus RS was introduced on Rally Deutschland. Style changes to the front grill area reflected the looks of the new Focus RS road car, while a new turbo and crankshaft gave a small power increase. The differences

DÉJÀ VU AT SUBARU

THE TEAM'S supporters didn't need reminding of this, but the fact is Subaru's last proper world championship rally win was in Mexico in 2005. Since then, the Banbury-based team and its drivers Petter Solberg and Chris Atkinson have been unable to worry the WRC frontrunners for any significant length of time – and won't even be trying to in 2009.

Yes, there were flashes of speed, the odd stage win (23 in 2008, actually) and they always found something to feel positive about after every rally, but for some reason the improvement never seemed to gather momentum and sooner or later it was back to disappointment and frustration. In short, Subaru seemed trapped in rallying's version of Groundhog Day.

Quite how it got into such a mess wasn't clear, nor was the reason why it didn't turn things around after four years. End-of-stage comments from Solberg and Atkinson only added to the mystery. Solberg gave us everything from his resigned "this is part of the game" to tears of utter frustration, while Chris had a good selection of sarcastic replies to "how's it going?"

What made the situation worse was that last year's new from the ground up Impreza WR2008 seemed to have inherited handling shortcomings similar to those of its predecessor. Sure, a brand new car can't be expected to be on the money straight away, but three months after its launch the team had a miserable time in Finland and New Zealand. Six months on and it was been unable to match its debut form.

What caused the problem? Well, the team consistently denied that one single area of the old or new car was to blame – although it did admit dampers had something to do with it.

The team had used off-the-shelf units from Bos Engineering since the WRC2007 – or S12 – was launched at Rally Mexico in 2007. Results with that car were disappointing and both Solberg and Atkinson complained of inconsistent handling. A number of damper unit failures were reported, too. The team responded with an increase in test and development work, much of which was focused on dampers. Bos continued as supplier for the Impreza WRC2008 (S14) when it replaced the S12 in Greece. But although the car propelled Solberg to the podium on its debut, some of the drivers' cryptic comments thereafter had had a familiar ring to them.

Dampers are one of the most important areas of a modern-day WRC car. While the tyre on the ground is ultimately responsible for grip, the damper is the link between the car and tyre. "Damper technology has moved on in recent years and you've got more and more technology in terms of settings and options," says Ford's technical director Christian Loriaux. "You can have different damping at high speed, low speed and at different parts of the travel. There are hydraulic bump stops and things like that, but the most important thing is to have a consistent characteristic. A damper will behave very differently when it is hot from when it's cold, for instance. If you don't compensate for that then you lose the characteristics."

In Finland Subaru revealed that it had taken over management of the damper project from Bos and was instead assembling 'collaborative' units in-house. The team's technical director David Lapworth maintained the latest generation of Prodrive/Bos dampers were more reliable and consistent than before. "Dampers have been the focus of our attention, that's the area where we've had to do the most catching up, but the inconsistencies haven't been an issue for a long time," he said. "There might be issues about how it can be improved but we did all of Rally Japan with Petter on one set of dampers – and the same in GB."

In October Subaru decided to stop working with Bos beyond the current homologation and had instead agreed a deal with Swedish firm – and seasoned WRC competitor - Ohlins to produce a damper for the 2009 season...

According to Lapworth, the damper is only part of the reason the latest car hasn't been able to save the day. "It's been very difficult to get to the bottom of what it is the drivers are looking for to get their confidence," he says. "Some of it has been around dampers and some of it has been around trying to find a set-up that suited them. We've gone around in circles with the set-up trying to find something that is responsive enough when it's twisty, and yet stable and easy to drive when it's fast or bumpy. Despite lots of comparative work to reassure us that the new car was a big step forward, for some reason – and dampers is part of the story - they weren't able to find a set-up in the car for Finland/New Zealand that gave them confidence in tricky conditions."

"There's no one thing we can point at and say that was the mistake. We've moved on a little bit – we did a little work on the set-up of the car and gradually things improved. And that's been a trend all the way through and still right up to Rally GB. If you look through the rallies you'll see that our stage times are pretty competitive when the conditions are predictable, and when the conditions get unpredictable - when grip levels are variable - they drop off. The situation got better from Japan where we set some really good stage times in difficult conditions. And in GB we had some really good sections and some good splits where we were on the pace of Loeb and Latvala. But still they haven't quite been able to put it together when the conditions are changeable and really tricky."

The S15 was expected to appear in March. Who knows how different things would have been if the Subaru team had got hold of that.

Left: Petter Solberg was second in the new Impreza in Greece, but it was something of a false dawn.
Photograph: PHOTO4

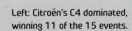

Left: Citroën's C4 dominated, winning 11 of the 15 events.

Above: Nobuhiro 'Monster' Tajima was replaced at the helm of the Suzuki WRC team after a troubled debut.

Top: The handling of the C4 was highly praised and owed much to the design of the car's suspension.

Middle left: Toni Gardemeister led the Suzuki team but was often frustrated by a lack of progress.
Photographs: PHOTO4

Top left: The FIA's efforts to improve driver safety continued in 2008 with in-car safety netting.
Photograph: SWRT.com

were slight but kept the Focus at the sharp end of what was possible under WRC regulations.

"Everybody is looking to get better and better, but it's getting difficult now," admits Loriaux. "We're getting to the point where it's a law of diminishing returns and everybody struggled to make much improvement. You keep tweaking a bit here and there, you have to keep on moving. We know we've improved a bit, but for sure they [Citroën] have improved too."

Citroën began the season with a freshly homologated C4 WRC. The car was fitted with a new EW series engine, replacing the ageing XU unit which had reached the end of its development cycle. The 2008 C4 also featured lighter front and rear sub-frames, and changes to the front wings and bumper to improve airflow. Unlike Ford, Suzuki and Subaru, which began the season taking dampers from third party suppliers (Reiger, Reiger and Bos respectively), Citroën continued to design, build and develop its own units in-house. Some parts were bought in from specialists (such as XTC), but Citroën Sport in Paris made the majority of components.

The combination of Citroën's own damper development and testing programme, plenty of asphalt rally experience and drivers with a deep understanding of the surface meant the C4 was best suited to the new asphalt tyres on Rallye Monte Carlo. On gravel the Citroën came off second best to the Ford early on, but turned the situation around by Rally Jordan after making set-up refinements.

Following two development outings in 2007, Suzuki's first (and so far only) full season with the SX4 WRC turned out to be a tricky one. Things took a turn for the worse before the year had begun, when the team's technical manager and the SX4's designer Michel Nandan left. Nandan's position was taken by Shusuke Inagaki, who managed the project from the team's base in Japan, where the bodyshells and most of the complete cars were built before being shipped to the team's other base in Paris.

Most people expected the SX4 to have a few new car issues at the start of the year. And they were right. Without much pre-event testing, Suzuki ended up doing most of it on the stages. The first three rallies were marked by a series of engine failures – later traced to a faulty batch of head gaskets. The gaskets forced Toni Gardemeister's retirement in Monte Carlo, P-G Andersson's exit from Rally Sweden and, worst of all, a double retirement on Rally Mexico.

Suzuki's team principal, Nobuhiro Tajima, felt that regulations brought in to cut costs were hampering Suzuki's efforts to fix the fault. "It's clear that we have an issue with the engines, but under the current engine linking regulations we are not permitted to change the engine during or in between the rallies to try and understand the problem," he said.

In response, the FIA eased certain parts restrictions for manufacturers in their first year of entering the championship. Instead of having to stick rigidly to the rules concerning engine pairing and the supply of spares like transmissions, steering racks and sub-frames, Suzuki could use two additional engines and change other parts without penalty. The team's two Suzuki SX4 WRCs arrived on the next event, Rally Argentina, with a revised head gasket. From that moment on the engine was generally reliable, albeit down on torque and driveability compared to the competition.

Being a tall car, the SX4 also struggled with a high centre of gravity and poor aerodynamics. Even after running regulation polycarbonate windows and weight-saving composite body panels there was still a lot of weight high up. "It should have been lower," says Toni Gardemeister. "We tried to do that from the start – even a few centimetres makes a big difference. But the depth of the under body protection meant we didn't have a lot of ground clearance. If we took the car

THE FUTURE'S GREEN, BUT WHICH GREEN?

IN OCTOBER Citroën took the wraps off its C4 WRC HYmotion4 - a hybrid power concept car that it believes could lead the way in eco-friendly rallying.

Whether the future will be pan out according to Citroën's vision no one can yet say, but the C4's arrival, plus a flurry of activity coming from the Formula 1 paddock, got people talking about the green route world rallying might take in the future.

Citroën's concept employs a hybrid energy recovery system – similar to the KERS (Kinetic Energy Recovery System) under development in F1. The key components of Citroën's set-up - known as HYmotion4 - are a 125kW electric motor-generator connected to the rear differential and a pack of 990-cell lithium-ion 400V batteries positioned over the fuel tank. Citroën reckons the system is more efficient than a petrol engine, provides more torque and a 30 per cent reduction in fuel consumption. It also added the dizzying possibility of a boost mode where both the petrol and electric motors are run simultaneously, generating an additional 300Nm-1 of torque.

But while the C4 HYmotion4 is the first proper stab at an environmentally conscious rally car, the technical route Citroën has gone down isn't the only one available. There are dozens out there. Determining which one is right for the WRC is just one of the hurdles which need to be cleared before these machines are whizzing silently through the forests, leaving nothing but tyre marks.

"It's raised a philosophical debate within the WRC community," says David Lapworth, technical director of the ill-fated Subaru team. "The simple answer is yes, we should be embracing new technology and helping to pioneer things in this area. But if you think about the history of rallying, what we are normally doing is demonstrating existing technologies and influencing people's choice of cars by showing them how good a particular brand or model is. Until now we've been basing our cars on road cars that you can buy today, not the ones you will be able to buy in five years' time."

Assuming the philosophical debate can be settled – and in favour of boundary-pushing environmentally friendly cars – that still leaves the question of which technology to back. Ask a few car manufacturers how their cars will be powered in five years' time and you'll get a variety of answers ranging from hydrogen fuel cells to purely electric - if they'll tell you at all. Trying to make a single set of WRC regulations for the widest possible number of manufacturers to buy into is almost impossible.

Then there are the costs. It's a fact that developing new technology is expensive. "It needs to be done in a controlled way," says one manufacturer source. "If you allow something like the KERS system then we would all embark on massive research programmes." Not an activity that sits well with the current drive to reduce costs.

So while there's general agreement that the sport should try to move forward as fast as it can on eco matters, for now the answer seems to be by taking small steps and being faster to react where there is consensus. Which, in the short term, means further debate on issues like biofuels and the trend towards reduced capacity engines.

Above: Citroën showed off this hybrid version of its all-conquering C4 World Rally Car – and showed the sport's ability to think green.

Below: The car has been driven on the road, and the French manufacturer is investigating an extensive testing programme.
Photographs: Citroën Communication

too low we kept hitting the ground and lifting the front wheels off the road."

In the first half of the year the car also proved susceptible to hydraulic problems, which in turn affected the power steering and gearbox. The car took a big step forward on Rally Finland when Suzuki homologated new hydraulic components, a new sump design to give better under body clearance and revised rear suspension geometry. In the second half of the year the team also embarked on an aggressive weight-saving programme – even removing the interior heater on Wales Rally GB. "It wasn't a lot of fun – the only thing that was heated was the windscreen," recalls Gardemeister.

Subaru began the season with the S12; the last of the saloon Imprezas and the car Petter Solberg and Chris Atkinson had struggled to get consistent performance from in 2007. Small changes had been made to the suspension geometry over the winter, designed to improve mechanical grip, but otherwise changes were limited to safety systems and a few ongoing damper developments. For the first five months of the season Subaru travelled to WRC events with a slimmed down team and a no-frills service area. Development of the S12 was frozen from the start of the year.

"In the early part of the year we weren't really looking for performance," says Lapworth. "If we identified problems we couldn't ignore them, but from Christmas onwards we were putting as much resource as possible into the new car." Markko Märtin signed up as the team's official test driver in January and conducted all of the early testing work before handing over to Solberg and Atkinson at the end of April.

Billed by the team as the most radically different Subaru World Rally Car in 15 years, the Impreza WRC2008 made its eagerly anticipated debut in Greece – two rallies earlier than expected. Based on the hatchback Impreza road car introduced in June 2007, the WRC2008 was a new car from the ground up. Underneath the five-door bodyshell, however, the car retained Subaru's horizontally opposed engine and symmetrical four-wheel-drive system. In common with its predecessor, dampers were supplied by the French firm, Bos.

Compared to the S12, the WRC2008 had a longer wheelbase, shortened front and rear overhangs and improved aerodynamics. It was also the first Impreza World Rally Car not to be fitted with the trademark bonnet scoop. Instead, the front-mounted intercooler and engine air intake were fed from an opening in the front bumper. Apart from new manifolds, coolant and intercooler systems, the engine was the only major component to be carried over from the S12. This was mated to a revised Prodrive-built electo-hydraulic gearbox, which continued to be the only one in the championship to utilise an H-pattern shift system.

Despite trying to keep expectations for the car to a minimum, Petter Solberg's second place debut suggested that, technically at least, Subaru had turned a corner with the new car. But over the following eight rallies neither driver was able to match the first result. Since introduction no major changes have been made to the WRC2008. There have been a host of minor set-up changes and the team brought production of the Bos dampers in-house, but the major suspension components, cross members, bodyshell, engine and gearbox remained the same. Now that Subaru has pulled out of the WRC, we won't know if the team could have turned a corner in 2009. If the manufacturer's stated aim of returning to the world's stages in the not-too-distant future comes to fruition, maybe we will find out.

Rule changes and economic influences will make for an evolving World Rally Championship in 2009 and beyond. Plus there's the small matter of who might eventually overhaul Mr Loeb... By David Evans

Race&motion

WHILE THE World Rally Championship is set for a transitional season before new technical regulations are introduced in 2010, this year's title battle is set to be an epic with young stars Mikko Hirvonen, Jari-Matti Latvala and Dani Sordo all determined to prevent Sébastien Loeb from claiming a sixth consecutive honour.

But it's not just the drivers' fight that will make 2009 enthralling. A new rotational calendar will be introduced, giving events such as Rally Poland a chance to appear on the global stage for the first time in more than three decades. Changes to the rules will allow rallies to run on mixed surfaces, while new teams and drivers are set to emerge.

The season will also mark the 30th anniversary of the crowning of the first drivers' world champion and the fastest pilots on the planet will be plying their trade on some of the bumpiest and trickiest strips of asphalt anywhere in the world when Rally Ireland kicks off the campaign.

Five-time world champion Loeb always commands massive interest. He's a titan of the sport, but he's going to be hunted like never before throughout this season. His fellow Citroën driver Dani Sordo has another year's experience under his belt and is certain to threaten the established order of the French team. But that's not it for Citroën in 2009 – not by a long shot.

Over the closed season, the Citroën Junior Team has emerged with some of the quickest and most entertaining young drivers around. Sébastien Ogier, the reigning Junior World Rally Champion who led for much of the opening day on Rally GB last December, is set to enter the opening six rallies. His deal for the second half of the year has yet to be concluded, but he's going to be well worth watching as he aims to deliver at the highest level.

The rivalry in the Citroën Junior Team is going to be fierce. And the benchmark is likely to be set – on Rally Ireland at least – by Chris Atkinson. The Australian's initial deal is for Ireland only, but it is expected he will be seen in a C4 WRC on more than one occasion as the season progresses. And Atkinson's pace is well known. He regularly outpaced his former world champion Subaru team-mate Petter Solberg during the past two seasons and is desperate to break his victory duck in the WRC.

The man in the team who has the most experience of the car is Conrad Rautenbach. The former FIA African Rally Champion showed well on occasion last season, most notably taking his C4 to fourth overall on Rally Argentina which was at its most testing last year. The season was all about the step up from Juniors to a full World Rally Championship programme for Rautenbach. This year is about maximising everything he has learned. By his own admission, this is a very important time for the 24-year-old Zimbabwean.

The fourth and final Citroën Junior driver is Evgeniy Novikov, one of the most exciting young

Above: Ford's Jari-Matti Latvala is among a new generation of drivers who have the potential to be world champion.

Top: The benchmark in the WRC is still Sébastien Loeb, who will chase a sixth straight drivers' title in 2009.

Right: Mikko Hirvonen remains at the head of Ford's driver line-up for the coming season.

Above right: Conrad Rautenbach has spent the past season gaining valuable experience in the Citroën C4 WRC. Expect him to make further progress.

Photographs: PHOTO4 unless specified

talents around. Still only 18 years old, the Russian sensation came within an ace of winning a Production Car World Rally Championship round in Japan last season. And this term, he gets his big chance when he starts at least eight rallies in the C4 WRC.

Moving over to Ford, it's more of the same for the BP Abu Dhabi squad with Hirvonen – the first driver ever to finish every single round of a season in the points – again joined by fellow Finn Jari-Matti Latvala. Both Ford drivers are aiming at one man through 2009: Loeb. They know the Frenchman can be beaten, but for the coming year it's going to be a case of picking their fights and working together as

Race&motion

they attempt to steal the manufacturers' crown back for the Blue Oval.

Hirvonen and Latvala should go to every event with a view to winning after they both regularly demonstrated the speed on gravel to trouble Loeb last year. The loss of Rallye Deutschland and the Tour de Corse in 2009, both strong asphalt rallies for Loeb, could well play into the hands of the Focus drivers in terms of the season-long standings.

The voice of youth is echoed in the Stobart VK M-Sport Ford World Rally Team, where the emerging Urmo Aava will join Matthew Wilson. Wilson is a familiar face around the WRC service park now, entering his fourth season at the top level. Building on his experience, Wilson will be looking for points on every round – and his first ever WRC podium. But he's going to come up against some fierce opposition from his Estonian team-mate as he chases that maiden top three. Aava's results in a Mitsubishi Lancer WRC and a Citroën C4 in the last two years have marked him out as one of the sport's burgeoning talents.

And there are more Fords. The Munchi's team will be back with the likeable and dependable Federico Villagra. Henning Solberg, one of the most entertaining drivers to emerge in recent seasons, will back him up.

No sooner will a classic 2009 season be completed than the wraps will come off 2010, when the WRC is set to really take to the skies. It's when the governing body of world motorsport, the FIA, will look to further reduce the costs of competing in the sport's top echelon. The cars will be considerably less expensive to produce, thanks to regulations restricting the use of highly expensive materials and technology. The upshot of these new rules is that the WRC will offer increased accessibility and therefore greater competition and more spectacle.

Already, manufacturers around the world are eagerly awaiting the final technical regulations to be published so they can begin planning a new campaign to show off their products in the most extreme of conditions the WRC provides.

Those cars and drivers will be given a vast platform for achieving worldwide exposure courtesy of new commercial agreements being discussed by the FIA to deliver a global promoter to the WRC. A new dawn is coming, but even the pre-dawn is looking exciting.

And finally, the rallies. For 2009, the WRC returns to Ireland, where the fans are among the most knowledgeable and fervent anywhere in the world. After that, the series heads back to Norway –another great success story among the WRC debutants in 2007.

Cyprus is next on the schedule, but in a much-altered state having missed out on a slot since 2006. For the first time in years, a WRC round will be split between asphalt and gravel – making the island event one of the most challenging rounds of the season. As if it wasn't already…

And for round four, it's back to Portugal, where the locals will be trying to out-do their Irish counterparts to make this the most popular round of the series. The fifth and final returning rally is Australia. But while the Rally Australia title remains, everything else is new as the September event has shifted from Western Australia to the Gold Coast in the east.

Poland is the only completely new round of the championship in a season that concludes uncharacteristically early, with Rally GB running at the end of October. Dates and rallies might have been tweaked and changed, but that only adds to the intrigue and excitement of the year to come.

Race&motion

Shades of **genius**

Newcomer Sébastien Ogier's Junior world title triumph not only won him plaudits among the WRC regulars, but also fuelled comparisons to a certain other Seb. By Rob Wilkins

HE MAY not have been very well known at the start of the year, but by the end of it Sébastien Ogier had established himself as a real star. And he wasn't referred to as the 'new Seb' – a nod to fellow countryman and five-time world champion, Sébastien Loeb – for nothing.

Indeed Ogier blitzed the opposition en route to the 2008 FIA Junior World Rally Championship title – and all in his maiden year in the WRC.

Just how much potential Ogier has he convincingly underlined on the season-ending Wales Rally GB, his debut outing in a World Rally Car, when he won his first stage in the Citroën C4 WRC and actually led overall until SS6, despite the horrendous weather conditions.

Rewind back to last March, and Rally Mexico, the opening round in the JWRC, and the signs were ominous. Ogier dominated in his PH Sport-run Citroën C2 S1600, easily taking the Junior win and also incidentally becoming the first JWRC driver to score a world championship point when he finished eighth.

He followed that up with his second win in succession in Jordan, and while he only took one more victory – in Germany – his speed was unquestionable. He won 50 JWRC stages in total, more than double that of his closest rival.

Errors in Sardinia and Catalunya – where he was leading by more than a minute at the end of the second day and heading for the Junior title – showed he wasn't yet the finished article. This was something that his accident on the first stage on day two in Wales highlighted again. But in his first year it was more than forgivable. It is not what people will remember either. What they will recall is that Ogier won first time out, repeated that success second time out, won the JWRC title and flew on Rally GB.

There's a new Seb on the block, and he's just as quick...

Q Sébastien, you've enjoyed a great season, but did you expect to do so well and dominate the JWRC in the way you did?
A "At the start of the season I had hoped to have a year like this. But when I came in I hadn't done any WRC events and I knew practically nothing. What can I say? I was happy to have a season like this."

You started fantastically in Mexico where you not only won the JWRC category but also finished eighth overall. That was some debut, wasn't it?
"It was a perfect start for me and to begin my career in the WRC with a record was really very exciting. It was a great way to start 2008."

For most people, prior to this year, you were relatively unknown. What championships had you competed in before this season and how did that experience help you?
"I did two seasons in the French championship with a Peugeot 206 and I won the Peugeot 206 Cup in 2007. It is a perfect championship for a young driver to get experience in because it has some events on gravel and some on Tarmac. It was a very good place to learn."

You have enjoyed the backing of the FFSA and Citroën this year. How critical has that support been?
"This support was really important for me because without it I wouldn't have been able to do anything in the world championship. It is really thanks to Citroën and the French federation that I could do this season."

Above: 2008 was a breakthrough year for Sébastien Ogier, who began his Junior title campaign as a relative unknown.

Right: Ogier's win in Germany was his third of the season.

Below and middle right: His debut win in Mexico marked Ogier out as the WRC's latest hot property.

Above right: Ogier was brought down to earth in Sardinia when he punctured a tyre by hitting a rock and finished fifth as a result

Top right: The young Frenchman's celebrates his title success in Corsica.

Far right: A step up to a World Rally Car posed little problem for Ogier after he led for much of the opening day in Wales.
Photographs: PHOTO4 unless specified

Race&motion

Race&motion

Race&motion

Race&motion

Race&motion

What do you think you would you have done without that backing?
"I don't know – and I've never thought about that because I knew I had this programme really early, at the end of 2007."

You are sometimes labelled the 'new Seb' and people like to make comparisons between you and Sébastien Loeb. Just how much has he helped you?
"It is difficult to say how much. But Sébastien is a really good man and since I have known him he has given me some advice about the WRC. It is important for me to be in the same team as him."

While it must be a major compliment to be compared to the most successful driver in WRC history, that's got to be quite daunting too. How do you cope with it?
"It is good for me to be compared to him because he is the best rally driver, as you say. But many times I've pointed out that it will be very difficult for me to have the same career as him. One day everybody must see me as another driver, as Sébastien Ogier, not as a new Seb."

You dominated the JWRC, so how hard did you have to push to stay in front of the competition and was it as easy as you made it look?
"It is not easy to win rallies and to set good stage times. But I had a really good car and a really good team with me and this helped a lot. I never had any problems with my car either and that was a good advantage."

In the end you had to wait until the final JWRC event in Corsica to win the title. What did it mean to clinch the crown on home soil?
"It was the perfect end to the year and to win the championship at home was brilliant. I had a lot of fun on this rally. My family and friends were there and I was very happy to win it."

The error in Catalunya put you under a bit of pressure. Would you have preferred not to have crashed in Spain and won the title with one round to spare?
"Yes, it would have been better to have won in Catalunya. But I made a mistake and afterwards I had to be prudent in Corsica, and that is what I did. Nobody likes to make an error. It was annoying for me. But the important thing was to win the title after this rally."

You made your debut in a World Rally Car on Rally GB – a reward from Citroën for winning the 2008 JWRC title. How was that?
"It was a good opportunity for me to get experience and to drive a WRC car for the first time. I started rallying three years ago and my progression at the moment is very fast. I was really happy to get a start in a WRC car."

Were you pleased with how you got on in Great Britain?
"I was happy to do this rally but it was really, really difficult because of the weather. I think the tyres weren't very good for the conditions. It was hard. I was very surprised at the end of the first day, too. It was crazy to lead my first rally in a WRC car. But I think that was thanks to my position on the road. I know it will be difficult in the future to beat the best drivers in the WRC. I need to get experience at the moment. However, I was really happy with it."

How did the Citroën C4 WRC compare to the Citroën C2 S1600?
"There are a lot of differences. The C2 S1600 is a good car in its category. But the C4 is a really efficient car and there is a lot of power. The difference on the stages is you carry a lot more speed and sometimes it's difficult to stay on the road. I must change something with my pacenotes for next year now because the speed makes it really hard."

As well as competing in the JWRC with the C2 S1600 and doing Rally GB with the C4 WRC, you have also contested a number of events in the C2-R2 Max such as the Ulster Rally and Rally Finland. Did you enjoy those outings and how have they helped you develop?
"I did enjoy driving the C2-R2 Max. Citroën gave me a good opportunity to get some more experience. This car is quite similar to the C2 S1600 and for me it was a nice way to get some more mileage."

How important a role did your regular co-driver, Julien Ingrassia, play in your success?
"It is important to have a good co-driver who doesn't do any mistakes. Julien had a good season and it is also thanks to him that we won."

What is your target for 2009?
"I hope to drive the C4 on a lot of rallies, and I think for me it will be important to do a lot of kilometres with this car and to finish as many events as possible. I need to get experience and then I can be competitive for 2010. My ultimate goal is to become world champion one day. I have time and now it is crucial to just get experience."

Race&motion

The stuff of legends

Good friends and fellow world champions went stage-side to honour the much-missed Colin McRae and Richard Burns in 2008. By David Evans

TWO CHAMPIONS and two rallies. The lives of Britain's World Rally Champions Colin McRae and Richard Burns were celebrated in fine style last September. The McRae event was, naturally, held in his native Scotland and attracted a bevy of world champions, while the Burns rally was in Norfolk and played host to the Subaru World Rally Team.

The Richard Burns Memorial Rally was a two-day event run at RAF Marham on September 13/14. The main attraction was the Impreza WRC2008 crewed by Burns' close friends Markko Märtin and Robert Reid. Given that RB collected his 2001 world title in Subaru blue, it was fitting that it was on 'his' rally that the car not only made its competitive debut in Britain, but also took its maiden win.

While Märtin has busied himself recently with the odd event here and there and a Subaru test contract, the Richard Burns Memorial Rally marked Reid's first time back as a co-driver in a World Rally Car since he and Richard carried out a pre-Rally GB test that

fateful November back in 2003. It was as though Robert have never left the office.

Emotions aside, he and Märtin set about a clinical win. There was plenty more on offer beyond the new Subaru, Märtin and Reid, however. A complete collection of Richard's rally cars were on show for fans to admire, along with RB's dad Alex co-driving Gordon Jarvis in a replica of the Sunbeam in which Burns had cut his teeth in the late 1980s.

As well as providing some fine early autumn entertainment, the event also raised pots of cash for the Richard Burns Foundation and the RAF Benevolent Fund.

A fortnight later and the focus turned north, to Perth and the Colin McRae Forest Stages Rally.

The event organisers had aimed for a star-studded 15-car line-up to run at the head of the usual Scottish Rally Championship round – and the rally world duly delivered. Four world champions (Ari Vatanen, Hannu Mikkola, Björn Waldegård and Louise Aitken-Walker joined a party already boasting British and American heroes to turn on the style one more time. That day of sport in the Perthshire woods is already the stuff of legend. Alister McRae's flat-chat and super-spectacular Ford Escort finished joint winner of the legends category, while Matthew Wilson won the event outright in a 2005 Focus WRC.

The results were largely unimportant though. This was about the occasion. From the pre-event forum to an increasingly boisterous post-event dinner, auction and party, this was a gathering at which Colin would have not only been mighty proud, but also right in the middle of.

Above left: It was apt that Colin McRae's brother Alister (centre) would finish as the leading celebrity driver on the rally held in the late Scot's memory. He's joined here by Björn Waldegård (right) and Hannu Mikkola who were second and third respectively in the invitation class.

Main: Ari Vatanen and David Richards were reunited in competition for the first time since they won the world championship together in 1980. Vatanen was a close friend of McRae's after partnering him in the Subaru team which Richards managed.

Left: Waldegård, seen here driving a Porsche 911, won the world championship in 1979, 16 years before McRae claimed the prestigious accolade. Photographs: Jacob Ebrey

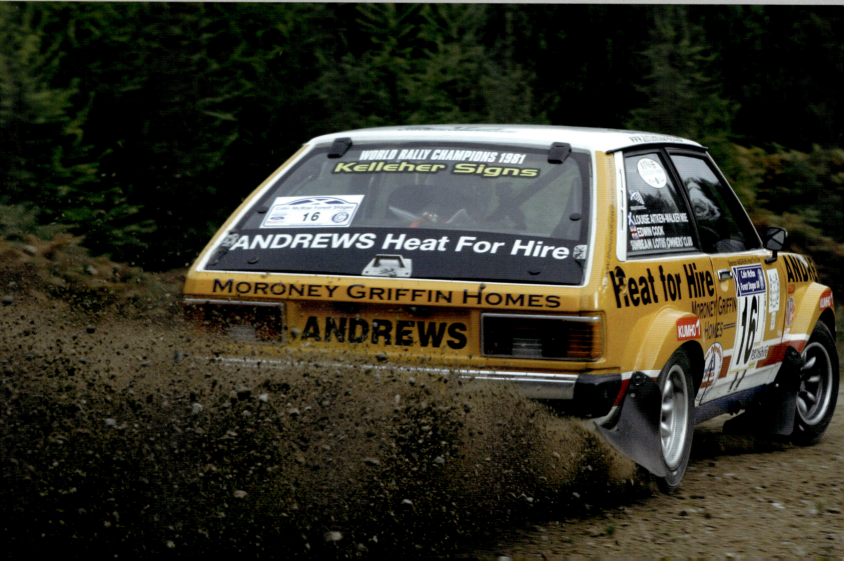

THE RICHARD BURNS MEMORIAL RALLY

Above: Matthew Wilson and Scott Martin idolised Colin McRae, and were able to provide a fitting tribute to their hero by winning the event overall in a Ford Focus World Rally Car loaned to them on the eve of the event.

Left: Former Ladies' World Rally Champion Louise Aitken-Walker hadn't driven in anger since 1993, but was happy to take a break from her day job of running a garage to turn out in honour of McRae.

Top: Colin's father Jimmy's rally ended at the bottom of a ravine after he left the road on a right-hand bend one mile from the end of the final stage, which forced the event to be halted prematurely. Fortunately neither McRae nor his co-driver Andy Richardson were hurt.

Top left: Colin's former business manager Campbell Roy joined Alister in his Ford Escort MkII. Their rally ran largely without a hitch apart from when their car's intercom failed on the opening stage.

Photographs: Jacob Ebrey

Above: Markko Märtin and Robert Reid combined forces to remember their good friend Richard Burns in some style by winning with ease in Subaru's latest Impreza World Rally Car. Reid was Burns' co-driver and hadn't competed since Rally Catalunya in 2003.

Left: Reid (right) and Märtin (left) are congratulated by Alex Burns, Richard's father. The event raised more than £40,000 for the Richard Burns Foundation and the RAF Benevolent Fund.

Below left: The rally was designed to give club drivers the chance to pay their tribute to Burns and more than 100 responded, including second-placed Tom Morris.

Photographs: Joe Bridge

Pirelli takes control

The Italian tyre manufacturer became the WRC's sole supplier in 2008 and excelled, winning over its doubters along the way. By Russell Atkins

'TERRIFIC', 'EXCELLENT' and 'a good job' – that is a selection of the plaudits used to describe Pirelli Competizioni's maiden season as the FIA World Rally Championship's control tyre supplier. But for Paul Hembery, the Italian company's success came as no surprise at all.

Prior to 2008 Pirelli had been absent from the WRC service park for a year, and in 2006 had provided rubber for just one of the sport's six teams, Subaru. Against chief adversary BFGoodrich, no victories had been forthcoming over the course of the 16 rounds, even if Petter Solberg did finish runner-up on three occasions.

So there was undeniably some unease – and not a little anger – when it was the Milanese who were awarded the three-year contract to become the WRC's first single-tyre supplier by the governing body the following February, rather than their Michelin-owned rivals. Thus adding the WRC supply to its expansive portfolio – one encompassing the British Rally Championship, World Superbike Championship and British Superbike Championship – Pirelli embarked upon this new test. It was one that it handled with aplomb.

"From our point of view it was a great success," says Hembery, Pirelli's motorsport director. "It was obviously a challenge and quite a different one to previous years, to come into a championship where historically we've maybe had one or two or, at one stage, teams, to go from having say six cars to up to between 60 or 70 on an event."

Hembery acknowledges that there were a number of concerns expressed at the start of the year, most notably to do with the banning of tyre mousse inserts and the manufacturer's ability to handle the logistics of both looking after the teams and producing just two tyre types to cope with all the demands of a diverse

WRC calendar. That meant dealing with everything from icy Welsh forests to the deluges of Argentina, snow in Japan and the sheer heat and abrasive surfaces of Turkey and the Acropolis, where Hembery admits "tyre wear was on the limit because we hadn't been able to test to those extremes in our preparation for the championship". Any such fears, however, were soon assuaged.

"Pre-season, people were talking a lot about punctures," he says, "but in reality we saw very few overall, and certainly a lot less than you would have had when we had mousse, because the tyres are very heavily reinforced. Often when people were speaking of punctures, the reality was it was wheels that had been damaged, and we could actually re-fit the tyres back onto a new rim and have no issues. It was less of a problem than people had anticipated. Also, on the asphalt events in particular, drivers learned to take fewer cuts – which would have aided safety – and it was no surprise that certain drivers had no punctures whatsoever. There was a level of adapting their driving style to allow for a margin of error."

There was some criticism fired at Pirelli before Rally Argentina over the tyre choice for that event. But, says Hembery, "when everybody's on the same product, they're all going to suffer to the same degree".

He adds: "You can optimise the product, which is what we would have done in recent years – providing a bespoke product for each event in every condition – but we didn't really have any major issues. Sometimes the teams have had a lot to adapt to, more maybe so than we've had, because you need to bear in mind that we've competed in national championships with control tyres for many years, and as a manufacturer we're used to having one tyre for all situations. You can imagine from the teams' point of view that they're going from almost an open book of opportunities in

Above: Pirelli's first year as the WRC's control tyre supplier was judged an outstanding success.

Right: The Italian firm's tyres performed well on all surfaces, with few punctures reported.

Middle right: Pirelli provided equal service to four different manufacturers, including Suzuki whose former team boss Nobuhiro Tajima is pictured right.

Top: A long-running tradition with the tyre company has been its celebrated 'Pirelli girls'.

Right: A Subaru team technician checks tyre pressures in Argentina.

Far right top: Pirelli's motorsport director Paul Hembery believes the upcoming move to Super 2000 rules is a step in the right direction for the WRC.
Photographs: PHOTO4

PAUL HEMBERY: THERE'S VALUE IN THE WRC

"WHERE DOES the World Rally Championship need to go? There are a lot of good things the sport is doing, but it's also clearly in a stage of transition. We have new regulations coming into force over the next couple of years, taking us through to the Super 2000 era, and judging by the number of people that have built S2000 cars, it's clearly something that has excited a lot more manufacturers than the current WRC regulations. That's a good basis from which to move forward.

"You then consider how much it costs to compete. That's something we will understand better when we see the real running costs of Super 2000, with the bolt-on kit of performance parts. Those costs are going to determine the number of competitors we have.

"It's not necessarily the case that a well-organised event will have lots of competitors, so the sport needs to look at what it has to provide to make people want to spend money and compete. That opens up the bigger question of what events should be included in the WRC? If you talk to people who are either involved in the sport or are fans, they would expect to see a number of the classic rallies. Everybody would like to see Monte Carlo, a lot of people are coming round to the fact that we lost a very unique event in Africa, the Safari Rally – which provided a backdrop to rallying that no other sporting event really did – and you then have to add that the sport should be venturing into new territories, like Formula 1 has done.

"Rallying has been a bit tardy getting into countries such as Brazil, Russia, India and China. It's not only from the manufacturers' point of view – we have to remember that the sport is also about sponsors and investors, and there are a lot of major businesses that want to be seen in those countries. That's where they want to expand their businesses.

"Regarding the event format, I think we lost a strong element when the rules were changed to provide a permanent service park. We used to move around a country, which created a spectacle when you saw the whole show on the road. People took notice, and it also meant you reached more members of the public.

"There were a number of events last year where we said goodbye to the crews in the morn-ing, and they turned up again late in the evening, so you have eight or maybe 10 hours of being in a service park where there are no competitors or cars. That's not logical when you're trying to attract people into the service park.

"You have to question whether we should be moving to two- instead of three-day events, because Friday is a dead day. People are working, the public isn't there and there's the extra distance that the crews travel.

"The other key area for the championship is young talent. Any sport is only as healthy as the talent that is being developed in it, and rallying at the moment doesn't have a high-level formula for demonstrating driver talent in equivalent vehicles. Where we need to learn from Formula 1 and circuit racing is that they're starting from karting and going through the various formulas, with GP2 just before F1, where the cars are the same, allowing young talent to be showcased well.

"I'd love to see a WRC2 category, with a control vehicle and maybe five or six events – all in Europe to keep the costs down – where young drivers need to raise 300,000 to 400,000 max, knowing that if they compete on those events and beat their rivals there's going to be a strong chance that they'll get a WRC drive. That's what GP2 has been doing for F1 and rallying desperately needs the same thing.

"You can't ignore the current economic climate. Rallying is relatively cheap compared to other world championship events, and it can still provide exceptional value to competitors, so the cost bene-fit analysis should reveal that rallying provides a significant return on investment for manufacturers and teams.

"We saw a number of privateer teams running last year who have had extremely good media coverage, and that has been valuable for them. If a brand wants to promote itself through sport, rallying is still a platform for any sponsor to gain strong recognition around the world.

"Rallying does need to be careful about its costs, but it is reducing the number of events next year, the move to Super 2000 is another step in the right direction and I think the actual value provided against the cost at this moment in timeis such that rallying still offers value for money."

Race&motion

terms of tyre compound choices and structures and designs, to a point where they're using just one tyre. It's maybe been difficult for them to understand that they'd have to slow down or drive in a different way to cope with having only one tyre choice rather than four or five per event. Now they have to look after the tyres, it becomes another element to manage like many other components on the car.

"Overall, there have been very few lows, fortunately, and many highs. We've had very few punctures, few technical issues and we've had extremely kind comments from the competitors and other people involved in the championship."

That much is corroborated by the teams, who speak positively of Pirelli's control tyre debut. Suzuki World Rally Team director Shusuke Inagaki had been enthusiastic about the parity and 'equivalence' that was generated by the move (prior to the team's withdrawal form the WRC), while BP Ford Abu Dhabi World Rally Team director Malcolm Wilson says there have been no major problems, adding that in his opinion the lack of competition between tyre manufacturers in the championship has barely been missed.

"If you look at what they've had to cope with in their first year, they've done a terrific job," says the 1994 British Rally Champion. "In a short space of time they've made tyres to cope with every condition that

the WRC throws at you and I don't think there's another motorsport discipline that offers so many variations. Okay, when you've got a situation like we had on Wales Rally GB a control tyre does make things difficult [the tyres weren't designed for such icy conditions], but maybe we can learn from this and have an emergency tyre for adverse conditions. Really, though, apart from that they've done an excellent job.

"From our side it's terrific because it's a level playing field. Everybody is on the same tyre, so you can clearly identify where the performance is coming from – whether it's the car, the driver or a combination of the two. I think in 2009 they'll just build on the progress made. Obviously 2008 was the first year so they will have learned a lot, and there are some events where we can maybe use different compounds to what we used then, but again that is all about experience and learning."

Like Wilson, Prodrive boss David Lapworth thinks that the provision of an emergency third compound needs investigating. But he agrees with Hembery until then the onus is on drivers and teams to react accordingly in extreme conditions.

"Really, people thought that to come up with just two tyres to cover the whole season was expecting too much, but in fact I think the drivers have been surprised at how good they are considering the range of events," says the technical director of Subaru, which like Suzuki will be missing from the 2009 WRC line-up.

"The tyre we used in Wales was also used in Finland at 25 degrees Celsius, and we were using it in Wales at minus something. That is perhaps an extreme ask, but in 95 per cent of the conditions the two tyres have done everything that we could have expected. I think the drivers have been surprised that not only do they work, but the performance is good too."

Lapworth doesn't believe there is an issue with the gap in performance between the hard and soft compound. "We saw in Japan on the first day that we expected too much in snowy and icy conditions," he says. "If you draw the parallel with road cars, we're all used to the idea that we don't need to change to wets when we get up to go to work in the morning and it's raining, but I think everybody accepts that if you were to drive up into the mountains in the winter, then you should fit winter tyres.

"These tyres have done really well, but ice and snow is just a bit too far. Everybody recognises that we need a third option for extreme conditions, but it's a tricky balance. At the moment everybody is talking about costs, and the whole idea behind the control tyre was cost reduction. It's achieved that, so what we don't want to do is start re-introducing tyre choices, weather crews and people driving through stages to make a tyre selection. What we've asked for is an emergency tyre that is not at our discretion. The clerk of the course or the stewards – somebody neutral – gets up in the morning, looks at the stage conditions

PIRELLI STAR DRIVERS 2008

Nicos Thomas
From: Cyprus
Age: 20
Won the Middle East Rally Championship nomination over the course of the season. Along the way, Thomas became the youngest ever winner of the Cyprus Rally – and only the second local to win the island's biggest motorsport event. He also won the Cypriot title in his first season in the sport.

Jon Williams
From: South African
Age: 25
Williams was the first nomination to be made this season after impressing the organisers of the FIA African Rally Championship sufficiently for them to put him forward as their competitor. Competing for five years, 2008 was his first campaign at the highest level of African rallying – where he drove a VW Polo S2000.

Mark Tapper
From: New Zealand
Age: 27
Aucklander Mark Tapper won his drive over two rounds of the Asia-Pacific series, the Rally of Whangarei and the Malaysia Rally. One of New Zealand's most promising drivers, he sacrificed his entry on this year's Rally New Zealand in order to save his car for Malaysia. It paid handsome dividends. He's relocating to Europe for 2009.

Martin Semerad
From: Czech Republic
Age: 18
Won one of two seats at the European Pirelli Star Driver shoot-out while still in his first full season of rallying. Demonstrated massive ability at the wheel of his Mitsubishi Lancer, despite extremely limited experience. Only knew he was in the final a week before, following Martin Prokop's exclusion for being over qualified.

Jarkko Nikara
From: Finland
Age: 22
The second European Star Driver Shoot-out winner. Has turned heads with extraordinary car control all year – but then underlined his pace with a stunning 10th overall –in a Group N Fiesta – on the Colin McRae Stages in Scotland earlier this year. Season ended on a bit of a low when he crashed out of the Fiesta Shoot-out in Cumbria.

PIRELLI'S SEARCH FOR A WRC STAR

PIRELLI MOTORSPORT director Paul Hembery believes that the tyre manufacturer's Star Driver programme can help to develop some genuine world championship challengers in the coming years.

Launched in conjunction with the FIA in mid-2008, the initiative's goal was to discover and nurture the crème de la crème of young rallying talent around the globe. It is a scheme that builds on the Italian company's long-held reputation for furthering the careers of up-and-coming drivers in a variety of motorsport spheres.

Five drivers have been chosen from the 2008 selection process to compete on the world championship rallies in Portugal, Italy, Greece, Finland, Spain and Great Britain in a fleet of identical Group N-specification Mitsubishi Lancers serviced by Ralliart Italy. Two were plucked from an 18-driver shoot-out event in Europe, with the other three coming from the FIA's Africa, Asia Pacific and Middle East regional championships.

Hembery hopes the project will blaze a trail in terms of enabling promising young drivers to break into the WRC ranks. "The first year of any scheme has teething problems," he says, "and we all had some learning to do along the way. We had little time to set it up, as we were focused on getting the WRC tyre programme up and running. But we've worked well with the FIA in creating a channel for identifying drivers who will be coming through in 2009. It's a

sign that the sport is starting to recognise the need for youth development. We're not just looking for future Sébastien Loebs; we're trying to create interest in world rallying at a grass roots level.

"Have we found a future Loeb? We'll see. Everyone would like to think so, and these sorts of schemes go from strength to strength the longer they continue. We will publicise it more in the future, and we'll try and get more people involved."

While the European section of the scheme was decided by a two-day assessment in Friestadt, Austria, in late October, the highest placed driver under the age of 27 in the African and Middle East championships was rewarded with a drive for this season. The Asia Pacific winner was decided by adding together the results of two rounds of the series in New Zealand and Malaysia. Hembery hopes to run European-style shoot-out events in all regions in the future, with drivers being judged on their performances behind the wheel and their ability to deal with the media.

"You're looking at dramatically different regional championships," he says. "Europe is a hotbed for rallying – always has been – so it made sense to go for the shoot-out, which made it very exciting because that created an event where you had a significant number of drivers as potential winners. The negative is that there's an element of interpretation in an evaluation, which you can always be criticised for, but I think the drivers that were chosen will be worthy contenders next season.

"The other regional events differ, in the sense that if you take Asia, for example, geographically it's enormous. The Asia Pacific Championship is almost like a mini world championship because the distances between the events are so vast, so it wouldn't have made much practical sense to try to bring together all the regional candidates. Africa was a different type of challenge. There was a great level of interest generated through the scheme, but the organisers felt that there was no need to create a bespoke shoot-out event.

"Each region had its own ideas. There will be further discussions about creating one format for all the regions, and this is really FIA-driven, because their members make the decisions. As to what was the best format, I don't think they've fully decided what they want to do, but personally I think there's great merit in the shoot-out process because it does create an event, it creates a clear focus for everybody and it creates a lot of discussion and media value."

Hembery hopes the scheme will continue on an annual basis, providing his company continues as the WRC's exclusive tyre supplier. "Certainly the take-up

has been fantastic, and there's been a warm reception from the media. They recognise that it's a scheme the FIA and Pirelli have put together that is going to benefit the sport. Maybe if we won another tender for the supply of tyres for a further three years we could get to a point where there are some genuine world championship talents being developed through the scheme."

A QUESTION OF QUALITY CONTROL

GEORGE BLACK'S mood mirrored his name when he that discovered Pirelli was to become the FIA World Rally Championship's first control tyre supplier in 2008. He feared the Italian manufacturer would not be up to the task of furnishing the entire field with equal products, but, 12 months on, he's been forced to admit he was wrong.

"I was concerned," says the BP Ford Abu Dhabi tyre engineer. "The performance of the product had been good in the past, but Pirelli's reputation for quality control hadn't always been the best, so I was worried about how they would cope with the sheer logistical size of the programme when they got the contract to supply everybody."

While admitting that he has missed the added variable of tyre competition between different manufacturers – "It used to be a big talking point at the end of every stage, and you got quite a buzz if you made the correct call on tyres" – Black reflects that there were no major issues during the year and that Pirelli dealt with a demanding task "incredibly well".

"The whole operation has been much better than expected," he says. "Logistically they've coped well with the product as regards quality control, and the product has been consistent all the way through. The only problems we've had, which were outside Pirelli's control, were associated with having a control tyre. The FIA decided that you could have one hard and one soft gravel tyre, so it was rare that you were ever going to have the correct tyre for the conditions, because you're always going to be in a compromised situation, but the FIA and Pirelli have learned from that. Some drivers and teams accepted it more easily than others, and some were saying 'we should have this' or 'we should have that', but for me we're all in the same boat."

Black says there were a few issues on the first gravel rally in Argentina, when "we were on the wrong compound. We were on the hard tyre, it was spring, it rained which left it quite muddy in places and we should have been on the soft

tyre, no doubt. But my guys accepted that's the way it is – you just slow down and drive accordingly – and there were no major problems."

On a more positive note Black says: "One of the biggest things with the tyre is that it improved in reliability and strength. We had punctures, sure, but most of them were related to broken wheels rather than tyre failures. Tyre failures really have been very few.

"I don't think there's a lot of room for big changes," he adds, "because we're getting accustomed to running without the mousse inserts. We've got information from the events we've done, and we know we can go long distances now on the soft tyre in sandier conditions like in Finland and Argentina. If we have a very warm Acropolis Rally, we may be on the limit with durability, but there's no point in having a knee-jerk reaction and going away to try and make something different."

World Rally Champion Sébastien Loeb had never driven on Pirelli rubber before the start of last year. The Frenchman admits to some difficulty in adjusting to the tyres initially, having predominantly used Michelin/BFGoodrich rubber during his WRC career, but he was full of praise for what Pirelli has achieved, even though he too misses the element of competition between tyre companies.

"For me tyre choice has always been an interesting part of the rally," says the Citroën star, "but I think Pirelli has done a good job. At the start we had to work on the suspension to find good grip, but since then it's been okay. With only two tyre compounds to do all the rallies, it was not easy for them. On Rally GB it wasn't completely okay because we didn't have any cuts, but that's not the fault of Pirelli – it's a regulations issue because we are not allowed to cut the tyres. That made that rally tricky, but overall Pirelli have done a great job."

Above: Ford's tyre technician George Black admits his initial concerns over Pirelli's control tyres were unfounded. Photograph: PHOTO4

and says 'today guys, you're going to use the emergency tyre'. That will mean we don't have a choice, we don't have any tactical debates, we don't have to have weather crews or whatever – we just get on with it.

"Even talking to the drivers, I don't think that from their point of view it's a big issue in terms of not having tyre choice. Over the years they've got used to the fact that sometimes it will rain and you'll be on the wrong tyre and so forth."

Such constructive criticism, Hembery insists, has been taken on board as Pirelli looks to the future. There is always room for improvement, but throughout the course of last season the company that many believed wouldn't be able to cope with the demands of being the WRC's control tyre supplier silenced its doubters. "Looking at the stage times, we've seen some events where the times have been comparable – and in some cases quicker – than in previous years," says Hembery. "That wasn't intentional – what we tried to do was provide products that would operate across a broad range of conditions and temperatures, and the main thing was that we provided stability and safety. They were the main objectives, which we feel we've achieved.

"We still want to provide greater wear resistance for the really tough endurance rallies, because that was where we felt maybe we needed to provide more safety. Obviously it's hard, because every year each rally changes – you never have the same weather conditions, so you're never quite sure what you're going to encounter. There is going to be some ongoing development in wear resistance, but other than that the product will stay the same for the next three years.

"The big challenge is that you can only test so far; you can't replicate every event, no matter how many kilometres you do, if you're using roads that aren't the same as the ones you're going to compete on. In many cases you're on roads that are similar, but not the same. I'm not saying it's a stab in the dark, because we've been in rallying for 30 years so we have a pretty good idea of how the events are going to be.

"The development programme in 2008 went to plan, and it was successful in the sense that we didn't have any events where we had an extreme problem. Of course we learned through the year, as you're bound to in the first year of such a demanding championship, but overall I'm happy with the way it went."

Below: Pirelli also provided tyres to the Production championship field. This is Toshi Arai's Subaru Impreza. Photograph: PHOTO4

OFFICIAL MERCHANDISE

WRC Sparco Trainers
Sizes:- 40, 41, 42, 43, 44, 45, 46
Price:- £50.00
Code:- WRCS-SHOE

WRC Sparco Sweatshirt
Sizes: -XS, S, M, L, XL, XXL
Price: - £59.95
Code: - WRCS-SS

WRC Umbrella
One Size
Price:- £23.95
Code:- WRC-U

Wheelspin T-Shirt
Sizes: - S,M,L,XL,XXL, 3XL
Price: - £16.95
Code: - WRC-WHEEL

WRC Sparco Lightweight Jacket
Sizes: - XS, S, M, L, XL, XXL
Price: - £119.95
Code: - WRCS-LW

WRC Wallet
One Size
Price:- £4.95
Code:- WRC-WALLET

Cap
One Size
Price: - £12.95
Code: - WRC-CAP05

WRC Keyring
One Size
Price:- £4.95
Code:- WRC-KEY

Mug
One Size
Price: - £5.95
Code: - WRC-MUG3

Order online at -
www.wrc.com
www.performance-clothing.com
or call + 44 (0) 1597 822884

Performance Clothing UK Ltd
5 Heart of Wales Business Park
Llandrindod Wells
LD1 5AB
United Kingdom

OBITUARIES

OVE ANDERSSON
JANUARY 3RD, 1938 TO JUNE 11TH, 2008

MECHANIC, RALLY driver, team manager, company chairman; international rallies and races, Le Mans and Formula 1 – the roles and disciplines through which Ove Andersson moved during his 45 years of active participation in the highly-competitive world of motorsport cover almost everything. And yet a more unassuming and modest man it would have been hard to find.

Ove started out by owning his own tiny business servicing and repairing cars in eastern Sweden, outside Uppsala. His early motoring experiences were with a motorbike that he had bought in direct contravention of his father's wishes. He later ascribed his ability on mixed surfaces to having been in intimate contact with gravel, ice and snow, often with the motorbike uppermost. His first rally car was a two-stroke Saab 96 in which he drove small rallies in the local area. These T-races had short, rough stages, and so the young Andersson got a good training in driving the Saab on rally roads and in fixing it afterwards.

His progress as a driver was such that he was offered a BMC Sweden Cooper S for the 1963 Swedish Rally and won his class. This and other results in his own Saab came to the notice of the Saab factory team, which took him on for the 1965 season. He was sixth overall on the Swedish and got to do several European events, for instance the Acropolis where he and his co-driver drove the rally car all the way from Sweden to Athens. They did not finish and the same was true in both Poland and the RAC Rally. Sharing a team with such experienced people as Erik Carlsson, Pat Moss and Carl Orrenius was not easy and Ove decided to find an outfit where he could be accorded better status. He wrote to Cesare Fiorio at the newborn Lancia team and, much to his surprise, was accepted. The Swedes thought he must have sought special favour and nicknamed him Påven – the Pope.

His first rally for Lancia was the 1966 Monte Carlo – the one where the Minis, Cortinas and Imps were excluded – and, when all the dust had settled, he found his Flavia classified third. He repeated that placing on the Sanremo with one of the new Fulvia Coupés and took one to fourth on the Acropolis. At that time, the Fulvias had 1200cc engines, so it was pretty amazing that he finished the year by so nearly winning the RAC Rally. After a string of mechanical problems he finished seventh, but his special stage record told a better story.

The following year was even better. Ove opened his account with the new 1.3 Fulvia by nearly snatching the Monte win from Rauno Aaltonen's Mini Cooper S, finally finishing just 13 seconds behind him. In Sanremo and Acropolis he was third and then won the Spanish Rally outright. In the course of the year he had some drives for Ford in the Mk2 Lotus Cortina and in quick succession he won Britain's endurance forest event, the Gulf London, and then took fourth place on the 1000 Lakes. No surprise then that a Ford contract loomed for 1968, but first

he did Monte and Sestriere for Lancia finishing sixth and fourth respectively, before taking an Escort Twin Cam to third in Sanremo on its international debut. Other good results followed, with second on the Tulip and Gulf London before missing the RAC Rally to do the London-Sydney with Roger Clark in a Mk 2 Lotus Cortina. Victory was in sight until the axle broke in Australia and they finished 10th.

The two years that followed were not the most productive of Ove's career. He won the Welsh International for Ford in 1969 and was third on the Acropolis in 1970, but elsewhere results were hard to come by and he now felt that he was very much third priority behind Ford's two Finns. Thus he once again looked elsewhere and discovered that Jacques Cheinisse at Alpine was prepared to give him a drive. It might have been for only one rally – Ove never discovered – but since that first rally was the 1971 Monte Carlo that he won, a drive chez Alpine was certain. In fact, over the next 12 months, Ove and the Alpine A110 were the sensations of the rally world. He won Sanremo, the Austrian Alpine and the Acropolis, thus helping Alpine to victory in the FIA International Manufacturers' Rally Championship.

For the next season, Alpine increased the power of its engines but failed to uprate the transmission. Ove often led rallies but equally often failed to finish. Then came Renault, which bought Alpine and only wanted French drivers. Ove did the 1973 Monte Carlo and finished second to his victorious team-mate but that was that. In 1972, Ove had driven the Safari for Datsun, finishing 12th in a car that had the habit of remaining stationary for long periods. His thoughts now turned to another Japanese company and, knowing that his contract with Renault Alpine was ending, he drove a Toyota Celica to ninth place on the 1972 RAC Rally. With a small group of Swedish friends he did other rallies during '73, retiring in Portugal and Greece but finishing seventh in Austria and 12th on the RAC.

The next hurdle was the "petrol crisis" of 1973/74. Toyota wanted to stop competition so Ove flew to Japan – not for the last time – and persuaded them to continue. For 1974 Toyota Team Europe was the result. Gradually the results improved, with Ove fourth in Portugal and Björn Waldegård fourth on the RAC. In 1975, Hannu Mikkola won the 1000 Lakes in a Corolla and thus TTE had won its first WRC event, something that could also be said of Ove who had won the Safari in a Peugeot 504 some months earlier. However, the business of running TTE gradually meant that Ove did less driving and he finally hung up his helmet in 1980 after a sixth on the Acropolis and DNF on the Ivory Coast.

From now on it was management all the way and, with the arrival of its Group B Celica Turbo, TTE was soon winning regularly in Africa. In fact there were three Safari wins on the trot between 1984-86. With the end of Group B, Ove managed to persuade the factory to build a mass-production 4WD

turbocharged Celica and in 1990 it carried Carlos Sainz to his first WRC drivers' title. Three more titles followed in 1991-93 for Sainz, Juha Kankkunen and Didier Auriol, and manufacturers' titles in 1993/94. Up until 1993, TTE had belonged to Ove, but then Toyota bought him out and in 1997 expanded the operation to design and build a sportscar to race at Le Mans. Before that, at Catalunya in 1995, there was a major trauma when it was discovered that, in an attempt to keep the ageing Celica competitive, a rogue element within TTE had introduced a cheat turbo restrictor. Toyota lost all its points from 1995 and was banned from the 1996 season. Under Ove's direction it bounced back, introducing the Corolla World Rally Car in 1997 and using it to win the manufacturers' title for a third time in 1999.

Ove oversaw Toyota's participation at Le Mans, when its best result was second in 1999 with an all-Japanese squad in a GT-One. Then Toyota turned to Formula 1 and made its debut in the 2002 season again with Ove at the helm. But he finally decided to retire at the end of 2003 and moved to South Africa in 2007. He died at the wheel of a Volvo PV444 doing a classic rally with a friend when, ironically, they were involved in a road accident with a Toyota.

JOHN DAVENPORT

Photographs: PHOTO4

ROB ARTHUR
DECEMBER 6TH, 1949 – SEPTEMBER 24TH, 2008

IN THE partnership that is a rally crew, the co-driver is frequently seen as a kind of boffin ministering to both the technical and personal needs of the driver. Rob Arthur was a very successful co-driver who, while carrying out all the functions of a boffin, was also a very sociable person to have in a team. While others ostentatiously announced that they were retiring to their hotel rooms to copy pacenotes, look over maps, or run through petrol consumption calculations, Rob would be recounting an anecdote in the bar or recommending a trip to a special restaurant that he happened to know. He would do all this, and yet the following day he would arrive with all his notes, maps and calculations pristine. There was a rumour that he never slept...

Rob's rally career started with British rallies at the end of the 1970s. For some years he juggled the twin demands of a job and his hobby, navigating and co-driving for a variety of drivers at a time that British rallying was gradually weaning itself off the old night-time events and converting to the new stage events. He thus had an excellent background in working off maps as well as road books and pacenotes.

His burgeoning career nearly came to a sudden and fiery end in 1976 while he was competing on the Epynt Stages Rally with Peter Waldon in a Ford Escort Twin Cam. They were coming down the Esgair Dyfed forest stage behind Llanwrtyd Wells when the Escort left the road and rolled down a grassy bank. In the accident the externally-mounted fuel cap was

knocked off, causing petrol to be spilled onto dry grass and a hot exhaust. In seconds the car was alight. Rob just got out but Peter was trapped and, since no one could reach him, he died in the fire. Dave Whittock was the co-driver in the next car and this meeting in such unfortunate circumstances led to the pair mounting a collection for Peter's family at that year's RAC.

This was not the last instance of Rob's charitable deeds, but for the time being he returned to rallying. He accepted the task of co-driving Basil Wadham's Peugeot 504 on the 1977 London-Sydney Marathon and it was largely due to his good organisation that they were 25th out of 47 finishers. This endurance event gave Rob the chance to meet a lot of the people involved in European rallying, including Andrew Cowan.

Back in the UK things went on much as before with Rob occasionally adding to his co-driving experience by helping others organise their participation, as on the 1980 RAC Rally where he assisted Terry Kaby's Datsun effort. A few months later he got a call from Kaby saying that Whittock couldn't do Corsica due to work commitments, and would Rob like to step in? The answer was, of course, yes. Rob took to WRC rallying like a fish to water and their Datsun finished fifth. He and Kaby came back to the UK and promptly won the Manx National in a Chevette. His ability did not go unnoticed by a Datsun team-mate from Corsica, Tony Pond, and soon Rob was invited to rally with him in various Austin Rover, Vauxhall and Nissan drives. The latter took Rob as far

away as New Zealand and, in 1983, to eighth place in Portugal and sixth in Corsica.

For 1984 he and Pond signed for Austin Rover and started driving Rovers and eventually the MG Metro 6R4. Rob's first taste of Rover motoring was with Colin Malkin on the Circuit of Ireland where they retired but, after its launch, the 6R4 started to enter national events. With the Rover, he and Pond won Group A on the Hunsruck and Manx, but on the RAC Rally their first stage was their last. The following year they had a proper go at winning the Group A Open Championship, and would have done so easily had they repeated their 1984 performance on the Manx. Sadly they crashed out, but still finished sixth in the overall championship and ahead of the car that won Group A.

But 1985 was when the 'proper' version of the 6R4 was launched and, after winning the Gwynedd in the old car, they went on to win two more events before tackling the RAC. This was a dream WRC debut for them, in that their 6R4 captured the imagination of the nation and finished third behind the two Lancia S4s. Sadly this promise was not maintained in 1986 when the 6R4 proved to be both unreliable and off the pace. The fatalities of the season did not help and at the end of the year – and the end of Group B – Pond decided that he, like Austin Rover, was going to stop. Rob was back as a freelance.

He got a ride on the RAC Rally with Sepp Haider in a GM Euro Sport Kadett that ended when the gearbox broke. Then for 1988 he linked up with

Jimmy McRae to crew a Shell-sponsored Sierra RS Cosworth, with which they won four of the six British Open events and took the title. In 1989 they won the Circuit of Ireland and finished third in the championship, as well as having a one-off drive with Mitsubishi on the Acropolis Rally where they came a very creditable fourth in a Galant VR-4.

At this point Rob's active rallying tailed off, but he found plenty to replace it. He became president of the Southern Car Club and instigated the famous Foot Rallies that raised money for charity. At various times he was route devisor for classic rallies, clerk of the course of the Classic Marathon and service co-ordinator for Mitsubishi Ralliart. It was this last task at which he was totally in his element. Once visited a town and all its facilities were indelibly inscribed on Rob's mental database, while his wide co-driving experience meant that he was a canny man with the logistics on the old type of rallies where a judiciously-placed service point could make all the difference. Tommi Mäkinen's world titles depended considerably on the background work from guys like Rob. He then co-ordinated the Ka and Puma championships for Ford before moving to France and almost complete retirement. Sadly this was something that he was only allowed to enjoy for a few years.

Within the rally community, where he was a never-ending source of information and anecdotes from past events, Rob Arthur will be sadly missed.

JOHN DAVENPORT

PAT MOSS-CARLSSON
DECEMBER 27TH, 1934 – OCTOBER 15TH, 2008

EVEN IN the 21st century we struggle to define equality when it comes to a matter of the sexes. The British Government tried with the 1975 Sex Discrimination Act. But there are outstanding females who do not need Acts of Parliament to proclaim their equality, and one shining example in the masculine world of motorsport was Pat Moss.

One could be forgiven for supposing that she began her competitive life behind the wheel, for she was the daughter of parents who had both competed in motorsport and her elder brother, Stirling, was headed towards a major career in motor racing. Instead the purchase of a black Shetland pony set her on a career in horse riding and specifically show jumping where she soon excelled. In 1952 Pat got the summons to join the British show jumping team and it was that same year that she learnt to drive using the Land Rover that served for general use around the farm. For her 17th birthday her father bought her a Morris Ten and, after a couple of attempts, she passed her test. But still, motorsport did not appeal and it took Ken Gregory, Stirling's manager, to suggest that she join him as one of the passengers in his Standard Vanguard Estate for an evening treasure hunt before the bug bit.

A Minor Coupé replaced the Ten and in 1954 Pat did her first rally as a driver. That summer she bought a TR2 with prize money from show jumping and was soon doing more rallies, winning her first event in January 1955. An approach to Triumph for a works drive on the RAC Rally yielded a TR but no expenses, so when BMC offered an MG TF and expenses Pat accepted. This was a relationship that lasted almost nine years and involved Pat driving a bewildering variety of cars from an A90 Westminster to a Mini Cooper, and an MGA to an A40 Farina.

It would have been too like Hollywood if on that first RAC Rally Pat had shot to prominence by winning the Ladies' Award. As it was she finished third, learning a lot about driving long distances in bad weather in a sportscar and getting lost. But her name figured high on the special test results, which was a good omen for the future. In the ensuing years two people came into her life who were to help her enormously: Marcus Chambers, competition manager of BMC, and Ann Wisdom, her regular co-driver. Chambers gave her the opportunity to gain experience in major European events and Ann kept her on the right road. Nowhere was this more evident than on the 1957 Liège-Rome-Liège where, in a 1000c Morris Minor, the pair not only finished this tough event at their first try but were 23rd overall and fourth in class.

For 1958 Chambers decided that Pat should go for the European Ladies' title. Things started badly, with the Minor 1000 crashing out of the Monte Carlo. But on the RAC Rally, again in a Minor, Pat was fourth overall. A fourth overall on the Liège – plus the team prize – and eighth on the Alpine were gained in the new Austin Healey 100/6, and when added to results from the Tulip (Riley 1.5) and Viking (Minor 1000) Pat had won the European title, an achievement she was to repeat in 1960, '62, '64 and '65. For her, probably the most important event of the year was doing the Swedish Rally in an MGA and meeting Erik Carlsson for the first time.

There was more variety in 1959 with rallies in Canada and Portugal added to the usual ones, but results were harder to come by with Lady Luck playing her part. The following year did not start well with a nasty crash on the Solitude circuit during the Lyons-Charbonniéres in an Austin Healey 3000. First on the scene to rescue his girlfriend was Erik Carlsson, who ripped off the side-screen to haul her to safety. Rather typically of Pat, she tore him off a strip for wrecking "the only Healey side-screen that had ever fitted properly". A sixth place on the Geneva Rally and second on the Alpine in Healeys restored her confidence and prepared her for her greatest achievement, winning the Liège outright. This was an incredible achievement since the four-day, four-night practically non-stop Liège was the defining rally of the era and one that every driver aspired to win.

Anything that came after that was bound to be an anti-climax. Pat had driven a borrowed Saab on the 1000 Lakes in 1960 and was now "persuaded" by her fiancé, Carlsson, to buy her own Saab rally car. While continuing to rally for BMC and winning the European Ladies' title for the third time, Pat and Erik took their respective Saabs down to East Africa and drove in the 1962 Safari Rally. Both had trouble, with Carlsson finishing sixth, but Pat was leading when she hit an antelope and dropped to second before getting penalised at the brake test at the finish and falling to third.

During 1962 Marcus Chambers had retired and BMC competitions was now under the management of Stuart Turner, who did not believe Pat when she told him that Ford had offered her a very attractive contract for 1963. He did not outbid them and Pat's days at BMC were over. However, she made her move about four years too early for the development of the Cortina and had a rather unimpressive year in the new Ford. At the end of 1963, Ford tried to lure Carlsson into its team but instead, Pat –since March 3rd Mrs Moss-Carlsson – decided to leave and join her husband at Saab.

There followed three very satisfying years with a Saab 96 two-stroke. In 1964 Pat finished fifth in Monte Carlo, second in Sanremo, third on the Acropolis, and fourth on the Liège and RAC. However, her outstanding achievement in a Saab came the following year when she finished third on the legendary, blizzard-struck Monte Carlo. This was a performance of great distinction, typical of the endurance and skill that made her stand out among her peers in the rally world.

With the arrival of the Saab 96 V4, Carlsson chose to retire and Pat took up an offer from Lancia to drive a Fulvia Coupé in 1968. She finished second in Sanremo, won the Sestriére and took sixth place on the 1969 Monte Carlo, but later that year she gave birth to a daughter, Suzy, and rallying took a back seat. She returned on several occasions during the next few years and finished tenth on the 1972 Monte Carlo in an Alpine Renault A110. But, as Suzy grew up and became interested in horse riding, so Pat's participation in rallies stopped entirely.

Pat's superstitions about competition numbers, her naming of her rally cars – the Minor 1000 was called 'Granny's' – and her frequent separation from her handbag were legendary and proper feminine traits. But there was nothing feminine about her driving style. It was only a few years into her career that there was no more talk of the Ladies' classification. For her, it was the overall classification that mattered – as a great number of gentlemen rally drivers discovered to their cost.

JOHN DAVENPORT

World Rally Championship 2008

Photograph: PHOTO4

Race&motion

SÉBASTIEN LOEB was mildly irked, his Citroën team-mate Dani Sordo even more so. It was late morning on the second day of the Monte Carlo Rally and Ford's Mikko Hirvonen had found a reason to be cheerful. Having followed the Spaniard into the St Martial stage, he'd seen tyre marks on the road. Dani, it seemed, had been off.

Questioning the driver of the number two C4 drew a blank. "Me, off? No. Why? Who said so?" was the general gist of the conversation. Hirvonen had said so, Sordo was told, which only incited a general ribbing of the assembled hack pack. "So, you hear a Citroën has been off and it has to be me. Not Seb, eh? Okay..."

When the same question was put to Loeb, he looked equally bemused. "I don't see what the questions are all about," he replied. "On the road section up to the stage, I told Daniel [Elena, his co-driver] that I thought I was braking too early. I wanted to brake later. In this corner, I found there was a lot of space, some good run-off area, so I braked later and locked the wheels. I found the limit for the brake; I won't do that again. I went to the edge of the road, but I didn't go off."

Forgive the protracted explanation of what turned out to be a brief flurry of excitement, but rumours of Loeb making a mistake on the Monte are few and far between. Yes, he did bin it here two years ago, but since the C4 became the new Xsara, he has not put a wheel wrong. He didn't this year, either.

Last season, Sordo had come close to threatening Loeb on Friday morning. This time around, there wasn't a hope of that. The four-times champion was on scintillating form on the dry, snow-free roads – and was only beaten on the Burzet stage when the Citroën Sport team fed him some duff split times. And even if Sordo had of got the better of him, he needn't have worried: the second Citroën hit turbo trouble in SS11. After a brief peak under the bonnet, Sordo was up for continuing in the now naturally aspirated C4, but the team commanded otherwise. He parked up and 'super-allied' his way through the final day to collect the single point Citroën needed to edge Subaru in the manufacturers' championship.

Hirvonen was the chief beneficiary of Sordo's trouble. The Ford man had never been able to mount a serious challenge to the pair ahead, but he kept his nose clean to take second – a result he openly admitted was as much as he could have hoped for in the French Alps.

Subaru's apparent Renaissance – despite the team still using the aged Impreza S12B (which given that this was another homologation, should really have been the S12C) – came courtesy of another inspired effort from Chris Atkinson. Twelve months ago, he had punched well above his weight to edge Hirvonen for fourth. This time around, he outpaced the returning François Duval (Stobart Ford) in a classic scrap for the final podium spot. The result went right down to the final dash around the harbour section of the Monaco Grand Prix track, but when the pair set exactly the same time, the third and final bottle of champagne was handed to the Australian.

Above: Sébastien Loeb talks set-up with his engineers.

Above left: Toni Gardemeister's Suzuki debut was curtailed by engine failure after 14 stages.

Top: François Duval missed out on a podium finish by 1.1 seconds.

Opposite page: Loeb led from the second stage to score a record-breaking fifth win in the Principality.
Photographs: PHOTO4 unless specified

Right: Petter Solberg's engine dropped onto three cylinders on the second day, but he struggled on to fifth.

Far right: Jari-Matti Latvala was the first driver to suffer a tyre deflation on the very first stage....

Below right: Mikko Hirvonen inherited second place after Dani Sordo's turbo malfunction.

Below: It was Gigi Galli's first asphalt outing for almost two years, but he was sixth despite a loss of power-steering fluid on day two.

Photographs: PHOTO4 unless specified

Race&motion

Rallye Automobile Monte Carlo Results

24–27 JANUARY 2008 | FIA WORLD RALLY CHAMPIONSHIP ROUND 1

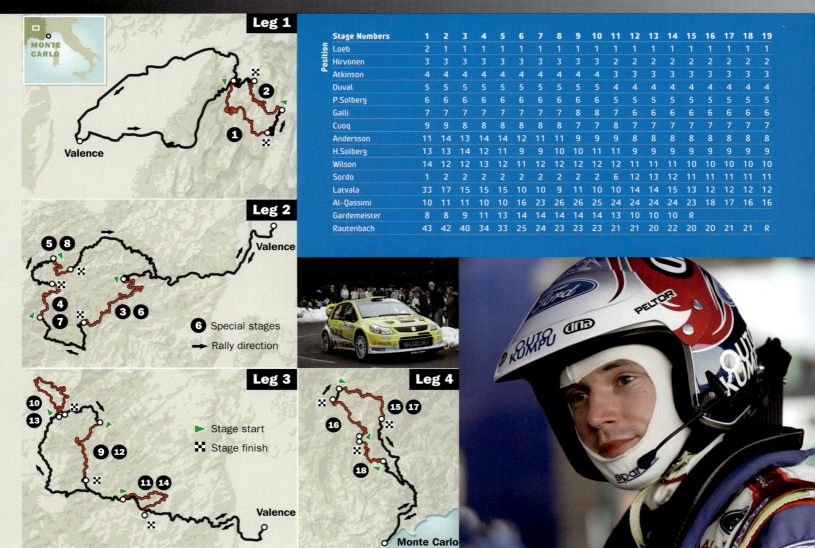

Leg 1 — Valence

Leg 2 — Valence

6 Special stages
→ Rally direction

Leg 3 — Valence

Leg 4 — Monte Carlo

▶ Stage start
🏁 Stage finish

MONTE CARLO

Position / Stage Numbers	1	2	3	4	5	6	7	8	9	10	11	12	13	14	15	16	17	18	19
Loeb	2	1	1	1	1	1	1	1	1	1	1	1	1	1	1	1	1	1	1
Hirvonen	3	3	3	3	3	3	3	3	3	3	2	2	2	2	2	2	2	2	2
Atkinson	4	4	4	4	4	4	4	4	4	4	3	3	3	3	3	3	3	3	3
Duval	5	5	5	5	5	5	5	5	5	5	5	4	4	4	4	4	4	4	4
P.Solberg	6	6	6	6	6	6	6	6	6	6	6	5	5	5	5	5	5	5	5
Galli	7	7	7	7	7	7	7	7	8	8	7	6	6	6	6	6	6	6	6
Cuoq	9	9	9	8	8	8	8	8	7	7	8	7	7	7	7	7	7	7	7
Andersson	11	14	13	14	14	12	11	11	9	9	9	8	8	8	8	8	8	8	8
H.Solberg	13	13	14	12	11	9	9	10	10	11	11	9	9	9	9	9	9	9	9
Wilson	14	12	12	13	12	11	12	12	12	12	11	11	10	10	10	10	10	10	10
Sordo	1	2	2	2	2	2	2		2	2		12	11	11	11	11	11	11	11
Latvala	33	17	15	15	10	10	10	9	11	10	10	14	14	15	13	12	12	12	12
Al-Qassimi	10	11	11	11	10	10	16	23	26	26	25	24	24	24	23	18	17	16	16
Gardemeister	8	8	9	11	13	14	14	14	14	14	13	10	10	10	R				
Rautenbach	43	42	40	34	33	25	24	24	23	23	21	20	22	20	20	20	21	21	R

Above middle: P-G Andersson claimed his and Suzuki's first WRC points at the top level on the Japanese manufacturer's debut.

Above right: Latvala wound up 12th after his early indiscretion.
Photographs: PHOTO4

FINISH LINES...

François Duval's appearance on the opening round of the championship came courtesy of a Belgian-based sponsor. The former Rally Australia winner took a while to get to know his 'guest' co-driver Eddy Chevailler, but once the event moved into more familiar terrain to the south of Valence, Duval was able to stretch his legs and explore the limits of the Stobart Ford. Heading south and into the Alpes Maritimes for four Sunday stages, and he was sensational, reeling Atkinson in – only to miss out on third by 1.1 seconds... Petter Solberg scored his best ever Monte Carlo result with fifth overall, adding to Subaru's manufacturers' tally, which left the Banbury outfit closer to the front of the makes' race than it had been since Tommi Mäkinen won this event in 2002... Gigi Galli's debut for the Stobart team was slightly less inspired than that of Duval, but the Italian fulfilled his brief to bring the car to the finish in one piece. Ardeche driver Jean-Marie Cuoq delivered another strong performance in his Peugeot 307 WRC, finishing in the top 10 for the second year running. This time, however, his seventh overall on the Monte was overshadowed by the news that he had been stripped of his 2007 French National title after being found guilty of illegal reconnaissance... Nothing, however, could take the shine off Suzuki's Monte effort. Per-Gunnar Andersson was eighth overall, taking a point – and a fifth fastest time – on his first World Rally Car outing. Both his SX4 WRC and the sister car of Toni Gardemeister had suffered mechanical troubles, but both had spent time in the top 10.

RUNNING ORDER

1	Sébastien Loeb / Daniel Elena	Citroën C4 WRC / A8
3	Mikko Hirvonen / Jarmo Lehtinen	Ford Focus RS WRC 07 / A8
2	Daniel Sordo / Marc Martí	Citroën C4 WRC / A8
5	Petter Solberg / Phil Mills	Subaru Impreza WRC2007 / A8
6	Chris Atkinson / Stéphane Prévot	Subaru Impreza WRC2007 / A8
4	Jari-Matti Latvala / Miikka Anttila	Ford Focus RS WRC 07 / A8
8	François Duval / Eddy Chevaillier	Ford Focus RS WRC 07 / A8
11	Toni Gardemeister / Tomi Tuominen	Suzuki SX4 WRC / A8
7	Gigi Galli / Giovanni Bernacchini	Ford Focus RS WRC 07 / A8
12	P-G Andersson / Jonas Andersson	Suzuki SX4 WRC / A8
14	Henning Solberg / Cato Menkerud	Ford Focus RS WRC 07 / A8
16	Matthew Wilson / Scott Martin	Ford Focus RS WRC 07 / A8
18	Jean-Marie Cuoq / Philippe Janvier	Peugeot 307 WRC / A8
19	Khalid Al-Qassimi / Michael Orr	Ford Focus RS WRC 07 / A8
20	Conrad Rautenbach / David Senior	Citroën Xsara WRC / A8
61	Frédéric Romeyer /	Peugeot 206 WRC
64	Riccardo Errani / Stefano Casadio	Skoda Octavia WRC / A8
65	Laurent Carbonaro / Marc-Emilien Choudey	Peugeot 307 WRC / A8
66	Frédéric Combe / Hubert Brun	Renault Clio RS / A7
67	Marc Dessi / Michel Fieschi	Renault Clio RS / A7

SPECIAL STAGE TIMES

SS1 St Jean en Royans - Col de La Chau (28.12km)
1 D.Sordo/M.Martí (Citroën C4 WRC) 14m08.9s; 2 S.Loeb/D.Elena (Citroën C4 WRC) 14m12.7s; 3 M.Hirvonen/J.Lehtinen (Ford Focus RS WRC 07) 14m29.0s; 4 C.Atkinson/ S.Prévot (Subaru Impreza WRC2007) 14m39.9s; 5 F.Duval/E.Chevaillier (Ford Focus RS WRC 07) 14m47.6s; 6 P.Solberg/P.Mills (Subaru Impreza WRC2007) 14m50.1s

SS2 La Cime du Mas - Col de Gaudissart (17.58km)
1 Loeb/Elena (Citroën) 9m25.7s; 2 Sordo/Martí (Citroën) 9m42.2s; 3 Hirvonen/Lehtinen (Ford) 9m53.4s; 4 Atkinson/Prévot (Subaru) 9m57.1s; 5 P.Solberg/Mills (Subaru) 10m02.8s; 6 Duval/Chevaillier (Ford) 10m04.3s

SS3 St Pierreville - Col de la Fayolle (29.52km)
1 Loeb/Elena (Citroën) 18m54.4s; 2 Sordo/Martí (Citroën) 19m02.7s; 3 Hirvonen/Lehtinen (Ford) 19m04.5s; 4 Duval/Chevaillier (Ford) 19m22.2s; 5 Atkinson/ Prévot (Subaru) 19m34.2s; 6 J-M.Latvala/M.Anttila (Ford Focus RS WRC 07) 19m34.4s

SS4 Burzet – Lachamp Raphael (16.30km)
1 Sordo/Martí (Citroën) 9m37.1s; 2 Loeb/Elena (Citroën) 9m39.8s;
3 Hirvonen/Lehtinen (Ford) 9m44.6s; 4 P.Solberg/Mills (Subaru)
9m50.4s; 5 Atkinson/Prévot (Subaru) 9m51.0s; 6 Duval/Chevaillier
(Ford) 9m53.5s

SS5 St Martial – Le Chambon – Beleac (12.66km)
1 Loeb/Elena (Citroën) 8m06.2s; 2 Sordo/Martí (Citroën) 8m11.4s;
3 Hirvonen/Lehtinen (Ford) 8m12.0s; 4 P.Solberg/Mills (Subaru)
8m17.9s; 5 Atkinson/Prévot (Subaru) 8m18.8s; 6
G.Galli/G.Bernacchini (Ford Focus RS WRC 07) 8m19.8s

SS6 St Pierreville – Col de la Fayolle (29.52km)
1 Loeb/Elena (Citroën) 18m41.8s; 2 Duval/Chevaillier (Ford)
18m51.1s; 3 Hirvonen/Lehtinen (Ford) 18m51.9s; 4 Sordo/Martí
(Citroën) 18m52.6s; 5 Atkinson/Prévot (Subaru) 18m54.2s; 6
Latvala/Anttila (Ford) 19m01.3s

SS7 Burzet – Lachamp Raphael (16.30km)
1 Loeb/Elena (Citroën) 9m40.7s; 2 Hirvonen/Lehtinen (Ford)
9m43.0s; 3 Atkinson/ Prévot (Subaru) 9m45.3s; 4 Sordo/Martí
(Citroën) 9m48.1s; 5 Duval/Chevaillier (Ford) 9m50.8s; 6
H.Solberg/C.Menkerud (Ford Focus RS WRC 07) 9m 54.3s

SS8 St Martial – Le Chambon – Beleac (12.66km)
1 Loeb/Elena (Citroën) 8m03.6s; 2 Hirvonen/Lehtinen (Ford)
8m09.3s; 3 Atkinson/Prévot (Subaru) 8m13.0s; 4 Duval/Chevaillier
(Ford) 8m18.1s; 5 Sordo/Martí (Citroën) 8m18.5s; 6
P.Solberg/Mills (Subaru) 8m19.7s

SS9 Labatie d'Andaure – Lalouvesc (19.37km)
1 Sordo/Martí (Citroën) 11m18.1s; 2 Loeb/Elena (Citroën)
11m20.1s; 3 Atkinson/Prévot (Subaru) 11m24.4s; 4
Hirvonen/Lehtinen (Ford) 11m24.9s; 5 P.Andersson/J.Andersson
(Suzuki SX4 WRC) 11m30.6s; 6 P.Solberg/Mills (Subaru) 11m33.9s

SS10 St Bonnet – St Bonnet (25.36km)
1 Loeb/Elena (Citroën) 12m39.0s; 2 Sordo/Martí (Citroën)
12m40.2s; 3 Duval/Chevaillier (Ford) 12m45.0s; 4
Hirvonen/Lehtinen (Ford) 12m46.8s; 5 P.Solberg/Mills (Subaru)
12m48.3s; 6 Atkinson/Prévot (Subaru) 12m49.7s

SS11 Lamastre – Gilhoc – Alboussiere (21.66km)
1 Loeb/Elena (Citroën) 12m59.8s; 2 Duval/Chevaillier (Ford)
13m08.7s; 3 Hirvonen/Lehtinen (Ford) 13m17.9s; 4 P.Solberg/Mills
(Subaru) 13m21.0s; 5 Atkinson/Prévot (Subaru) 13m21.5s; 6
Galli/Bernacchini (Ford) 13m23.9s

SS12 Labatie d'Andaure – Lalouvesc (19.37km)
1 Loeb/Elena (Citroën) 11m12.0s; 2 Atkinson/Prévot (Subaru)
11m14.6s; 3 Duval/Chevaillier (Ford) 11m18.1s; 4
Hirvonen/Lehtinen (Ford) 11m18.6s; 5 P.Solberg/Mills (Subaru)
11m19.3s; 6 Galli/Bernacchini (Ford) 11m21.5s

SS13 St Bonnet – St Bonnet (25.36km)
1 Atkinson/Prévot (Subaru) 12m23.9s; 2 Duval/Chevaillier (Ford)
12m31.4s; 3 Loeb/Elena (Citroën) 12m34.6s; 4 P.Solberg/Mills
(Subaru) 12m35.8s; 5 Hirvonen/Lehtinen (Ford) 12m36.6s; 6
T.Gardemeister/T.Tuominen (Suzuki SX4 WRC) 12m51.0

SS14 Lamastre – Gilhoc – Alboussiere (21.66km)
1 Loeb/Elena (Citroën) 13m08.4s; 2 Duval/Chevaillier (Ford)
13m12.8s; 3 Atkinson/Prévot (Subaru) 13m13.8s; 4
Hirvonen/Lehtinen (Ford) 13m16.9s; 5 P.Solberg/Mills (Subaru)
13m17.8s; 6 Galli/Bernacchini (Ford) 13m27.0s

SS15 La Bollene Vesubie – Moulinet (22.68km)
1 Duval/Chevaillier (Ford) 15m48.6s; 2 Sordo/Martí (Citroën)
15m53.0; 3 Loeb/Elena (Citroën) 15m57.0s; 4 Latvala/Anttila
(Ford) 16m00.2s; 5 Atkinson/Prévot (Subaru) 16m00.7s; 6
Hirvonen/Lehtinen (Ford) 16m07.2s

SS16 Luceram – Loda (15.34km)
1 Sordo/Martí (Citroën) 10m51.7; 2 Duval/Chevaillier (Ford)
10m53.8s; 3 Latvala/Anttila (Ford) 10m56.4s; 4 Atkinson/Prévot

(Subaru) 10m57.8s; 5 Loeb/Elena (Citroën) 10m58.3s; 6
P.Solberg/Mills (Subaru) 10m59.1s

SS17 La Bollene Vesubie – Moulinet (22.68km)
1 Duval/Chevaillier (Ford) 15m27.7s; 2 Atkinson/Prévot (Subaru)
15m28.2s; 3 Sordo/Martí (Citroën) 15m29.0; 4 Loeb/Elena
(Citroën) 15m33.6s; 5 Hirvonen/Lehtinen (Ford) 15m42.5s; 6
Latvala/Anttila (Ford) 15m47.0s

SS18 Luceram – Col des Portes (6.25km)
1 Duval/Chevaillier (Ford) 4m24.4s; 2 Latvala/Anttila (Ford)
4m24.6s; 3 Loeb/Elena (Citroën) 4m25.6s; 4 Hirvonen/Lehtinen
(Ford) 4m26.1s; 5 P.Solberg/Mills (Subaru) 4m26.7s; 6
Atkinson/Prévot (Subaru) 4m26.8s

SS19 Monaco – Circuit (2.70km)
1= Atkinson/Prévot (Subaru), Duval/Chevaillier (Ford) 1m40.7s; 3
Latvala/Anttila (Ford) 1m40.9s; 4 P.Solberg/Mills (Subaru)
1m41.3s; 5 Hirvonen/Lehtinen (Ford) 1m42.7s; 6 Galli/Bernacchini
(Ford) 1m43.4s

Cars that retired and subsequently restarted and were classified
under SuperRally regs:

19	Al-Qassimi/Orr	Ford Focus RS WRC 07		
	Off road	SS6	A8	
2	Sordo/ Martí	Citroën C4 WRC		
	Engine	SS11	A8	
4	Latvala/Anttila	Ford Focus RS WRC 07		
	Mechanical	SS12	A8	

MAJOR RETIREMENTS

11	Gardemeister/Tuominen	Suzuki SX4 WRC	
	Mechanical	SS14	A8
20	Rautenbach/Senior	Citroën Xsara WRC	
	Off road	SS19	A8

FIA CLASS WINNERS

A8	Over 2000cc	Loeb/Elena
		Citroën C4 WRC
A7	1600-2000cc	Broccoli/Cicognini
		Renault Clio
A6	1400-1600cc	Moretti/Doglio
		Renault Clio
N4	Over 2000cc	Artru/Virieux
		Mitsubishi Lancer Evo IX

RALLY LEADERS
Overall: SS1 Sordo; SS2-19 Loeb

SPECIAL STAGE ANALYSIS

	1st	2nd	3rd	4th	5th	6th
Loeb (Citroën)	10	3	3	1	1	-
Duval (Ford)	4	5	2	2	2	2
Sordo (Citroën)	4	5	1	2	1	-
Atkinson (Subaru)	2	2	4	3	6	2
Hirvonen (Ford)	-	2	7	5	3	1
Latvala (Ford)	-	1	2	1	-	3
P.Solberg (Subaru)	-	-	-	5	5	4
Andersson (Suzuki)	-	-	-	-	1	-
Galli (Ford)	-	-	-	-	-	5
H.Solberg (Ford)	-	-	-	-	-	1
Gardemeister (Suzuki)	-	-	-	-	-	1

TYRES
Tyres: Pirelli Pzero – studded winter tyre – un-studded winter tyre
Compounds: soft
Number of tyres available per car: 54

WORLD CHAMPIONSHIP POINTS
Drivers
1 Loeb 10; 2 Hirvonen 8; 3 Atkinson 6; 4 Duval 5; 5 P.Solberg 4; 6
Galli 3; 7 Cuoq 2; 8 Andersson 1
Manufacturers
1 Citroën Total WRT 11; 2 Subaru WRT 10; 3= BP Ford Abu Dhabi
WRT / Stobart VK M-Sport Ford RT 8; 5 Suzuki WRT 2

ROUTE DETAILS
Total route of 1481.25km of which 365.09km were competitive on
19 stages
Leg 1 Thursday 24 January, 2 special stages totalling 45.70km
Leg 2 Friday 25 January, 6 special stages totalling 116.96 km
Leg 3 Saturday 26 January, 6 special stages totalling 132.78 km
Leg 4 Sunday 27 January, 5 special stages totalling 69.65 km

RESULTS

1	Sébastien Loeb/	Citroën C4 WRC	
	Daniel Elena	3h39m17.0s	A8
2	Mikko Hirvonen/	Ford Focus RS WRC 07	
	Jarmo Lehtinen	3h41m51.4s	A8
3	Chris Atkinson/	Subaru Impreza WRC2007	
	Stéphane Prévot	3h42m15.6s	A8
4	François Duval/	Ford Focus RS WRC 07	
	Eddy Chevaillier	3h42m16.7s	A8
5	Petter Solberg/	Subaru Impreza WRC2007	
	Phil Mills	3h43m57.9s	A8
6	Gigi Galli/	Ford Focus RS WRC 07	
	Giovanni Bernacchini	3h48m03.5	A8
7	Jean Marie Cuoq/	Peugeot 307 WRC	
	Philippe Janvier	3h49m41.8	A8
8	P-G Andersson/	Suzuki SX4 WRC	
	Jonas Andersson	3h50m36.5	A8
9	Henning Solberg/	Ford Focus RS WRC 07	
	Cato Menkerud	3h52m00.6	A8
10	Matthew Wilson/	Ford Focus RS WRC 07	
	Scott Martin	3h53m17.1	A8

47 starters, 34 finishers

RECENT WINNERS

1964	Paddy Hopkirk/Henry Liddon	Mini Cooper S
1965	Timo Mäkinen/Paul Easter	Mini Cooper S
1966	Pauli Toivonen/Ensio Mikander	Citroen DS21
1967	Rauno Aaltonen/Henry Liddon	Mini Cooper S
1968	Vic Elford/David Stone	Porsche 911T
1969	Björn Waldegård/Lars Helmer	Porsche 911S
1970	Björn Waldegård/Lars Helmer	Porsche 911T
1971	Ove Andersson/David Stone	Alpine Renault A110
1972	Sandro Munari/Mauro Mannucci	Lancia Fulvia
1973	Jean-Claude Andruet/'Biche'	Alpine Renault A110
1975	Sandro Munari/Mauro Mannucci	Lancia Stratos
1976	Sandro Munari/Silvio Maiga	Lancia Stratos
1977	Sandro Munari/Silvio Maiga	Lancia Stratos
1978	Jean-Pierre Nicolas/Vincent Laverne	Porsche 911 Carrera
1979	Bernard Darniche/Alan Mahé	Lancia Stratos
1980	Walter Röhrl/Christian Geistdörfer	Fiat 131 Abarth
1981	Jean Ragnotti/Jean-Marc Andrié	Renault 5 Turbo
1982	Walter Röhrl/Christian Geistdorfer	Opel Ascona 400
1983	Walter Röhrl/Christian Geistdorfer	Lancia Rally 037
1984	Walter Röhrl/Christian Geistdorfer	Audi Quattro A2
1985	Ari Vatanen/Terry Harryman	Peugeot 205 Turbo 16
1986	Henri Toivonen/Sergio Cresto	Lancia Delta S4
1987	Miki Biasion/Tiziano Siviero	Lancia Delta HF 4x4
1988	Bruno Saby/Jean-François Fauchille	Lancia Delta HF 4x4
1989	Miki Biasion/Tiziano Siviero	Lancia Delta Integrale
1990	Didier Auriol/Bernard Occelli	Lancia Delta Integrale 16v
1991	Carlos Sainz/Luis Moya	Toyota Celica GT4
1992	Didier Auriol/Bernard Occelli	Lancia Delta HF Integrale
1993	Didier Auriol/Bernard Occelli	Toyota Celica Turbo 4wd
1994	François Delecour/Daniel Grataloup	Ford Escort RS Cosworth
1995	Carlos Sainz/Luis Moya	Subaru Impreza 555
1996	Patrick Bernardini/Bernard Occelli	Ford Escort RS Cosworth
1997	Piero Liatti/Fabrizia Pons	Subaru Impreza WRC97
1998	Carlos Sainz/Luis Moya	Toyota Corolla WRC
1999	Tommi Mäkinen/Risto Mannenmäki	Mitsubishi Lancer E6
2000	Tommi Mäkinen/Risto Mannenmäki	Mitsubishi Lancer E6
2001	Tommi Mäkinen/Risto Mannenmäki	Mitsubishi Lancer Evo
2002	Tommi Mäkinen/Kaj Lindström	Subaru Impreza WRC2001
2003	Sébastien Loeb/Daniel Elena	Citroën Xsara WRC
2004	Sébastien Loeb/Daniel Elena	Citroën Xsara WRC
2005	Sébastien Loeb/Daniel Elena	Citroën Xsara WRC
2006	Marcus Grönholm/Timo Rautiainen	Ford Focus RS WRC 06
2007	Sébastien Loeb/Daniel Elena	Citroën C4 WRC

THE ABSENCE of winter on the World Rally Championship's only winter rally was of no concern to the man standing on the roof of his Ford Focus RS WRC 07. He couldn't have cared less that it hadn't snowed and the temperature had remained obstinately above freezing for the last three days. Jari-Matti Latvala didn't care because he'd just won his first round of the WRC.

At 22 years old, success at the highest level came with another slant as he broke the record – previously held by the then 24-year-old Henri Toivonen – for being the youngest winner of a WRC round. When Latvala talked of his maiden victory and scratching Toivonen's name from the record books, his voice was almost tinged with guilt. Toivonen had been his hero when he was growing up. His guilt eased slightly when Henri's brother Harri texted Latvala to congratulate him.

The accolades for Latvala didn't stop there. And neither should they have. He had carved out this win for himself by driving faster than anybody. Anybody. Sure, round one winner and reigning world champion Sébastien Loeb had retired from the event on the second day, but his early bath came courtesy of a fourth-stage roll – as the Frenchman pushed his Citroën beyond its limit in an effort to keep pace with the Finn.

Latvala's senior team-mate Mikko Hirvonen had planned to chop into his rival's 48-second lead on Saturday morning and score enough points to lead the drivers' championship for the first time come Sunday afternoon. Half of that happened. Through the Horssjon and Hagfors stages which opened leg two, Hirvonen couldn't get it together, while the nerveless Latvala nailed it and put his Ford out of reach. There was a general expectation that Ford team principal Malcolm Wilson would step in and find favour with his team leader. But he didn't. He let the sport take its course and left the door open for a famous Finnish win.

There were smiles whichever way you turned at Ford: Latvala's win, Hirvonen's championship lead, Gigi

Galli third, helping the Stobart team to an early second in the makes' race – second that is to the BP Ford team. Wilson's weekend really was almost perfect. The only spoiler was his son Matthew's penultimate-stage departure from fifth place with a throttle problem. Five Fords in the top six became four in the top five as Andreas Mikkelsen picked up where Wilson Jr had left off. And there was another record broken as Mikkelsen, at 18, became the youngest driver ever to score WRC points.

Across the border in Norway, Mikkelsen was making all the headlines – rather than his countryman, and former world champion, Petter Solberg. Solberg had beaten him home, but the torment remained for the Subaru driver. A perfectly driveable Impreza WRC2007 had been transformed into his worst nightmare on Saturday courtesy of a new set of dampers. A further suspension revision for Sunday returned the car to its former glory, but this was another unsatisfactory event for driver and team.

There were two crumbs of comfort for Solberg: he had beaten both his brother Henning and team-mate Chris Atkinson, both of whom fell off the road in the course of the three days.

Above left: Jari-Matti Latvala celebrates becoming the WRC's youngest ever winner with Ford team-mates Gigi Galli (left) and Mikko Hirvonen.

Main: Warm temperatures meant there was little snow on the road, but the 22-year-old Finn led from the first forest stage on Friday morning.

Left: Norwegian fans made the short journey across the border to cheer on Petter Solberg to fourth.
Photographs: PHOTO4

Race&motion

Left: Solberg kept out of trouble unlike his team-mate Chris Atkinson, who got stuck in a snow bank for 15 minutes on day one.

Far left: Sébastien Loeb retired from day one after rolling on the third stage – a rare error from the reigning world champion.

Below: Hirvonen couldn't match team-mate Latvala's pace but second place gave him the championship lead.
Photographs: PHOTO4 unless specified

Below left: After Henning Solberg crashed, Galli inherited third place to complete Ford's podium lockout.
Julian Gonzalez/PHOTO4

Uddeholm Swedish Rally Results

07-10 FEBRUARY 2008 | FIA WORLD RALLY CHAMPIONSHIP ROUND 2

Position / Stage Numbers	1	2	3	4	5	6	7	8	9	10	11	13	14	15	16	17	19	20
Latvala	2	1	1	1	1	1	1	1	1	1	1	1	1	1	1	1	1	1
Hirvonen	3	2	2	2	2	2	2	2	2	2	2	2	2	2	2	2	2	2
Galli	6	6	5	4	4	4	4	4	3	3	3	3	3	3	3	3	3	3
P.Solberg	1	7	6	5	5	5	5	5	5	4	4	4	4	4	4	4	4	4
Mikkelsen	10	13	12	9	9	9	9	9	8	8	6	6	6	6	6	6	5	5
Sordo	60	60	54	38	31	24	18	18	12	11	8	7	7	7	7	7	6	6
Gardemeister	8	10	8	6	7	7	8	8	7	7	11	10	8	8	8	8	7	7
Hänninen	19	17	16	13	12	11	11	11	10	10	10	9	9	9	9	9	8	8
Östberg	9	4	9	8	6	6	6	28	22	19	18	14	14	13	11	10	9	9
Ketomaa	24	14	13	10	11	13	14	15	11	12	12	11	10	10	10	10	10	9
H.Solberg	5	5	4	3	3	3	3	3	4	4	7	14	18	18	18	16	14	13
Rautenbach	28	22	22	19	18	16	15	14	19	17	16	16	15	16	18	16	16	16
Aava	12	12	10	45	38	32	39	43	38	36	32	31	28	25	25	22	20	18
Atkinson	14	9	60	56	54	49	46	45	40	37	35	32	29	26	26	26	22	21
Van Merksteijn	28	25	25	23	25	22	24	24	21	18	18	19	25	24	24	24	24	25
Al-Qassimi	13	15	14	12	13	12	12	12	33	34	31	36	33	31	30	30	29	26
Wilson	11	11	11	7	8	8	7	7	6	6	5	5	5	5	5	5	5	R
Loeb	4	3	3	29	45	47	48	50	47	45	R							
Andersson	6	8	7	R														

Leg 1 / Leg 2 / Leg 3 (Route map)

- **7** Stages
- → Rally direction
- ▶ Stage start
- ✖ Stage finish
- Karlstad

Race&motion

Above: Rising star Andreas Mikkelsen was a fine fifth driving a privateer Focus.

Above right: Gigi Galli dedicated his third place in Sweden to Andrew Tinkler of sponsor Stobart Group.

Photograph: PHOTO4 unless specified

FINISH LINES...

The lack of snow and freezing temperatures hit the organisers of the Swedish Rally hard, with renewed calls for the event to be shifted much further north in search of snow-sure roads. While clerk of the course Bertil Klarins maintained there was never a risk of a repeat of the warm weather-enforced cancellation of 1990, there would be the loss of two stages and the national rally which had been scheduled to run on the back of the WRC qualifier... Citroën's chances of victory in Sweden were effectively halved before the start, when the Versailles team elected to change the engine on Dani Sordo's C4 WRC. The turbo damage done to the motor in Monte Carlo was worse than first thought but a five-minute penalty was imposed for the engine change. Despite that Sordo turned in a fine performance, which would have netted him third place without the penalty... Another legacy of round one that returned in Sweden was the head gasket failure that sidelined Toni Gardemeister's Suzuki. This time, however, it nobbled the sister SX4 WRC of local hero Per-Gunnar Andersson. After a major build-up from the Swedish media, the double Junior champion's participation was over by lunchtime on Friday. The only positive to take from it all was that he had been seventh and in the points when he retired. Gardemeister's car kept running despite ongoing hydraulic problems and he would take Suzuki's best-ever result in seventh position... Mitsubishi man Juho Hanninen eclipsed the memory of his exclusion from the top step of the Group N podium 12 months earlier by once again being quickest through the stages – this time, though, his Lancer Evo IX was deemed legal at the post-event scrutiny. Not only did he bag 10 points in the first round of the Production race, he also collect-

ed the final point in the drivers' WRC. Hanninen's early efforts were thwarted by a fine debut from Patrik Sandell in a Peugeot 207 S2000. The Swede belied his lack of experience in the Super 2000 car to lead, but then lost two minutes after going off the road in the second run at Vargasen. He battled back to third, with notice served of his potential for the rest of the season.

RUNNING ORDER

1	Sébastien Loeb/ Daniel Elena	Citroën C4 WRC A8
3	Mikko Hirvonen/ Jarmo Lehtinen	Ford Focus RS WRC 07 A8
6	Chris Atkinson/ Stéphane Prévot	Subaru Impreza WRC2007 A8
5	Petter Solberg/ Phil Mills	Subaru Impreza WRC2007 A8
7	Gigi Galli/ Giovanni Bernacchini	Ford Focus RS WRC 07 A8
12	P-G Andersson/ Jonas Andersson	Suzuki SX4 WRC A8
8	Henning Solberg/ Cato Menkerud	Ford Focus RS WRC 07 A8
16	Matthew Wilson/ Scott Martin	Ford Focus RS WRC 07 A8
2	Daniel Sordo/ Marc Martí	Citroën C4 WRC A8
4	Jari-Matti Latvala/ Miikka Anttila	Ford Focus RS WRC 07 A8
23	Khalid Al Qassimi/ Michael Orr	Ford Focus RS WRC 07 A8
21	Conrad Rautenbach/ David Senior	Citroën C4 WRC A8
11	Toni Gardemeister/ Tomi Tuominen	Suzuki SX4 WRC A8
17	Andreas Mikkelsen/ Ola Fløene	Ford Focus RS WRC 06 A8
19	Mads Østberg/ Ole Kristian Unnerud	Subaru Impreza WRC2007 A8
20	Urmo Aava/ Kuldar Sikk	Citroën C4 WRC A8
22	Peter van Merksteijn/ Hans van Beek	Ford Focus RS WRC 06 A8
31	Toshi Arai/ Glenn Macneall	Subaru Impreza N4
52	Juho Hänninen/ Mikko Markkula	Mitsubishi Lancer Evo IX N4
39	Nasser Al-Attiyah/ Chris Patterson	Subaru Impreza N4

SPECIAL STAGE TIMES

SS1 Karstad Superspecial 1 (1.89km)

1 P.Solberg/P.Mills (Subaru Impreza WRC2007) 1m28.9s; 2 J-M.Latvala/M.Anttila (Ford Focus RS WRC 07) 1m29.4s; 3 M.Hirvonen/J.Lehtinen (Ford Focus RS WRC 07) 1m29.8s; 4 S.Loeb/D.Elena (Citroën C4 WRC) 1m30.0s; 5 H.Solberg/C.Menkerud (Ford Focus RS WRC 07) 1m30.4s; 6 G.Galli/G.Bernacchini (Ford Focus RS WRC 07) 1m30.9s; PC U.Nittel/D.Ruf (Mitsubishi Lancer Evo IX) 1m38.2s

SS2 Stensjon 1 (15.5km)

1 Latvala/Anttila (Ford) 7m24.0s; 2 Hirvonen/Lehtinen (Ford) 7m27.3s; 3 M. Østberg/O.K.Unnerud (Subaru Impreza WRC2007) 7m28.3s; 4 Loeb/Elena (Citroën) 7m30.7s; 5 H.Solberg/Menkerud (Ford) 7m31.0s; 6 Galli/Bernacchini (Ford) 7m32.2s PC J.Ketomaa/M.Teiskonen (Subaru Impreza) 7m58.5s

SS3 Bjalverud 1 (21.57km)

1 Latvala/Anttila (Ford) 10m33.7s; 2 Hirvonen/Lehtinen (Ford)

10m35.6s; 3 Loeb/Elena (Citroën) 10m38.3s; 4 H.Solberg/Menkerud (Ford) 10m41.6s; 5 Galli/Bernacchini (Ford) 10m47.6s; 6 P.Solberg/Mills (Subaru) 10m53.0s PC P.Sandell/E.Axelsson (Peugeot 207) 11m29.5s

SS4 Mangen 1 (22.09km)
1 Latvala/Anttila (Ford) 12m20.7s; 2 H.Solberg/Menkerud (Ford) 12m37.1s; 3 Hirvonen/Lehtinen (Ford) 12m38.1s; 4 Galli/Bernacchini (Ford) 12m45.4s; 5 P.Solberg/Mills (Subaru) 12m51.9s; 6 M.Wilson/S.Martin (Ford Focus WRC RS 07) 12m54.8s; PC Sandell/Axelsson (Peugeot) 13m12.1s

SS5 Stensjon 2 (15.5km)
1 Latvala/Anttila (Ford) 7m22.3s; 2 Galli/Bernacchini (Ford) 7m26.5s; 3 H.Solberg/Menkerud (Ford) 7m26.7s; 4 Hirvonen/Lehtinen (Ford) 7m28.4s; 5 Ostberg/Unnerud (Subaru) 7m29.5s; 6 D.Sordo/M.Martí (Citroën C4 WRC) 7m31.5s; PC Sandell/Axelsson (Peugeot) 7m57.8s

SS6 Bjalverud (21.57km)
1 Latvala/Anttila (Ford) 10m32.4s; 2 H.Solberg/Menkerud (Ford) 10m39.9s; 3 Galli/Bernacchini (Ford) 10m40.0s; 4 Hirvonen/Lehtinen (Ford) 10m40.4s; 5 P.Solberg/Mills (Subaru) 10m48.0s; 6 Sordo/Martí (Citroën) 10m49.4s; PC J.Hänninen/M.Markkula (Mitsubishi Lancer Evo IX) 11m27.9s

SS7 Mangen 2 (22.09km)
1 Latvala/Anttila (Ford) 12m21.2s; 2 Galli/Bernacchini (Ford) 12m24.5s; 3 Sordo/Martí (Citroën) 12m28.3s; 4 Ostberg/Unnerud (Subaru) 12m30.7s; 5 Hirvonen/Lehtinen (Ford) 12m32.1s; 6 H.Solberg/Menkerud (Ford) 12m33.5s; PC Sandell/Axelsson (Peugeot) 13m10.7s

SS8 Karlstad 2 (1.89km)
1 Galli/Bernacchini (Ford) 1m28.2s; 2 P.Solberg/Mills (Subaru) 1m29.2s; 3 H.Solberg/Menkerud (Ford) 1m29.4s; 4 Latvala/Anttila (Ford) 11m29.6s; 5 Hirvonen/Lehtinen (Ford) 1m29.8s; 6 C.Atkinson/S.Prévot (Subaru Impreza WRC2007) 1m30.3s; PC Hänninen/Markkula (Mitsubishi) 1m39.1s

SS9 Horrsjon (14.89km)
1 Loeb/Elena (Citroën) 9m18.1s; 2 Sordo/Martí (Citroën) 9m18.6s; 3 A.Mikkelsen/O.Fløene (Ford Focus RS WRC) 9m23.4s; 4 Latvala/Anttila (Ford) 9m25.0s; 5 Hirvonen/Lehtinen (Ford) 9m29.9s; 6 T.Gardemeister/T.Tuominen (Suzuki SX4) 9m31.3s; PC Hänninen/Markkula (Mitsubishi) 9m41.1s

SS10 Hagfors (14.92km)
1 Sordo/Martí (Citroën) 11m45.8s; 2 Latvala/Anttila (Ford) 11m47.4s; 3 H.Solberg/Menkerud (Ford) 11m47.4s; 4 Loeb/Elena (Citroën) 11m50.4s; 5 Mikkelsen/Fløene (Ford) 11m52.0s; 6 Galli/Bernacchini (Ford) 11m52.1s; PC Sandell/Axelsson (Peugeot) 12m25.0s

SS11 Vargasen 1 (24.62km)
1 Loeb/Elena (Citroën) 13m49.1s; 2 Hirvonen/Lehtinen (Ford) 13m50.1s; 3 Latvala/Anttila (Ford) 13m58.3; 4 Sordo/Martí (Citroën) 13m59.1s; 5 Atkinson/Prévot (Subaru) 14m02.6s; 6 Galli/Bernacchini (Ford) 14m04.9s; PC Hänninen/Markkula (Mitsubishi) 14m36.2s

SS12 Horrsjon 2 (14.89km)
Cancelled due to mild weather.

SS13 Hagfors 2 (20.92km)
1 Sordo/Martí (Citroën) 11m30.1s; 2 Latvala/Anttila (Ford) 11m31.8s; 3 Hirvonen/Lehtinen (Ford) 11m33.1s; 4 P.Solberg/Mills (Subaru) 11m35.1s; 5 Galli/Bernacchini (Ford) 11m38.2s; 6 Mikkelsen/Fløene (Ford) 11m39.7s; PC Sandell/Axelsson (Peugeot) 12m15.4s

SS14 Vargasen 2 (24.62km)
1 Hirvonen/Lehtinen (Ford) 13m32.5s; 2 Latvala/Anttila (Ford) 13m37.9s; 3 Atkinson/Prévot (Subaru) 13m38.1s; 4 Sordo/Martí (Citroën) 13m38.5s; 5 P.Solberg/Mills (Subaru) 13m41.5s; 6 Galli/Bernacchini (Ford) 13m45.1s; PC A.Aigner/K.Wicha (Mitsubishi Lancer Evo IX) 14m40.8s

SS15 Ullen 1 (16.25km)
1 H.Solberg/Menkerud (Ford) 8m21.7s; 2 P.Solberg/Mills (Subaru) 8m27.0s; 3 Hirvonen/Lehtinen (Ford) 8m28.7s; 4 Latvala/Anttila (Ford) 8m28.8s; 5 Ostberg/Unnerud (Subaru) 8m29.3s; 6 Sordo/Martí (Citroën) 8m31.9s; PC Ketomaa/Teiskonen (Subaru) 9m09.6s

SS16 Lesjofors 1 (10.48km)

1 H.Solberg/Menkerud (Ford) 5m54.5s; 2 Latvala/Anttila (Ford) 5m56.4s; 3 Ostberg/Unnerud (Subaru) 5m58.4s; 4 Atkinson/Prévot (Subaru) 5m59.9s; 5 U.Aava/K.Sikk (Citroën C4 WRC) 6m00.4s; 6 Hirvonen/Lehtinen (Ford) 6m01.2s; PC P.Flodin/G.Bergsten (Subaru Impreza) 6m16.4s

SS17 Rammen 1 (21.87km)
1 H.Solberg/Menkerud (Ford) 11m14.4s; 2 Latvala/Anttila (Ford) 11m22.6s; 3 Hirvonen/Lehtinen (Ford) 11m23.7s; 4 Aava/Sikk (Citroën) 11m26.7s; 5 Sordo/Martí (Citroën) 11m27.0s; 6 Ostberg/Unnerud (Subaru) 11m27.1s; PC Sandell/Axelsson (Peugeot) 12m07.2s

SS18 Ullen 2 (16.25km)
Cancelled due to mild weather.

SS19 Lesjofors 2 (10.48km)
1 H.Solberg/Menkerud (Ford) 5m43.8s; 2 P.Solberg/Mills (Subaru) 5m46.2s; 3 Sordo/Martí (Citroën) 5m46.2s; 4 Atkinson/Prévot (Subaru) 5m48.2s; 5 Latvala/Anttila (Ford) 5m48.3s; 6 Ostberg/Unnerud (Subaru) 5m49.0s; PC Sandell/Axelsson (Peugeot) 6m11.1s

SS20 Rammen 2 (21.87km)
1 H.Solberg/Menkerud (Ford) 11m07.1s; 2 Latvala/Anttila (Ford) 11m11.4s; 3 Hirvonen/Lehtinen (Ford) 11m11.4s; 4 P.Solberg/Mills (Subaru) 11m15.1s; 5 Aava/Sikk (Citroën) 11m19.1s; 6 Sordo/Martí (Citroën) 11m20.2s; PC Sandell/Axelsson (Peugeot) 11m56.1s

Cars that retired and subsequently restarted and were classified under SuperRally regs:

13	Solberg/Menkerud	Ford Focus RS WRC 07	
	Accident	SS11	A8
18	Aava/Sikk	Citroën C4 WRC	
	Mechanical	SS7	A8

MAJOR RETIREMENTS

7	Loeb/Elena	Citroën C4 WRC	
	Mechanical	SS4/SS11	A8
16	Andersson/Andersson	Suzuki SX4 WRC	
	Mechanical	SS14	A8
17	Wilson/Martin	Ford Focus WRC RS 07	
	Mechanical	SS19	A8

FIA CLASS WINNERS

A8	Over 2000cc	Latvala/Anttila
		Ford Focus RS WRC 07
A7	1600-2000	Raschi/Cadore
		Renault Clio R3
A6	1400-1600cc	Dautov/Danilova
		Citroën C2
N4	Over 2000cc	Hänninen/Markkula
		Mitsubishi Lancer Evo IX
N3	1600-2000cc	Storm/Storm
		Renault Clio Ragnotti
N2	1400-1600cc	Hytönen/Larsson
		Suzuki Swift Sport

RALLY LEADERS
Overall: SS1 P.Solberg; SS2-20 Latvala

PC: SS1 U.Nittel; SS2-4 Ketomaa; SS5-13 Sandell; Hänninen SS14-20

SPECIAL STAGE ANALYSIS

	1st	2nd	3rd	4th	5th	6th
Latvala (Ford)	6	8	-	3	1	-
H.Solberg (Ford)	5	3	1	1	2	1
Hirvonen (Ford)	2	2	6	2	3	1
Sordo (Citroën)	2	1	3	1	1	4
P.Solberg (Subaru)	1	3	-	2	3	1
Galli (Ford)	1	2	1	1	3	4
Loeb (Citroën)	1	-	1	3	-	-
Ostberg (Subaru)	-	-	2	1	2	2
Mikkelsen (Ford)	-	-	1	-	1	1
Atkinson (Subaru)	-	-	1	3	-	1
Aava (Citroën)	-	-	-	1	2	1
Gardemeister (Suzuki)	-	-	-	-	-	1
Wilson (Ford)	-	-	-	-	-	1

TYRES
Tyres: Pirelli studded snow tyre
Compound: soft
Number of tyres available per car: 42

WORLD CHAMPIONSHIP POINTS
Drivers

1 Hirvonen 16; 2= Latvala, Loeb 10 16; 4= P.Solberg, Galli 9; 6 Atkinson 6; 7 Duval 5; 8 Mikkelsen 4; 9 Sordo 3; 10= Gardemeister, Cuoq 2 etc

Manufacturers

1 BP Ford Abu Dhabi WRT 26; 2= Subaru WRT, Stobart VK M-Sport Ford RT 16; 4 Citroën Total WRT 15; 6; 5 Suzuki WRT 5

Production Car World Rally Championship

1 Hänninen 10; 2 Ketomaa 8; 3 Sandell 6; 4 Prokop 5; 5 Nittel 4; 6 Arai 3; 7 Aráujo 2; 8 Sousa 1

ROUTE DETAILS
Total route of 1440.08km of which 340.18km were competitive on 20 stages

Leg 1 Thursday 7-Friday 8 February, 8 Special Stages totalling 122.12km

Leg 2 Saturday 9 February, 6 Special Stages totalling 120.86km

Leg 3 Sunday 10 February, 6 Special Stages totalling 97.20km

RESULTS

1	Jari-Matti Latvala/	Ford Focus RS WRC 07	
	Miikka Anttila	2h46m41.2s	A8
2	Mikko Hirvonen	Ford Focus RS WRC 07	
	Jarmo Lehtinen	2h47m39.5s	A8
3	Gigi Galli/	Ford Focus RS WRC 07	
	Giovanni Bernacchini	2h49m04.4s	A8
4	Petter Solberg/	Subaru Impreza WRC2007	
	Phil Mills	2h49m40.6s	A8
5	Andreas Mikkelsen/	Ford Focus RS WRC 06	
	Ola Fløene	2h52m27.2s	A8
6	Dani Sordo/	Citroën C4 WRC	
	Marc Martí	2h53m54.3s	A8
7	Toni Gardemeister/	Suzuki SX4 WRC	
	Tomi Tuominen	2h57m16.5s	A8
8	Juho Hänninen/	Mitsubishi Lancer Evo IX	
	Mikko Markkula	2h59m08.7s	N4
9	Mads Ostberg/	Subaru Impreza WRC2007	
	Ole Kristian Unnerud	3h00m09.7s	A8
10	Jari Ketomaa/	Subaru Impreza	
	Miika Teiskonen	3h00m31.9s	N4

61 starters, 49 finishers

RECENT WINNERS

Mexico was the setting for
a career-best second place
for Chris Atkinson in the
ageing Subaru Impreza.
Photograph: Race&motion

Main: Third-placed Jari-Matti Latvala led after the first day, but couldn't hold off the charging Loeb.

Top right: Loeb tried to hide from the furore under traditional Mexican headwear.

Bottom right: Sébastien Loeb's third win on the bounce in Mexico was shrouded in controversy after a five-minute penalty for an engine linking infringement was rescinded. Photographs: PHOT04 unless specified

Race&motion

THERE WAS an air of confidence surrounding championship leader Mikko Hirvonen as he landed in León for the third round of the series. The Ford man talked of having 'the feeling'. It was the same feeling, he said, as when he had arrived home in Jyvaskyla for last year's Rally Finland. On that occasion he delivered a drive of epic proportions. This time around, he was way off beam. Maybe his Mexican feeling had come from one too many fajitas...

At the end of leg one there was, indeed, a BP-backed Ford Focus RS WRC out front. But it was the sister car of Jari-Matti Latvala, who was following up his round two win in the best possible fashion by leading on the WRC's first dirt date of the season. So what about Sébastien Loeb?

After a nightmare run at the start of the event, the Frenchman admitted he was happy to be venturing into the Mexican outback, where he could focus on driving his Citroën as fast as possible. The problem for the reigning champion had been a fuel injection system failure at shakedown. As if that and the loss of pre-event running time weren't bad enough, Citroën then found itself on the wrong end of a five-minute penalty. The team pointed out that it had been badly advised on the matter of changing the engine and would it help if they put the old motor back in Loeb's C4? The FIA deemed that to be agreeable and off they went.

Despite Loeb's favourable position of third on the road, behind the Fords of Hirvonen and Latvala, it was Jari-Matti who took the advantage. Running first on the road after an unsurprisingly dry winter in Central America was taking its toll on Hirvonen. To compile the agony, he suffered three punctures (two on the same

stage after running front and rear wheels over the same razor-sharp rock) during the event. He emerged from three torrid days still in the championship lead, but by the narrowest of margins.

Having heard his team-mate's tales of woe, Latvala was forced to run first on the road on leg two. He lasted one more stage before Loeb powered past. In a flurry of fastest times, Loeb built a big lead – helped no end by the fact that Latvala had dropped two minutes with a broken turbo pipe. He went from first, to second, to third. The Finn remained on the bottom step of the podium until the end.

That took the pressure off Loeb, who had looked deeply stressed throughout the event. Part of this was due to his far-from-ideal start to the rally, and part due to the fact that his team-mate Dani Sordo and fellow C4 WRC driver Conrad Rautenbach had both suffered suspension failures on their cars. Loeb tiptoed his way around the biggest of the Mexican boulders to his second win of the year.

With just over a minute between himself and runner-up Chris Atkinson, Loeb could afford to take it easy. Atkinson's second place was a mixed blessing. Yes, it was his best WRC result ever and the Australian was pleased with that, and yes, the Impreza WRC's handling had improved since Sweden. But this still wasn't enough. Still, there were niggling problems slowing the Subaru. Having been in the thick of the fight for the lead, Atko was a little demoralised at not being able to maintain that momentum.

Behind Latvala, Henning Solberg had hoped to keep Hirvonen out of fourth position, but a right-front puncture in Comanjilla put paid to that.

Right: Henning Solberg had hoped to beat Mikko Hirvonen to fourth, but a puncture in the penultimate stage put paid to that.

Bottom Right: The winners are almost lost in the podium confetti in Léon.

Below: Running first on the road hurt fourth-placed Hirvonen's chances, and he wasn't helped by a series of punctures.

Photographs: PHOTO4 unless specified

Corona Rally Mexico Results

28 FEBRUARY – 02 MARCH 2008 | FIA WORLD CHAMPIONSHIP ROUND 3

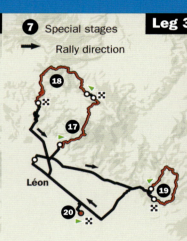

Stage Numbers	1	2	3	4	5	6	7	8	9	10	11	12	13	14	15	16	17	19	20
Loeb	4	2	2	2	2	2	2	2	2	1	1	1	1	1	1	1	1	1	1
Atkinson	2	3	3	3	3	3	3	3	3	3	3	3	2	2	2	2	2	2	2
Latvala	1	1	1	1	1	1	1	1	1	2	2	2	3	3	3	3	3	3	3
Hirvonen	5	5	4	4	5	5	5	5	5	5	5	5	5	5	5	5	5	5	4
H.Solberg	7	10	9	7	7	6	6	6	6	6	5	5	4	4	4	4	4	4	5
Wilson	9	8	7	6	6	7	7	7	7	6	6	6	6	6	6	6	6	6	6
Villagra	19	12	11	8	8	8	8	8	8	8	9	9	7	7	7	7	7	7	7
Ogier	12	13	12	10	10	10	10	10	10	10	10	10	10	9	9	9	9	9	8
Mölder	14	15	14	11	11	11	11	11	11	12	12	11	11	10	10	10	10	10	9
Kosciuszko	13	16	15	13	12	12	12	12	12	11	11	12	11	11	11	11	11	11	10
P.Solberg	6	6	5	5	4	4	4	4	4	7	7	9	12	14	12	14	13	12	11
Rautenbach	10	9	18	19	19	20	21	22	20	19	19	19	18	16	16	16	16	16	15
Sordo	28	27	28	26	24	23	23	23	23	21	20	20	20	18	18	17	17	17	16
TriviÀo	11	11	10	9	9	9	9	9	9	9	9	8	8	8	8	8	8	8	EX
Galli	3	4	8	R															
Andersson	8	7	6	R															
Gardemeister	31	32	33	R															

Leg 1   ▶ Stage start   ✖ Stage finish
Leg 2   ⑦ Special stages   → Rally direction
Leg 3

MEXICO

Léon

Top: Sébastien Ogier claimed his first Junior WRC victory on his series debut and also took the final point when Ricardo Triviño was excluded.

Above right: Beer company Corona continued its sponsorship of its home rally.
Photographs: PHOTO4

FINISH LINES...

Matthew Wilson continued to impress with his 2008 form in Mexico. Having come within an ace of collecting fifth place in Sweden, he did bag sixth in Central America. And that was despite the best efforts of the local hooligan and canine population. The 21-year-old hit a dog early in the event and then had a rock hurled at the screen of his Focus RS WRC in the Duarte stage. Understandably furious, Wilson battled on to register his first points of the season... Points were something that Subaru's Petter Solberg would dearly have loved in León. When he also hit a dog, this time in stage one, the 2003 champion should have known this wasn't going to be his event. Severe brake problems hindered him further in the first loop before a broken driveshaft put him out on the second stage of day two. The former Mexico winner was deeply – and understandably – depressed with his trip across the Atlantic... The list of those suffering from the misery of retirement grew and grew: Gigi Galli held a top three position early on, before binning his Focus on the third stage and then again on SS4 – this time permanently after scrutineers discovered roll cage damage. But the Italian's despair was nothing compared to that of Suzuki. Both SX4 WRCs retired with engine failures – the same problem which had stopped Toni Gardemeister in Monte and Per-Gunnar Andersson in Sweden. Andersson was sixth after the first loop, until his engine dropped onto three cylinders on the run back to León and he retired in service. Gardemeister's car managed eight kilometres of SS4 before

giving up the ghost. Given that throttle problems had slowed the Finn to 40kp/h for the first three stages, he was hardly about to leapfrog his way from 33rd to the lead, but the ignominy of the early bath hit just as hard... It wasn't even as though there was a Junior result for Suzuki to fall back on, as Citroën's new superstar Sébastien Ogier hit the ground running to win his first ever JWRC round in a C2 Super 1600. Ogier's result got even better a fortnight after the finish, when eighth-placed local driver Ricardo Trivino was excluded for wearing the wrong driving gloves in his Peugeot 206 WRC, promoting Ogier to a point-scoring position.

RUNNING ORDER

3	Mikko Hirvonen/ Jarmo Lehtinen	Ford Focus RS WRC 07 / A8
4	Jari-Matti Latvala/ Mikka Anttila	Ford Focus RS WRC 07 / A8
1	Sébastien Loeb/ Daniel Elena	Citroën C4 WRC / A8
7	Gigi Galli/ Giovanni Bernacchini	Ford Focus RS WRC 07 / A8
5	Petter Solberg/ Phil Mills	Subaru Impreza WRC2007 / A8
6	Chris Atkinson/ Stéphane Prévot	Subaru Impreza WRC2007 / A8
2	Daniel Sordo/ Marc Martí	Citroën C4 WRC / A8
11	Toni Gardemeister/ Tomi Tuominen	Suzuki SX4 WRC / A8
12	Per-Gunnar Andersson/ Jonas Andersson	Suzuki SX4 WRC / A8
10	Henning Solberg/ Cato Menkerud	Ford Focus RS WRC 07 / A8
8	Matthew Wilson/ Scott Martin	Ford Focus RS WRC 07 / A8
9	Federico Villagra/ Jorge Pérez Companc	Ford Focus RS WRC 07 / A8
14	Conrad Rautenbach/ David Senior	Citroën C4 WRC / A8
31	Martin Prokop/ Jan Tománek	Citroën C2 S1600 / A6
41	Patrik Sandell/ Emil Axelsson	Renault Clio S1600 / A6
32	Jaan Mölder/ Frédéric Miclotte	Suzuki Swift S1600 / A6
33	Aaron Burkart/ Michael Kölbach	Citroën C2 S1600 / A6
35	Michal Kosciuszko/ Maciek Szczepaniak	Suzuki Swift S1600 / A6
46	Shaun Gallagher/ Michael Morrissey	Citroën C2 S1600 / A6
42	Sébastien Ogier/ Julien Ingrassia	Citroën C2 S1600 / A6

SPECIAL STAGE TIMES

SS1 Alfaro 1 (22.96km)
1 J-M.Latvala/M.Anttila (Ford Focus RS WRC 07) 14m14.6s; 2 C.Atkinson/S.Prévot (Subaru Impreza WRC2007) 14m17.6s; 3 G.Galli/G.Bernacchini (Ford Focus RS WRC 07) 14m21.9s; 4 S.Loeb/D.Elena (Citroën C4 WRC) 14m22.0s; 5 M.Hirvonen/J.Lehtinen (Ford Focus RS WRC 07) 14m24.4s; 6 P.Solberg/P.Mills (Subaru Impreza WRC2007) 14m25.0s; JC S.Ogier/J.Ingrassia (Citroën C2 S1600) 15m56.1s

SS2 Ortega 1 (23.83km)

1 Loeb/Elena (Citroën) 14m11.8s; 2 Galli/Bernacchini (Ford) 14m13.4s; 3 Latvala/Anttila (Ford) 14m14.3s; 4 Atkinson/Prévot (Subaru) 14m17.1s; 5 Hirvonen/Lehtinen (Ford) 14m17.4s; 6 P.Solberg/Mills (Subaru) 14m33.1s; JC Ogier/Ingrassia (Citroën) 15m48.9s

SS3 El Cubilete 1 (18.87km)
1 Loeb/Elena (Citroën) 11m51.5s; 2 Latvala/Anttila (Ford) 11m52.0s; 3 H.Solberg/C.Menkerud (Ford Focus RS WRC 07) 11m56.2s; 4 Atkinson/Prévot (Subaru) 11m57.4s; 5 Hirvonen/Lehtinen (Ford) 11m57.8s; 6 M.Wilson/S.Martin (Ford Focus RS WRC 07) 12m07.6s; JC Ogier/Ingrassia (Citroën) 12m59.2s

SS4 Alfaro 2 (22.96km)
1 P.Solberg/Mills (Subaru) 14m02.5s; 2 Latvala/Anttila (Ford) 14m06.2s; 3 Atkinson/Prévot (Subaru) 14m08.3s; 4 Loeb/Elena (Citroën) 14m08.8s; 5 Hirvonen/Lehtinen (Ford) 14m10.9s; 6 H.Solberg/Menkerud (Ford) 14m12.5s; JC Ogier/Ingrassia (Citroën) 15m45.5s

SS5 Ortega 2 (23.83km)
1 Latvala/Anttila (Ford) 14m00.1s; 2 Loeb/Elena (Citroën) 14m02.4s; 3 Atkinson/Prévot (Subaru) 14m02.8s; 4 P.Solberg/Mills (Subaru) 14m09.4s; 5 H.Solberg/Menkerud (Ford) 14m09.7s; 6 Wilson/Martin (Ford) 14m31.7s; JC Ogier/Ingrassia (Citroën) 15m33.3s

SS6 El Cubilete 2 (18.87km)
1 Latvala/Anttila (Ford) 11m45.5s; 2 Loeb/Elena (Citroën) 11m47.4s; 3 Atkinson/Prévot (Subaru) 11m47.8s; 4 H.Solberg/Menkerud (Ford) 11m49.7s; 5 P.Solberg/Mills (Subaru) 11m50.8s; 6 Hirvonen/Lehtinen (Ford) 11m50.8s; JC Ogier/Ingrassia (Citroën) 12m50.3s

SS7 Superspecial 1 (2.21km)
1 P.Solberg/Mills (Subaru) 1m41.7s; 2 Loeb/Elena (Citroën) 1m42.3s; 3 F.Villagra/J.P.Companc (Ford Focus RS WRC 07) 1m42.8s; 4 Atkinson/Prévot (Subaru) 1m42.8s; 5 Wilson/Martin (Ford) 1m43.6s; 6 Latvala/Anttila (Ford) 1m43.6s; JC J.Mölder/F.Miclotte (Suzuki Swift 1600) 1m54.1s

SS8 Superspecial 2 (2.21km)
1 Loeb/Elena (Citroën) 1m42.0s; 2 Latvala/Anttila (Ford) 1m42.3s; 3 H.Solberg/Menkerud (Ford) 1m42.3s; 4 P.Solberg/Mills (Subaru) 1m42.3; 5 Villagra/Companc (Ford) 1m42.4s; 6 Wilson/Martin (Ford) 1m42.6s; JC M.Kosciuszko/M.Szczepaniak (Suzuki Swift S1600) 1m53.0s

SS9 Ibarilla 1 (29.90km)
1 Loeb/Elena (Citroën) 18m35.7s; 2 Hirvonen/Lehtinen (Ford) 18m39.4s; 3 Atkinson/Prévot (Subaru) 18m42.4s; 4 D.Sordo/M.Martí (Citroën C4 WRC) 18m44.0s; 5 P.Solberg/Mills (Subaru) 18m44.7s; 6 Latvala/Anttila (Ford) 18m45.2s; JC P.Sandell/E.Axelsson (Renault Clio S1600) 21m06.4s

SS10 Duarte 1 (23.27km)
1 Loeb/Elena (Citroën) 18m19.6s; 2 Sordo/Martí (Citroën) 18m20.1s; 3 Latvala/Anttila (Ford) 18m24.3s; 4 Atkinson/Prévot (Subaru) 18m26.0s; 5 Hirvonen/Lehtinen (Ford) 18m26.4s; 6 H.Solberg/Menkerud (Ford) 18m46.7s; JC Sandell/Axelsson (Renault) 20m17.3s

SS11 Derramadero 1 (23.28km)
1 Sordo/Martí (Citroën) 14m04.6s; 2 Loeb/Elena (Citroën) 14m05.1s; 3 Hirvonen/Lehtinen (Ford) 14m06.3s; 4 Latvala/Anttila (Ford) 14m06.3s; 5 Atkinson/Prévot (Subaru) 14m07.4s; 6 H.Solberg/Menkerud (Ford) 14m14.8s; JC Sandell/Axelsson (Renault) 15m44.5s

SS12 Ibarilla 2 (29.90km)
1 Loeb/Elena (Citroën) 18m21.0s; 2 Latvala/Anttila (Ford) 18m28.1s; 3 Atkinson/Prévot (Subaru) 18m29.5s; 4 Sordo/Martí (Citroën) 18m30.5s; 5 H.Solberg/Menkerud (Ford) 18m40.5s; 6 Wilson/Martin (Ford) 19m04.5s; JC Mölder/Miclotte (Suzuki) 20m50.6s

SS13 Duarte 2 (23.27km)
1 Sordo/Martí (Citroën) 17m56.2s; 2 Loeb/Elena (Citroën) 18m04.4s; 3 H.Solberg/Menkerud (Ford) 18m10.8s; 4 Hirvonen/Lehtinen (Ford) 18m12.9s; 5 Atkinson/Prévot (Subaru) 18m26.2s; 6 Wilson/Martin (Ford) 18m27.9s; JC Sandell/Axelsson (Renault) 19m47.3s

SS14 Derramadero 2 (23.28km)
1 H.Solberg/Menkerud (Ford) 13m52.9s; 2 Sordo/Martí (Citroën) 13m55.1s; 3 Hirvonen/Lehtinen (Ford) 13m57.3s; 4 Loeb/Elena (Citroën) 14m03.1s; 5 Atkinson/Prévot (Subaru) 14m05.3s; 6 Wilson/Martin (Ford) 14m28.5s; JC Ogier/Ingrassia (Citroën) 15m41.7s

SS15 Superspecial 3 (2.21km)
1 H.Solberg/Menkerud (Ford) 1m41.9s; 2 Loeb/Elena (Citroën) 1m41.9s; 3 Hirvonen/Lehtinen (Ford) 1m42.4s; 4 Atkinson/Prévot 1m42.6s; 5 Sordo/Martí (Citroën) 1m43.2s; 6 Villagra/Companc (Ford) 1m43.4s; JC Ogier/Ingrassia (Citroën) 1m55.4s

SS16 Superspecial 4 (2.21km)
1 Atkinson/Prévot (Subaru) 1m40.8s; 2 Loeb/Elena (Citroën) 1m40.8s; 3 Sordo/Martí (Citroën) 1m41.4s; 4 H.Solberg/Menkerud (Ford) 1m41.7s; 5 Hirvonen/Lehtinen (Ford) 1m41.7s; 6 Villagra/Companc (Ford) 1m42.4s; JC Sandell/Axelsson (Renault) 1m53.5s

SS17 Leon (16.09km)
1 Latvala/Anttila (Ford) 10m43.3s; 2 P.Solberg/Mills (Subaru) 10m43.5s; 3 Hirvonen/Lehtinen (Ford) 10m46.2s; 4 Sordo/Martí (Citroën) 10m46.7s; 5 H.Solberg/Menkerud (Ford) 10m52.9s; 6 Loeb/Elena (Citroën) 10m53.8s; JC Mölder/Miclotte (Suzuki) 12m14.5s

SS18 Guanajuatito (22.30km)
Cancelled due to excessive crowd numbers.

SS19 Comanjilla (17.88km)
1 Hirvonen/Lehtinen (Ford) 10m12.7s; 2 Latvala/Anttila (Ford) 10m13.7s; 3 Sordo/Martí (Citroën) 10m14.2s; 4 H.Solberg/Menkerud (Ford) 10m24.4s; 5 Loeb/Elena (Citroën) 10m31.9s; 6 Wilson/Martin (Ford) 10m35.9s; JC Sandell/Axelsson (Renault) 11m32.3s

SS20 Superspecial 5 (4.42km)
1 Sordo/Martí (Citroën) 3m19.3s; 2 Atkinson/Prévot (Subaru) 3m20.8s; 3 Villagra/Companc (Ford) 3m22.4s; 4 Hirvonen/Lehtinen (Ford) 3m22.4s; 5 Loeb/Elena (Citroën) 3m24.4s; 6 Wilson/Martin (Ford) 3m25.7s; JC Kosciuszko/Szczepaniak (Suzuki) 3m44.8s

MAJOR RETIREMENTS

7	Galli/Bernacchini Mechanical	Ford Focus RS WRC 07 SS4 Gr A8
17	Gardemeister/Tuominen Engine	Suzuki SX4 WRC SS4 Gr A8
18	Andersson/Andersson Engine	Suzuki SX4 WRC SS4 Gr A8
15	TriviÀo/Salom Excluded	Peugeot 206 WRC SS20 Gr A8

FIA CLASS WINNERS

A8	Over 2000 cc	Loeb/Elena Citroën C4 WRC
A7	1600-2000cc	Komljenovic/Jeremic Renault Clio R3
A6	1400-1600cc	Ogier/Ingrassia Citroën C2 S1600
N4	Over 2000 cc	Guerra/Gonzalez Mitsubishi Lancer Evo VIII
N3	1600-2000cc	Espinoza/Suarez Renault Clio RS

RALLY LEADERS
Overall: SS1-9 Latvala; SS10-20 Loeb
JWRC: SS1-20 Ogier

SPECIAL STAGE ANALYSIS

	1st	2nd	3rd	4th	5th	6th
Loeb (Citroën)	8	5	-	3	2	1
Latvala (Ford)	4	5	2	1	1	1
Sordo (Citroën)	3	2	2	3	1	-
P.Solberg (Subaru)	2	2	-	1	2	2
H.Solberg (Ford)	2	1	2	3	3	3
Hirvonen (Ford)	1	3	3	4	2	-
Atkinson (Subaru)	1	2	6	4	3	-
Galli (Ford)	-	1	1	-	-	-
Villagra (Ford)	-	-	2	-	1	2
Wilson (Ford)	-	-	-	-	1	8

TYRES
Tyres: Pirelli Scorpion
Compound: hard
Number of tyres available per car: 36

WORLD CHAMPIONSHIP POINTS
Drivers
1 Hirvonen 21; 2 Loeb 20; 3 Latvala 16; 4 Atkinson 14; 5= P.Solberg, Galli 9; 7 Duval 5; 8= H.Solberg, Mikkelsen 4; 10= Sordo, Wilson 3 etc
Manufacturers
1 BP Ford Abu Dhabi WRT 37; 2= Citroën Total WRT, Subaru WRT 25; 4 Stobart VK M-Sport Ford RT 19; 5 Munchi's Ford WRT 6; 6 Suzuki WRT 5
Junior World Rally Championship
1 Ogier 10; 2 Mölder 8; 3 Kosciuszko 6; 4 Burkart 5; 5 Sandell 4; 6 Gallagher 3; 7 Prokop 2; 8 Fanari 1
Production Car World Rally Championship
1 Hänninen 10; 2 Ketomaa 8; 3 Sandell 6; 4 Prokop 5; 5 Nittel 4; 6 Arai 3; 7 Aráujo 2; 8 Sousa 1

ROUTE DETAILS
Total route of 830.83km of which 353.75km were competitive on 20 stages
Leg 1 Friday 29 February, 8 Special Stages totalling 135.74km
Leg 2 Saturday 1 March, 8 Special Stages totalling 157.32km
Leg 3 Sunday 2 March, 4 Special Stages totalling 60.69km

RESULTS

1	Sébastien Loeb/ Daniel Elena	Citroën C4 WRC 3h33m29.9s A8
2	Chris Atkinson/ Stéphane Prévot	Subaru Impreza WRC2007 3h34m36.0s A8
3	Jari-Matti Latvala/ Mikka Anttila	Ford Focus RS WRC 07 3h35m09.6s A8
4	Mikko Hirvonen/ Jarmo Lehtinen	Ford Focus RS WRC 07 3h37m08.6s A8
5	Henning Solberg/ Cato Menkerud	Ford Focus RS WRC 07 3h38m27.8s A8
6	Matthew Wilson/ Scott Martin	Ford Focus RS WRC 07 3h39m58.8s A8
7	Federico Villagra/ Jorge Pérez Companc	Ford Focus RS WRC 07 3h52m32.9s A8
8	Sébastien Ogier/ Julien Ingrassia	Citroën C2 S1600 3hr58.54.8s A6
9	Jaan Mölder/ Frédéric Miclotte	Suzuki Swift S1600 4hr00m26.7s A6
10	Michal Kosciuszko/ Maciek Szczepaniak	Suzuki Swift S1600 4hr02m00.0s A6

40 starters, 28 finishers

RECENT WINNERS

1999*	Gabriel Marin/Javier Marin	Mitsubishi Lancer Evo VI
2000*	Douglas Gore/Mark Nelson	Mitsubishi Lancer Evo VI
2001*	Ramon Ferreyros/Raul Velit	Toyota Celica GT4
2002*	Harri Rovanperä/Risto Pietiläinen	Peugeot 206 WRC
2003*	Marcos Ligato/Ruben Garcia	Mitsubishi Lancer Evo VI
2004	Markko Märtin/Michael Park	Ford Focus RS WRC 03
2005	Petter Solberg/Phil Mills	Subaru Impreza WRC2005
2006	Sébastien Loeb/Daniel Elena	Citroën Xsara WRC
2007	Sébastien Loeb/Daniel Elena	Citroën C4 WRC

*Non-championship event

Race&motion

MIKKO HIRVONEN could scarcely believe his morning. Wiping the sweat from his eyes at the end of the opening stage, the championship-leading Finn raised his eyes heaven-wards. "That was one long stage," he grimaced. "We could have gained a minute or lost a minute in there."

At the start of the week, the southern hemisphere stages had been bathed in late summer sunshine for the recce. Then out of nowhere – and simultaneous to the start of the rally proper – autumn had arrived with a vengeance. Rain, fog, cloud – the drivers had to contend with the lot on Friday morning north of Villa Carlos Paz. But it appeared that as bad as the conditions had been for Hirvonen, they deteriorated further once the Ford was through. His words were bang on. Almost. He hadn't quite lifted a minute out of reigning world champion Sébastien Loeb, but he had taken 50.7 seconds. Hirvonen's team-mate Jari-Matti Latvala was an early second, just ahead of Loeb, but the second of Ford's Finns rolled off he road and dropped eight minutes on the very next stage.

If Hirvonen had looked exasperated, Loeb was even more so when he heard how much time he'd lost to his rival. "I think we have some work to do..." was all the Frenchman offered before nosing his Citroën down the road and into stage two.

Loeb's miserable morning continued, however, and he was unable to post a fastest time until the conditions had brightened for the second run through the stages in the afternoon. It wasn't just the weather that showed a sunnier outlook, either. Loeb was all smiles and sitting on a hefty lead after Hirvonen had smacked a rock not far into SS5, shearing the bolts on the track control. In an instant, his rally appeared over. His lead gone – in the rally and the championship. That he would recover to fifth after a slightly insane weekend of weather came as little consolation. He had, after all, been staring at his first win of the season.

"The rock wasn't in my notes," was about all Hirvonen could or would offer on the subject.

Loeb sympathised, set fastest time and then throttled back to control a lead that would mushroom to more than two minutes by Sunday afternoon. After the flurry of excitement which had surrounded

Hirvonen's lead in the drivers' championship and Latvala's first win in Sweden, Loeb hit back and put the rest of the WRC firmly in its place in Argentina. He let his results do the talking – and at three wins from four starts and a five-point advantage at the top of the table, they made fairly dismal reading for his rivals.

Finishing second for the second event in succession was Subaru's Chris Atkinson. The Australian had held the position for much of day one, relinquishing it on day two when his team-mate Petter Solberg edged ahead. Understandably, team principal David Richards was enormously keen to claim two of the three steps on the podium and told the drivers to hold station. Unfortunately for Subaru, a possible 14 points became eight when Solberg's Impreza WRC suffered an electrical glitch within sight of the finish.

That promoted Loeb's Citroën partner Dani Sordo to third. The Spaniard had spent most of the event recovering from power steering failure on the opening leg – but even he admitted he hadn't expected third. Stories of drivers returning from Argentina with better-than-expected results were commonplace throughout the top 10, especially in the case of Conrad Rautenbach. Twenty-first after the opening stage, the Zimbabwean had tamed his C4 WRC – on only his second event in the car – and the conditions to end the rally an astonished but elated fourth.

Above: Chris Atkinson emerged as an outside bet for the title by scoring his third podium finish from four starts.

Below: The Australian gets used to the taste of champagne courtesy of winning co-driver Daniel Elena.

Opposite page: Loeb's Citroën C4 sported Red Bull livery for the first time.
Photographs: PHOTO4 unless specified

Right: Jari-Matti Latvala rolled out of second place on the opening morning. He was 15th after retiring again on day two with a damaged starter motor.

Below: Conrad Rautenbach avoided all the pitfalls to claim his first world championship points in fourth overall.

Middle Right: A build-up of smoke in the cockpit of Gigi Galli's Ford Focus slowed him on Saturday and dropped him to seventh.

Far Right: Dani Sordo battled back from recent disappointments to finish third.

Bottom Right: Federico Villagra was the first local driver home in sixth place.

Photographs: PHOTO4 unless specified

Race&motion

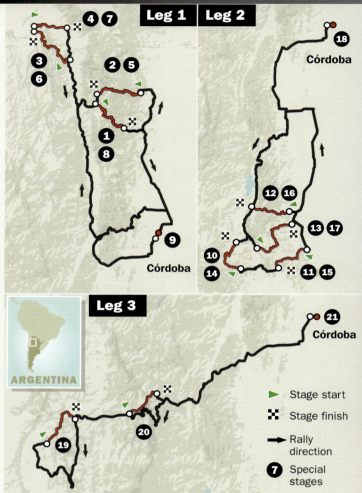

Leg 1 | Leg 2

Córdoba

Córdoba

Leg 3

Córdoba

ARGENTINA

▶ Stage start

▣ Stage finish

→ Rally direction

⑦ Special stages

Stage Numbers	1	2	3	4	5	6	7	8	9	10	11	12	13	14	15	16	17	18	19	20	21
Loeb	3	2	2	2	1	1	1	1	1	1	1	1	1	1	1	1	1	1	1	1	1
Atkinson	4	3	3	3	2	2	2	2	2	3	3	5	5	5	4	4	3	3	3	2	2
Sordo	7	6	6	5	4	4	4	5	5	4	4	4	4	4	5	4	4	4	4	3	3
Rautenbach	21	16	13	13	11	10	10	10	9	9	9	9	9	8	6	5	5	5	4	4	4
Hirvonen	1	1	1	1	8	11	19	20	25	21	18	17	17	15	14	10	7	6	5	5	5
Villagra	8	7	7	7	6	6	6	6	6	7	7	7	6	9	9	8	9	8	6	6	6
Galli	6	5	5	6	5	5	5	4	4	4	4	4	5	5	6	6	11	8	7	7	
Aigner	13	12	12	12	13	13	12	12	10	10	10	10	10	10	9	8	7	7	8	8	
Beltrán	19	19	16	16	17	15	15	14	12	11	11	11	11	12	11	11	10	10	9	9	
Ketomaa	25	23	20	20	21	20	18	18	15	14	14	14	13	14	12	12	11	10	10		
Latvala	2	30	22	21	15	12	11	8	8	8	8	7	P	8	13	15	16	14	12	12	
Andersson	34	33	33	35	38	36	36	36	35	31	31	30	30	29	30	30	31	32	28	24	24
Wilson	10	10	10	10	9	8	8	7	7	6	6	6	6	7	14	15	13	R			
Gardemeister	9	9	9	9	9	14	9	14	16	16	16	17	18	18	19	20	19	R			
P.Solberg	5	4	4	4	3	3	3	3	3	2	2	2	2	2	2	2	2	2	R		
H.Solberg	11	9	8	8	12	21	24	26	29	25	24	23	19	20	21	22	22	24	R		
Companc	14	11	11	11	10	9	9	9	11	16	R										

Above right: A delighted Andreas Aigner scored his first Production win.
Photographs: PHOTO4

FINISH LINES...

Local hero Federico Villagra was sixth in his Munchi's Ford Focus RS WRC 07. Ordinarily he would have been chuffed to bits with that, except he could have been fourth had it not been for an electrical glitch with the car. Matthew Wilson shared those sentiments. The Briton had battled hard with Villagra and passed him on SS10, only for his Focus's wiring loom to go up in smoke on SS14... Gigi Galli suffered the same fate at the same time, but limped back to service despite the cockpit filling with choking smoke. With the problem duly rectified, the Italian continued to collect seventh place and two points... For the second rally in a row, the lead driver in the WRC support series – this time the Production Car WRC – claimed the final point. Austrian Andreas Aigner turned in a faultless drive to win his first P-WRC round for the Red Bill Mitsubishi team. Two-time champion Toshi Arai led after stage one, but dropped back with suspension problems. Subaru's hopes of a return to Group N fortune took a big hit with Arai's demise, but Nasser Al-Attiyah overcame engine troubles on day one to power his way up the order and into second – only for the gremlins to return and halt him in his tracks on the final day. Second in P-WRC and ninth overall therefore went to Argentinian ace Sebastian Beltran. Jari Ketomaa was third in Group N in his Impreza, rounding out the overall top 10... Notable by its absence from the finishers' list was a Suzuki SX4 WRC. This was another disastrous event for the Japanese firm: P-G Andersson didn't make the first stage before retirement beckoned, while team-mate Toni Gardemeister struggled through 15 stages before calling it a day with hydraulic problems.

RUNNING ORDER

3	Mikko Hirvonen/ Jarmo Lehtinen	Ford Focus RS WRC 07 A8
1	Sébastien Loeb/ Daniel Elena	Citroën C4 WRC A8
4	Jari-Matti Latvala/	Ford Focus RS WRC 07

	Mikka Anttila	A8
6	Chris Atkinson/ Stéphane Prévot	Subaru Impreza WRC2007 A8
7	Gigi Galli/ Giovanni Bernacchini	Ford Focus RS WRC 07 A8
5	Petter Solberg/ Phil Mills	Subaru Impreza WRC2007 A8
8	Henning Solberg/ Cato Menkerud	Ford Focus RS WRC 07 A8
16	Matthew Wilson/ Scott Martin	Ford Focus RS WRC 07 A8
2	Daniel Sordo/ Marc Martí	Citroën C4 WRC A8
11	Toni Gardemeister/ Tomi Tuominen	Suzuki SX4 WRC A8
9	Federico Villagra/ Jorge Pérez Companc	Ford Focus RS WRC 07 A8
12	Per-Gunnar Andersson/ Jonas Andersson	Suzuki SX-4 A8
9	Luis Pérez Companc/ José María Volta	Ford Focus RS WRC 07 A8
17	Conrad Rautenbach/ David Senior	Citroën C4 WRC A8
46	Jari Ketomaa/ Miika Teiskonen	Subaru Impreza N4
55	Patrik Sandell/ Emil Axelsson	Peugeot 207 S2000 N4
33	Martin Prokop/ Jan Tománek	Mitsubishi Lancer Evo IX N4
53	Uwe Nittel/ Detlet Ruf	Mitsubishi Lancer Evo IX N4
31	Toshihiro Arai/ Glenn Macneall	Subaru Impreza N4
32	Mirco Baldacci/ Giovanni Agnese	Mitsubishi Lancer Evo IX N4

SPECIAL STAGE TIMES

SS1 Lu Cumbre 1 (18.70km)

1 M.Hirvonen/J.Lehtinen (Ford Focus RS WRC 07) 16m29.3s; 2 J-M.Latvala/M.Anttila (Ford Focus RS WRC 07) 17m17.4s; 3 S.Loeb/D.Elena (Citroën C4 WRC) 17m20.0s; 4 C.Atkinson/S.Prévot (Subaru Impreza WRC2007) 17m44.1s; 5 P.Solberg/P.Mills (Subaru Impreza WRC2007) 18m03.1s; 6 G.Galli/G.Bernacchini (Ford Focus RS WRC 07) 18m04.6s; PC T.Arai/G.Macneall (Subaru Impreza) 19m15.2s

SS2 Ascochinga 1 (23.28km)

1 Hirvonen/Lehtinen (Ford) 14m59.6s; 2 Loeb/Elena (Citroën) 15m11.2s; 3 Atkinson/Prévot (Subaru) 15m13.2s; 4 P.Solberg/Mills (Subaru) 15m13.2s; 5 Galli/Bernacchini (Ford) 15m35.6s; 6 D.Sordo/M.Martí (Citroën) 15m37.4s; PC A.Aigner/K.Wicha (Mitsubishi Lancer Evo IX) 17m41.6s

SS3 Capilla Del Monte 1 (22.95km)

1 Latvala/Anttila (Ford) 17m39.7s; 2 Loeb/Elena (Citroën) 17m42.7s; 3 Galli/Bernacchini (Ford) 17m46.2s; 4 Hirvonen/Lehtinen (Ford) 17m46.9s; 5 Sordo/Martí (Citroën) 17m47.7s; 6 Atkinson/Prévot (Subaru) 17m48.5s; PC Aigner/Wicha (Mitsubishi) 18m57.8s

SS4 San Marcos (9.61km)

1 Hirvonen/Lehtinen (Ford) 6m38.3s; 2 Sordo/Martí (Citroën) 6m38.9s; 3 H.Solberg/C.Menkerud (Ford) 6m39.9s; 4 Loeb/Elena (Citroën) 6m40.6s; 5 P.Solberg/Mills (Subaru) 6m42.9s; 6 Galli/Bernacchini (Ford) 6m43.5s; PC M.Ligato/R.García (Mitsubishi Lancer Evo IX) 7m15.0s

SS5 Ascochinga 2 1 (23.28km)

1 Loeb/Elena (Citroën) 14m51.3s; 2 Galli/Bernacchini (Ford) 15m01.8s; 3 Sordo/Martí (Citroën) 15m02.6s; 4 Atkinson/Prévot (Subaru) 15m03.0s; 5 P.Solberg/Mills (Subaru) 15m05.0; 6 Latvala/Anttila (Ford) 15m08.2s; PC P.Sandell/E.Axelsson (Peugeot 207 S2000) 16m18.8s

SS6 Capilla Del Monte 2 (22.95km)

1 Latvala/Anttila (Ford) 17m23.1s; 2 Galli/Bernacchini (Ford)

17m24.0s; 3 Atkinson/Prévot (Subaru) 17m28.2s; 4 Sordo/Martí (Citroën) 17m29.1s; 5 Loeb/Elena (Citroën) 17m30.2s; 6 P.Solberg/Mills (Subaru) 17m36.9s; PC B.Sousa/C.Magalhães (Mitsubishi Lancer Evo IX) 18m53.1s

SS7 San Marcos 2 (9.61km)
1 Galli/Bernacchini (Ford) 6m33.5s; 2 Atkinson/Prévot (Subaru) 6m33.9s; 3 Latvala/Anttila (Ford) 6m34.6s; 4 Sordo/Martí (Citroën) 6m34.7s; 5 Loeb/Elena (Citroën) 6m35.6s; 6 P.Solberg/Mills (Subaru) 6m39.2s; PC Sandell/Axelsson (Peugeot) 7m08.3s

SS8 La Cumbre 2 (18.70km)
1 Latvala/Anttila (Ford) 17m02.3s; 2 Loeb/Elena (Citroën) 17m05.0s; 3 Galli/Bernacchini (Ford) 17m05.3s; 4 P.Solberg/Mills (Subaru) 17m08.1s; 5 Sordo/Martí (Citroën) 17m32.6s; 6 Atkinson/Prévot (Subaru) 17m46.2s; PC N.Al-Attiyah/C.Patterson (Subaru Impreza) 18m46.9s

SS9 Cordoba Stadium 1 (1.78km)
1 Atkinson/Prévot (Subaru) 1m39.4s; 2 P.Solberg/Mills (Subaru) 1m39.7s; 3 Latvala/Anttila (Ford) 1m40.7s; 4 Loeb/Elena (Citroën) 1m41.0s; 5 Galli/Bernacchini (Ford) 1m41.2s; 6 Sordo/Martí (Citroën) 1m42.8s; PC Al-Attiyah/Patterson (Subaru) 1m49.1s

SS10 Santica Monica 1 (22.71km)
1 P.Solberg/Mills (Subaru) 12m02.7s; 2 Atkinson/Prévot (Subaru) 12m16.7s; 3 Loeb/Elena (Citroën) 12m18.2s; 4 Hirvonen/Lehtinen (Ford) 12m22.6; 5 Latvala/Anttila (Ford) 12m24.0s; 6 Sordo/Martí (Citroën) 12m24.8s; PC Al-Attiyah/Patterson (Subaru) 13m37.9s

SS11 Villa Del Dique 1 (16.41km)
1 Loeb/Elena (Citroën) 9m10.0s; 2 P.Solberg/Mills (Subaru) 9m14.4s; 3 Atkinson/Prévot (Subaru) 9m17.8s; 4 Sordo/Martí (Citroën) 9m19.3s; 5 Galli/Bernacchini (Ford) 9m20.6s; 6 Hirvonen/Lehtinen (Ford) 9m23.8s; PC J.Ketomaa/M.Teiskonen (Subaru Impreza) 10m22.0s

SS12 San Augustin 1 (16.31km)
1 Loeb/Elena (Citroën) 11m26.5s; 2 Atkinson/Prévot (Subaru) 11m31.5s; 3 P.Solberg/Mills (Subaru) 11m33.2s; 4 Hirvonen/Lehtinen (Ford) 11m40.3s; 5 Sordo/Martí (Citroën) 11m43.8s; 6 F.Villagra/JP.Companc (Ford Focus RS WRC 07) 11m55.2s; PC Sandell/Axelsson (Peugeot) 12m53.6s

SS13 Santa Rosa 1 (21.41km)
1 Atkinson/Prévot (Subaru) 13m37.3s; 2 P.Solberg/Mills (Subaru) 13m40.6s; 3 Hirvonen/Lehtinen 13m40.8s (Ford); 4 Loeb/Elena (Citroën) 13m42.7s; 5 Galli/Bernacchini (Ford) 13m51.4s; 6 Sordo/Martí (Citroën) 13m52.1s; PC Al-Attiyah/Patterson (Subaru) 15m13.1s

SS14 Villa Del Dique 2 (22.17km)
1 P.Solberg/Mills (Subaru) 11m37.2s; 2 Loeb/Elena (Citroën) 11m44.8s; 3 Hirvonen/Lehtinen (Ford) 11m45.8s; 4 Atkinson/Prévot (Subaru) 11m47.2s; 5 Sordo/Martí (Citroën) 11m48.3; 6 M.Wilson/S.Martin (Ford Focus RS WRC 07) 12m16.9s; PC Al-Attiyah/Patterson (Subaru) 13m03.3s

SS15 Santa Rosa 1 (16.41km)
1 Loeb/Elena (Citroën) 8m57.8s; 2 P.Solberg/Mills (Subaru) 8m58.1s; 3 Hirvonen/Lehtinen (Ford) 9m06.0s; 4 Atkinson/Prévot (Subaru) 9m06.1s; 5 Sordo/Martí (Citroën) 9m07.3s; 6 C.Rautenbach/D.Senior (Citroën C4 WRC); PC Al-Attiyah/Patterson (Subaru) 10m04.3s

SS16 San Augustin 2 (16.31km)
1 P.Solberg/Mills (Subaru) 11m18.8s; 2 Loeb/Elena (Citroën) 11m19.2s; 3 Hirvonen/Lehtinen (Ford) 11m28.4s; 4 Sordo/Martí (Citroën) 11m32.5s; 5 Atkinson/Prévot (Subaru) 11m33.0; 6 Rautenbach/Senior (Citroën) 12m06.4s; PC Sandell/Axelsson (Peugeot) 12m41.5s

SS17 Santa Rosa 2 (21.41km)
1 P.Solberg/Mills (Subaru) 13m23.6s; 2 Hirvonen/Lehtinen (Ford) 13m25.3s; 3 Loeb/Elena (Citroën) 13m28.2s; 4 Atkinson/Prévot (Subaru) 13m34.2s; 5 Sordo/Martí (Citroën) 13m39.8s; 6 Rautenbach/Senior (Citroën) 14m38.1s; PC Al-Attiyah/Patterson (Subaru) 14m45.2s

SS18 Cordoba Stadium 2 (1.78km)
1 P.Solberg/Mills (Subaru) 1m40.6s; 2 Loeb/Elena (Citroën) 1m41.1s; 3 Atkinson/Prévot (Subaru) 1m42.6s; 4 Hirvonen/Lehtinen (Ford) 1m44.3s; 5 Rautenbach/Senior (Citroën)

1m45.1s; 6 Sordo/Martí (Citroën) 1m46.0; PC Al-Attiyah/Patterson (Subaru) 1m49.5s

SS19 Mina Clavero 1 (24.70km)
1 Latvala/Anttila (Ford) 19m57s; 2 Sordo/Martí (Citroën) 20m06.1s; 3 Galli/Bernacchini (Ford) 20m06.5s; 4 Hirvonen/Lehtinen (Ford) 20m07.8s; 5 Loeb/Elena (Citroën) 20m08.6s; 6 Villagra/Companc (Ford) 20m10.3s; PC S.Beltrán/R.Rojas (Mitsubishi Lancer Evo IX) 21m27.4s

SS20 El Condor 1 (15.99km)
1 Loeb/Elena (Citroën) 15m08.6s; 2 Latvala/Anttila (Ford) 15m19.3s; 3 Atkinson/Prévot (Subaru) 15m27.9s; 4 Galli/Bernacchini (Ford) 15m28.4s; 5 Sordo/Martí (Citroën) 15m37.6s; 6 Hirvonen/Lehtinen (Ford) 15m41.1s; PC Aigner/Wicha (Mitsubishi) 17m07.6s

SS21 Cordoba Stadium 3 (1.98km)
1 Latvala/Anttila (Ford) 2m13.3s; 2 Hirvonen/Lehtinen (Ford) 2m14.0s; 3 Loeb/Elena (Citroën) 2m14.9s; 4 S.Campedelli/D.Fappani (Mitsubishi Lancer Evo IX) 2m15.1s; 5 Galli/Bernacchini (Ford) 2m15.1s; 6 E.Akasakov/A.Kornilov (Mitsubishi Lancer Evo IX) 2m16.1s; PC Campedelli/Fappani (Mitsubishi) 2m15.1s

Cars that retired and subsequently restarted and were classified under SuperRally regs:

12	Andersson/Andersson	Suzuki SX4 WRC		
	Electrical	SS1/SS14	A8	
3	Hirvonen/Lehtinen	Ford Focus RS WRC 07		
	Accident	SS5	A8	
8	H.Solberg/Menkerud	Ford Focus RS WRC 07		
	Accident	SS5	A8	
11	Gardemeister/Tuominen	Suzuki SX4 WRC		
	Accident	SS8/SS16	A8	
7	Galli/Bernacchini	Ford Focus RS WRC 07		
	Accident damage	SS14	A8	
4	Latvala/Anttila	Ford Focus RS WRC 07		
	Over time limit	SS14	A8	
16	Wilson/Martin	Ford Focus RS WRC 07		
	Suspension	SS15	A8	

MAJOR RETIREMENTS

10	Companc/Volta	Ford Focus RS WRC 07		
	Accident	SS10	A8	
5	Solberg/Mills	Subaru Impreza WRC2007		
	Electrical	SS19	A8	
8	Solberg/Menkerud	Ford Focus RS WRC 07		
	Stopped in stage	SS19	A8	
11	Gardemeister/Tuominen	Suzuki SX4 WRC		
	Stopped in stage	SS20	A8	
16	Wilson/Martín	Ford Focus RS WRC 07		
	Suspension	SS20	A8	

FIA CLASS WINNERS

A8	Over 2000cc	Loeb/Elena Citroën C4 WRC
A6	1400-1600cc	Bottazzini/De Luca Renault Clio
N4	Over 2000 cc	Aigner/Wicha Mitsubishi Lancer Evo IX
N3	1600-2000cc	Durante/Casajus Renault Clio

RALLY LEADERS
Overall: SS1 – SS4 Hirvonen; SS5-21 Loeb

PC: SS1 Arai; SS2-SS21 Aigner

SPECIAL STAGE ANALYSIS

	1st	2nd	3rd	4th	5th	6th
Loeb (Citroën)	5	5	4	3	3	-
P.Solberg (Subaru)	5	4	1	2	3	2
Latvala (Ford)	5	2	2	-	3	1
Hirvonen (Ford)	3	2	4	5	-	2
Atkinson (Subaru)	2	3	5	3	1	2
Galli (Ford)	1	2	3	1	4	3
Sordo (Citroën)	-	2	1	4	7	4
H.Solberg (Ford)	-	-	1	-	-	-
Campedelli (Mitsubishi)	-	-	-	1	-	-
Rautenbach (Citroën)	-	-	-	-	-	3
Villagra (Ford)	-	-	-	-	-	2

| Wilson (Ford) | - | - | - | - | - | 1 |
| Akasakov (Mitsubishi) | - | - | - | - | - | 1 |

TYRES
Tyres: Pirelli Scorpion
Compound: hard
Number of tyres available per car: 36

WORLD CHAMPIONSHIP POINTS
Drivers
1 Loeb 30; 2 Hirvonen 25; 3 Atkinson 22; 4 Latvala 16; 5 Galli 11; 6= P.Solberg, Sordo 9; 8= Duval, Rautenbach, Villagra 5 etc
Manufacturers
1 BP Ford Abu Dhabi WRT 44; 2 Citroën Total WRT 41; 3 Subaru WRT 33; 3 Stobart VK M-Sport Ford RT 22; 5 Munchi's Ford WRT 10; 6 Suzuki WRT 6
Junior World Rally Championship
1 Ogier 10; 2 Mölder 8; 3 Kosciuszko 6; 4 Burkart 5; 5 Sandell 4; 6 Gallagher 3; 7 Prokop 2; 8 Fanari 1
Production Car World Rally Championship
1 Ketomaa 14; 2= Aigner, Hänninen 10; 4 Beltran 8; 5 Prokop 7; 6 Sandell 6; 7 Nutahara 5; 8= Rauam, Nittel 4 ; 10= Arai, Farrah 3 etc

ROUTE DETAILS
Total route of 1619.45km of which 347.91km were competitive on 21 stages
Leg 1 Friday 28 March, 9 Special Stages totalling 150.86km
Leg 2 Saturday 29 March, 9 Special Stages totalling 154.38km
Leg 3 Sunday 30 March, 3 Special Stages totalling 42.67km

RESULTS

1	Sébastien Loeb/ Daniel Elena	Citroën C4 WRC 4h05m48.6s A8
2	Chris Atkinson/ Stéphane Prévot	Subaru Impreza WRC2007 4h08m21.8s A8
3	Dani Sordo/ Marc Martí	Citroën C4 WRC 4h09m53.3s A8
4	Conrad Rautenbach/ David Senior	Citroën C4 WRC 4h25m52.1s A8
5	Mikko Hirvonen/ Jarmo Lehtinen	Ford Focus RS WRC 07 4h31m03.9s A8
6	Federico Villagra/ Jorge Pérez Companc	Ford Focus RS WRC 07 4h33m30.6s A8
7	Gigi Galli/ Giovanni Bernacchini	Ford Focus RS WRC 07 4h33m40.4s A8
8	Andreas Aigner/ Klaus Wicha	Mitsubishi Lancer Evo IX 4h34m47.09 N4
9	Sebastián Beltrán/ Ricardo Rojas	Mitsubishi Lancer Evo IX 4h35m53.5s N4
10	Jari Ketomaa/ Miika Teiskonen	Subaru Impreza 4h37m41.2s N4

56 starters, 31 finishers

PREVIOUS WINNERS
1979*Jean Guichet/Jean Todt — Peugeot 504
1980 Walter Röhrl/Christian Geistdörfer — Fiat 131 Abarth
1981 Guy Fréquelin/Jean Todt — Talbot Sunbeam Lotus
1983 Hannu Mikkola/Arne Hertz — Audi Quattro A1
1984 Stig Blomqvist/Björn Cederberg — Audi Quattro A2
1985 Timo Salonen/Seppo Harjanne — Peugeot 205 Turbo 16
1986 Miki Biasion/Tiziano Siviero — Lancia Delta S4
1987 Miki Biasion/Tiziano Siviero — Lancia Delta HF 4x4
1988 Jorge Recalde/Jorge Del Buono — Lancia Delta Integrale
1989 Mikael Ericsson/Claes Billstam — Lancia Delta Integrale
1990 Miki Biasion/Tiziano Siviero — Lancia Delta Integrale 16v
1991 Carlos Sainz/Luis Moya — Toyota Celica GT4
1992 Didier Auriol/Bernard Occelli — Lancia Delta HF Integrale
1993 Juha Kankkunen/Nicky Grist — Toyota Celica Turbo 4wd
1994 Didier Auriol/Bernard Occelli — Toyota Celica Turbo 4wd
1995 Jorge Recalde/Märtin Christie — Lancia Delta HF Integrale
1996 Tommi Mäkinen/Seppo Harjanne — Mitsubishi Lancer E3
1997 Tommi Mäkinen/Seppo Harjanne — Mitsubishi Lancer E4
1998 Tommi Mäkinen/Risto Mannisenmäki — Mitsubishi Lancer E5
1999 Juha Kankkunen/Juha Repo — Subaru Impreza WRC99
2000 Richard Burns/Robert Reid — Subaru Impreza WRC2000
2001 Colin McRae/Nicky Grist — Ford Focus RS WRC
2002 Carlos Sainz/Luis Moya — Ford Focus RS WRC02
2003 Marcus Grönholm/Timo Rautiainen — Peugeot 206 WRC
2004 Carlos Sainz/Marc Martí — Citroën Xsara WRC
2005 Sébastien Loeb/Daniel Elena — Citroën Xsara WRC
2006 Sébastien Loeb/Daniel Elena — Citroën Xsara WRC
2007 Sébastien Loeb/Daniel Elena — Citroën C4 WRC
*Non-championship event

SÉBASTIEN LOEB is a straight-down-the-line fella. He's not really into game-playing, scheming or conniving. Which is probably why he looked a touch uncomfortable at the end of leg one of the inaugural WRC-qualifying Jordan Rally. He was just 1.1 seconds behind Citroën team-mate and rally leader Dani Sordo. One-point-one seconds? Hmm, wasn't that just a bit too close? Were tactics being deployed here? Was the four-times champion trying to pull a fast one to ensure Sordo would have to sweep a car's worth of loose gravel off the slippery surface of the Jordanian stages the following day?

As Loeb came over all 'Who me sir?' the rest of the service park drew its own conclusions. If Loeb had really been pushing as hard as he said he had, the gap would be fairly static the following morning. Except it wasn't.

As had been expected – and as any sensible tactician would – Loeb and Citroën had done a bit of manoeuvring. But the big question now was how to play Saturday. Road position was even more important going into the third and final day – complete with the longest and most slippery stages of the entire event. It was reckoned a spot around fifth on the road would be about right, but that would mean a day of calculations and mathematics. Loeb preferred to do what he did best. He preferred to go hell-for-leather and build a lead on Saturday, then defend it from the front on Sunday.

One stage down on Saturday and he was out in front. He'd absolutely caned everybody. From 1.1s down, he was now 8.1s up. A stage later and the margin was 16.3s. Then came the big one: Shuna, the longest stage of the day. Privately, it emerged later, Loeb had talked of his hopes of putting 30 seconds

between himself and his nearest rival before he went to bed on Saturday night. Emerging from SS11 11.3s faster than anybody else, he'd allowed himself a wry smile. And why not? The job was almost done.

Seconds later, the smile was wiped from his face. Going through his post-stage routine of removing crash helmet, taking a drink and chatting to his engineer on the radio, he'd just clicked his seat belts back in when he motored into a right-hander. Simultaneously, Conrad Rautenbach was going through his pre-stage routine, motoring into a left-hander on the same stretch of road. Both corners were blind. Both cars in the middle of the road. The inevitable happened and the two C4s were out. Both drivers had stood on the brakes, slashing the impact speed to a meagre 10mph. But the damage was done. Two radiators became one and what had already been a miserable event for Rautenbach got even worse. As for Loeb, all his hard work had been for nothing.

Once the dust had settled, there was a dawning realisation that there was now one hell of a fight on for this fifth round of the season. If Loeb and Citroën had been canny about their approach to tactics on Friday night, Ford men Mikko Hirvonen and Jari-Matti Latvala were blatant in their efforts to ensure Sordo remained first on the road. They succeeded, much to the Spaniard's chagrin. There was nothing the likeable Sordo could do on Sunday. But as Hirvonen motored to his first win of the season, Latvala's hopes of scoring his second success in four starts went out of the window when he clattered a rock in Kafrain, the day's opener. The left-rear of the Focus collapsed and he lost minutes. A potential win became a disconsolate seventh.

Main: Hirvonen's victory put him five points clear of Sébastien Loeb in the championship.

Inset: Ford team boss Malcolm Wilson congratulates Mikko Hirvonen. Road position tactics had helped the Finn to overhaul Dani Sordo for his first win of the season. Photographs: Race&motion

Right: Young Brit Matthew Wilson finished fifth despite a left-rear puncture on the final morning.

Above: Sordo fought back to second when Jari-Matti Latvala broke his Ford's suspension on Sunday's second stage.

Opposite top: The podium finishes continued for Subaru's Chris Atkinson. Subaru team boss David Richards (left) doesn't look that impressed...

Opposite middle & bottom: Loeb was leading by 35 seconds when he collided with Conrad Rautenbach's similar Citroën on a road section on day two.
Photographs: PHOTO4 unless specified

Race&motion

Jordan Rally Results

24-27 APRIL 2008 | FIA WORLD RALLY CHAMPIONSHIP ROUND 5

	Stage Numbers	1	2	3	4	5	6	7	8	9	10	11	12	13	14	15	16	17	18	19	20	21	22
Position	Hirvonen	3	4	4	5	4	4	4	4	4	4	3	2	2	2	3	2	1	1	1	1		
	Sordo	1	1	1	1	1	1	1	1	2	2	2	1	3	3	3	3	2	2	2	2		
	Atkinson	7	7	6	6	6	5	5	5	5	5	5	4	4	4	3	3	3	3				
	H.Solberg	12	13	12	13	11	9	8	8	8	8	8	7	7	7	7	7	6	4	4	4		
	Wilson	11	9	9	9	9	8	7	7	7	7	6	6	6	6	6	6	5	5	5	5		
	Villagra	10	11	11	11	12	11	10	9	9	9	9	8	8	8	7	6	6	6	6	6		
	Latvala	4	3	3	2	2	3	3	3	3	2	1	1	1	1	1	3	8	8	9	7		
	Galli	6	6	7	7	7	6	13	18	14	13	12	11	11	10	10	10	10	9	9	8		
	Al-Qassimi	13	14	13	12	13	12	11	10	10	10	10	9	9	9	9	9	9	8	7	7	9	
	Loeb	5	5	5	3	3	2	2	2	1	1	1	7	10	12	17	20	18	17	12	11	10	10
	Clark	38	29	24	24	22	20	17	15	18	18	18	17	18	18	18	15	14	15	15	14	13	12
	Rautenbach	14	12	10	10	10	10	9	27	23	22	28	33	36	36	34	33	32	32	29	28	27	26
	Aava	8	6	8	8	7	6	6	6	5	5	5	5	5	5	5	5	5	5				
	Andersson	54	54	53	53	53	53	53	53	49	49	49	47	46	44	41	39	37	37	R			
	P.Solberg	2	2	2	4	5	15	27	32	28	25	22	22	21	17	16	R						
	Gardemeister	9	10	R																			

Leg 1

Leg 2

Leg 3

- ▶ Stage start
- ✕ Stage finish
- **7** Special stages
- ➡ Rally direction

JORDAN

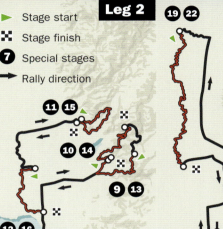

Top: Junior WRC contender Patrik Sandell was two minutes clear when he crashed out of the category lead in his Renault Clio.

Above right: Local fans got their first stage of WRC action once the dust had cleared.
Photographs: PHOTO4

FINISH LINES...

The final podium position went to Subaru's Chris Atkinson, but the Australian appeared genuinely bemused at how the place had come to him. Being five minutes adrift of the winner, Atkinson pointed out that he really had no business spraying champagne on Sunday afternoon. It had been another tricky event for Subaru. After a couple of quiet rallies, Atkinson's team-mate Petter Solberg had let rip with another spectacular volley of curses. And not without just cause. On the first two days of the event, he'd had three dampers burst on him – the last one showering the inside of the car with damper oil. Things went from bad to worse when he rolled out on Sunday... Sunday's 41km Jordan River stage had been billed as a killer before the event. And so it transpired. Matthew Wilson was on for a career-best fourth before he had to stop and change a puncture; Suzuki's P-G Andersson crashed off the road, compiling what had been a truly awful event for Suzuki – team-mate Toni Gardemeister had retired on Friday with a damaged engine... Eventually, it was Henning Solberg who collected fourth, with Wilson fifth and Federico Villagra repeating his sixth place of the previous round... If you thought the WRC class had been exciting, it was nothing compared with the battle for Junior honours. Round one winner Sébastien Ogier was engaged in an early tussle with Patrik Sandell, despite worrying fuel pump problems aboard his Citroën. The Frenchman's hopes of back-to-back wins appeared to have gone south when he stopped to change a puncture in stage six. That left Sandell with a comfortable two-minute lead, until a Sunday morning shunt handed the win to Ogier, who had to be given credit forturning in one of the comeback drives of the season.

RUNNING ORDER

1	Sébastien Loeb/ Daniel Elena	Citroën C4 WRC A8	
3	Mikko Hirvonen/ Jarmo Lehtinen	Ford Focus RS WRC 07 A8	
6	Chris Atkinson/ Stéphane Prévot	Subaru Impreza WRC2007 A8	
4	Jari-Matti Latvala/ Mikka Anttila	Ford Focus RS WRC 07 A8	
7	Gigi Galli/ Giovanni Bernacchini	Ford Focus RS WRC 07 A8	
2	Daniel Sordo/ Marc Martí	Citroën C4 WRC A8	
5	Petter Solberg/ Phil Mills	Subaru Impreza WRC2007 A8	
18	Conrad Rautenbach/ David Senior	Citroën C4 A8	
9	Federico Villagra/ Jorge Pérez Companc	Ford Focus RS WRC 07 A8	
8	Henning Solberg/ Cato Menkerud	Ford Focus RS WRC 07 A8	
16	Matthew Wilson/ Scott Martin	Ford Focus RS WRC 07 A8	
11	Toni Gardemeister/ Tomi Tuominen	Suzuki SX4 WRC A8	
12	Per-Gunnar Andersson/ Jonas Andersson	Suzuki SX4 WRC A8	
14	Khalid Al-Qassimi/ Michael Orr	Ford Focus RS WRC 07 A8	
17	Urmo Aava/ Kuldar Sikk	Citroën C4 WRC A8	
10	Barry Clark/ Luis Diaz	Ford Focus RS WRC 07 A8	
42	Sébastien Ogier/ Julien Ingrassia	Citroën C2 S1600 A6	
32	Jaan Mölder/	Suzuki Swift S1600	

	Frédéric Miclotte	A6
35	Michal Kosciuszko/ Maciek Szczepaniak	Suzuki Swift S1600 A6
41	Patrik Sandell/ Emil Axelsson	Renault Clio S1600 A6

SPECIAL STAGE TIMES

SS1 Suwayma 1 (13.03km)
1 D.Sordo/M.Marti (Citroën C4 WRC) 6m40.2s; 2 P.Solberg/P.Mills (Subaru Impreza WRC2007) 6m40.2; 3 M.Hirvonen/J.Lehtinen (Ford Focus RS WRC 07) 6m40.7s; 4 J-M.Latvala/M.Anttila (Ford Focus RS WRC 07); 5 S.Loeb/D.Elena (Citroën C4 WRC) 6m44.8s; 6 G.Galli/G.Bernacchini (Ford Focus RS WRC 07) 6m53.2s; JC P.Sandell/E.Axelsson (Renault Clio S1600) 7m23.7s

SS2 Mahes 1 (20.00km)
1 Sordo/Marti (Citroën) 13m54.8s; 2 P.Solberg/Mills (Subaru) 14m00.2s; 3 Latvala/Anttila (Ford) 14m03.7s; 4 Hirvonen/Lehtinen (Ford) 14m06.1s; 5 Loeb/Elena (Citroën) 14m07.4s; 6 U.Aava/K.Sikk (Citroën C4 WRC) 14m07.5s; JC S.Ogier/J.Ingrassia (Citroën C2 S1600) 14m58.3s

SS3 Mount Nebo 1 (11.10km)
1 Sordo/Marti (Citroën) 8m02.9s; 2 Loeb/Elena (Citroën) 8m07.9s; 3 Latvala/Anttila (Ford) 8m08.6s; 4 Hirvonen/Lehtinen (Ford) 8m09.4s; 5 C.Atkinson/S.Prévot (Subaru Impreza WRC2007) 8m09.4s; 6 P.Solberg/Mills (Subaru) 8m12.6s; JC Sandell/Axelsson (Renault) 8m37.7s

SS4 Mal'n 1 (13.46km)
1 Loeb/Elena (Citroën) 9m55.4s; 2 Latvala/Anttila (Ford) 10m00.4s; 3 Hirvonen/Lehtinen (Ford) 10m01.2s; 4 P.Solberg/Mills (Subaru) 10m02.8s; 5 Sordo/Martí (Citroën) 10m02.8s; 6 Atkinson/Prévot (Subaru) 10m14.5s; JC Sandell/Axelsson (Renault) 10m58.4s

SS5 Suwayma 2 (13.03km)
1 Latvala/Anttila (Ford) 6m37.7s; 2 Loeb/Elena (Citroën) 6m38.7s;
3 Hirvonen/Lehtinen (Ford) 6m39.7s; 4 Sordo/Martí (Citroën)
6m41.7s; 5 Atkinson/Prévot (Subaru) 6m42.1; 6 P.Solberg/Mills
(Subaru) 6m43.5s; JC Ogier/Ingrassia (Citroën) 7m20.0s

SS6 Mahes 2 (20.00km)
1 Loeb/Elena (Citroën) 13m38.5s; 2 Sordo/Martí (Citroën)
13m39.6s; 3 Latvala/Anttila (Ford) 13m41.1s; 4 Hirvonen/Lehtinen
(Ford) 13m45.6s; 5 Atkinson/Prévot (Subaru) 13m48.2; 6
Aava/Sikk (Citroën) 13m57.9s; JC Sandell/Axelsson (Renault)
14m51.4s

SS7 Mount Nebo 2 (11.10km)
1 Loeb/Elena (Citroën) 7m52.6s; 2 Latvala/Anttila (Ford) 7m56.3s;
3 Hirvonen/Lehtinen (Ford) 7m57.7s; 4 Sordo/Martí (Citroën)
7m58.3s; 5 Atkinson/Prévot (Subaru) 8m03.2s; 6 Aava/Sikk
(Citroën) 8m10.3s; JC Ogier/Ingrassia (Citroën) 8m32.5s

SS8 Mal'n 2 (13.46km)
1 Hirvonen/Lehtinen (Ford) 9m46.7s; 2 Loeb/Elena (Citroën)
9m49.8s; 3 Latvala/Anttila (Ford) 9m52.6s; 4 Sordo/Martí (Citroën)
9m53.4s; 5 Atkinson/Prévot (Subaru) 9m56.0s; 6 Aava/Sikk
(Citroën) 10m03.9s; JC Ogier/Ingrassia (Citroën) 10m50.2s

SS9 Turki 1 (14.13km)
1 Loeb/Elena (Citroën) 8m18.1s; 2 Latvala/Anttila (Ford) 8m23.2s;
3 Hirvonen/Lehtinen (Ford) 8m26.1s; 4 Sordo/Martí (Citroën)
8m27.3; 5 P.Solberg/Mills (Subaru) 8m29.3s; 6 Galli/Bernacchini
(Ford) 8m38.5s; JC Ogier/Ingrassia (Citroën) 9m12.2s

SS10 Erak Elamir 1 (12.47km)
1 Loeb/Elena (Citroën) 8m40.9s; 2 Hirvonen/Lehtinen (Ford)
8m47.6s; 3 Sordo/Martí (Citroën) 8m49.1s; 4 Latvala/Anttila (Ford)
8m51.6s; 5 Galli/Bernacchini (Ford) 8m52.9s; 6 P.Solberg/Mills
8m54.8s; JC Ogier/Ingrassia (Citroën) 9m32.1s

SS11 Shuna 1 (15.19km)
1 Loeb/Elena (Citroën) 11m54.9s; 2 Latvala/Anttila (Ford)
12m06.2s; 3 Hirvonen/Lehtinen (Ford) 12m06.3s; 4 Sordo/Martí
(Citroën) 12m12.7s; 5 Galli/Bernacchini (Ford) 12m14.5s; 6
Aava/Sikk (Citroën) 12m18.1s; JC M.Kosciuszko/M.Szczepaniak
(Suzuki Swift 1600) 12m58.6s

SS12 Baptism Site 1 (13.13km)
1 Sordo/Martí (Citroën) 6m42.2s; 2 Latvala/Anttila (Ford)
6m42.5s; 3 Hirvonen/Lehtinen (Ford) 6m43.9s; 4 Galli/Bernacchini
(Ford) 6m47.4s; 5 Aava/Sikk (Citroën) 6m53.0s; 6 Atkinson/
Prévot (Subaru) 6m54.2s; JC Ogier/Ingrassia (Citroën) 7m28.9s

SS13 Turki 2 (14.13km)
1 Hirvonen/Lehtinen (Ford) 8m15.7s; 2 Latvala/Anttila (Ford)
8m17.5s; 3 Sordo/Martí (Citroën) 8m22.1s; 4 P.Solberg/Mills
(Subaru) 8m23.1s; 5 Galli/Bernacchini (Ford) 8m24.8s; 6
Atkinson/Prévot (Subaru) 8m26.2s; JC Ogier/Ingrassia (Citroën)
9m01.4s

SS14 Erak Elamir 2 (12.47km)
1 Galli/Bernacchini (Ford) 8m40.8s; 2 Hirvonen/Lehtinen (Ford)
8m42.3s; 3 Latvala/Anttila (Ford) 8m43.8s; 4 P.Solberg/Mills
(Subaru) 8m46.2s; 5 Sordo/Martí (Citroën) 8m 46.3s; 6
H.Solberg/C.Menkerud (Ford Focus RS WRC 07); JC Ogier/Ingrassia
(Citroën) 9m23.1s

SS15 Shuna 2 (15.19km)
1 Galli/Bernacchini (Ford) 11m57.8s; 2 Latvala/Anttila (Ford)
12m00.7s; 3 Atkinson/Prévot (Subaru) 12m02.7s; 4
Hirvonen/Lehtinen (Ford) 12m03.3s; 5 Sordo/Martí (Citroën)
12m05.4s; 6 P-G.Andersson/J.Andersson (Suzuki SX4 WRC)
12m09.7; JC Ogier/Ingrassia (Citroën) 12m42.7s

SS16 Baptism Site 2 (13.13km)
1 Galli/Bernacchini (Ford) 6m41.2s; 2 Sordo/Martí (Citroën)
6m44.1s; 3 Solberg/Menkerud (Ford) 6m48.4s; 4 Atkinson/Prévot
(Subaru) 6m48.7s; 5 Aava/Sikk (Citroën) 6m49.1; 6
M.Wilson/S.Martin (Ford Focus RS WRC 07) 6m50.4s; JC
Ogier/Ingrassia (Citroën) 7m28.4s

SS17 Kafrain 1 (16.49km)
1 Hirvonen/Lehtinen (Ford) 11m02.5s; 2 Latvala/Anttila (Ford)
11m04.1s; 3 Loeb/Elena (Citroën) 11m06.0s; 4 Sordo/Martí
(Citroën) 11m15.0s; 5 Galli/Bernacchini (Ford) 11m16.5s; 6
F.Villagra/J.P.Companc (Ford Focus RS WRC 07) 11m26.9s; JC
Ogier/Ingrassia (Citroën) 12m11.8s

SS18 Wadi Shueib 1 (9.18km)

1 Loeb/Elena (Citroën) 7m10.1s; 2 Galli/Bernacchini (Ford)
7m16.5s; 3 Hirvonen/Lehtinen (Ford) 7m19.4s; 4
Andersson/Andersson (Suzuki) 7m21.9s; 5 Sordo/Martí (Citroën)
7m22.7s; 6 Wilson/Martin (Ford) 7m29.1s; JC S.Gallagher/P.Kiely
(Citroën C2 S1600) 8m02.0s

SS19 Jordan River 1 (41.45km)
1 Loeb/Elena (Citroën) 28m32.8s; 2 Hirvonen/Lehtinen (Ford)
28m36.8s; 3 Sordo/Martí (Citroën) 28m39.1s; 4 Galli/Bernacchini
(Ford) 29m02.7s; 5 H.Solberg/Menkerud (Ford) 29m10.2s; 6
Atkinson/Prévot (Subaru) 29m25.8s; JC Ogier/Ingrassia (Citroën)
31m02.9s

SS20 Kafrain 2 (16.49km)
1 Latvala/Anttila (Ford) 11m00.4s; 2 Loeb/Elena (Citroën)
11m06.4s; 3 Hirvonen/Lehtinen (Ford) 11m08.9s; 4
Galli/Bernacchini (Ford) 11m12.3s; 5 Sordo/Martí (Citroën)
11m22.0; 6 H.Solberg/Menkerud (Ford) 11m27.2s; JC
Ogier/Ingrassia (Citroën) 12m22.9s

SS21 Wadi Shueib 2 (9.18km)
1 Loeb/Elena (Citroën) 7m04.8s; 2 Galli/Bernacchini (Ford)
7m08.7s; 3 Hirvonen/Lehtinen (Ford) 7m17.9s; 4 Sordo/Martí
(Citroën) 7m20.8s; 5 H.Solberg/Menkerud (Ford) 7m21.6s; 6
Wilson/Martin (Ford) 7m25.5s; JC Ogier/Ingrassia (Citroën) 7m59.2

SS22 Jordan River 2 (41.45km)
1 Hirvonen/Lehtinen (Ford) 28m09.1s; 2 Loeb/Elena (Citroën)
28m19.5s; 3 Latvala/Anttila (Ford) 28m30.2s; 4 Galli/Bernacchini
(Ford) 28m43.0s; 5 H.Solberg/Menkerud (Ford) 20m00.4s; 6
Sordo/Martí (Citroën) 29m01.1s; JC Ogier/Ingrassia (Citroën)
31m29.6s

Cars that retired and subsequently restarted and were classified
under SuperRally regs:

12	Andersson/Andersson	Suzuki SX4 WRC		
	Accident	SS1	A8
5	P.Solberg/Mills	Subaru Impreza WRC2007	
	Hit a rock	SS6	A8
7	Galli/Bernacchini	Ford Focus RS WRC 07	
	Lost a wheel	SS7	A8
18	Rautenbach/Senior	Citroën C4 WRC	
	Clutch	SS9	A8
18	Rautenbach/Senior	Citroën C4 WRC	
	Road section crash	SS11	A8
1	Loeb/Elena	Citroën C4 WRC	
	Road section crash	SS11	A8

MAJOR RETIREMENTS

11	Gardemeister/Tuominen	Suzuki SX4 WRC	
	Engine	SS3	A8
5	P.Solberg/Mills	Subaru Impreza WRC2007	
	Accident	SS16	A8
12	Andersson/Andersson	Suzuki SX4 WRC	
	Accident	SS19	A8
17	Aava/Sikk	Citroën C4 WRC	
	Suspension	SS19	A8

FIA CLASS WINNERS

A8	Over 2000cc	Hirvonen/Lehtinen
		Ford Focus RS WRC 07
A7	1600 – 2000cc	Schammel/Jamoul
		Renault Clio R3
A6	1400-1600cc	Ogier/Ingrassia
		Citroën C2 S1600
N4	Over 2000 cc	A.Al-Qassimi/Gocentas
		Mitsubishi Lancer Evo IX

RALLY LEADERS
Overall: SS1-8 Sordo; SS9-11 Loeb; SS12 Sordo; SS13-15 Latvala;
SS16 Sordo; SS17 Latvala; SS18-22 Hirvonen

JWRC: SS1 Sandell; SS2 Ogier; SS3-16 Sandell; SS17-22 Ogier

SPECIAL STAGE ANALYSIS

	1st	2nd	3rd	4th	5th	6th
Loeb (Citroën)	9	5	1	-	2	-
Sordo (Citroën)	4	2	4	8	4	1
Hirvonen (Ford)	4	3	10	4	-	-
Galli (Ford)	3	2	-	4	4	2
Latvala (Ford)	2	8	6	2	-	-
P.Solberg (Subaru)	1	1	-	3	1	3
Atkinson (Subaru)	-	-	1	1	5	3
H.Solberg (Ford)	-	-	1	-	3	2
Andersson (Suzuki)	-	-	-	1	-	1
Aava (Citroën)	-	-	-	-	2	5

| Wilson (Ford) | - | - | - | - | - | 3 |
| Villagra (Ford) | - | - | - | - | - | 1 |

TYRES
Tyres: Pirelli Scorpion
Compound: hard
Number of tyres available per car: 54

WORLD CHAMPIONSHIP POINTS
Drivers
1 Hirvonen 35; 2 Loeb 30; 3 Atkinson 28; 4 Latvala 18; 5 Sordo 17;
6 Galli 12; 7= P.Solberg, H.Solberg 9; 9 Villagra 8; 10 Wilson 7 etc
Manufacturers
1 BP Ford Abu Dhabi WRT 57; 2 Citroën Total WRT 50; 3 Subaru
WRT 39; 4 Stobart VK M-Sport Ford RT 29; 5 Munchi's Ford WRT 14;
6 Suzuki WRT 6 etc
Junior World Rally Championship
1 Ogier 20; 2 Gallagher 11; 3 Mölder 8; 4= Schammel, Kosciuszko 6;
6= Niegel, Burkart 5; 8= Albertini, Sandell 4; 10 Bertolini 3 etc
Production Car World Rally Championship
1 Ketomaa 14; 2= Aigner, Hänninen 10; 4 Beltrán 8; 5 Prokop 7; 6
Sandell 6; 7 Nutahara 5; 8= Rauam, Nittel 4; 10= Arai, Farrah 3 etc

ROUTE DETAILS
Total route of 983.44km of which 359.26km were competitive on
22 stages
Leg 1 Friday 25 April, 8 Special Stages totalling 115.18km
Leg 2 Saturday 26 April, 8 Special Stages totalling 109.84km
Leg 3 Sunday 27 April, 6 Special Stages totalling 134.24km

RESULTS

1	Mikko Hirvonen/	Ford Focus RS WRC 07	
	Jarmo Lehtinen	4h02m47.9s	A8
2	Dani Sordo/	Citroën C4 WRC	
	Marc Martí	4h04m03.6s	A8
3	Chris Atkinson/	Subaru Impreza WRC2007	
	Stéphane Prévot	4h07m47.4s	A8
4	Henning Solberg/	Ford Focus RS WRC 07	
	Cato Menkerud	4h10m23.7s	A8
5	Matthew Wilson/	Ford Focus RS WRC 07	
	Scott Martin	4hr13m29.6s	A8
6	Federico Villagra/	Ford Focus RS WRC 07	
	Jorge Pérez Companc	4h14m10.1s	A8
7	Jari-Matti Latvala/	Ford Focus RS WRC 07	
	Miika Anttila	4h15m03.5s	A8
8	Gigi Galli/	Ford Focus RS WRC 07	
	Giovanni Bernacchini	4h15m12.3s	A8
9	Khalid Al-Qassimi/	Ford Focus RS WRC 07	
	Michael Orr	4h21m53.6s	A8
10	Sébastien Loeb/	Citroën C4 WRC	
	Daniel Elena	4h26m26.0s	A8

54 starters, 33 finishers

RECENT WINNERS
1981*Michel Saleh/Tony Samia   Toyota Celica GT
1982*Michel Saleh/Tony Samia   Toyota Celica GT
1983*Saeed Al-Hajiri/John Spiller   Opel Manta 400
1984*Mohammed bin Sulayem/Hasan Bin Shadour
                                       Toyota Celica Twin Cam Turbo
1985*Saeed Al-Hajiri/John Spiller   Porsche 911 SC RS
1986*Saeed Al-Hajiri/John Spiller   Porsche 911 SC RS
1987*Mohammed bin Sulayem/John Spiller
                                       Toyota Celica Twin Cam Turbo
1988*Mohammed bin Sulayem/Ronan Morgan
                                       Toyota Celica Twin Cam Turbo
1990*Mohammed bin Sulayem/Ronan Morgan   Toyota Celica GT 4
1992*Abbas Al-Mosawi/Benny Smythe   Toyota Celica GT 4
1993*Sheikh Hammad Al-Thani/Abdullah Al Mani
                                       Mitsubishi Galant VR 4
1994*Mohammed Bin Sulayem/Phillip Mills Ford Escort RS Cosworth
1995*Abdullah Bakhashab/Bobby Willis   Ford Escort RS Cosworth
1996*Mohammed Bin Sulayem/Ronan Morgan
                                       Ford Escort RS Cosworth
1997*Mohammed Bin Sulayem/Ronan Morgan
                                       Ford Escort RS Cosworth
1998*Mohammed Bin Sulayem/Ronan Morgan Ford Escort Cosworth
1999*Mohammed Bin Sulayem/Ronan Morgan Ford Escort Cosworth
2000*Mohammed Bin Sulayem/Ronan Morgan   Ford Focus WRC
2001*Mohammed Bin Sulayem/Khalid Zakaria   Ford Focus WRC
2002*Mohammed Bin Sulayem/John Spiller   Ford Focus WRC
2003*Nasser Al-Attiyah/Chris Patterson   Ford Focus WRC
2004*Amjad Farrah/Khalid Zakaria   Mitsubishi Lancer Evo VII
2005*Nasser Al-Attiyah/Chris Patterson   Subaru Impreza WRC
2006*Nasser Al-Attiyah/Chris Patterson   Subaru Impreza WRC
2007*Khalid Al-Qassimi/Michael Orr   Subaru Impreza WRX STi
*Non-championship event

Rally d'Italia Sardegna

A puncture on the opening morning for Stobart driver Gigi Galli cost him a shot at victory on his home event.
Photograph: PHOTO4

Race&motion

WAS THAT right? Could that be right? Yes and yes. Sébastien Loeb had just taken 18 seconds out of everybody through the Crastazza stage. He'd demolished the rest of the field in one go. With everybody else on the back foot, Loeb was now ready to push further and try to win the event on Friday afternoon. The Frenchman did just that. He suffered through Saturday and Sunday, running first on the road, but the C4 driver's day-one dash had netted him enough time to hold on until the finish. Just.

Loeb's attack on Friday had been reminiscent of what he had attempted to do on Saturday morning in Jordan. This time around, though, there would be no chance, head-on meeting with another C4. This time, Loeb banged in the fastest times to build a day-one lead of 35 seconds.

Jari-Matti Latvala had been the quickest of the Ford drivers, the Finn on an absolute mission through the first stage of the rally (he was seven seconds quicker than anybody – including Loeb...). It all went wrong for J-ML on SS2, though. Sliding into a bank on a downhill right-hander forced the left-rear Pirelli from its rim, leaving him with meaningful drive from only three of the four wheels. He slipped down the leaderboard, as did fellow Ford driver Gigi Galli. In an identical incident Galli trashed the left-rear tyre on his Stobart car.

Latvala was deeply disappointed with himself. He sought to make up for his blunder in the only way he knew how by braking less. And he did that in some style through the second day in Sardinia. Fastest on every stage, he moved back up to head into Sunday in joint second place with team-mate Mikko Hirvonen.

Both Fords had been on a rollercoaster journey through days one and two. Latvala had been the more headline grabbing in terms of drama; Hirvonen had been on more of an emotional journey. Running first on the road courtesy of his championship lead, Hirvonen had struggled with sweeping the loose gravel on the surface. He'd looked all at sea on the opening day, talking about checking data or in discussion with his engineers. In short, there was nothing wrong with car or driver; it was just the road surface – and subsequently Hirvonen's head. He got everything into gear on Saturday and was second fastest to Latvala every time.

With four long stages and a short televised stage still to come on Sunday, this rally was far from over. With his lead under the half-minute mark, Loeb was concerned, particularly as the pendulum had certainly swung in favour of the Fords through day two. It was the Finns who were now in the groove and the Frenchman out front sweeping the loose gravel from the stages.

Dropping 10 seconds on Sunday's opener forced Loeb to pull out all the stops for the next stage, where he pegged them back by four seconds. It was more of the same through Monte Olbia 2 as he dropped another nine seconds to Hirvonen. But with 23sec still in hand, Loeb and the Ford men knew the job was done. The Frenchman had survived, but it had been a close-run thing. For Ford's Finns, there was thinking to be done. Hirvonen's subject was self-confidence and the need for more of it, while Latvala's was a more straightforward lesson in keeping air in the tyres.

Above: Mikko Hirvonen lost time through running first on the road on Friday. He finished 10 seconds behind winner Sébastien Loeb.

Above left: Ford team-mate Jari-Matti Latvala led after the first stage before suffering a puncture, but later recovered to third.

Left: Galli's fan club was out in force.

Far Left: Dani Sordo was slowed by understeer on Friday morning and reported a loss of traction on Saturday, but still finished fifth.

Photographs: PHOTO4 unless specified

Above: Suzuki's P-G Andersson made it to the finish in ninth despite the SX4's front brakes overheating on Friday.

Above middle: Henning Solberg had an unremarkable run to seventh and two points on his preferred gravel surface.

Above right: Chris Atkinson added to his points haul with sixth place aboard the works Impreza.
Photographs: PHOTO4

Main: Loeb hit the big 4-0 in terms of WRC victories with another faultless display of driving.
Photograph: Race&motion

Race&motion

Position / Stage Numbers	1	2	3	4	5	6	7	8	9	10	11	12	13	14	15	16	17
Loeb	4	1	1	1	1	1	1	1	1	1	1	1	1	1	1	1	1
Hirvonen	8	3	3	3	4	4	3	2	2	2	2	2	2	2	2	2	2
Latvala	1	14	9	9	7	7	6	4	3	3	3	2	3	3	3	3	3
Galli	3	10	7	6	6	6	4	5	5	5	4	4	4	4	4	4	4
Sordo	2	2	2	2	2	2	2	2	4	4	5	5	5	5	5	5	5
Atkinson	7	4	3	5	5	5	5	6	6	6	6	6	6	6	6	6	6
H.Solberg	12	8	8	8	9	8	8	7	7	7	7	7	7	7	7	7	7
Aava	10	7	6	7	8	9	9	8	8	8	8	8	8	8	8	8	8
Andersson	11	9	10	10	11	11	11	10	10	10	9	9	9	9	9	9	9
P.Solberg	6	5	5	4	3	3	7	14	14	14	11	10	10	12	11	10	10
Ostberg	9	11	16	15	15	15	15	15	15	12	12	12	11	10	11	11	
Wilson	16	16	15	14	14	14	12	12	11	10	11	11	10	12	12	12	
Rautenbach	15	12	13	13	12	12	13	11	11	12	14	14	14	13	13	13	13
Villagra	14	13	12	12	13	13	12	13	13	13	13	13	14	14	14	14	14
Al-Qassimi	17	15	14	24	28	33	32	28	24	24	24	22	19	18	18	16	16
Gardemeister	13	6	11	11	10	10	10	9	9	9	27	33	29	28	R		
Van Merksteijn	18	R															
Mikkelsen	5	R															

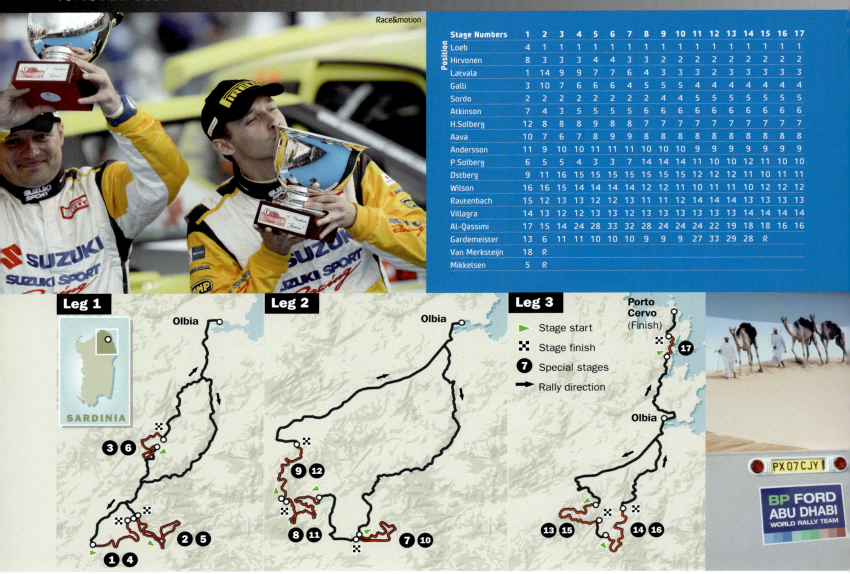

Leg 1 — Olbia · SARDINIA — stages 1, 4, 2, 5, 3, 6

Leg 2 — Olbia — stages 9, 12, 8, 11, 7, 10

Leg 3 — Porto Cervo (Finish), Olbia — stages 17, 13, 15, 14, 16

▶ Stage start
✖ Stage finish
7 Special stages
→ Rally direction

PX 07 CJY

BP FORD ABU DHABI WORLD RALLY TEAM

Above: The fight for JWRC honours was between Michal Kosciuszko and Martin Prokop, who lost out when fuel pressure problems struck on the final stage.

Above right: This is the rear of the Abu Dhabi hospitality unit, in case you were wondering...

Opposite: Swedish fans were out in force to cheer on Patrik Sandell's run to third in the PWRC.
Photographs: PHOTO4 unless specified

FINISH LINES...

Galli recovered from his early puncture to collect fourth on his home round of the World Rally Championship... Citroën's Dani Sordo was fifth with top Subaru man Chris Atkinson sixth. This was another difficult event for the Impreza WRC, as Petter Solberg could manage no better than 10th after an event troubled by suspension problems... Henning Solberg (Stobart Ford) and Urmo Aava (PH Sport Citroën) rounded out the points-paying positions... There was some solace for the Suzuki team, as P-G Andersson made up for his brace of crashes on the previous round in Jordan by placing his SX4 WRC in ninth overall... If Suzuki could find little to cheer in the overall standings, Michal Kosciuszko's first ever win in the Junior World Rally Championship raised a smile in the Japanese team. The Polish driver had done an incredible job for the entire event at the wheel of his Swift S1600. He and Martin Prokop had been separated by seconds for the best part of three days, only for the latter's Citroën C2 S1600 to suffer fuel pump problems within sight of the finish. While the rest of us rued the lack of a fight to the absolute finish, Kosciuszko celebrated an exceptional maiden win at this level...

RUNNING ORDER

No	Driver / Co-driver	Car
3	Mikko Hirvonen / Jarmo Lehtinen	Ford Focus RS WRC 07 — A8
1	Sébastien Loeb / Daniel Elena	Citroën C4 WRC — A8
6	Chris Atkinson / Stéphane Prévot	Subaru Impreza WRC2007 — A8
4	Jari-Matti Latvala / Mikka Anttila	Ford Focus RS WRC 07 — A8
2	Dani Sordo / Marc Martí	Citroën C4 WRC — A8
7	Gigi Galli / Giovanni Bernacchini	Ford Focus RS WRC 07 — A8
10	Henning Solberg / Cato Menkerud	Ford Focus RS WRC 07 — A8
5	Petter Solberg / Phil Mills	Subaru Impreza WRC2007 — A8
9	Federico Villagra / Jorge Pérez Companc	Ford Focus RS WRC 07 — A8
8	Matthew Wilson / Scott Martin	Ford Focus RS WRC 07 — A8
15	Conrad Rautenbach / David Senior	Citroën C4 WRC — A8
18	Andreas Mikkelsen / Maria Andersson	Ford Focus WRC 06 — A8
11	Toni Gardemeister / Tomi Tuominen	Suzuki SX4 WRC — A8
12	Per-Gunnar Andersson / Jonas Andersson	Suzuki SX4 WRC — A8
14	Khalid Al-Qassimi / Michael Orr	Ford Focus RS WRC 07 — A8
16	Urmo Aava / Kuldar Sikk	Citroën C4 WRC — A8
19	Mads Østberg / Ole Kristian Unnerud	Subaru Impreza WRC2007 — A8
20	Peter van Merksteijn / Hans van Beek	Ford Focus RS WRC 06 — A8
42	Sébastien Ogier / Julien Ingrassia	Citroën C2 S1600 — A6
46	Shaun Gallagher / Claire Mole	Citroën C2 S1600 — A6

SPECIAL STAGE TIMES

SS1 Monte Corvos 1 (16.43km)
1 J-M.Latvala/M.Anttila (Ford Focus RS WRC 07) 11m24.3s; 2 D.Sordo/M.Martí (Citroën C4 WRC) 11m31.3s; 3 G.Galli/G.Bernacchini (Ford Focus RS WRC 07) 11m31.7s; 4 S.Loeb/D.Elena (Citroën C4 WRC) 11m32.1s; 5 A.Mikkelsen/M.Andersson (Ford Focus WRC 06) 11m33.9s; 6 P.Solberg/P.Mills (Subaru Impreza WRC2007); JC P.Sandell/E.Axelsson (Renault Clio S1600) 12m33.8s

SS2 Crastazza 1 (33.96km)
1 Loeb/Elena (Citroën) 23m56.1s; 2 Sordo/Martí (Citroën) 24m14.3s; 3 M.Hirvonen/J.Lehtinen (Ford Focus RS WRC 07) 24m17.0s; 4 C.Atkinson/S.Prévot (Subaru Impreza WRC2007) 24m21.3s; 5 P.Solberg/Mills (Subaru) 24m25.2s; 6 T.Gardemeister/T.Tuominen (Suzuki SX4 WRC) 24m33.0s; JC M.Prokop/J.Tománek (Citroën C2 S1600) 26m17.6s

SS3 Terranova (15.39km)

1 Loeb/Elena (Citroën) 10m48.3s; 2 Latvala/Anttila (Ford) 10m52.7s; 3 Galli/Bernacchini (Ford) 10m52.9s; 4 Sordo/Martí (Citroën) 10m53.4s; 5 Atkinson/Prévot (Subaru) 10m56.7s; 6 Hirvonen/Lehtinen (Ford) 10m58.0s; JC M.Kosciuszko/M.Szczepaniak (Suzuki Swift S1600) 12m02.2s

SS4 Monte Corvos 2 (16.43km)

1 Galli/Bernacchini (Ford) 11m07.3s; 2 Latvala/Anttila (Ford) 11m08.8s; 3 P.Solberg/Mills (Subaru) 11m11.2s; 4 Sordo/Martí (Citroën) 11m15.8s; 5 Hirvonen/Lehtinen (Ford) 11m16.3s; 6 Loeb/Elena (Citroën) 11m16.3s; JC Sandell/Axelsson (Renault) 12m17.0s

SS5 Crastazza 2 (33.96km)

1 Loeb/Elena (Citroën) 23m21.4s; 2 Latvala/Anttila (Ford) 23m24.9s; 3 Galli/Bernacchini (Ford) 23m25.0s; 4 Sordo/Martí (Citroën) 23m28.9s; 5 P.Solberg/Mills (Subaru) 23m31.1s; 6 Hirvonen/Lehtinen (Ford) 23m33.2s; JC Prokop/Tománek (Citroën) 25m37.1s

SS6 Terranova 2 (20.00km)

1 Latvala/Anttila (Ford) 10m30.9s; 2 Loeb/Elena (Citroën) 10m34.5s; 3 Galli/Bernacchini (Ford) 10m34.5s; 4 H.Solberg/C.Menkerud (Ford Focus RS WRC 07) 10m37.8s; 5 P.Solberg/Mills (Subaru) 10m38.3s; 6 Sordo/Martí (Citroën) 10m39.6s; JC Kosciuszko/Szczepaniak (Suzuki) 11m44.8s

SS7 Punta Pianedda 1 (11.10km)

1 Latvala/Anttila (Ford) 11m27.8s; 2 Hirvonen/Lehtinen (Ford) 11m36.2s; 3 Galli/Bernacchini (Ford) 11m40.5s; 4 Loeb/Elena (Citroën) 11m40.9s; 5 Sordo/Martí (Citroën) 11m41.9s; 6 Atkinson/Prévot (Subaru) 11m46.5s; JC Prokop/Tománek (Citroën) 12m47.9

SS8 Monte Lerno 1 (13.46km)

1 Latvala/Anttila (Ford) 19m46.3s; 2 Hirvonen/Lehtinen (Ford) 19m51.7s; 3 Loeb/Elena (Citroën) 19m57.1s; 4 Galli/Bernacchini (Ford) 20m05.1s; 5 Sordo/Martí (Citroën) 20m08.3s; 6 Atkinson/Prévot (Subaru) 20m21.8s; JC Kosciuszko/Szczepaniak (Suzuki) 21m52.2s

SS9 Su Filigosu 1 (14.13km)

1 Latvala/Anttila (Ford) 12m43.3s; 2 Hirvonen/Lehtinen (Ford) 12m49.3s; 3 Galli/Bernacchini (Ford) 12m51.4s; 4 Loeb/Elena (Citroën) 12m56.1s; 5 Sordo/Martí (Citroën) 13m04.0s; 6 U.Aava/K.Sikk (Citroën C4 WRC) 13m09.8s; JC Kosciuszko/Szczepaniak (Suzuki) 15m57.7s

SS10 Punta Pianedda 2 (12.47km)

1 Latvala/Anttila (Ford) 11m09.3s; 2 Hirvonen/Lehtinen (Ford) 11m14.6s; 3 Loeb/Elena (Citroën) 11m18.4s; 4 Galli/Bernacchini (Ford) 11m18.8s; 5 Sordo/Martí (Citroën) 11m23.2s; 6 Atkinson/Prévot (Subaru) 11m33.7s; JC S.Ogier/J.Ingrassia (Citroën C2 S1600) 12m30.1s

SS11 Monte Lerno 2 (15.19km)

1 Latvala/Anttila (Ford) 19m19.9s; 2 Hirvonen/Lehtinen (Ford) 19m24.2s; 3 Galli/Bernacchini (Ford) 19m32.3s; 4 Loeb/Elena (Citroën) 19m32.3s; 5 Sordo/Martí (Citroën) 19m45.7s; 6 Atkinson/Prévot (Subaru) 19m47.4s; JC Prokop/Tománek (Citroën) 21m25.1s

SS12 Su Filigosu 2 (13.13km)

1 Latvala/Anttila (Ford) 12m25.6s; 2 Hirvonen/Lehtinen (Ford) 12m28.4s; 3 Loeb/Elena (Citroën) 12m29.1s; 4 Galli/Bernacchini (Ford) 12m33.1s; 5 P.Solberg/Mills (Subaru) 12m43.2s; 6 Atkinson/Prévot (Subaru) 12m45.3s; JC Kosciuszko/Szczepaniak (Suzuki) 13m36.0s

SS13 Monte Olia 1 (14.13km)

1 Hirvonen/Lehtinen (Ford) 14m03.2s; 2 Latvala/Anttila (Ford) 14m08.3s; 3 Loeb/Elena (Citroën) 14m13.5s; 4 Galli/Bernacchini (Ford) 14m21.5s; 5 Sordo/Martí (Citroën) 14m23.0s; 6

P.Solberg/Mills (Subaru) 14m28.3s; JC Kosciuszko/Szczepaniak (Suzuki) 15m53.5s

SS14 Sorilis 2 (12.47km)

1 Loeb/Elena (Citroën) 13m58.9s; 2 Hirvonen/Lehtinen (Ford) 14m02.8s; 3 Latvala/Anttila (Ford) 14m03.2s; 4 Sordo/Martí (Citroën) 14m08.2s; 5 Galli/Bernacchini (Ford) 14m10.1s; 6 C.Rautenbach/D.Senior (Citroën C4 WRC) 14m25.3s; JC Prokop/Tomanek (Citroën) 15m37.4s

SS15 Monte Olia 2 (15.19km)

1 Latvala/Anttila (Ford) 13m46.2s; 2 Hirvonen/Lehtinen (Ford) 13m48.9s; 3 Galli/Bernacchini (Ford) 13m55.5s; 4 Loeb/Elena (Citroën) 13m55.7s; 5 Sordo/Martí (Citroën) 14m02.6s; 6 P.Solberg/Mills (Subaru) 14m03.7s; JC Kosciuszko/Szczepaniak (Suzuki) 15m22.3s

SS16 Sorilis 2 (13.13km)

1 Hirvonen/Lehtinen (Ford) 13m45.0s; 2 Loeb/Elena (Citroën) 13m48.3s; 3 Latvala/Anttila (Ford) 13m49.1s; 4 Sordo/Martí (Citroën) 13m52.6s; 5 Galli/Bernacchini (Ford) 13m56.3s; 6 P.Solberg/Mills (Subaru) 13m56.4s; JC J.Mölder/F.Miclotte (Suzuki Swift 1600) 15m15.5s

SS17 Liscia Ruja (16.49km)

1 Latvala/Anttila (Ford) 1m54.8s; 2 P.Solberg/Mills (Subaru) 1m56.7s; 3 Hirvonen/Lehtinen (Ford) 1m57.0s; 4 Galli/Bernacchini (Ford) 1m57.1s; 5 Loeb/Elena (Citroën) 1m59.3s; 6 P-G.Andersson/J.Andersson (Suzuki SX4 WRC) 2m01.1s; JC Notional time given to all competitors

Cars that retired and subsequently restarted and were classified under SuperRally regs:

14	Al-Qassimi/Orr	Ford Focus WRC 07		
	Lost a wheel	SS4	A8	
11	Gardemeister/Tuominen	Suzuki SX4 WRC		
	Suspension	SS11	A8	

MAJOR RETIREMENTS

11	Gardemeister/Tuominen	Suzuki SX4 WRC		
	Suspension	SS14	A8	
18	Mikkelsen/Andersson	Ford Focus WRC 06		
	Accident	SS2	A8	
20	Van Merksteijn/Van Beek	Ford Focus WRC 06		
	Accident	SS4	A8	

FIA CLASS WINNERS

A8	Over 2000cc	Loeb/Elena
		Citroën C4 WRC
A7	1600 – 2000cc	Bettega/Scattolin
		Renault Clio R3
A6	1400-1600cc	Kosciuszko/Szczepaniak
		Suzuki Swift S1600
N4	Over 2000cc	Moreno/Rosseto
		Mitsubishi Lancer Evo IX
N3	1600-2000cc	Baranauskas/Celiesius
		Ford Fiesta ST
N1	Up to 1400cc	Donadio/Brondolo
		MG ZR 105

RALLY LEADERS

Overall: SS1 Latvala; SS2-17 Loeb
JWRC: SS1 Sandell; SS2-8 Prokop; SS9-10 Kosciuszko; SS11 Prokop; SS12-17 Kosciuszko

SPECIAL STAGE ANALYSIS

	1st	2nd	3rd	4th	5th	6th
Latvala (Ford)	10	4	2	-	-	-
Loeb (Citroën)	4	2	4	5	2	-
Hirvonen (Ford)	2	8	2	-	1	2
Galli (Ford)	1		8	5	2	-
Sordo (Citroën)	-	2	-	5	7	1
P.Solberg (Subaru)	-	1	1	-	4	4
Atkinson (Subaru)	-	-	-	1	1	5

H.Solberg (Ford)	-	-	-	1	-	-
Andersson (Suzuki)	-	-	-	-	-	1
Aava (Citroën)	-	-	-	-	1	-
Rautenbach (Citroën)	-	-	-	-	1	-
Mikkelsen (Ford)	-	-	-	-	1	-
Gardemeister (Suzuki)	-	-	-	-	-	1

TYRES

Tyres: Pirelli Scorpion
Compound: hard
Number of tyres available per car: 36

WORLD CHAMPIONSHIP POINTS

Drivers
1 Hirvonen 43; 2 Loeb 40; 3 Atkinson 31; 4 Latvala 24; 5 Sordo 21; 6 Galli 17; 7 H.Solberg 11; 8 P.Solberg 9; 9 Villagra 8; 10 Wilson 7 etc

Manufacturers
1 BP Ford Abu Dhabi WRT 71; 2 Citroën Total WRT 64; 3 Subaru WRT 42; 4 Stobart VK M-Sport Ford RT 34; 5 Munchi's Ford WRT 16; 6 Suzuki WRT 7 etc

Junior World Rally Championship
1 Ogier 24; 2= Gallagher, Kosciuszko 16; 4 Burkart 11; 5= Mölder, Bettega 8; 7 Albertini 7; 8= Schammel, Sandell 6; 10 Niegel 5 etc

Production Car World Rally Championship
1 Ketomaa 14; 2= Aigner, Hänninen 10; 4 Beltrán 8; 5 Prokop 7; 6 Sandell 6; 7 Nutahara 5; 8= Nittel, Rauam 4; 10= Arai, Farrah 3 etc

ROUTE DETAILS

Total route of 1040.35km of which 344.73km were competitive on 17 stages
Leg 1 Friday 16 May, 6 Special Stages totalling 131.56km
Leg 2 Saturday 17 May, 6 Special Stages totalling 134.68km
Leg 3 Sunday 18 May, 5 Special Stages totalling 78.57km

RESULTS

1	Sébastien Loeb/	Citroën C4 WRC	
	Daniel Elena	3h57m17.2s	A8
2	Mikko Hirvonen/	Ford Focus RS WRC 07	
	Jarmo Lehtinen	3h57m27.8s	A8
3	Jari-Matti Latvala/	Ford Focus RS WRC 07	
	Miika Anttila	3h57m32.5s	A8
4	Gigi Galli/	Ford Focus RS WRC 07	
	Giovanni Bernacchini	3h58m59.7s	A8
5	Dani Sordo/	Citroën C4 WRC	
	Marc Martí	3h59m22.8s	A8
6	Chris Atkinson/	Subaru Impreza WRC2007	
	Stéphane Prévot	4h02m25.8s	A8
7	Henning Solberg/	Ford Focus RS WRC 07	
	Cato Menkerud	4h03m18.2s	A8
8	Urmo Aava/	Citroën C4 WRC	
	Kuldar Sikk	4h03m38.5s	A8
9	Per-Gunnar Andersson/	Suzuki SX4 WRC	
	Jonas Andersson	4h05m05.9s	A8
10	Petter Solberg/	Subaru Impreza WRC2007	
	Phil Mills	4h06m58.2s	A8

57 starters, 38 finishers

RECENT WINNERS

2004 Petter Solberg/Phil Mills   Subaru Impreza WRC2004
2005 Sébastien Loeb/Daniel Elena   Citroën Xsara WRC
2006 Sébastien Loeb/Daniel Elena   Citroën Xsara WRC
2007 Marcus Grönholm/Timo Rautiainen   Ford Focus RS WRC 06

Race&motion

Three manufacturers were on the podium again, but one again Citroën took the top spot.
Photograph: PHOTO4

Above: Sébastien Loeb lost 30 seconds and the lead to Dani Sordo courtesy of a left-rear puncture, but came back to win and reclaim the championship lead.

Opposite: Mikko Hirvonen's hopes for victory ended against a rock on Friday's penultimate stage. The resulting damage restricted him to third.

Right: Petter Solberg is congratulated by Loeb after finishing second on the debut of the new Impreza.

Below: Sixty-two crews tackled the 55th running of the Acropolis Rally.
Photographs: PHOTO4 unless specified

SÉBASTIEN Loeb couldn't talk at the moment. He was on the phone, to his mother. It was Sunday morning in the cut-and-thrust of another World Rally Championship round, but the four-time champion had found time on the run back into service to catch up on family life. Ford team principal Malcolm Wilson described Loeb's 41st career win in Greece as masterful. It was hard to argue.

As had been the case a fortnight earlier in Sardinia, championship leader Mikko Hirvonen had been sacrificed as the road-sweeper at the head of the field. This time, the Ford driver didn't let his head drop or start questioning the car, the tyres, the weather, his own ability, etc. He just took the pragmatic view that he'd have to get on it through day two and take the time back out of Loeb.

Unfortunately, that plan went out of the window on the last significant corner of the opening day. Both Hirvonen and his Ford team-mate Jari-Matti Latvala pitted suspension parts against one of Greece's well-grounded rocks, and man-made material lost out. Comprehensively. The Focus RS WRC 07s made it to the superspecial that concluded the Friday action, but both dropped the thick end of a minute hobbling around through the 4.5km test.

That left Loeb with a day two advantage of 15.7 seconds over his team-mate Dani Sordo. Stung by criticism of his performance on the previous round, the Spaniard was on form on the Acropolis, admitting he found the more consistent grip of the Greek roads to his liking. And he only had one answer for those service park sceptics who suspected he might spend the day running as Loeb's wingman: to halve the gap between the C4s in the longest stage of the event which opened Saturday morning.

One stage and a Loeb puncture later and Sordo was out front – and by some margin. With close to half a minute in hand, there was talk of broken ducks north of Athens. A brace of late Saturday deflations put paid to such discussions, as Sordo dropped from first to seventh in two stages. He only had to look next door to see the perfect way to preserve tyres.

Loeb was back to the front in time for the most difficult afternoon of action in this year's WRC.

Baked hard by the scorching sun, the likes of Aghii Theodori had the Pirelli engineers looking nervous prior to Saturday's second run through the stages. This was going to be the biggest test yet of the hard-compound Scorpion rubber. And Loeb was the perfect ambassador for the Italian firm. He picked his way through the sharpest stones, plotting the perfect route through three agonisingly rough stages and bringing the car home in one piece with four air-filled and non-too-shoddy-looking covers sitting beneath it.

With that loop done and dusted, Loeb cantered through Sunday to move back into the lead of the world championship. This being his 41st career win you could understand it if Loeb was beginning to feel a little jaded at this endless champagne business. Behind him, the feeling couldn't have been more different. For Petter Solberg and the new Subaru Impreza WRC2008, the taste of the podium bubbly couldn't have been sweeter. The much-anticipated new Subaru had delivered. Partly. That it shared more than the odd damper part with the old car, some handling 'characteristics' remained. Solberg's face occasionally explained that perfectly, but on the whole this was a solid showing from the new machine.

Sordo's downfall elevated Hirvonen to third – which helped him to contain Loeb's championship lead to a single point. Even Mikko admitted he'd been granted something of a 'get out of jail card' on this one.

Above: Not even a propshaft failure could deny Matthew Wilson a top-six finish.
Photograph: PHOTO4

Stage Numbers	1	2	3	4	5	6	7	8	9	10	11	12	13	14	15	16	17	18	19	20
Loeb	3	3	2	1	1	1	1	.	1	2	2	2	2	1	1	1	1	1	1	1
P.Solberg	5	5	5	5	6	5	3	3	3	3	3	3	2	2	2	2	2	2	2	2
Hirvonen	3	4	4	4	4	4	7	6	6	8	5	5	4	4	4	3	3	3	3	3
Aava	11	6	7	7	7	7	5	13	11	11	7	6	5	5	5	5	5	4	4	4
Sordo	2	2	2	3	2	3	2	2	1	1	1	2	7	7	7	6	6	5	5	5
Wilson	7	9	13	12	11	12	12	11	10	9	8	7	6	6	6	7	6	6	6	6
Latvala	1	1	1	3	3	2	6	4	4	9	8	8	8	8	8	8	8	7	7	7
H.Solberg	10	7	6	6	5	6	4	5	5	5	4	4	3	3	3	3	7	8	8	8
Gardemeister	12	12	11	11	12	11	11	9	10	10	10	10	9	9	9	9	9	9	9	9
Rautenbach	15	13	14	14	14	14	14	13	12	12	11	9	10	10	10	10	10	10	10	10
Andersson	9	10	10	10	10	10	10	10	7	7	6	9	13	12	12	12	12	12	11	11
Al-Qassimi	17	15	15	15	15	19	17	15	14	13	12	11	11	11	11	11	11	11	12	12
Villagra	14	11	10	10	10	10	10	9	8	6	11	14	20	20	16	14	13	13	13	13
Østberg	8	51	51	52	46	46	47	46	44	40	39	34	34	33	30	27	27	26	26	24
Galli	13	49	50	50	45	45	46	43	39	35	36	37	36	34	33	29	26	R		
Atkinson	6	8	8	8	8	8	8	7	12	18	22	22	25	25	23	R				
Vovos	16	14	12	13	13	13	13	12	R											

Above middle: Urmo Aava finished a career-best fourth driving a works-supported Citroën C4 WRC.

Above right: Pirelli's tyre technicians were well prepared for the searing heat and gruelling stages.
Photographs: PHOT04

FINISH LINES...

Estonian C4 privateer Urmo Aava turned in his drive of the year to place his PH Sport-run Citroën in fourth overall, setting the fastest time on the second run at Pissia. Aava had begun the final day in fifth place, but benefited when Henning Solberg's Focus suffered continued electrical issues. Despite the Stobart team changing just about everything containing electrical current, the Norwegian Ford faltered and dropped to eighth – a single point being scant reward when he'd started Sunday safely on the podium... Matthew Wilson's solid sixth provided some comfort for Stobart fans, although Gigi Galli registered a no-score after suffering a brace of TCA failures aboard the lead Stobart car... Andreas Aigner collected his second consecutive Production Car World Rally Championship win in his Red Bull-backed Mitsubishi Lancer. Coming off the back of his Argentinian success, 10 points in Greece elevated him to the top of the PWRC stack. The Austrian admitted he'd never expected to win after breaking the intercooler on his car on the opening loop and dropping to 20th in class. A fightback drive that was sensibly pacey allied to problems for his PWRC rivals ensured him of success... Subaru's miserable PWRC run with its new Impreza WRX continued in Greece, when Nasser Al-Attiyah led but dropped out with catastrophic suspension failure on Saturday... Estonian Martin Rauam was excluded from second place after the brakes on his Lancer were found to be illegal – this elevated Aigner's Red Bull team-mate Bernardo Sousa to a career best second in the Production category.

RUNNING ORDER

3	Mikko Hirvonen/	Ford Focus RS WRC 07
	Jarmo Lehtinen	A8
1	Sébastien Loeb/	Citroën C4 WRC
	Daniel Elena	A8
6	Chris Atkinson/	Subaru Impreza WRC2008
	Stéphane Prévot	A8
4	Jari-Matti Latvala/	Ford Focus RS WRC 07
	Miikka Anttila	A8
2	Daniel Sordo/	Citroën C4 WRC
	Marc Martí	A8
7	Gigi Galli/	Ford Focus RS WRC 07
	Giovanni Bernacchini	A8
8	Henning Solberg/	Ford Focus RS WRC 07
	Cato Menkerud	A8
5	Petter Solberg/	Subaru Impreza WRC2008
	Phil Mills	A8
9	Federico Villagra/	Ford Focus RS WRC 07
	Jorge Pérez Companc	A8
16	Matthew Wilson/	Ford Focus RS WRC 07
	Scott Martin	A8
18	Conrad Rautenbach/	Citroën C4 WRC
	David Senior	A8
11	Toni Gardemeister/	Suzuki SX4 WRC
	Tomi Tuominen	A8
14	Khalid Al-Qassimi/	Ford Focus RS WRC 07
	Michael Orr	A8
12	P-G Andersson/	Suzuki SX4 WRC
	Jonas Andersson	A8
15	Urmo Aava/	Citroën C4 WRC
	Kuldar Sikk	A8
17	Mads Østberg/	Subaru Impreza WRC2007
	Ole Kristian Unnerud	A8
10	Aris Vovos/	Ford Focus RS WRC 07
	'EL-EM'	A8
46	Jari Ketomaa/	Subaru Impreza
	Miika Teiskonen	N4
41	Andreas Aigner/	Mitsubishi Lancer Evo IX
	Klaus Wicha	N4
52	Juho Hänninen/	Mitsubishi Lancer Evo IX
	Mikko Markkula	N4

SPECIAL STAGE TIMES

SS1 Schimatari 1 (11.57km)
1 J-M Latvala/M.Anttila (Ford Focus RS WRC 07) 10m34.3s; 2 D.Sordo/M.Martí (Citroën C4 WRC) 10m39.5s; 3= M.Hirvonen/J.Lehtinen (Ford Focus RS WRC 07), S.Loeb/D.Elena (Citroën C4 WRC) 10m40.1s; 5 P.Solberg/P.Mills (Subaru Impreza WRC2008) 10m43.6s; 6 C.Atkinson/S.Prévot (Subaru Impreza WRC2008) 10m46.4s; PC M.Baldacci/G.Agnese (Mitsubishi Lancer Evo IX) 11m09.0s

SS2 Thiva 1 (23.76km)
1 Loeb/Elena (Citroën) 17m15.2s; 2 Sordo/Martí (Citroën) 17m15.5s; 3 Latvala/Anttila (Ford) 17m19.5s; 4 U.Aava/K.Sikk (Citroën C4 WRC) 17m23.5s; 5 H.Solberg/C.Menkerud (Ford Focus RS WRC 07) 17m26.1s; 6 P.Solberg/Mills (Subaru) 17m26.8s; PC J.Hänninen/M.Markkula (Mitsubishi Lancer Evo IX) 18m14.4s

SS3 Psatha 1 (17.41km)
1 Latvala/Anttila (Ford) 11m28.7s; 2 Loeb/Elena (Citroën) 11m31.4s; 3 Sordo/Martí (Citroën) 11m33.7s; 4 P.Solberg/Mills (Subaru) 11m39.5s; 5 Hirvonen/Lehtinen (Ford) 11m40.1s; 6 H.Solberg/Menkerud (Ford) 11m42.1s; PC Hänninen/Markkula (Mitsubishi) 12m36.3s

SS4 Schimatari 2 (11.57km)
1 Loeb/Elena (Citroën) 10m26.7s; 2 Sordo/Martí (Citroën) 10m28.0s; 3 Hirvonen/Lehtinen (Ford) 10m31.3s; 4 H.Solberg/Menkerud (Ford) 10m32.6s; 5 P.Solberg/Mills (Subaru) 10m36.7s; 6= M.Wilson/S.Martin (Ford Focus RS WRC 07), Latvala/Anttila (Ford) 10m37.5s; PC A.Aigner/K.Wicha (Mitsubishi Lancer Evo IX) 10m56.2s

SS5 Thiva 2 (23.76km)
1 Loeb/Elena (Citroën) 16m53.8s; 2 Sordo/Martí (Citroën) 16m57.7s; 3 Latvala/Anttila (Ford) 16m58.3s; 4 H.Solberg/Menkerud (Ford) 17m05.1s; 5 Atkinson/Prévot (Subaru) 17m06.9s; 6 Hirvonen/Lehtinen (Ford) 17m08.3s; PC Hänninen/Markkula (Mitsubishi) 18m05.8s

SS6 Psatha 2 (17.41km)
1 Loeb/Elena (Citroën) 11m12.5s; 2 Latvala/Anttila (Ford) 11m14.2s; 3 Sordo/Martí (Citroën) 11m20.8s; 4 Hirvonen/Lehtinen (Ford) 11m21.1s; 5 P.Solberg/Mills (Subaru) 11m21.7s; 6 Atkinson/Prévot (Subaru) 11m26.5s; PC N.Al-Attiyah/C.Patterson (Subaru Impreza) 12m27.1s

SS7 SSS Tatoi 1 (4.60km)
1 Aava/Sikk (Citroën) 3m31.3s; 2 P.Solberg/Mills (Subaru) 3m33.7s; 3 Loeb/Elena (Citroën) 3m35.1s; 4= Sordo/Martí

(Citroën), C.Rautenbach/D.Senior (Citroën C4 WRC) 3m35.3s; 6 H.Solberg/Menkerud (Ford) 3m35.5s; PC= Hänninen/Markkula (Mitsubishi), F.Nutahara/D.Barritt (Mitsubishi Lancer Evo IX) 3m42.1s

SS8 Aghii Theodori 1 (32.16km)
1 Hirvonen/Lehtinen (Ford) 22m42.1s; 2 Latvala/Anttila (Ford) 22m43.9s; 3 P.Solberg/Mills (Subaru) 22m46.7s; 4 Atkinson/Prévot (Subaru) 22m48.0s; 5 Sordo/Martí (Citroën) 22m51.2s; 6 Loeb/Elena (Citroën) 22m58.2s; PC Hänninen/Markkula (Mitsubishi) 24m12.6s

SS9 Pissia 1 (16.60km)
1 G.Galli/G.Bernacchini (Ford Focus RS WRC 07) 12m17.2s; 2 Latvala/Anttila (Ford) 12m17.5s; 3 Aava/Sikk (Citroën) 12m21.6s; 4 P.Solberg/Mills (Subaru) 12m22.8s; 5 H.Solberg/Menkerud (Ford) 12m23.2s; 6 Sordo/Martí (Citroën) 12m23.4s; PC Hänninen/Markkula (Mitsubishi) 12m53.1s

SS10 Aghia Triada 1 (10.80km)
1 Galli/Bernacchini (Ford) 7m46.1s; 2 Loeb/Elena (Citroën) 7m46.5s; 3 Latvala/Anttila (Ford) 7m46.9s; 4 H.Solberg/Menkerud (Ford) 7m49.0s; 5 Sordo/Martí (Citroën) 7m49.5s; 6 Aava/Sikk (Citroën) 7m54.0s; PC Hänninen/Markkula (Mitsubishi) 8m16.9s

SS11 Aghii Theodori 2 (32.16km)
1 Hirvonen/Lehtinen (Ford) 22m36.1s; 2 P.Solberg/Mills (Subaru) 22m39.3s; 3 H.Solberg/Menkerud (Ford) 22m40.7s; 4 Sordo/Martí (Citroën) 22m42.9s; 5 Aava/Sikk (Citroën) 22m49.8s; 6 Loeb/Elena (Citroën) 22m54.0s; PC Aigner/Wicha (Mitsubishi) 24m31.7s

SS12 Pissia 2 (16.60km)
1 Aava/Sikk (Citroën) 12m13.9s; 2 Loeb/Elena (Citroën) 12m16.3s; 3 Hirvonen/Lehtinen (Ford) 12m20.1s; 4 P.Solberg/Mills (Subaru) 12m27.1s; 5 Wilson/Martin (Ford) 12m31.1s; 6 H.Solberg/Menkerud (Ford) 12m32.6s; PC L.Athanassoulas/N.Zakheos (Subaru Impreza) 13m02.5s

SS13 Aghia Triada 2 (10.80km)
1 Hirvonen/Lehtinen (Ford) 7m45.4s; 2 Loeb/Elena (Citroën) 7m49.8s; 3 P.Solberg/Mills (Subaru) 7m52.9s; 4 Rautenbach/Senior (Citroën) 7m59.8s; 5 K.Al-Qassimi/M.Orr (Ford Focus RS WRC 07) 8m05.9s; 6 Wilson/Martin (Ford) 8m06.4s; PC M.Prokop/J.Tománek (Mitsubishi Lancer Evo IX) 8m21.2s

SS14 Avlonas 1 (15.14km)
1 Atkinson/Prévot (Subaru) 9m09.6s; 2 Latvala/Anttila (Ford) 9m16.0s; 3 Loeb/Elena (Citroën) 9m16.9s; 4 Hirvonen/Lehtinen (Ford) 9m21.5s; 5 Galli/Bernacchini (Ford) 9m22.3s; 6 Sordo/Martí (Citroën) 9m34.7s; PC Hänninen/Markkula (Mitsubishi) 10m00.6s

SS15 Assopia 1 (18.52km)
1 Latvala/Anttila (Ford) 11m39.9s; 2 Galli/Bernacchini (Ford) 11m46.8s; 3 Hirvonen/Lehtinen (Ford) 11m48.6s; 4 Sordo/Martí (Citroën) 11m54.0s; 5 Loeb/Elena (Citroën) 12m00.5s; 6 P-G.Andersson/J.Andersson (Suzuki SX4 WRC) 12m05.7s; PC Hänninen/Markkula (Mitsubishi) 12m30.8s

SS16 Aghia Sotira 1 (15.20km)
1 Galli/Bernacchini (Ford) 9m47.2s; 2 Latvala/Anttila (Ford) 9m48.7s; 3 Hirvonen/Lehtinen (Ford) 9m52.5s; 4 Sordo/Martí (Citroën) 10m05.1s; 5 Aava/Sikk (Citroën) 10m10.1s; 6 P.Solberg/Mills (Subaru) 10m11.8s; PC Hänninen/Markkula (Mitsubishi) 10m38.1s

SS17 Avlonas 2 (15.14km)
1 Galli/Bernacchini (Ford) 9m00.9s; 2 Latvala/Anttila (Ford) 9m01.5s; 3 Sordo/Martí (Citroën) 9m10.2s; 4 Aava/Sikk (Citroën) 9m13.3s; 5 Hirvonen/Lehtinen (Ford) 9m15.9s; 6 Andersson/Andersson (Suzuki) 9m18.7s; PC Hänninen/Markkula (Mitsubishi) 9m47.1s

SS18 Assopia 2 (18.52km)
1 Latvala/Anttila (Ford) 11m26.6s; 2 Sordo/Martí (Citroën) 11m36.9s; 3 Hirvonen/Lehtinen (Ford) 11m39.2s; 4 Loeb/Elena (Citroën) 11m44.4s; 5 M.Ostberg/O.Unnerud (Subaru Impreza WRC) 11m49.8s; 6 F.Villagra/J.P.Companc (Ford Focus RS WRC 07) 11m49.9s; PC Hänninen/Markkula (Mitsubishi) 12m19.2s

SS19 Aghia Sotira 2 (15.20km)
1 Latvala/Anttila (Ford) 9m52.2s; 2 Aava/Sikk (Citroën) 10m01.5s;

3 Sordo/Martí (Citroën) 10m05.5s; 4 Hirvonen/Lehtinen (Ford) 10m07.6s; 5 Andersson/Andersson (Suzuki) 10m12.0s; 6 P.Solberg/Mills (Subaru) 10m16.7s; PC Hänninen/Markkula (Mitsubishi) 10m47.0s

SS20 SSS Tatoi 2 (4.60km)
1 Sordo/Martí (Citroën) 3m33.0s; 2 Hirvonen/Lehtinen (Ford) 3m33.2s; 3 Ostberg/Unnerud (Subaru) 3m34.1s; 4 T.Gardemeister/T.Tuominen (Suzuki SX4 WRC) 3m34.4s; 5 Latvala/Anttila (Ford) 3m34.9s; 6 Aava/Sikk (Citroën) 3m35.3s; PC E.Novikov/D.Chumak (Mitsubishi Lancer Evo IX) 3m48.7s

Cars who retired and subsequently restarted and were classified under SupeRally regs:

17	Ostberg/Unnerud	Subaru Impreza WRC2007		
	Differential	SS2	A8
9	Villagra/Companc	Ford Focus RS WRC 07		
	Suspension	SS11	A8
12	Andersson/Andersson	Suzuki SX4 WRC		
	Suspension	SS11	A8

MAJOR RETIREMENTS

7	Galli/Bernacchini	Ford Focus RS WRC 07		
	Suspension	SS2	A8
6	Atkinson/Prévot	Subaru Impreza WRC2008		
	Electrical	SS8/9	A8
10	Vovos/'EL-EM'	Ford Focus RS WRC 07		
	Steering	SS9	A8
7	Galli/Bernacchini	Ford Focus RS WRC 07		
	Hydraulics	SS11	A8
6	Atkinson/Prévot	Subaru Impreza WRC2008		
	Mechanical	SS16	A8
7	Galli/Bernacchini	Ford Focus RS WRC 07		
	Suspension	SS18	A8

FIA CLASS WINNERS

A8	Over 2000cc	Loeb/Elena
		Citroën C4 WRC
A6	1400-1600cc	Zounis/Demertzis
		MG Rover 25
A5	Up to 1400cc	G.Ladogiannis/N.Ladogiannis
		Fiat Seicento
N4	Over 2000cc	Aigner/Wicha
		Mitsubishi Lancer Evo IX

RALLY LEADERS
Overall: SS1-3 Latvala; SS4-8 Loeb; SS9-11 Sordo; SS12-20 Loeb
PC: SS1 Baldacci; SS2 Al-Attiyah; SS3-5 Hänninen; SS6-8 Al-Attiyah
N: SS9-10 Hänninen; SS11-20 Aigner

SPECIAL STAGE ANALYSIS

	1st	2nd	3rd	4th	5th	6th
Latvala (Ford)	5	6	3	-	1	1
Loeb (Citroën)	4	4	3	1	1	2
Galli (Ford)	4	1	-	-	1	-
Hirvonen (Ford)	3	1	5	4	2	1
Aava (Citroën)	2	1	1	2	2	2
Sordo (Citroën)	1	5	4	4	2	2
Atkinson (Subaru)	1	-	-	1	1	2
P.Solberg (Subaru)	-	2	2	3	3	3
H.Solberg (Ford)	-	-	1	2	2	3
Ostberg (Subaru)	-	-	1	-	1	-
Rautenbach (Citroën)	-	-	-	2	-	-
Gardemeister (Suzuki)	-	-	-	1	-	-
Wilson (Ford)	-	-	-	-	1	2
Andersson (Suzuki)	-	-	-	-	1	2
Al-Qassimi (Ford)	-	-	-	-	1	-
Villagra (Ford)	-	-	-	-	-	1

TYRES
Tyres: Pirelli Scorpion
Compound: hard
Number of tyres available per car: 42

WORLD CHAMPIONSHIP POINTS
Drivers
1 Loeb 50; 2 Hirvonen 49; 3 Atkinson 31; 4 Latvala 26; 5 Sordo 25; 6= Galli, P.Solberg 17; 8 H.Solberg 12; 9 Wilson 10; 10 Villagra 8 etc
Manufacturers
1 BP Ford Abu Dhabi WRT 81; 2 Citroën Total WRT 79; 3 Subaru WRT 50; 4 Stobart VK M-Sport Ford RT 37; 5 Munchi's Ford WRT 16;

6 Suzuki WRT 10 etc
Junior World Rally Championship
1 Ogier 24; 2= Kosciuszko, Gallagher 16; 4 Burkart 11; 5= Mölder, Bettega 8; 7 Albertini 7; 8= Schammel, Sandell 6; 10 Niegel 5 etc
Production Car World Rally Championship
1 Aigner 20; 2 Ketomaa 14; 3 Hänninen 12; 4= Nutahara, Sousa 10; 6= Beltrán, Araújo 8; 8 Prokop 7; 9 Sandell 6; 10 Nittel 4 etc

ROUTE DETAILS
Total Route of 1311.32km of which 331.52km were competitive on 20 stages
Leg 1 Friday 30 May, 7 special stages totalling 110.08km
Leg 2 Saturday 31 May, 6 special stages totalling 119.12km
Leg 3 Sunday 1 June, 7 special stages totalling 102.32km

RESULTS

1	Sébastien Loeb/	Citroën C4 WRC		
	Daniel Elena	3h54m54.7s	A8
2	Petter Solberg/	Subaru Impreza WRC2008		
	Phil Mills	3h56m04.2s	A8
3	Mikko Hirvonen/	Ford Focus RS WRC 07		
	Jarmo Lehtinen	3h56m50.8s	A8
4	Urmo Aava/	Citroën C4 WRC		
	Kuldar Sikk	3h59m14.4s	A8
5	Dani Sordo/	Citroën C4 WRC		
	Marc Martí	3h54m44.1s	A8
6	Matthew Wilson/	Ford Focus RS WRC 07		
	Scott Martin	4h01m06.0s	A8
7	Jari-Matti Latvala/	Ford Focus RS WRC 07		
	Miikka Anttila	4h01m42.2s	A8
8	Henning Solberg/	Ford Focus RS WRC 07		
	Cato Menkerud	4h04m08.7s	A8
9	Toni Gardemeister/	Suzuki SX4 WRC		
	Tomi Tuominen	4h05m08.5s	A8
10	Conrad Rautenbach/	Citroën C4 WRC		
	David Senior	4h08m23.8s	A8

60 starters, 42 finishers

RECENT WINNERS

1965	Carl-Magnus Skogh/'Tandlakare'	Volvo 122S
1966	Bengt Söderström/Gunnar Palm	Ford Lotus Cortina
1967	Paddy Hopkirk/Ron Crellin	Mini Cooper S
1968	Roger Clark/Jim Porter	Ford Escort TC
1969	Pauli Toivonen/Matti Kolari	Porsche 911S
1970	Jean-Luc Thérier/Marcel Callewaert	Alpine Renault A110
1971	Ove Andersson/Arne Hertz	Alpine Renault A110
1972	Håkan Lindberg/Helmut Eisendle	Fiat 124 Spyder
1973	Jean-Luc Thérier/Christian Delferrier	Alpine Renault A110
1975	Walter Röhrl/Jochen Berger	Opel Ascona
1976	Harry Kallström/Claes-Goran Andersson	Datsun 160J
1977	Björn Waldegård/Hans Thorszelius	Ford Escort RS
1978	Walter Röhrl/Christian Geistdörfer	Fiat 131 Abarth
1979	Björn Waldegård/Hans Thorszelius	Ford Escort RS
1980	Ari Vatanen/David Richards	Ford Escort RS
1981	Ari Vatanen/David Richards	Ford Escort RS
1982	Michèle Mouton/Fabrizia Pons	Audi Quattro
1983	Walter Röhrl/Christian Geistdörfer	Lancia Rally 037
1984	Stig Blomqvist/Björn Cederberg	Audi Quattro A2
1985	Timo Salonen/Seppo Harjanne	Peugeot 205 Turbo 16
1986	Juha Kankkunen/Juha Piironen	Peugeot 205 Turbo 16 E2
1987	Markku Alén/Ilkka Kivimäki	Lancia Delta HF 4x4
1988	Miki Biasion/Tiziano Siviero	Lancia Delta Integrale
1989	Miki Biasion/Tiziano Siviero	Lancia Delta Integrale
1990	Carlos Sainz/Luis Moya	Toyota Celica GT4
1991	Juha Kankkunen/Juha Piironen	Lancia Delta Integrale 16v
1992	Didier Auriol/Bernard Occelli	Lancia Delta HF Integrale
1993	Miki Biasion/Tiziano Siviero	Ford Escort RS Cosworth
1994	Carlos Sainz/Luis Moya	Subaru Impreza 555
1995	Aris Vovos/Kostas Stefanis	Lancia Delta HF Integrale
1996	Colin McRae/Derek Ringer	Subaru Impreza 555
1997	Carlos Sainz/Luis Moya	Ford Escort RS WRC
1998	Colin McRae/Nicky Grist	Subaru Impreza WRC98
1999	Richard Burns/Robert Reid	Subaru Impreza WRC99
2000	Colin McRae/Nicky Grist	Ford Focus RS WRC
2001	Colin McRae/Nicky Grist	Ford Focus RS WRC 01
2002	Colin McRae/Nicky Grist	Ford Focus RS WRC 02
2003	Markko Märtin/Michael Park	Ford Focus RS WRC 03
2004	Petter Solberg/Phil Mills	Subaru Impreza WRC2004
2005	Sébastien Loeb/Daniel Elena	Citroën Xsara WRC
2006	Marcus Grönholm/Timo Rautiainen	Ford Focus RS WRC 06
2007	Marcus Grönholm/Timo Rautiainen	Ford Focus RS WRC 06

Ford's road position tactics helped Mikko Hirvonen to a second victory of the season.
Photograph: Race&motion

Above: Dust filled Henning Solberg's Ford after he tore a hole in the wheel arch by hitting a rock, but he fought on to fifth place.

Top right: An under-fire Hirvonen and team boss Malcolm Wilson kept their joy in check after the Finn retook the championship lead.

Right: Conrad Rautenbach battled an overheating engine to take the final point in eighth place.

Far right: Funnily enough Hirvonen looks a little happier in this picture...
Photographs: PHOTO4

CITROËN SPORT team principal Olivier Quesnel could barely conceal his anger. So he didn't bother trying. The Frenchman let rip with a tirade of verbal assaults. He'd just watched his man Sébastien Loeb being forced to run first on the road – the worst possible position – by the Ford team. Mikko Hirvonen had cast a 20-second lead aside to drop to fifth place ahead of day two of the Rally of Turkey.

It was tactical genius from the Ford team. And Quesnel hated it.

"It's stupid," he said. "A stupid regulation and if that's the only way Ford can win, then that's up to them. The good thing for me is that they obviously don't have a car which is fast enough to beat ours in a straight fight."

Ouch.

Ford team principal Malcolm Wilson took it on the chin. "I can see his point," said the Cumbrian. "But I'll bet he'd do the same thing in our position."

The answer to that was: "Non." Quesnel added: "We have won five from seven rallies completed so far this season and we have never used those tactics."

His argument was undermined on two parts, the first being Loeb's admittance that he thought Ford's tactical approach was common sense. Then his team-mate Dani Sordo veered significantly off message when he came on the radio saying he'd slowed down in the last stage so he could run behind Henning Solberg's Ford on the final day. Wilson pointed this out to Quesnel at the end-of-leg press conference. The Frenchman departed, seeking a word with his Spanish charge.

Unfortunately, the talk of tactics did detract slightly from what was an exceptional team performance from the BP Ford men. Hirvonen took a 34-second lead into the final day and carried the fight to Loeb. The reigning champion had no answer to his Ford rival's sure-footed and uber-fast approach to the rough and horribly hot Turkish roads. Hirvonen's team-mate did the perfect job for the team, bringing his car home in second with Loeb third.

Latvala could well have won this rally – and from the front as early as Friday. He punctured in the first long stage, but hit back with a quite astonishing time on the next one. He then collected a second deflation in the afternoon, which cost more time. He'd listened intently to the instruction about driving in the middle of the road. Asked what had gone wrong at the end of the day, he looked sheepish and said: "I put my crash helmet on..."

Beyond the tactics, the foundations for Hirvonen's second win of the season were laid with a brace of inch-perfect runs through the Silyon test. Sixteen seconds quicker than Loeb, Hirvonen was in a confident mood when it came to his turn – as rally leader – to lead the field into Sunday.

Stalling at the start of Sunday's Olympos opener might have rattled Hirvonen 12 months ago, but he didn't bat an eyelid this time. He simply got his head down and drove. Depsite being first in, he only lost another two seconds on top of the time sat waiting for the Ford to fire on the line. An overshoot in the penultimate stage ruled out a last-gasp charge from Latvala, and when all three leading cars destroyed their tyres in that test, the deal was done: Hirvonen was back in the lead of the championship.

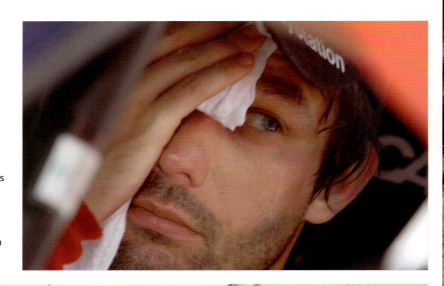

Right: Sébastien Loeb was unhappy after Ford's strategy robbed him of victory.

Below: Loeb's C4 ran faultlessly, but he had to settle for third.
Photographs: PHOTO4

Right: Gigi Galli and Giovanni Bernacchini had no requirements for their crash helmets on Sunday after the onset of heat exhaustion forced the driver to withdraw.

Opposite page: Jari-Matti Latvala bounced back from a string of troubled rallies to make it a one-two for Ford.
Photographs: PHOTO4

Rally of Turkey Results

12-15 JUNE 2008 | FIA WORLD RALLY CHAMPIONSHIP ROUND 8

Position	Stage Numbers	1	2	3	4	5	6	7	8	9	10	11	12	13	14	15	16	17	18	19
	Hirvonen	3	1	1	1	1	2	1	1	5	4	1	1	1	1	1	1	1	1	1
	Latvala	4	14	4	2	3	1	2	2	3	2	2	2	2	2	2	2	2	2	2
	Loeb	1	6	5	5	6	4	3	4	1	1	5	3	3	3	3	3	3	3	3
	Sordo	5	3	3	6	5	5	8	8	8	7	7	6	5	5	5	5	4	4	4
	H.Solberg	8	7	6	4	4	6	5	5	2	5	5	4	4	4	4	4	5	5	5
	P.Solberg	2	5	8	7	7	7	6	6	6	6	6	6	5	6	6	6	6	6	6
	Wilson	14	9	7	8	8	8	7	7	7	8	8	8	7	7	7	7	7	7	7
	Rautenbach	27	13	12	12	12	11	11	11	10	10	9	9	9	9	9	9	8	8	8
	Villagra	7	15	14	14	14	13	12	12	11	11	10	10	10	10	10	10	9	9	9
	Clark	16	18	15	15	15	14	13	13	12	13	11	11	11	11	11	11	10	10	10
	Atkinson	6	11	10	10	9	10	17	24	26	25	22	21	21	19	20	20	15	15	13
	Mikkelsen	34	8	11	11	11	26	30	27	25	24	20	17	15	14	14	11	11	19	
	Aava	29	4	29	37	39	40	39	38	37	35	32	30	27	27	25	25	20	20	R
	Galli	8	2	2	2	3	2	4	3	4	3	4	8	8	8	8	R			
	Andersson	32	12	9	9	10	9	9	9	13	12	R								
	Gardemeister	10	10	13	13	13	12	10	10	10	9	9	R							

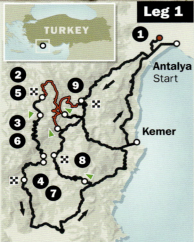
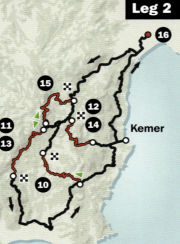
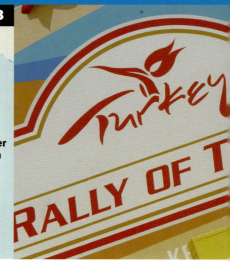

Leg 1 — TURKEY — Antalya Start — Kemer

Leg 2 — Kemer

Leg 3 — Kemer Finish

▶ Stage start
✖ Stage finish
7 Special stages
→ Rally direction

Above: There was a record-equalling third successive victory in the Production championship for Andreas Aigner.

Above right: Turkey returned to the WRC after a year's break.
Photographs: PHOTO4

FINISH LINES...

Citroën did the best job possible in containing Ford's lead in the man-ufacturers' championship: if there was no chance of a C4 finishing in the top two, then third and fourth would have to do. Loeb and team-mate Dani Sordo filled those places respectively. Sordo was again looking good to play himself into the fight at the front, until he tweaked the rear suspension on his C4 and dropped three places to eighth place on the second run at Kumluca as a result. Sordo fought on and posted some tidy times to rocket his way back into fourth by the close of play... After losing out to his younger brother in a tight Acropolis fight a fortnight earlier (or it was tight before the electrics on Henning's Focus fell apart), Henning took his revenge on Petter this time around. He brought his Ford home 14.5 seconds up on Petter's Subaru... Subaru's event was another mixed bag, with the lows ultimately outweighing the highs. Solberg's sixth place was a fair reflection on where the team was at with the new car in Turkey, but suspension failure put paid to team-mate Chris Atkinson's rally at the end of SS6. He returned under SuperRally rules and it was the times that the Australian set which provided most of the highlights for the British team...Stobart driver Matthew Wilson was seventh, one position further back than he had been in Greece, but this was a much better drive from the Briton. Dogged by a cold throughout the event, Wilson turned in a fine and gritty drive – one that included fastest sec-tor times. His father and team principal Malcolm reckoned this was his best showing in the WRC to date... Conrad Rautenbach scored points for the second time in his C4 WRC. Unfortunately, the reigning FIA African champion couldn't manage the fourth overall he'd posted in Argentina, but eighth was a good result for a 23-year-old still learn-

ing his craft in only his ninth outing in the WRC's top category... For the third rally in succession, Andreas Aigner won the PWRC category. The Austrian made the most of transmission trouble which knobbled Patrik Sandell's Peugeot 207 S2000 on Saturday afternoon. Before Sandell's broken driveshaft there had been nothing to chose between the top two, but come Sunday afternoon it was Aigner who led the series by 16 points.

RUNNING ORDER

1	Sébastien Loeb/ Daniel Elena	Citroën C4 WRC A8
3	Mikko Hirvonen/ Jarmo Lehtinen	Ford Focus RS WRC 07 A8
6	Chris Atkinson/ Stéphane Prévot	Subaru Impreza WRC2008 A8
4	Jari-Matti Latvala/ Miikka Anttila	Ford Focus RS WRC 07 A8
2	Daniel Sordo/ Marc Martí	Citroën C4 WRC A8
5	Petter Solberg/ Phil Mills	Subaru Impreza WRC2008 A8
7	Gigi Galli/ Giovanni Bernacchini	Ford Focus RS WRC 07 A8
8	Henning Solberg/ Cato Menkerud	Ford Focus RS WRC 07 A8
16	Matthew Wilson/ Scott Martin	Ford Focus RS WRC 07 A8
9	Federico Villagra/ Jorge Pérez Companc	Ford Focus RS WRC 07 A8
17	Urmo Aava/ Kuldar Sikk	Citroën C4 WRC A8
14	Conrad Rautenbach/ David Senior	Citroën C4 WRC A8
15	Andreas Mikkelsen/ Ola Fløene	Ford Focus RS WRC 06 A8
11	Toni Gardemeister/ Tomi Tuominen	Suzuki SX4 WRC A8
12	P-G Andersson/ Jonas Andersson	Suzuki SX4 WRC A8
10	Barry Clark/ Paul Nagle	Ford Focus RS WRC 07 A8
41	Andreas Aigner/ Klaus Wicha	Mitsubishi Lancer Evo IX N4
50	Armindo Arájuo/ Miguel Ramalho	Mitsubishi Lancer Evo IX N4
33	Martin Prokop/ Jan Tománek	Mitsubishi Lancer Evo IX N4
55	Patrik Sandell/ Emil Axelsson	Peugeot 207 S2000 N4

SPECIAL STAGE TIMES

SS1 Antalya SSS 1 (2.60km)

1 S.Loeb/D.Elena (Citroën C4 WRC) 2m07.6s; 2 P.Solberg/P.Mills (Subaru Impreza WRC2008) 2m08.3s; 3 M.Hirvonen/J.Lehtinen (Ford Focus RS WRC 07) 2m08.7s; 4 J-M Latvala/M.Anttila (Ford Focus RS WRC 07) 2m09.9s; 5 D.Sordo/M.Martí (Citroën C4 WRC) 2m10.5s; 6 C.Atkinson/S.Prévot (Subaru Impreza WRC2008) 2m11.3s; PC M.Baldacci/G.Agnese (Mitsubishi Lancer Evo IX) 2m13.0s

SS2 Perge 1 (22.43km)

1 U.Aava/K.Sikk (Citroën C4 WRC) 16m03.6s; 2 G.Galli/G.Bernacchini (Ford Focus RS WRC 07) 16m05.2s; 3 A.Mikkelsen/O.Fløene (Ford Focus RS WRC 06) 16m05.8s; 4 Hirvonen/Lehtinen (Ford) 16m05.9s; 5 Sordo/Martí (Citroën) 16m10.5s; 6 P-G.Andersson/J.Andersson (Suzuki SX4 WRC) 16m12.3s; PC A.Aigner/K.Wicha (Mitsubishi Lancer Evo IX) 16m56.7s

SS3 Myra 1 (24.15km)

1 Latvala/Anttila (Ford) 21m05.3s; 2 Sordo/Martí (Citroën)

21m20.5s; 3 Galli/Bernacchini (Ford) 21m22.0s; 4 H.Solberg/C.Menkerud (Ford Focus RS WRC 07) 21m22.9s; 5 Hirvonen/Lehtinen (Ford) 21m24.1s; 6 Loeb/Elena (Citroën) 21m24.8s; PC U.Nittel/M.Wenzel (Mitsubishi Lancer Evo IX) 22m26.9s

SS4 Kumluca 1 (9.90km)
1 Galli/Bernacchini (Ford) 7m47.4s; 2 Latvala/Anttila (Ford) 7m48.3s; 3 H.Solberg/Menkerud (Ford) 7m48.4s; 4 Loeb/Elena (Citroën) 7m50.4s; 5= Atkinson/Prévot (Subaru), Hirvonen/Lehtinen (Ford) 7m50.9s; PC Nittel/Wenzel (Mitsubishi) 8m11.5s

SS5 Perge 2 (22.43km)
1 Galli/Bernacchini (Ford) 15m42.8s; 2 Latvala/Anttila (Ford) 15m43.7s; 3 Hirvonen/Lehtinen (Ford) 15m44.5s; 4 H.Solberg/Menkerud (Ford) 15m44.7s; 5 Sordo/Martí (Citroën) 15m47.2s; 6 Loeb/Elena (Citroën) 15m48.4s; PC Aigner/Wicha (Mitsubishi) 16m46.5s

SS6 Myra 2 (24.15km)
1 Latvala/Anttila (Ford) 20m46.0s; 2 Hirvonen/Lehtinen (Ford) 20m56.4s; 3 Loeb/Elena (Citroën) 20m57.2s; 4 Sordo/Martí (Citroën) 20m57.7s; 5 Galli/Bernacchini (Ford) 21m01.0s; 6 Andersson/Andersson (Suzuki) 21m09.3s; PC P.Sandell/E.Axelsson (Peugeot 207 S2000) 22m10.9s

SS7 Kumluca 2 (9.90km)
1 Loeb/Elena (Citroën) 7m38.9s; 2 Hirvonen/Lehtinen (Ford) 7m40.2s; 3 Galli/Bernacchini (Ford) 7m44.4s; 4 H.Solberg/Menkerud (Ford) 7m45.6s; 5 P.Solberg/Mills (Subaru) 7m50.9s; 6 M.Wilson/S.Martin (Ford Focus RS WRC 07) 7m51.7s; PC Aigner/Wicha (Mitsubishi) 8m09.2s

SS8 Chimera 1 (16.94km)
1 Galli/Bernacchini (Ford) 12m21.5s; 2 H.Solberg/Menkerud (Ford) 12m21.6s; 3 Latvala/Anttila (Ford) 12m23.9s; 4 Andersson/Andersson (Suzuki) 12m30.4s; 5 Hirvonen/Lehtinen (Ford) 12m31.2s; 6 P.Solberg/Mills (Subaru) 12m31.5s; PC Aigner/Wicha (Mitsubishi) 13m16.0s

SS9 Phaselis 1 (22.40km)
1 H.Solberg/Menkerud (Ford) 17m49.3s; 2 Sordo/Martí (Citroën) 17m53.5s; 3 Wilson/Martin (Ford) 17m56.1s; 4 Loeb/Elena (Citroën) 17m58.1s; 5 T.Gardemeister/ T.Tuominen (Suzuki SX4 WRC) 18m00.0s; 6 P.Solberg/Mills (Subaru) 18m03.9s; PC Nittel/Wenzel (Mitsubishi) 18m44.4s

SS10 Chimera 2 (16.94km)
1 Hirvonen/Lehtinen (Ford) 11m57.3s; 2 Latvala/Anttila (Ford) 12m00.2s; 3 Loeb/Elena (Citroën) 12m01.2s; 4 Galli/Bernacchini (Ford) 12m01.5s; 5 Sordo/Martí (Citroën) 12m03.4s; 6 P.Solberg/Mills (Subaru) 12m11.3s; PC Aigner/Wicha (Mitsubishi) 13m01.4s

SS11 Silyon 1 (27.36km)
1 Hirvonen/Lehtinen (Ford) 21m53.5s; 2 Galli/Bernacchini (Ford) 21m59.1s; 3 Latvala/Anttila (Ford) 21m59.2s; 4 Aava/Sikk (Citroën) 22m02.8s; 5 Loeb/Elena (Citroën) 22m10.1s; 6 Atkinson/Prévot (Subaru) 22m16.0s; PC N.Al-Attiyah/C.Patterson (Subaru Impreza) 23m30.2s

SS12 Kemer 1 (20.50km)
1 Aava/Sikk (Citroën) 15m06.9s; 2 Atkinson/Prévot (Subaru) 15m07.8s; 3 Hirvonen/Lehtinen (Ford) 15m10.4s; 4 Sordo/Martí (Citroën) 15m11.8s; 5= Loeb/Elena (Citroën), P.Solberg/Mills (Subaru) 15m15.7s; PC Nittel/Wenzel (Mitsubishi) 16m10.0s

SS13 Silyon 2 (27.36km)
1 Hirvonen/Lehtinen (Ford) 21m36.8s; 2 Latvala/Anttila (Ford) 21m40.3s; 3 Sordo/Martí (Citroën) 21m46.9s; 4 Loeb/Elena (Citroën) 21m52.6s; 5 Atkinson/Prévot (Subaru) 21m53.5s; 6 H.Solberg/Menkerud (Ford) 21m54.1s; PC Al-Attiyah/Patterson (Subaru) 23m10.9s

SS14 Kemer 2 (20.50km)
1 Latvala/Anttila (Ford) 14m49.4s; 2 Hirvonen/Lehtinen (Ford)

14m50.0s; 3 Sordo/Martí (Citroën) 14m50.7s; 4 Loeb/Elena (Citroën) 14m51.7s; 5 Aava/Sikk (Citroën) 14m52.3s; 6 P.Solberg/Mills (Subaru) 14m56.9s; PC Baldacci/Agnese (Mitsubishi) 15m53.3s

SS15 Phaselis 2 (22.40km)
1= Loeb/Elena (Citroën), Hirvonen/Lehtinen (Ford) 17m19.2s; 3 Latvala/Anttila (Ford) 17m23.1s; 4 Sordo/Martí (Citroën) 17m29.4s; 5 Aava/Sikk (Citroën) 17m38.3s; 6 P.Solberg/Mills (Subaru) 17m45.8s; PC Baldacci/Agnese (Mitsubishi) 18m34.0s

SS16 Antalya SSS 2 (2.60km)
1 Loeb/Elena (Citroën) 2m06.3s; 2 H.Solberg/Menkerud (Ford) 2m07.8s; 3 Hirvonen/Lehtinen (Ford) 2m08.5s; 4 P.Solberg/Mills (Subaru) 2m09.1s; 5= Galli/Bernacchini (Ford), Latvala/Anttila (Ford) 2m09.3s; PC Baldacci/Agnese (Mitsubishi) 2m15.8s

SS17 Olympos 1 (31.03km)
1 Aava/Sikk (Citroën) 25m07.5s; 2 Mikkelsen/Fløene (Ford) 25m11.4s; 3 Sordo/Martí (Citroën) 25m13.3s; 4 Latvala/Anttila (Ford) 25m14.9s; 5 Loeb/Elena (Citroën) 25m15.7s; 6 P.Solberg/Mills (Subaru) 25m22.3s; PC S.Campedelli/D.Fappani (Mitsubishi Lancer Evo IX) 26m28.0s

SS18 Camyuva (5.50km)
1 Loeb/Elena (Citroën) 4m11.2s; 2 Hirvonen/Lehtinen (Ford) 4m12.1s; 3 Atkinson/Prévot (Subaru) 4m15.1s; 4 Latvala/Anttila (Ford) 4m17.3s; 5 Mikkelsen/Fløene (Ford) 4m18.0s; 6 Aava/Sikk (Citroën) 4m18.3s; PC Campedelli/Fappani (Mitsubishi) 4m38.8s

SS19 Olympos 2 (31.03km)
1 Latvala/Anttila (Ford) 24m48.9s; 2 Hirvonen/Lehtinen (Ford) 24m53.7s; 3 Loeb/Elena (Citroën) 24m53.9s; 4 Solberg/Mills (Subaru) 24m59.8s; 5 Atkinson/Prévot (Subaru) 25m03.8s; 6 Sordo/Martí (Citroën) 25m05.0s; PC Campedelli/Fappani (Mitsubishi) 26m18.8s

Cars that retired and subsequently restarted and were classified under SuperRally regs:

6	Atkinson/Prévot	Subaru Impreza WRC2008		
	Suspension	SS6	A8	

MAJOR RETIREMENTS

15	Aava/Sikk	Citroën C4 WRC	
	Lost a wheel	SS3	A8
11	Gardemeister/Tuominen	Suzuki SX4 WRC	
	Mechanical	SS11	A8
12	Andersson/Andersson	Suzuki SX4 WRC	
	Mechanical	SS11	A8
7	Galli/Bernacchini	Ford Focus RS WRC 07	
	Illness	SS16D	A8
15	Aava/Sikk	Citroën C4 WRC	
	Retired	SS19	A8

FIA CLASS WINNERS

A8	Over 2000cc	Hirvonen/Lehtinen Ford Focus RS WRC 07
A7	1600-2000cc	Vatankhah/Ahmadi Ford Fiesta ST
A6	1400-1600cc	Unal/Gücenmez Fiat Punto S1600
A5	Upto 1400cc	Bostanci/Baydar Ford Ka
N4	Over 2000cc	Aigner/Wicha Mitsubishi Lancer Evo IX
N3	1600-2000cc	Çetinkaya/Güney Ford Fiesta ST
N2	Upto 1400cc	Onkök/Serim Fiat Palio

RALLY LEADERS
Overall: SS1 Loeb; SS2-5 Hirvonen; SS6 Latvala; SS7-8 Hirvonen; SS9-10 Loeb; SS11-19 Hirvonen
PC: SS1-3 Baldacci; SS4 Nittel; SS5 Baldacci; SS6 Nittel; SS7 Sandell P; SS8-19 Aigner

SPECIAL STAGE ANALYSIS

	1st	2nd	3rd	4th	5th	6th
Loeb (Citroën)	5	–	3	4	3	2
Hirvonen (Ford)	4	5	4	1	3	–
Latvala (Ford)	4	4	3	4	1	–
Galli (Ford)	3	2	2	1	2	–
Aava (Citroën)	3	–	–	1	2	1
H.Solberg (Ford)	1	2	1	3	–	1
Sordo (Citroën)	–	2	3	2	4	1
Atkinson (Subaru)	–	1	1	–	3	2
Mikkelsen (Ford)	–	1	1	–	1	–
P.Solberg (Subaru)	–	1	–	2	2	6
Wilson (Ford)	–	–	1	–	–	1
Andersson (Suzuki)	–	–	–	1	–	2
Gardemeister (Suzuki)	–	–	–	–	1	–

TYRES
Tyres: Pirelli Scorpion
Compound: hard
Number of tyres available per car: 48

WORLD CHAMPIONSHIP POINTS
Drivers
1 Hirvonen 59; 2 Loeb 56; 3 Latvala 34; 4 Atkinson 31; 5 Sordo 30; 6 P.Solberg 20; 7 Galli 17; 8 H.Solberg 16; 9 Wilson 12; 10 Villagra 8 etc
Manufacturers
1 BP Ford Abu Dhabi WRT 99; 2 Citroën Total WRT 90; 3 Subaru WRT 53; 4 Stobart VK M-Sport Ford RT 41; 5 Munchi's Ford WRT 19; 6 Suzuki WRT 10

Junior World Rally Championship
1 Ogier 24; 2= Kosciuszko, Gallagher 16; 4 Burkart 11; 5= Mölder, Bettega 8; 7 Albertini 7; 8= Schammel, Sandell 6; 10 Niegel 5 etc

Production Car World Rally Championship
1 Aigner 30; 2= Ketomaa, Sandell 14; 4= Hänninen, Araújo 12; 6= Nutahara, Sousa 10; 8 Rauam 9; 9 Beltrán 8; 10 Prokop 7 etc

ROUTE DETAILS
Total Route of 1263.74km of which 360.12km were competitive on 19 stages
Leg 1 Thursday 12 June - Friday 13 June, 9 special stages totalling 154.90km
Leg 2 Saturday 14 June, 7 special stages totalling 137.66km
Leg 3 Sunday 15 June, 3 special stages totalling 67.56km

RESULTS

1	Mikko Hirvonen/ Jarmo Lehtinen	Ford Focus RS WRC 07	4h42m07.1s A8
2	Jari-Matti Latvala/ Miikka Anttila	Ford Focus RS WRC 07	4h42m15.0s A8
3	Sébastien Loeb/ Daniel Elena	Citroën C4 WRC	4h42m32.8s A8
4	Dani Sordo/ Marc Martí	Citroën C4 WRC	4h44m32.7s A8
5	Henning Solberg/ Cato Menkerud	Ford Focus RS WRC 07	4h44m40.8s A8
6	Petter Solberg/ Phil Mills	Subaru Impreza WRC2008	4h44m55.3s A8
7	Matthew Wilson/ Scott Martin	Ford Focus RS WRC 07	4h46m31.3s A8
8	Conrad Rautenbach/ David Senior	Citroën C4 WRC	4h49m53.8s A8
9	Federico Villagra/ Jorge Pérez Companc	Ford Focus RS WRC 07	4h51m31.2s
10	Barry Clark/ Paul Nagle	Ford Focus RS WRC 07	4h56m55.9s A8

60 starters, 37 finishers

PREVIOUS WINNERS

2000*	Volkan Işık/Yusuf Avimelek	Subaru Impreza WRC
2001*	Serkan Yazici/Erkan Bodur	Toyota Corolla WRC
2002*	Ercan Kazaz/Cem Bakançocuklari	Subaru Impreza WRC
2003	Carlos Sainz/Marc Martí	Citroën Xsara WRC
2004	Sébastien Loeb/Daniel Elena	Citroën Xsara WRC
2005	Sébastien Loeb/Daniel Elena	Citroën Xsara WRC
2006	Marcus Grönholm/Timo Rautiainen	Ford Focus RS WRC 06

*Non-championship event, Anatolian Rally (WRC candidate event)

Main: Subaru's Chris
Atkinson was back on the
podium for the first time
since the Jordan Rally
in April.

Left: Sébastien Loeb
had been a podium finisher
in Finland three times
before but finally took his
maiden win.
Photographs: PHOTO4

Neste Oil Rally Finland 2008

Race&motion

Above: Mikko Hirvonen had been expected to win on home soil, but had no answer to Loeb's pace. Their relative fortunes were clear to see.

Right: Matti Rantanen shocked the establishment by claiming seventh place in a privateer Ford Focus.

Far right: Citroën team boss Olivier Quesnel offers his congratulations to Loeb.

Middle Right: Henning won the battle of the Solberg brothers in Finland, beating Petter to fifth by seven seconds.

Top right: Jari-Matti Latvala was devastated after crashing out on the first day of his home event.
Photographs: PHOTO4 unless specified

VELLIPOHJA, the fifth stage of Rally Finland, gave the best indication of where Sébastien Loeb's pace and priorities were. A technical glitch had robbed his Citroën C4 WRC of split times for the 17-kilometre test, forcing him to get his head down and drive the door handles off the car for fear of losing time to Mikko Hirvonen. Loeb was, essentially, driving in the dark. He wound the C4 WRC up and let rip, taking 2.7 seconds out of Ford's local hero.

At that point in the event, Loeb had still not been beaten on a stage. Was this really happening in Finland? In his pre-event spiel, Loeb had spoken about being more than happy with a podium finish – and the fact that he wasn't interested in winning the 'classic' events, just championships. Taking Hirvonen to the cleaners didn't sit easily with any of that.

Hirvonen did get a look in, eventually. But taking seven tenths of a second out of Loeb in stage eight turned out to be counter-productive, as the reigning world champion hit back harder on the next test. And that was how the event panned out. Hirvonen would nibble at Loeb's lead, but the Frenchman was able to maintain the gap to his title rival.

Hirvonen was by no means beaten out of sight. He did a fantastic job and forced Loeb to drive out of his comfort zone and faster than he has ever been in Finland before. The Jyväskylä lad's pace around his home town would have been enough to beat any other driver in the world – Marcus Grönholm included – but Loeb was on fire in Finland. There was simply no stopping the Frenchman.

"My car was perfect," said Loeb at the end. "After I struggled last year with the set-up, we had a long debrief and the team and I understood more about

what was needed this year. In the pre-event test, we went in the right direction and here we had a great car. I was comfortable and very confident in the car. This is how I could win. But Mikko pushed hard. Very hard. If Mikko had beaten me here, I wouldn't have been able to understand it."

And that was that. That was how Loeb became the first non-Nordic driver to win in these parts since Didier Auriol in 1992, and only the third in the history of the sport.

Hirvonen was pragmatic in defeat. He'd done everything he could. A Loeb spin on the penultimate stage had given him hope and urged him into an even greater effort, but it wasn't enough.

"Fair play," said Hirvonen, "he's beaten me and that's all there is to say."

Finland made one thing perfectly clear for Hirvonen and the Ford team, though. His pace and consistency across the three days of competition was indicative of a true team leader. There had been talk of Hirvonen's team-mate Jari-Matti Latvala troubling him at Ford this year, but the younger man's third-stage accident highlighted the fact that his Ford career is still a work in progress.

Finland was a deeply confusing event for Subaru. Petter Solberg struggled through the event, while team-mate Chris Atkinson was nowhere on Friday afternoon, but had made it onto the podium by the close of play. Even the Queenslander seemed a trifle confused about his elevation through days two and three. His fifth podium of the year hadn't come easily, though – he'd battled hard and out-driven Dani Sordo (fourth) and Henning Solberg (fifth), both of whom had looked good for third place before Atkinson's charge.

Race&motion

Leg 1

Leg 2

Leg 3

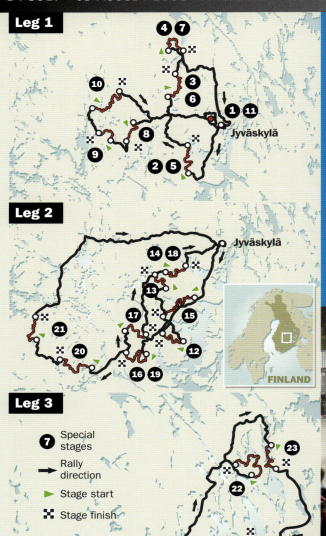

7 Special stages

→ Rally direction

▶ Stage start

✖ Stage finish

Jyväskylä

FINLAND

Position	Stage Numbers	1	2	3	4	5	6	7	8	9	10	11	12	13	14	15	16	17	18	19	20	21	22	23	24
	Loeb	1	1	1	1	1	1	1	1	1	1	1	1	1	1	1	1	1	1	1	1	1	1	1	1
	Hirvonen	3	2	2	2	2	2	2	2	2	2	2	2	2	2	2	2	2	2	2	2	2	2	2	2
	Atkinson	3	5	5	5	9	9	9	9	8	7	7	6	6	6	5	5	5	4	4	3	3	3	3	
	Sordo	2	4	3	4	3	3	3	4	5	5	4	4	4	4	4	4	3	3	3	4	4	4	4	
	H.Solberg	10	10	9	8	7	6	5	5	4	3	3	4	4	4	5	4	4	4	5	5	5	5	5	
	P.Solberg	5	8	8	8	8	8	8	7	6	6	6	7	7	7	6	6	6	6	6	6	6	6	6	
	Rantanen	15	17	13	13	13	12	12	12	11	10	9	10	9	8	7	7	7	7	7	7	7	7	7	
	Gardemeister	16	12	11	11	11	11	10	10	10	9	9	10	9	11	10	8	8	8	8	8	8	8	8	
	Wilson	13	13	14	14	14	13	13	13	12	11	11	12	11	10	11	9	9	9	9	9	9	9	9	
	Rautenbach	19	14	15	16	16	14	15	14	14	12	11	11	11	12	9	9	10	10	10	10	10	10	10	
	Al-Qassimi	16	19	18	18	18	17	17	17	16	15	15	15	16	14	13	13	13	12	12	11	11	11		
	Mikkelsen	8	6	6	5	6	7	7	7	6	20	42	34	32	26	24	17	17	16	15	14	13	13	12	
	Aava	7	7	4	3	4	5	6	6	24	43	58	50	46	41	36	32	31	30	26	19	19	16	16	15
	Latvala	6	3	85	94	93	91	88	88	88	87	87	82	79	75	73	68	64	62	57	51	47	42	42	38
	Companc	18	15	16	15	15	15	14	14	13	13	13	13	13	13	11	11	R							
	Villagra	12	18	17	17	17	16	16	16	15	14	14	14	14	14	12	12	12	12	R					
	Galli	9	9	7	6	5	4	4	3	3	4	4	3	3	3	3	R								
	Andersson	13	16	14	12	12	11	11	11	10	8	8	9	8	9	R									
	Östberg	11	11	10	10	10	R																		

146	Jan Lonegren	A8
	Jari Ketomaa/	Subaru Impreza
	Miika Teiskonen	N4

SPECIAL STAGE TIMES

SS1 SSS Killeri 1 (2.06km)
1 S.Loeb/D.Elena (Citroën C4 WRC) 1m20.5s; 2 D.Sordo/M.Martí (Citroën C4 WRC) 1m20.8s; 3= C.Atkinson/S.Prévot (Subaru Impreza WRC2008), M.Hirvonen/J.Lehtinen (Ford Focus RS WRC 07) 1m20.9s; 5 P.Solberg/P.Mills (Subaru Impreza WRC2008) 1m21.1s; 6 J-M Latvala/M.Anttila (Ford Focus RS WRC 07) 1m 21.3s; JC M.Prokop/J.Tománek (Citroën C2 S1600) 1m30.0s; PC J.Hänninen/M.Markkula (Mitsubishi Lancer Evo IX) 1m26.1s

SS2 Vellipohja 1 (17.16km)
1= Loeb/Elena (Citroën), Hirvonen/Lehtinen (Ford) 8m16.9s; 3 Latvala/Anttila (Ford) 8m20.1s; 4 Sordo/Martí (Citroën) 8m21.7s; 5 A.Mikkelsen/O.Fløene (Ford Focus RS WRC 06) 8m22.3s; 6 Atkinson/Prévot (Subaru) 8m22.4s; JC Prokop/Tománek (Citroën) 9m21.9s; PC Hänninen/Markkula (Mitsubishi) 8m59.0s

SS3 Mökkiperä 1 (11.38km)
1 Loeb/Elena (Citroën) 5m30.5s; 2 Hirvonen/Lehtinen (Ford) 5m31.6s; 3 G.Galli/G.Bernacchini (Ford Focus RS WRC 07) 5m34.5s; 4 U.Aava/K.Sikk (Citroën C4 WRC) 5m36.3s; 5 Sordo/Martí (Citroën) 5m36.7s; 6 P.Solberg/Mills (Subaru) 5m37.5s; JC M.Kosciuszko/M.Szczepaniak (Suzuki Swift S1600) 6m14.5s; PC J.Salo/M.Stenberg (Mitsubishi Lancer Evo IX) 5m59.5s

SS4 Palsankylä 1 (13.90km)
1 Loeb/Elena (Citroën) 7m12.7s; 2 Hirvonen/Lehtinen (Ford) 7m15.1s; 3 Aava/Sikk (Citroën) 7m17.0s; 4 H.Solberg/C.Menkerud (Ford Focus RS WRC 07) 7m18.2s; 5 Mikkelsen/Fløene (Ford) 7m18.9s; 6 Galli/Bernacchini (Ford) 7m19.1s; JC J.Mölder/F.Miclotte (Suzuki Swift S1600) 8m17.2s; PC Salo/Stenberg (Mitsubishi) 7m46.4s

SS5 Vellipohja 2 (17.16km)
1 Loeb/Elena (Citroën) 8m09.9s; 2 Hirvonen/Lehtinen (Ford) 8m12.6s; 3 Sordo/Martí (Citroën) 8m13.7s; 4 Galli/Bernacchini (Ford) 8m15.9s; 5 H.Solberg/Menkerud (Ford) 8m18.6s; 6 Mikkelsen/Fløene (Ford) 8m19.0s; JC Kosciuszko/Szczepaniak (Suzuki) 9m16.9s; PC Salo/Stenberg (Mitsubishi) 8m55.1s

SS6 Mökkiperä 2 (11.38km)
1= Loeb/Elena (Citroën), Hirvonen/Lehtinen (Ford) 5m28.8s; 3 Sordo/Martí (Citroën) 5m31.9s; 4 Galli/Bernacchini (Ford) 5m32.4s; 5 H.Solberg/Menkerud (Ford) 5m32.6s; 6 Aava/Sikk (Citroën) 5m36.4s; JC Kosciuszko/Szczepaniak (Suzuki) 6m16.1s; PC Salo/Stenberg (Mitsubishi) 6m00.6s

SS7 Palsankylä 2 (13.90km)
1 Loeb/Elena (Citroën) 7m07.8s; 2 Hirvonen/Lehtinen (Ford) 7m10.3s; 3 H.Solberg/Menkerud (Ford) 7m11.9s; 4 Galli/Bernacchini (Ford) 7m12.0s; 5 Sordo/Martí (Citroën) 7m14.5s; 6 Aava/Sikk (Citroën) 7m16.8s; JC Kosciuszko/Szczepaniak (Suzuki) 8m11.5s; PC Salo/Stenberg (Mitsubishi) 7m43.8s

SS8 Urria (12.65km)
1 Hirvonen/Lehtinen (Ford) 6m00.5s; 2 Loeb/Elena (Citroën) 6m01.2s; 3 H.Solberg/Menkerud (Ford) 6m01.9s; 4 Galli/Bernacchini (Ford) 6m03.3s; 5 Aava/Sikk (Citroën) 6m06.6s;

Above right: With title rival Andreas Aigner not counting the event as one of his scoring rounds, Juho Hänninen claimed a vital Production win.
Photograph: Race&motion

FINISH LINES...

This year's Rally Finland was an event for unearthing new talent on the world stage. Finland's Matti Rantanen was one such driver. The 27-year-old belied his complete lack of competitive experience in a World Rally Car of any flavour to place a Focus RS WRC 06 in seventh place on his debut. His only trouble had been a clutch problem, which caused him to stall the car at numerous startlines on the Saturday. Beyond that Rantanen's event was a dream... Suzuki had another rally to forget. Without the summer tests which had been planned, the SX4 WRC's development was severely restricted. In fairness, the cars were quicker and more reliable than they had been before. P-G Andersson was, once again, the quicker of Suzuki's two drivers and his car ran without fault until he ploughed into a tree in Kakaristo. Toni Gardemeister suffered, wait for it, power steering and yet more hydraulic problems on Saturday morning. That and a down-on-power engine meant that eighth was the best he could hope for... Juho Hänninen collected his second Production Car WRC win of the season, coming out on top after a cracking fight with fellow Mitsubishi Lancer driver Juha Salo. Salo had the edge early doors, but rolled his car out on the same corner as Andersson... Martin Prokop collected his first Junior win of the season. As in the Production class, the scrap for victory had been fascinating among the JWRC runners. As had been the case on the last rally, it was Prokop and Michal Kosciuszko who went head-to-head. The Suzuki man looked to have the beating of Prokop's C2 for the second event in succession, only to fall foul of a deceptive corner on Saturday's penultimate stage. Prokop won, Patrik Sandell (Renault) was second and Kosciuszko recovered to third.

RUNNING ORDER

3	Mikko Hirvonen/	Ford Focus RS WRC 07
	Jarmo Lehtinen	A8
1	Sébastien Loeb/	Citroën C4 WRC
	Daniel Elena	A8
4	Jari-Matti Latvala/	Ford Focus RS WRC 07
	Miikka Anttila	A8
6	Chris Atkinson/	Subaru Impreza WRC2008
	Stéphane Prévot	A8
2	Dani Sordo/	Citroën C4 WRC
	Marc Martí	A8
5	Petter Solberg/	Subaru Impreza WRC2008
	Phil Mills	A8
7	Gigi Galli/	Ford Focus RS WRC 07
	Giovanni Bernacchini	A8
8	Henning Solberg/	Ford Focus RS WRC 07
	Cato Menkerud	A8
16	Matthew Wilson/	Ford Focus RS WRC 07
	Scott Martin	A8
9	Federico Villagra/	Ford Focus RS WRC 07
	Jorge Pérez Companc	A8
14	Conrad Rautenbach/	Citroën C4 WRC
	David Senior	A8
15	Urmo Aava/	Citroën C4 WRC
	Kuldar Sikk	A8
19	Andreas Mikkelsen/	Ford Focus RS WRC 06
	Ola Fløene	A8
11	Toni Gardemeister/	Suzuki SX4 WRC
	Tomi Tuominen	A8
12	P-G Andersson/	Suzuki SX4 WRC
	Jonas Andersson	A8
17	Mads Østberg/	Subaru Impreza WRC 2007
	Ole Kristian Unnerud	A8
18	Khalid Al-Qassimi/	Ford Focus RS WRC 07
	Michael Orr	A8
10	Luis Pérez Companc/	Ford Focus RS WRC 07
	José María Volta	A8
20	Matti Rantanen/	Ford Focus RS WRC 06

6= Mikkelsen/Fløene (Ford), Atkinson/Prévot (Subaru) 6m07.6s; JC Kosciuszko/Szczepaniak (Suzuki) 6m43.5s; PC Salo/Stenberg (Mitsubishi) 6m27.0s

SS9 Lautaperä (7.87km)
1 Loeb/Elena (Citroën) 3m52.4s; 2 Hirvonen/Lehtinen (Ford) 3m53.1s; 3 H.Solberg/Menkerud (Ford) 3m55.5s; 4 Galli/Bernacchini (Ford) 3m58.2s; 5 Mikkelsen/Fløene (Ford) 3m58.4s; 6 P-G.Andersson/J.Andersson (Suzuki SX4 WRC) 3m58.5s; JC P.Sandell/E.Axelsson (Renault Clio S1600) 4m23.1s; PC Salo/Stenberg (Mitsubishi) 4m08.9s

SS10 Jukojärvi (22.18km)
1 Loeb/Elena (Citroën) 10m37.2s; 2 Hirvonen/Lehtinen (Ford) 10m41.2s; 3 H.Solberg/Menkerud (Ford) 10m43.4s; 4 Galli/Bernacchini (Ford) 10m46.8s; 5 Sordo/Martí (Citroën) 10m52.6s; 6 Atkinson/Prévot (Subaru) 10m53.1s; JC Sandell/Axelsson (Renault) 11m59.2s; PC Hänninen/Markkula (Mitsubishi) 11m26.0s

SS11 SSS Killeri 2 (2.06km)
1 Loeb/Elena (Citroën) 1m20.0s; 2= Atkinson/Prévot (Subaru), Sordo/Martí (Citroën) 1m20.6s; 4= P.Solberg/Mills (Subaru), H.Solberg/Menkerud (Ford) 1m21.1s; 6 Hirvonen/Lehtinen (Ford) 1m21.3s; JC Prokop/Tománek (Citroën) 1m30.0s; PC Hänninen/M.Markkula (Mitsubishi) 1m25.0s

SS12 Himos (15.35km)
1 Hirvonen/Lehtinen (Ford) 8m37.3s; 2 Loeb/Elena (Citroën) 8m40.3s; 3 Atkinson/Prévot (Subaru) 8m49.5s; 4 Galli/Bernacchini (Ford) 8m50.5s; 5 P.Solberg/Mills (Subaru) 8m51.8s; 6 M.Rantanen/J.Lonegren (Ford Focus RS WRC 06) 8m52.4s; JC Prokop/Tománek (Citroën) 9m55.4s; PC Hänninen/M.Markkula (Mitsubishi) 9m16.4s

SS13 Hirvimäki (10.67km)
1 Loeb/Elena (Citroën) 5m47.7s; 2 Hirvonen/Lehtinen (Ford) 5m51.4s; 3 Latvala/Anttila (Ford) 5m57.1s; 4 Sordo/Martí (Citroën) 5m58.4s; 5 Atkinson/Prévot (Subaru) 5m58.5s; 6 P.Solberg/Mills (Subaru) 6m00.6s; JC Kosciuszko/Szczepaniak (Suzuki) 6m47.6s; PC Salo/Stenberg (Mitsubishi) 6m17.5s

SS14 Surkee 1 (14.80km)
1 Loeb/Elena (Citroën) 8m03.4s; 2 Hirvonen/Lehtinen (Ford) 8m04.0s; 3 Latvala/Anttila (Ford) 8m08.8s; 4 Atkinson/Prévot (Subaru) 8m11.9s; 5= Sordo/Martí (Citroën), Galli/Bernacchini (Ford) 8m14.5s; JC Kosciuszko/Szczepaniak (Suzuki) 9m02.8s; PC Hänninen/M.Markkula (Mitsubishi) 8m32.0s

SS15 Leustu (21.43km)
1 Hirvonen/Lehtinen (Ford) 10m12.4s; 2 Loeb/Elena (Citroën) 10m17.0s; 3 Latvala/Anttila (Ford) 10m22.4s; 4 Sordo/Martí (Citroën) 10m26.1s; 5 P.Solberg/Mills (Subaru) 10m26.6s; 6 Atkinson/Prévot (Subaru) 10m26.7s; JC Prokop/Tománek (Citroën) 11m43.4s; PC Salo/Stenberg (Mitsubishi) 11m01.3s

SS16 Kakaristo 1 (20.09km)
1 Latvala/Anttila (Ford) 10m43.2s; 2 Loeb/Elena (Citroën) 10m48.3s; 3 Hirvonen/Lehtinen (Ford) 10m51.5s; 4 Atkinson/Prévot (Subaru) 11m02.1s; 5 Sordo/Martí (Citroën) 11m04.9s; 6 H.Solberg/Menkerud (Ford) 11m07.0s; JC Sandell/Axelsson (Renault) 11m58.2s; PC Hänninen/M.Markkula (Mitsubishi) 11m26.2s

SS17 Kaipolanvuori (13.64km)
1 Latvala/Anttila (Ford) 7m06.6s; 2 Hirvonen/Lehtinen (Ford) 7m06.9s; 3 Loeb/Elena (Citroën) 7m08.3s; 4 Atkinson/Prévot (Subaru) 7m11.1s; 5 Mikkelsen/Fløene (Ford) 7m12.4s; 6 Sordo/Martí (Citroën) 7m12.7s; JC Sandell/Axelsson (Renault) 7m55.6s; PC Hänninen/M.Markkula (Mitsubishi) 7m43.4s

SS18 Surkee 2 (14.80km)
1 Loeb/Elena (Citroën) 7m55.9s; 2 Hirvonen/Lehtinen (Ford) 7m57.8s; 3 Latvala/Anttila (Ford) 8m02.7s; 4 Latvala/Anttila (Ford) 8m03.7s; 5 H.Solberg/Menkerud (Ford) 8m04.5s; 6 P.Solberg/Mills (Subaru) 8m07.4s; JC Kosciuszko/Szczepaniak (Suzuki) 8m52.7s; PC S.Campedelli/D.Fappani (Mitsubishi Lancer Evo IX) 8m44.8s

SS19 Kakaristo 2 (20.09km)
1 Hirvonen/Lehtinen (Ford) 10m34.7s; 2 Latvala/Anttila (Ford) 10m35.9s; 3 Loeb/Elena (Citroën) 10m38.0s; 4 P.Solberg/Mills (Subaru) 10m46.1s; 5 Atkinson/Prévot (Subaru) 10m47.2s; 6 Sordo/Martí (Citroën) 10m50.3s; JC Kosciuszko/Szczepaniak (Suzuki) 11m51.2s; PC Hänninen/M.Markkula (Mitsubishi) 11m35.8s

SS20 Juupajoki (21.13km)
1 Latvala/Anttila (Ford) 10m57.4s; 2 Loeb/Elena (Citroën) 11m04.2s; 3 Hirvonen/Lehtinen (Ford) 11m06.8s; 4 Atkinson/Prévot (Subaru) 11m07.0s; 5 Mikkelsen/Fløene (Ford) 11m17.6s; 6 Sordo/Martí (Citroën) 11m17.7s; JC Prokop/Tománek

(Citroën) 12m27.7s; PC J.Ketomaa/M.Teiskonen (Subaru Impreza) 11m52.6s

SS21 Väärinmaja (16.25km)
1 Loeb/Elena (Citroën) 8m22.5s; 2 Hirvonen/Lehtinen (Ford) 8m26.6s; 3 Latvala/Anttila (Ford) 8m29.8s; 4 Atkinson/Prévot (Subaru) 8m31.4s; 5 Aava/Sikk (Citroën) 8m37.7s; 6= Sordo/Martí (Citroën), H.Solberg/Menkerud (Ford) 8m38.5s; JC Kosciuszko/Szczepaniak (Suzuki) 9m35.0s; PC Hänninen/M.Markkula (Mitsubishi) 9m07.7s

SS22 Lankamaa (23.09km)
1= Loeb/Elena (Citroën), Hirvonen/Lehtinen (Ford) 11m11.0s; 3 Latvala/Anttila (Ford) 11m11.9s; 4 Aava/Sikk (Citroën) 11m20.7s; 5 Atkinson/Prévot (Subaru) 11m20.8s; 6 P.Solberg/Mills (Subaru) 11m21.6s; JC Sandell/Axelsson (Renault) 12m38.8s; PC Ketomaa/Teiskonen (Subaru) 12m05.9s

SS23 Hannula (10.92km)
1 Latvala/Anttila (Ford) 5m43.8s; 2 Hirvonen/Lehtinen (Ford) 5m48.7s; 3 Mikkelsen/Fløene (Ford) 5m49.3s; 4 M.Wilson/S.Martin (Ford Focus RS WRC 07) 5m52.1s; 5 P.Solberg/Mills (Subaru) 5m52.9s; 6 Loeb/Elena (Citroën) 5m55.1s; JC Sandell/Axelsson (Renault) 6m28.0s; PC Ketomaa/Teiskonen (Subaru) 6m13.3s

SS24 Ruuhimäki (6.46km)
1 P.Solberg/Mills (Subaru) 3m12.9s; 2 Hirvonen/Lehtinen (Ford) 3m13.1s; 3 Aava/Sikk (Citroën) 3m13.2s; 4 Latvala/Anttila (Ford) 3m13.5s; 5 Loeb/Elena (Citroën) 3m15.9s; 6 Rantanen (Ford) 3m16.0s; JC Sandell/Axelsson (Renault) 3m36.9s; PC Hänninen/M.Markkula (Mitsubishi) 3m29.2s

Cars that retired and subsequently restarted and were classified under SupeRally regs:

4	Latvala/Anttila	Ford Focus RS WRC 07		
	Off road		SS3	A8
15	Aava/Sikk	Citroën C4 WRC		
	Off road		SS9	A8
19	Mikkelsen/Fløene	Ford Focus RS WRC 06		
	Off road		SS10	A8

MAJOR RETIREMENTS
17	Ostberg/Unnerud	Subaru Impreza WRC2007		
	Off road		SS6	A8
7	Galli/ Bernacchini	Ford Focus RS WRC 07		
	Off road		SS16	A8
12	Andersson/Andersson	Suzuki SX4 WRC		
	Off road		SS16	A8
9	Villagra/Companc	Ford Focus RS WRC 07		
	Off road		SS20	A8
10	Companc/Volta	Ford Focus RS WRC 07		
	Co-driver injured		SS21A	A8

FIA CLASS WINNERS
A8	Over 2000cc	Loeb/Elena
		Citroën C4 WRC
A7	1600-2000cc	Wilks/Pugh
		Honda Civic Type-R R3
A6	1400-1600cc	Prokop/Tománek
		Citroën C2 S1600
A5	Upto 1400cc	Laakso/Tarvainen
		VW Polo 16V
N4	Over 2000cc	Hänninen/Markkula
		Mitsubishi Lancer Evo IX
N3	1600-2000cc	Yurdakul/Erkal
		Ford Fiesta ST
N2	Upto 1400cc	Hytönen/Pietiläinen
		Suzuki Swift Sport

RALLY LEADERS
Overall: SS1-24 Loeb

JWRC: SS1-5 Prokop; SS6-11 Kosciuszko, SS12 Prokop, SS13-16 Kosciuszko, SS17 Prokop, SS18-19 Kosciuszko, SS20-24 Prokop
PC: SS1-2 Hänninen, SS3-15 Salo, SS16-24 Hänninen

SPECIAL STAGE ANALYSIS
	1st	2nd	3rd	4th	5th	6th
Loeb (Citroën)	15	5	2	-	1	1
Hirvonen (Ford)	7	13	3	-	-	1
Latvala (Ford)	4	1	6	2	-	1
P.Solberg (Subaru)	1	-	-	2	4	4
Sordo (Citroën)	-	2	2	3	5	4
Atkinson (Subaru)	-	1	3	5	3	4
H.Solberg (Ford)	-	-	4	2	3	2
Aava (Citroën)	-	2	2	2	2	-
Galli (Ford)	-	-	1	7	1	1
Mikkelsen (Ford)	-	-	1	-	5	2
Wilson (Ford)	-	-	-	1	-	-
Andersson (Suzuki)	-	-	-	-	-	1
Rantanen (Ford)	-	-	-	-	-	2

TYRES
Tyres: Pirelli Scorpion
Compound: soft
Number of tyres available per car: 36

WORLD CHAMPIONSHIP POINTS
Drivers
1 Hirvonen 67; 2 Loeb 66; 3 Atkinson 37; 4 Sordo 35; 5 Latvala 34; 6 P.Solberg 23; 7 H.Solberg 20; 8 Galli 17; 9 Wilson 12; 10 Villagra 8etc

Manufacturers
1 BP Ford Abu Dhabi WRT 108; 2 Citroën Total WRT 105; 3 Subaru WRT 62; 4 Stobart VK M-Sport Ford RT 45; 5 Munchi's Ford WRT 19; 6 Suzuki WRT 12

Junior World Rally Championship
1 Ogier 24; 2 Kosciuszko 22; 3 Gallagher 20; 4 Burkart 16; 5 Sandell 14; 6 Prokop 12; 7= Mölder, Bettega, Schammel 8; 10 Albertini 7 etc

Production Car World Rally Championship
1 Aigner 30; 2 Hänninen 22; 3 Ketomaa 20; 4= Sandell, Nutahara 14; 6 Araújo 12; 7 Sousa 10; 8 Rauam 9; 9= Beltrán, Välimäki 8 etc

ROUTE DETAILS
Total Route of 1461.58km of which 340.42km were competitive on 24 stages
Leg 1 Thursday 31 July - Friday 1 August, 11 special stages totalling 131.70km
Leg 2 Saturday 2 August, 10 special stages totalling 168.25km
Leg 3 Sunday 3 August, 3 special stages totalling 40.47km

RESULTS
1	Sébastien Loeb/	Citroën C4 WRC	
	Daniel Elena	2h54m05.5s	A8
2	Mikko Hirvonen/	Ford Focus RS WRC 07	
	Jarmo Lehtinen	2h54m14.5s	A8
3	Chris Atkinson/	Subaru Impreza WRC2008	
	Stéphane Prévot	2h57m22.5s	A8
4	Dani Sordo/	Citroën C4 WRC	
	Marc Martí	2h57m36.4s	A8
5	Henning Solberg/	Ford Focus RS WRC 07	
	Cato Menkerud	2h57m53.2s	A8
6	Petter Solberg/	Subaru Impreza WRC2008	
	Phil Mills	2h58m09.6s	A8
7	Matti Rantanen/	Ford Focus RS WRC 06	
	Jan Lonegren	3h00m16.6s	A8
8	Toni Gardemeister/	Suzuki SX4 WRC	
	Tomi Tuominen	3h02m24.2s	A8
9	Matthew Wilson/	Ford Focus RS WRC 07	
	Scott Martin	3h02m42.8s	A8
10	Conrad Rautenbach/	Citroën C4 WRC	
	David Senior	3h04m36.4s	A8

108 starters, 68 finishers

PREVIOUS WINNERS

FOR THE second time in as many weeks, Sébastien Loeb was toying with the assembled media. Just as he'd pulled a cover story about not being too bothered about winning Rally Finland a fortnight earlier, he was now trying to convince people of the threat posed by Ford's Mikko Hirvonen in Germany.

For a day in the Mosel vineyards, he had everybody convinced. The new Ford was less than 20 seconds behind Loeb's leading Citroën on Friday night. But then the event moved into the Saarland stages and Loeb simply drove away from his rivals. The Frenchman's mastery of these roads was utterly intact for the seventh straight season. The only change from years gone by was the weather. Despite predictions of monsoon-like conditions, the rain failed to show. Given that Loeb's previous six wins have included some of the most astonishing wet-weather driving ever seen, some considered the Citroën driver as being potentially vulnerable in the dry.

Forget it. Not a hope. Loeb was just as impressive when the sun was shining. His only 'moment' during the rally came in Birkenfelder Land, when he turned into a top-gear corner only to find the rally organisers had shifted the straw bale by 10cm. Such is Loeb's precision – even when the speeds are reading well into three figures – that he only clattered the bale, rattling the right-hand side of the C4 WRC down it. Beyond that, there was very little for him to talk about.

Mundane or not, he had broken his own record for the number of consecutive wins on a single rally and grabbed the lead in the drivers' championship back off Hirvonen.

The Ford man looked like he had the weight of the world on his shoulders as he readied himself for the final day. It was hardly surprising, having seen his second place fall to Loeb's team-mate Dani Sordo on the first Saturday stage. Then a puncture on that day's final test allowed François Duval to come past, demoting Hirvonen to fourth.

Sordo had struggled through the opening day, failing to find the right set-up for his C4. But on day two he reverted to the set-up he'd had on the pre-event test and found himself back in the zone. "I've got my car back," he grinned. And he made very good use of it. Hirvonen never threatened him again and his

runners-up spot contributed enormously to Citroën's efforts to regain the lead of the manufacturers' championship from Ford.

Duval, like Sordo, had not had the best of times in the vineyards. Returning to the Stobart team and the driving seat of a Focus RS WRC 07 for the first time since Monte Carlo, Duval wrestled with the car, battling against the wrong tyres here and too many clicks on the suspension there. As the event progressed, he admitted much of his trouble had come due to his road position – he was running much further back, battling with dirty roads muddied by the cars cutting corners ahead.

But he ran fourth at the end of day one, which meant fourth on the road through day two. Duval's times improved and he zoned in on Hirvonen, but until the Finn's deflation he didn't look likely to pass him. There was an expectation that the Fords would switch positions on the final day – and Duval said he would have no problem in doing that if team principal Malcolm Wilson asked him.

Wilson didn't, underlining the independence of the Stobart team from the BP boys. Just in case he might have been thinking about it, Duval gunned his Ford through the four main stages on Sunday, fastest on every one of them. The final podium position was his, and Hirvonen's misery was complete.

Main: Sébastien Loeb continued his domination in Germany, winning for the seventh time.

Left: Pirelli's Enrico Campioni had agreed to have his head shaved if Loeb won in Germany....

Above left: Mikko Hirvonen was a distant fourth on the German asphalt – not his favoured surface.
Photographs: PHOTO4

François Duval was third
for the Stobart team on his
first start since Monte
Carlo in January.
Photograph: PHOTO4

Left: Dani Sordo had to make do with second place to his more illustrious team-mate.

Above: The rally was based in Germany's oldest city Trier, which was founded by the Romans.

Top: Sébastien Ogier claimed his third Junior WRC win after Martin Prokop retired with alternator failure.

Far left: Ninth place marked another disappointing performance by Jari-Matti Latvala.

Top left: This was the new Impreza's debut on asphalt, and Chris Atkinson had an unhappy run to sixth after encountering several problems.
Photographs: PHOTO4

ADAC Rallye Deutschland Results

15-17 AUGUST 2008 | FIA WORLD RALLY CHAMPIONSHIP ROUND 10

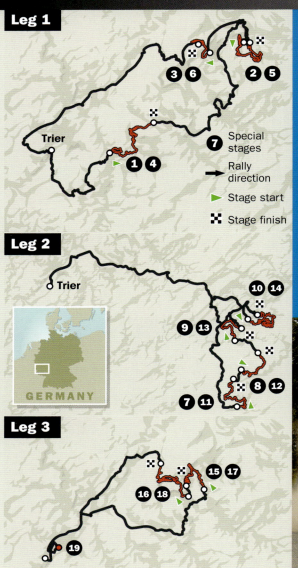

Leg 1

Trier

Special stages ▢✓

Rally direction →

Stage start ▶

Stage finish ▢✓

Leg 2

Trier

GERMANY

Leg 3

Position Stage Numbers	1	2	3	4	5	6	7	8	9	10	11	12	13	14	15	16	17	18	19
Loeb	1	1	1	1	1	1	1	1	1	1	1	1	1	1	1	1	1	1	1
Sordo	2	2	2	2	3	3	2	2	2	2	2	2	2	2	2	2	2	2	2
Duval	4	4	4	4	4	4	4	4	4	4	4	4	4	3	3	3	3	3	3
Hirvonen	3	3	2	3	2	2	3	3	3	3	3	3	3	4	4	4	4	4	4
P.Solberg	6	5	6	5	6	6	6	6	6	5	5	5	5	5	5	5	5	5	5
Atkinson	5	6	5	6	7	7	7	6	6	6	6	6	6	6	6	6	6	6	6
H.Solberg	9	8	8	8	8	8	8	8	7	7	7	7	7	7	7	7	7	7	7
Aava	10	10	10	10	9	9	9	9	8	8	8	8	8	8	8	8	8	8	8
Latvala	7	7	7	5	5	5	5	10	10	9	9	9	9	9	9	9	9	9	9
Gardemeister	11	11	12	11	10	10	10	10	9	9	10	10	10	10	10	10	10	10	10
Mikkelsen	12	13	13	13	12	12	12	12	11	11	11	11	11	12	12	11	11	11	11
Wilson	14	14	14	14	13	13	13	13	12	12	12	12	12	11	11	12	12	12	12
Rautenbach	16	15	16	15	14	14	14	14	13	13	13	13	13	13	13	13	13	13	13
Al-Qassimi	19	19	19	19	18	18	15	18	14	14	14	14	14	14	14	14	14	14	14
Andersson	13	12	11	12	11	11	11	11	17	19	17	17	16	15	15	15	15	15	15
Jones	24	21	20	20	19	19	22	21	19	18	19	19	17	17	16	16	16	16	16
Van Merksteijn	15	16	15	16	15	17	16	16	16	16	24	29	26	25	23	21	21		
Van Eldik	20	20	28	27	26	26	23	23	21	31	29	28	29	27	27	28	27	24	23
Wevers	16	17	17	17	16	16	18	17	15	15	15	15	30	32	31	29	28		
Galli	8	9	9	8	R														

Above left: Suzuki's P-G Andersson had to drive the fearsome Panzerplatte stage with a broken driveshaft, but made it to 15th.

Above right: Germany is always a crowd favourite, with fans flocking in from around Europe.
Photographs: PHOTO4

FINISH LINES...

The asphalt debut of Subaru's Impreza WRC2008 was always going to be a tricky affair, given that the team had only tested the car for four days – and one of those had been interrupted by Chris Atkinson's argument with a hinkelstein. On the rally there were the usual array of handling issues with the Impreza, but both Petter Solberg and Atkinson kept their cars in one piece and brought them home in fifth and sixth places without any major – or unexpected – technical issues... Henning Solberg turned in his most impressive asphalt showing to date, scoring points in seventh place. Unfortunately for his Stobart colleague Gigi Galli, the only thing the Italian would take home with him would be a broken left femur after a frightening top-gear accident in the Grafschaft stage. Galli's accident looked to have put him out for the remainder of the season... Suzuki actually fared quite well on asphalt, with neither SX4 WRC giving any major trouble. Toni Gardemeister was 10th, while P-G Andersson was 15th – a driveshaft had been pulled out after a particularly awkward entry into one of the many hairpins on the opening leg... Frenchman Sébastien Ogier took another giant leap towards this year's Junior World Rally Championship title when he scored his third win from four starts in his Citroën C2 Super 1600.

RUNNING ORDER

3 Mikko Hirvonen/ — Ford Focus RS WRC 08
Jarmo Lehtinen — A8

1 Sébastien Loeb/ — Citroën C4 WRC
Daniel Elena — A8

6 Chris Atkinson/ — Subaru Impreza WRC2008
Stéphane Prévot — A8

2 Dani Sordo/ — Citroën C4 WRC
Marc Martí — A8

4 Jari-Matti Latvala/ — Ford Focus RS WRC 08
Miikka Anttila — A8

5 Petter Solberg/ — Subaru Impreza WRC2008
Phil Mills — A8

15 Henning Solberg/ — Ford Focus RS WRC 07
Cato Menkerud — A8

7 Gigi Galli/ — Ford Focus RS WRC 07
Giovanni Bernacchini — A8

16 Matthew Wilson/ — Ford Focus RS WRC 07
Scott Martin — A8

17 Conrad Rautenbach/ — Citroën C4 WRC
David Senior — A8

18 Urmo Aava/ — Citroën C4 WRC
Kuldar Sikk — A8

8 François Duval/ — Ford Focus RS WRC 07
Patrick Pivato — A8

19 Andreas Mikkelsen/ — Ford Focus RS WRC 07
Ola Fløene — A8

11 Toni Gardemeister/ — Suzuki SX4 WRC
Tomi Tuominen — A8

12 P-G Andersson/ — Suzuki SX4 WRC
Jonas Andersson — A8

21 Khalid Al-Qassimi/ — Ford Focus RS WRC 07
Michael Orr — A8

22 Mark van Eldik/ — Subaru Impreza WRC2007
Michel Groenewoud — A8

23 Erik Wevers/ — Ford Focus RS WRC 06
Jalmar van Weeren — A8

24 Peter van Merksteijn/ — Ford Focus RS WRC 07
Hans van Beek — A8

25 Gareth Jones/ — Subaru Impreza WRC2007
David Moynihan — A8

SPECIAL STAGE TIMES

SS1 Ruwertal / Fell (21.22km)

1 S.Loeb/D.Elena (Citroën C4 WRC) 11m31.6s; 2 D.Sordo/M.Martí (Citroën C4 WRC) 11m37.4s; 3 M.Hirvonen/J.Lehtinen (Ford Focus RS WRC 08) 11m37.5s; 4 F.Duval/P.Pivato (Ford Focus RS WRC 07) 11m37.9s; 5 C.Atkinson/S.Prévot (Subaru Impreza WRC2008) 11m40.9s; 6 P.Solberg/P.Mills (Subaru Impreza WRC2008) 11m41.2s; JC S.Ogier/J.Ingrassia (Citroën C2 S1600) 12m39.9s

SS2 Grafschaft Veldenz (23.04km)

1 Loeb/Elena (Citroën) 13m14.4s; 2 Sordo/Martí (Citroën) 13m19.9s; 3 Hirvonen/Lehtinen (Ford) 13m21.1s; 4 J-M Latvala/M.Anttila (Ford Focus RS WRC 08) 13m27.8s; 5 P.Solberg/Mills (Subaru) 13m30.1s; 6 Atkinson/Prévot (Subaru) 13m30.8s; JC M.Prokop/J.Tománek (Citroën C2 S1600) 14m17.1s

SS3 Moselland (9.82km)

1 Loeb/Elena (Citroën) 5m29.3s; 2 Hirvonen/Lehtinen (Ford) 5m32.0s; 3 Duval/Pivato (Ford) 5m33.0s; 4 Sordo/Martí (Citroën) 5m33.3s; 5 Atkinson/Prévot (Subaru) 5m34.6s; 6 P.Solberg/Mills

(Subaru) 5m36.4; JC Prokop/Tománek (Citroën) 5m57.3s

SS4 Ruwertal / Fell (21.22km)
1 Loeb/Elena (Citroën) 11m28.7s; 2 Duval/Pivato (Ford) 11m30.9s; 3 Sordo/Martí (Citroën) 11m31.1s; 4 Hirvonen/Lehtinen (Ford) 11m32.1s; 5 G.Galli/G.Bernacchini (Ford Focus RS WRC 07) 11m33.3s; 6 Latvala/Anttila (Ford) 11m38.9s; JC Ogier/Ingrassia (Citroën) 12m30.5s

SS5 Grafschaft Veldenz (23.04km)*
1 Loeb/Elena (Citroën) 13m12.3s; 2 Hirvonen/Lehtinen (Ford) 13m12.4s; 3 Sordo/Martí (Citroën) 13m19.1s; 4 Duval/Pivato (Ford) 13m19.8s; 5 Latvala/Anttila (Ford) 13m20.9s; 6 Atkinson/Prévot (Subaru) 13m30.4s; JC Notional time given to all competitors

*Only 14 drivers completed the test at speed after it was stopped following Gigi Galli's accident. The rest were given notional times.

SS6 Moselland (9.82km)*
1 Loeb/Elena (Citroën) 5m26.2s; 2= Hirvonen/Lehtinen (Ford) 5m27.3s etc; 69 Atkinson/Prévot (Subaru) 5m56.4s; JC Notional time given to all competitors

*Only three drivers completed the test at speed - Loeb, Hirvonen and Atkinson - after the stage was cancelled due to the volume of spectators.

SS7 Bosenberg (19.12km)
1 Loeb/Elena (Citroën) 10m50.1s; 2 Sordo/Martí (Citroën) 10m50.4s; 3 Duval/Pivato (Ford) 10m54.2s; 4 Hirvonen/Lehtinen (Ford) 10m57.6s; 5 Latvala/Anttila (Ford) 11m01.5s; 6 Atkinson/Prévot (Subaru) 11m05.9s; JC Ogier/Ingrassia (Citroën) 12m05.5s

SS8 Freisen / Westrich (16.16km)
1 Loeb/Elena (Citroën) 9m26.9s; 2 Sordo/Martí (Citroën) 9m30.4s; 3 Duval/Pivato (Ford) 9m33.6s; 4 Hirvonen/Lehtinen (Ford) 9m34.6s; 5 Atkinson/Prévot (Subaru) 9m43.6s; 6 P.Solberg/Mills (Subaru) 9m44.4; JC Ogier/Ingrassia (Citroën) 10m40.2s

SS9 Birkenfelder Land (14.22km)
1 Loeb/Elena (Citroën) 7m57.1s; 2 Duval/Pivato (Ford) 7m57.6s; 3 Sordo/Martí (Citroën) 7m59.9s; 4 Hirvonen/Lehtinen (Ford) 8m00.7s; 5 U.Aava/K.Sikk (Citroën C4 WRC) 8m06.3s; 6 P.Solberg/Mills (Subaru) 8m06.5s; JC Ogier/Ingrassia (Citroën) 8m52.6s

SS10 Arena Panzerplatte (30.38km)
1 Loeb/Elena (Citroën) 17m44.5s; 2 Sordo/Martí (Citroën) 17m48.2s; 3 Hirvonen/Lehtinen (Ford) 17m56.1s; 4 P.Solberg/Mills (Subaru) 17m58.4s; 5 Atkinson/Prévot (Subaru) 18m05.3s; 6 Duval/Pivato (Ford) 18m12.2s; JC Ogier/Ingrassia (Citroën) 19m42.4s

SS11 Bosenberg (19.12km)
1 Loeb/Elena (Citroën) 10m50.6s; 2 Sordo/Martí (Citroën) 10m54.5s; 3 Hirvonen/Lehtinen (Ford) 10m56.1s; 4 Duval/Pivato (Ford) 10m56.2s; 5 P.Solberg/Mills (Subaru) 10m57.2s; 6 H.Solberg/C.Menkerud (Ford Focus RS WRC 07) 11m08.6s; JC Ogier/Ingrassia (Citroën) 12m09.5s

SS12 Freisen / Westrich (16.16km)
1 Loeb/Elena (Citroën) 9m30.4s; 2 Sordo/Martí (Citroën) 9m33.3s; 3 Hirvonen/Lehtinen (Ford) 9m35.0s; 4 Duval/Pivato (Ford) 9m35.1s; 5 Atkinson/Prévot (Subaru) 9m38.8s; 6 P.Solberg/Mills (Subaru) 9m39.7s; JC Ogier/Ingrassia (Citroën) 10m38.1s

SS13 Birkenfelder Land (14.22km)
1 Loeb/Elena (Citroën) 7m56.3s; 2 Sordo/Martí (Citroën) 7m56.6s; 3 Hirvonen/Lehtinen (Ford) 7m58.8s; 4 Duval/Pivato (Ford) 8m01.3s; 5 P.Solberg/Mills (Subaru) 8m01.5s; 6 Atkinson/Prévot (Subaru) 8m02.3s; JC A.Burkart/M.Kölbach (Citroën C2 S1600) 8m46.5s

SS14 Arena Panzerplatte (30.38km)
1 Sordo/Martí (Citroën) 17m41.5s; 2 Loeb/Elena (Citroën) 17m44.2s; 3 P.Solberg/Mills (Subaru) 17m49.7s; 4 Latvala/Anttila

(Ford) 17m54.0s; 5 Duval/Pivato (Ford) 17m55.5s; 6 Atkinson/Prévot (Subaru) 18m01.7s; JC Ogier/Ingrassia (Citroën) 19m26.6s

SS15 Dhrontal (22.22km)
1 Duval/Pivato (Ford) 14m23.1s; 2 Sordo/Martí (Citroën) 14m24.9s; 3 Hirvonen/Lehtinen (Ford) 14m25.3s; 4 Loeb/Elena (Citroën) 14m33.8s; 5 P.Solberg/Mills (Subaru) 14m35.4s; 6 Aava/Sikk (Citroën) 14m45.5s; JC Burkart/Kölbach (Citroën) 16m11.2s

SS16 Moselwein (18.08km)
1 Duval/Pivato (Ford) 10m43.9s; 2 Hirvonen/Lehtinen (Ford) 10m45.8s; 3 Loeb/Elena (Citroën) 10m46.9s; 4 Sordo/Martí (Citroën) 10m52.3s; 5 P.Solberg/Mills (Subaru) 10m54.0s; 6 Latvala/Anttila (Ford) 10m58.3s; JC Burkart/Kölbach (Citroën) 12m11.0s

SS17 Dhrontal (22.22km)
1 Duval/Pivato (Ford) 14m15.7s; 2 Hirvonen/Lehtinen (Ford) 14m19.4s; 3 Loeb/Elena (Citroën) 14m22.7s; 4 P.Solberg/Mills (Subaru) 14m25.8s; 5 Sordo/Martí (Citroën) 14m29.1s; 6 Latvala/Anttila (Ford) 14m30.3s; JC Ogier/Ingrassia (Citroën) 15m52.2s

SS18 Moselwein (18.08km)
1 Duval/Pivato (Ford) 10m45.4s; 2 Hirvonen/Lehtinen (Ford) 10m45.7s; 3 P.Solberg/Mills (Subaru) 10m46.1s; 4 Latvala/Anttila (Ford) 10m51.3s; 5 Loeb/Elena (Citroën) 10m51.3s; 6 Aava/Sikk (Citroën) 10m53.4s; JC Ogier/Ingrassia (Citroën) 11m53.0s

SS19 SSS Circus Maximus Trier (4.37km)
1= Loeb/Elena (Citroën), P.Solberg/Mills (Subaru), A.Mikkelsen/O.Fløene (Ford Focus RS WRC 07) 3m22.4s; 4 Aava/Sikk (Citroën) 3m22.5s; 5 Atkinson/Prévot (Subaru) 3m22.7s; 6 Hirvonen/Lehtinen (Ford) 3m22.8s; JC K.Abbring/B.Degandt (Renault Clio Sport R3) 3m37.7s

MAJOR RETIREMENTS
7	Galli/ Bernacchini	Ford Focus RS WRC 07	
	Accident	SS5	A8

FIA CLASS WINNERS
A8	Over 2000cc	Loeb/Elena Citroën C4 WRC
A7	1600-2000cc	Bettega/Scattolin Renault Clio R3
A6	1400-1600 cc	Ogier/Ingrassia Citroën C2 S1600
A5	Upto 1400cc	Hohlheimer/Kippe Fiat Seicento Sporting
N4	Over 2000 cc	Gaßner Jr./Wustenhagen Mitsubishi Lancer Evo IX
N3	1600-2000cc	Baranauskas/Celiesius Ford Fiesta ST
N2	1400-1600cc	Werner/Lembke Opel Corsa

RALLY LEADERS
Overall: SS1-19 Loeb
JWRC: SS1 Ogier; SS2-7 Prokop; SS8-19 Ogier

SPECIAL STAGE ANALYSIS
	1st	2nd	3rd	4th	5th	6th
Loeb (Citroën)	14	1	2	1	1	-
Duval (Ford)	4	2	3	5	1	1
Sordo (Citroën)	1	9	3	2	1	-
P.Solberg (Subaru)	1	-	2	2	5	5
Mikklesen (Ford)	1	-	-	-	-	-
Hirvonen (Ford)	-	5	7	4	-	1
Latvala (Ford)	-	-	-	3	2	3
Aava (Citroën)	-	-	-	1	1	2
Atkinson (Subaru)	-	-	-	-	6	5
Galli (Ford)	-	-	-	-	1	-
H.Solberg (Ford)	-	-	-	-	-	1

TYRES
Tyres: Pirelli Pzero

Compound: hard/soft
Number of tyres available per car: 60

WORLD CHAMPIONSHIP POINTS
Drivers
1 Loeb 76; 2 Hirvonen 72; 3 Sordo 43; 4 Atkinson 40; 5 Latvala 34; 6 P.Solberg 27; 7 H.Solberg 22; 8 Galli 17; 9 Wilson 12; 10 Duval 11 etc

Manufacturers
1 Citroën Total WRT 123; 2 BP Ford Abu Dhabi WRT 115; 3 Subaru WRT 69; 4 Stobart VK M-Sport Ford RT 51; 5 Munchi's Ford WRT 19; 6 Suzuki WRT 13

Junior World Rally Championship
1 Ogier 34; 2 Gallagher 25; 3 Burkart 24; 4 Kosciuszko 22; 5= Sandell, Bettega 14; 7 Prokop 12; 8= Mölder, Schammel 8; 10= Albertini, Bertolotti 7 etc

Production Car World Rally Championship
1 Aigner 30; 2 Hänninen 22; 3 Ketomaa 20; 4= Sandell, Nutahara 14; 6 Aráujo 12; 7 Sousa 10; 8 Rauam 9; 9= Beltrán, Välimäki 8 etc

ROUTE DETAILS
Total Route of 1174.91km of which 352.89km were competitive on 19 stages
Leg 1 Friday 15 August, 6 special stages totalling 108.16km
Leg 2 Saturday 16 August, 8 special stages totalling 159.76km
Leg 3 Sunday 17 August, 5 special stages totalling 84.97km

RESULTS
1	Sebastien Loeb/ Daniel Elena	Citroën C4 WRC 3h26m19.7s A8
2	Dani Sordo/ Marc Martí	Citroën C4 WRC 3h27m07.4s A8
3	François Duval/ Patrick Pivato	Ford Focus RS WRC 07 3h27m39.7s A8
4	Mikko Hirvonen/ Jarmo Lehtinen	Ford Focus RS WRC 08 3h27m49.8s A8
5	Petter Solberg/ Phil Mills	Subaru Impreza WRC2008 3h28m55.0s A8
6	Chris Atkinson/ Stéphane Prévot	Subaru Impreza WRC2008 3h31m05.6s A8
7	Henning Solberg/ Cato Menkerud	Ford Focus RS WRC 07 3h31m55.9s A8
8	Urmo Aava/ Kuldar Sikk	Citroën C4 WRC 3h31m57.5s A8
9	Jari-Matti Latvala/ Miikka Anttila	Ford Focus RS WRC 08 3h32m06.9s A8
10	Toni Gardemeister/ Tomi Tuominen	Suzuki SX4 WRC 3h33m36.5s A8

81 starters, 58 finishers

RECENT WINNERS
1982*	Erwin Weber/Matthias Berg	Opel Ascona 400
1983*	Walter Röhrl/Christian Geistdörfer	Lancia Rally 037
1984*	Hannu Mikkola/Christian Geistdörfer	Audi Sport Quattro
1985*	Kalle Grundel/Peter Diekmann	Peugeot 205T16
1986*	Michèle Mouton/Terry Harryman	Peugeot 205T16
1987*	Jochi Kleint/Manfred Hiemer	VW Golf GTI-16v
1988*	Robert Droogmans/Ronny Joosten	Ford Sierra RS Cosworth
1989*	Patrick Snijers/Dany Colebunders	Toyota Celica GT4
1990*	Robert Droogmans/Ronny Joosten	Lancia Delta Integrale
1991*	Piero Liatti/Luciano Tedeschini	Lancia Delta Integrale 16V
1992*	Erwin Weber/Manfred Hiemer	Mitsubishi Galant VR-4
1993*	Patrick Snijers/Dany Colebunders	Ford Escort RS Cosworth
1994*	Dieter Depping/Peter Thul	Ford Escort RS Cosworth
1995*	Enrico Bertone/Massimo Chiapponi	Toyota Celica Turbo4WD
1996*	Dieter Depping/Fred Berssen	Ford Escort RS Cosworth
1997*	Dieter Depping/Dieter Hawranke	Ford Escort RS Cosworth
1998*	Matthias Kahle/Dieter Schneppenheim	Toyota Corolla WRC
1999*	Armin Kremer/Fred Berßen	Subaru Impreza WRC97
2000*	Henrik Lundgaard/Jens Christian Anker	Toyota Corolla WRC
2001*	Philippe Bugalski/Jean-Paul Chiaroni	Citroën Xsara WRC
2002	Sébastien Loeb/Daniel Elena	Citroën Xsara WRC
2003	Sébastien Loeb/Daniel Elena	Citroën Xsara WRC
2004	Sébastien Loeb/Daniel Elena	Citroën Xsara WRC
2005	Sébastien Loeb/Daniel Elena	Citroën Xsara WRC
2006	Sébastien Loeb/Daniel Elena	Citroën Xsara WRC
2007	Sébastien Loeb/Daniel Elena	Citroën C4 WRC

*Non-championship event

THIS WAS supposed to be Ford's Rally. Not only had Ford drivers Mikko Hirvonen and Jari-Matti Latvala earned it, but Citroën had gifted it to them after Sébastien Loeb dropped time to run behind the two Finns on Sunday, and then dropped more time with a spin on the final day's opening test. Surely this one was in the back of the net. Er, no. The final stage of the event, the utterly spectacular run along Whaanga Coast, was a heartbreaker for the Cumbrian boys. First Latvala smacked a bank and damaged the steering; then Hirvonen clouted his right-rear tyre and punctured it. Ford's one-two was handed back to Citroën's Loeb and Dani Sordo; Hirvonen was a forgettable third.

The heavy rain that had pounded the North Island at least had the decency to stop just before the arrival of the World Rally Championship in Hamilton, but the damage had been done to some of the roads. Organisers were left with some re-routing to do after roads were hit by mudslides. First in the running order, Loeb was furious and mightily relieved in equal measure at the end of Friday's opening test. Concerned about how the stock hard-compound Pirelli would cope with the sodden Kiwi tracks, the Frenchman had come close to binning his C4 as he tried to get it slowed for a right-hander.

"I'm very lucky," he said. "The car was up on two wheels. I thought we were going to roll. We hit some big stones."

Pausing momentarily, more to compute the moment again rather than for dramatic effect, he added: "It's the tyres. The car is undriveable when there is so much gravel like this."

Funnily enough, the Ford drivers didn't exactly agree with that assessment of conditions. Running behind Loeb, Latvala was fastest and led after SS1, with Hirvonen in close attendance. Mikko was then fastest on SS2 to move past his team-mate, and he stayed ahead. If Loeb's day had started badly, it got a lot worse at the end, when his Citroën mysteriously failed to fire up ahead of the final test on Friday. After three minutes (which translates into a 30-second penalty on the road) Loeb figured that he could bump-start the car in reverse by rolling back down the hill.

"Tactics," cried the assembled service park. "Starter motor," replied Citroën. Ford team principal Malcolm Wilson smiled sagely, adding: "Maybe they need a Ford starter motor. The car would have started a bit quicker then..."

Despite the convenient imposition of a 30-second penalty, the Frenchman bounced back from an overnight second to hit the front on the penultimate Saturday stage of the day. But was the gap enough? Would Citroën really use tactics? They certainly did. Loeb had set himself a target time for the final sector of the Te Akau South stage; when he didn't meet it, he slowed and dropped time to ensure he would start Sunday third on the road. For the second time in as many days, Loeb had dropped out of the lead at the end of the leg.

"It's not nice for a driver to do this," said Loeb. "When I finished the stage, I went and said sorry to Mikko. For a driver, this is not what you want to do."

So, Citroën's tacticians had been outed. And now, it was a straightforward fight to the finish. Having dropped behind Latvala by 9.3 seconds, Hirvonen was four up on Loeb with 30 miles to run. Who would blink first?

There weren't many who expected it to be Loeb. But it was – the Citroën spun in Te Hutewai and lost 10 seconds. Hirvonen moved into the lead on the next stage and Ford's one-two looked to be a done deal until the last long stage of the rally, when its world turned upside down. Latvala's departure was a simple mistake and the Swedish Rally winner was inconsolable. Hirvonen clipped a bank not long after spotting his stricken colleague, but denied he'd been rattled. Whatever. The damage was done. The air left his tyre and first became third.

Loeb, Sordo and Citroën couldn't believe it. Having shot themselves in the foot, they'd then seen their rivals go and get an even bigger gun and shoot themselves in both feet. Astonishing. After the closest finish in the WRC's history 12 months earlier in New Zealand – when Marcus Grönholm beat Loeb by just 0.3sec – nobody thought this year's event could rival that for drama. Well, it did.

Dani Sordo took second after profiting from the factory Ford drivers' woes on the penultimate stage
Photograph: Race&motion

Left: Eighth place for Federico Villagra marked the final time the Argentine scored points in 2008.

Above: After dropping out of first place with two stages remaining, Mikko Hirvonen had little reason to celebrate with winning co-driver Daniel Elena.

Top: P-G Andersson made up for his crash in Finland with a fine run to sixth place.

Top left: Hopes of a second-place finish for Jari-Matti Latvala ended when he spun into a bank on the penultimate stage.

Far left: Former Junior championship rivals Andersson and Urmo Aava discuss life in the big league.
Photographs: PHOTO4

Right and bottom right: Petter Solberg finished fourth but his Subaru team couldn't pinpoint why the gap to the leaders was almost three minutes.

Below: Sébastien Loeb was all smiles at the finish, but some of his rivals suspected he had played foul to gain a better road position

Far right: Repco's sponsorship of Rally New Zealand added a touch of 'glamour'.

Photographs: PHOTO4 unless specified

Repco Rally New Zealand Results

28-31 AUGUST 2008 | FIA WORLD RALLY CHAMPIONSHIP ROUND 11

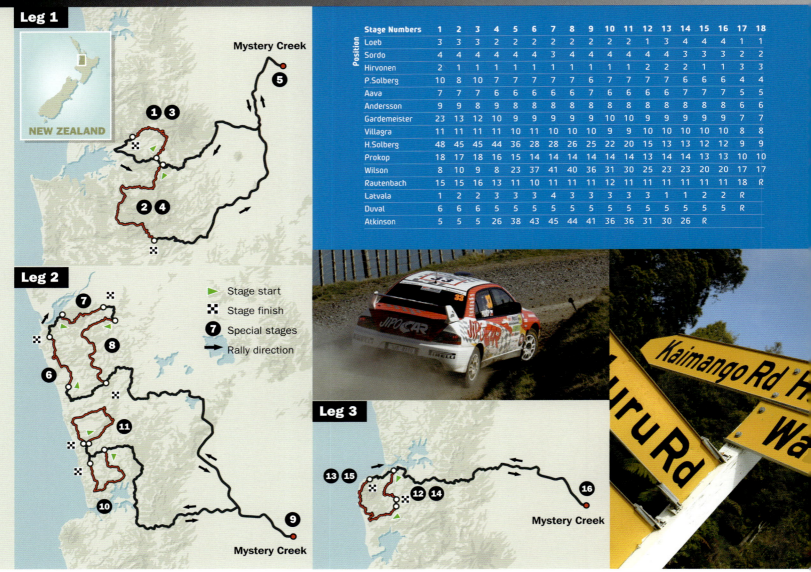

Leg 1

NEW ZEALAND

Mystery Creek ●5

●1 ●3

●2 ●4

Leg 2

●7

●8

●6

●11

●10

●9

Mystery Creek

▶ Stage start
✕ Stage finish
⑦ Special stages
→ Rally direction

Leg 3

●13 ●15

●12 ●14

●16

Mystery Creek

	Stage Numbers	1	2	3	4	5	6	7	8	9	10	11	12	13	14	15	16	17	18
Position	Loeb	3	3	3	2	2	2	2	2	2	2	2	2	1	3	4	4	1	1
	Sordo	4	4	4	4	4	4	3	4	4	4	4	4	3	3	3	2	2
	Hirvonen	2	1	1	1	1	1	1	1	1	1	1	1	2	1	1	3	3
	P.Solberg	10	8	10	7	7	7	7	7	6	7	7	7	6	6	6	4	4
	Aava	7	7	7	6	6	6	6	6	7	6	6	6	7	7	7	5	5
	Andersson	9	9	8	9	8	8	8	8	8	8	8	8	8	8	8	6	6
	Gardemeister	23	13	12	10	9	9	9	9	9	10	10	9	9	9	9	9	7	7
	Villagra	11	11	11	11	10	11	10	10	10	9	9	10	10	10	10	10	8	8
	H.Solberg	48	45	45	44	36	28	28	26	25	22	20	15	13	13	12	12	9	9
	Prokop	18	17	18	16	15	14	14	14	14	14	13	14	14	14	13	13	10	10
	Wilson	8	10	9	8	23	37	41	40	36	31	30	25	23	23	20	20	17	17
	Rautenbach	15	15	16	13	11	10	11	11	11	12	11	11	11	11	11	11	18	R
	Latvala	1	2	2	3	3	3	4	3	3	3	3	3	1	1	2	2	R
	Duval	6	6	6	5	5	5	5	5	5	5	5	5	5	5	5	R
	Atkinson	5	5	5	26	38	43	45	44	41	36	36.7s	36	31	30	26	R

Kaimango Rd
iru Rd
Wa

Above: Martin Prokop claimed his maiden Production championship victory.

Above right: New Zealand's roads are regarded as some of the finest in the world championship
Photographs: PHOTO4

FINISH LINES...

Petter Solberg's Subaru was fourth after another solid drive from the Norwegian. It had, however, been another troubled event for the British team. Solberg's team-mate Chris Atkinson had retired on the opening day with an engine fault in SS3, while the 2003 world champion was left hoping a switch to Finland-spec dampers would find him the speed to pass Urmo Aava's private Citroën. Solberg did just that to move into fifth. That result improved by one more position when François Duval added to Ford's woes by retiring his Stobart car against a tree on... yes, you've guessed it, the second run through Whaanga Coast... Suzuki celebrated its best result in the WRC to date, with P-G Andersson leading home the sister SX4 WRC of Toni Gardemeister in sixth place... Munchi's Ford driver Federico Villagra rounded out the points positions in eighth... Rally New Zealand had been billed as a crucial event in the outcome of the Production Car World Rally Championship. Both title protagonists Juho Hänninen and Andreas Aigner were present in Hamilton – and both went off the road on the opening stage. Aigner's Mitsubishi would not return, while Hänninen battled back from the double puncture his excursion cost him to end the rally fifth in the P-WRC standings... Fellow Mitsubishi man Martin Prokop registered the first P-WRC success of his career, following an accident involving early leader Mirco Baldacci... Patrik Sandell enjoyed his first taste of a turbocharged rally car, the Swede electing to hire a Lancer locally rather than ship his Peugeot 207

S2000 over from Europe. Sandell soon got to grips with the car, placing it second in class by Sunday afternoon.

RUNNING ORDER

1	Sébastien Loeb/ Daniel Elena	Citroën C4 WRC A8
3	Mikko Hirvonen/ Jarmo Lehtinen	Ford Focus RS WRC 08 A8
2	Dani Sordo/ Marc Martí	Citroën C4 WRC A8
6	Chris Atkinson/ Stéphane Prévot	Subaru Impreza WRC2008 A8
4	Jari-Matti Latvala/ Miikka Anttila	Ford Focus RS WRC 08 A8
5	Petter Solberg/ Phil Mills	Subaru Impreza WRC2008 A8
10	Henning Solberg/ Cato Menkerud	Ford Focus RS WRC 07 A8
8	Matthew Wilson/ Scott Martin	Ford Focus RS WRC 07 A8
7	François Duval/ Patrick Pivato	Ford Focus RS WRC 07 A8
9	Federico Villagra/ Jorge Pérez Companc	Ford Focus RS WRC 07 A8
14	Urmo Aava/ Kuldar Sikk	Citroën C4 WRC A8
15	Conrad Rautenbach/ David Senior	Citroën C4 WRC A8
11	Toni Gardemeister/ Tomi Tuominen	Suzuki SX4 WRC A8
12	P-G Andersson/ Jonas Andersson	Suzuki SX4 WRC A8

41	Andreas Aigner/ Klaus Wicha	Mitsubishi Lancer Evo IX N4
52	Juho Hänninen/ Mikko Markkula	Mitsubishi Lancer Evo IX N4
46	Jari Ketomaa/ Miika Teiskonen	Subaru Impreza N4
55	Patrik Sandell/ Emil Axelsson	Mitsubishi Lancer Evo IX N4
31	Toshi Arai/ Glenn Macneall	Subaru Impreza N4
56	Fumio Nutahara/ Daniel Barritt	Mitsubishi Lancer Evo IX N4

SPECIAL STAGE TIMES

SS1 (SS1) Pirongia West 1 (24.22km)

1. J-M Latvala/M.Anttila (Ford Focus RS WRC 08) 17m08.1s; 2 M.Hirvonen/J.Lehtinen (Ford Focus RS WRC 08) 17m09.3s; 3 S.Loeb/D.Elena (Citroën C4 WRC) 17m13.2s; 4 D.Sordo/M.Martí (Citroën C4 WRC) 17m16.7s; 5 C.Atkinson/S.Prévot (Subaru Impreza WRC2008) 17m26.4s; 6 F.Duval/P.Pivato (Ford Focus RS WRC 07) 17m31.6s; PC F.Nutahara/D.Barritt (Mitsubishi Lancer Evo IX) 18m12.9s

SS2 (SS2.1) Waitomo 1 part 1 (25.85km)

1 Hirvonen/Lehtinen (Ford) 15m12.5s; 2 Sordo/Martí (Citroën) 15m12.6s; 3 Loeb/Elena (Citroën) 15m13.9s; 4. Latvala/Anttila (Ford) 15m18.7s; 5 Atkinson/Prévot (Subaru) 15m18.9s; 6 Duval/Pivato (Ford) 15m28.0s; PC M.Baldacci/G.Agnese (Mitsubishi Lancer Evo IX) 16m01.3s

SS3 (SS2.2) Waitomo 1 part 2 (17.36km)

1 Hirvonen/Lehtinen (Ford) 14m13.5s; 2 Latvala/Anttila (Ford)

14m13.8s; 3 Sordo/Martí (Citroën) 14m17.0s; 4 Loeb/Elena (Citroën) 14m17.6s; 5 P-G.Andersson/J.Andersson (Suzuki SX4 WRC) 14m17.7s; 6 U.Aava/K.Sikk (Citroën C4 WRC) 14m20.4s; PC E.Novikov/D.Moscatt (Mitsubishi Lancer Evo IX) 14m36.8s

SS4 (SS3) Pirongia West 2 (24.22 km)
1 Loeb/Elena (Citroën) 16m35.8s; 2 Hirvonen/Lehtinen (Ford) 16m37.6s; 3 Latvala/Anttila (Ford) 16m41.4s; 4 Sordo/Martí (Citroën) 16m45.2s; 5 Duval/Pivato (Ford) 16m50.3s; 6 P.Solberg/P.Mills (Subaru Impreza WRC2008) 17m04.0s; PC J.Hänninen/M.Markkula (Mitsubishi Lancer Evo IX) 17m42.0s

SS5 (SS4.1) Waitomo 2 part 1 (25.85km)
1 Loeb/Elena (Citroën) 14m39.6s; 2 Hirvonen/Lehtinen (Ford) 14m46.5s; 3 Sordo/Martí (Citroën) 14m51.8s; 4 Latvala/Anttila (Ford) 14m52.7s; 5 Duval/Pivato (Ford) 14m57.6s; 6 P.Solberg/Mills (Subaru) 15m03.2s; PC Hänninen/Markkula (Mitsubishi) 15m40.2s

SS6 (SS4.2) Waitomo 2 part 2 (17.36km)
1 Loeb/Elena (Citroën) 13m37.8s; 2 Hirvonen/Lehtinen (Ford) 13m41.1s; 3 Sordo/Martí (Citroën) 13m47.0s; 4 Aava/Sikk (Citroën) 13m52.2s; 5 Duval/Pivato (Ford) 13m54.5s; 6 Latvala/Anttila (Ford) 13m55.2s; PC Hänninen/Markkula (Mitsubishi) 14m06.8s

SS7 (SS5) Mystery Creek 1 (3.14 km)
1 Hirvonen/Lehtinen (Ford) 3m03.8s; 2 Sordo/Martí (Citroën) 3m04.0s; 3 Loeb/Elena (Citroën) 3m04.2s; 4 Latvala/Anttila (Ford) 3m04.5s; 5 Andersson/Andersson (Suzuki) 3m05.2s; 6 Aava/Sikk (Citroën) 3m05.9s; PC Hänninen/Markkula (Mitsubishi) 3m08.1s

SS8 (SS6) Port Waikato (17.22 km)
1 H.Solberg/C.Menkerud (Ford Focus RS WRC 07) 10m02.2s; 2 Loeb/Elena (Citroën) 10m06.6s; 3 Latvala/Anttila (Ford) 10m06.7s; 4 Sordo/Martí (Citroën) 10m07.3s; 5 M.Wilson/S.Martin (Ford Focus RS WRC 07) 10m09.0s; 6 P.Solberg/Mills (Subaru) 10m09.2s; PC Hänninen/Markkula (Mitsubishi) 10m38.8s

SS9 (SS7) Possum (13.78 km)
1 Loeb/Elena (Citroën) 10m39.2s; 2 Hirvonen/Lehtinen (Ford) 10m42.3s; 3 Latvala/Anttila (Ford) 10m44.8s; 4 H.Solberg/Menkerud (Ford) 10m45.6s; 5 Sordo/Martí (Citroën) 10m48.0s; 6 Wilson/Martin (Ford) 10m51.5s; PC Hänninen/Markkula (Mitsubishi) 11m06.7s

SS10 (SS8) Franklin (31.58 km)
1 Latvala/Anttila (Ford) 22m02.7s; 2 Loeb/Elena (Citroën) 22m03.5s; 3 Sordo/Martí (Citroën) 22m10.8s; 4 Aava/Sikk (Citroën) 22m13.1s; 5 Wilson/Martin (Ford) 22m13.4s; 6 H.Solberg/Menkerud (Ford) 22m13.8s; PC M.Prokop/J.Tománek (Mitsubishi Lancer Evo IX) 22m53.1s

SS11 (SS9) Mystery Creek 2 (3.14 km)
1 H.Solberg/Menkerud (Ford) 2m58.0s; 2 Loeb/Elena (Citroën) 2m59.7s; 3 Hirvonen/Lehtinen (Ford) 3m01.2s; 4 Duval/Pivato (Ford) 3m01.6s; 5 Sordo/Martí (Citroën) 3m01.9s; 6= Latvala/Anttila (Ford), P.Solberg/Mills (Subaru) 3m02.0s; PC Hänninen/Markkula (Mitsubishi) 3m06.4s

SS12 (SS10) Te Akau South (31.92 km)
1 H.Solberg/Menkerud (Ford) 18m37.0s; 2 Sordo/Martí (Citroën) 18m43.5s; 3 Loeb/Elena (Citroën) 18m45.0s; 4 Latvala/Anttila (Ford) 18m45.3s; 5 Atkinson/Prévot (Subaru) 18m46.9s; 6 Duval/Pivato (Ford) 18m51.3s; PC Hänninen/Markkula (Mitsubishi) 19m31.1s

SS13 (SS11) Te Akau North (32.36 km)
1 H.Solberg/Menkerud (Ford) 17m29.7s; 2 Latvala/Anttila (Ford) 17m33.1s; 3 Atkinson/Prévot (Subaru) 17m35.0s; 4 P.Solberg/Mills (Subaru) 17m36.9s; 5 Sordo/Martí (Citroën) 17m38.9s; 6 Duval/Pivato (Ford) 17m40.8s; PC Hänninen/Markkula (Mitsubishi) 18m29.0s

SS14 (SS12) Te Hutewai 1 (11.23km)
1 H.Solberg/Menkerud (Ford) 8m03.0s; 2 Wilson/Martin (Ford) 8m04.8s; 3 Atkinson/Prévot (Subaru) 8m04.8s; 4 P.Solberg/Mills (Subaru) 8m09.3s; 5 Hirvonen/Lehtinen (Ford) 8m09.4s; 6 Sordo/Martí (Citroën) 8m10.0s; PC Hänninen/Markkula

(Mitsubishi) 8m20.4s

SS15 (SS13) Whaanga Coast 1 (29.72km)
1 H.Solberg/Menkerud (Ford) 21m26.4s; 2 Hirvonen/Lehtinen (Ford) 21m35.0s; 3 P.Solberg/Mills (Subaru) 21m36.9s; 4 Sordo/Martí (Citroën) 21m36.9s; 5 Loeb/Elena (Citroën) 21m38.1s; 6 Wilson/Martin (Ford) 21m42.7s; PC Hänninen/Markkula (Mitsubishi) 22m12.1s

SS16 (SS14) Te Hutewai 2 (11.23km)
1 Loeb/Elena (Citroën) 7m47.5s; 2 Hirvonen/Lehtinen (Ford) 7m49.8s; 3 H.Solberg/Menkerud (Ford) 7m50.9s; 4 Latvala/Anttila (Ford) 7m52.5s; 5 Wilson/Martin (Ford) 7m52.9s; 6 P.Solberg/Mills (Subaru) 7m53.3s; PC Hänninen/Markkula (Mitsubishi) 8m15.9s

SS17 (SS15) Whaanga Coast 2 (29.72km)
1 Loeb/Elena (Citroën) 20m47.0s; 2 H.Solberg/Menkerud (Ford) 21m01.7s; 3 P.Solberg/Mills (Subaru) 21m03.5s; 4 Sordo/Martí (Citroën) 21m05.7s; 5 Aava/Sikk (Citroën) 21m11.2s; 6 Wilson/Martin (Ford) 21m18.9s; PC Hänninen/Markkula (Mitsubishi) 22m19.3s

SS18 (SS16) Mystery Creek 3 (3.14km)
1 H.Solberg/Menkerud (Ford) 3m00.6s; 2 P.Solberg/Mills (Subaru) 3m03.3s; 3 Hirvonen/Lehtinen (Ford) 3m03.8s; 4 Wilson/Martin (Ford) 3m04.0s; 5 Loeb/Elena (Citroën) 3m04.1s; 6 F.Villagra/J.P.Companc (Ford Focus RS WRC 07) 3m05.0s; PC A.Aráujo/M.Ramalho (Mitsubishi Lancer Evo IX) 3m10.0s

Cars that retired and subsequently restarted under SuperRally regs:
6   Atkinson/Prévot   Subaru Impreza WRC2008
     Off road   SS4   A8

Cars that retired and subsequently restarted and were classified under SuperRally regs:
8   Wilson/Martin   Ford Focus RS WRC 07
     Gearbox   SS5   A8

MAJOR RETIREMENTS
6   Atkinson/Prévot   Subaru Impreza WRC2008
     Mechanical   SS15   A8
4   Latvala/Anttila   Ford Focus RS WRC 08
     Accident   SS17   A8
7   Duval/Pivato   Ford Focus RS WRC 07
     Off road   SS17   A8
15   Rautenbach/Senior   Citroën C4 WRC
     Mechanical   SS18   A8

FIA CLASS WINNERS
A8   Over 2000 cc   Loeb/Elena
                             Citroën C4 WRC
N4   Over 2000 cc   Prokop/Tománek
                             Mitsubishi Lancer Evo IX
N3   1600-2000cc   Reeves/Smyth
                             Ford Fiesta ST

RALLY LEADERS
Overall: SS1 Latvala; SS2-11 Hirvonen; SS12 Loeb; SS13-14 Latvala; SS15-16 Hirvonen; SS17-18 Loeb
PC: SS1 Nutahara; SS2-11 Baldacci; SS12-18 Prokop

SPECIAL STAGE ANALYSIS

	1st	2nd	3rd	4th	5th	6th
H.Solberg (Ford)	7	1	1	1	-	1
Loeb (Citroën)	6	3	4	1	2	1
Hirvonen (Ford)	3	7	2	-	1	-
Latvala (Ford)	2	2	3	5	-	2
Sordo (Citroën)	-	3	4	5	3	-
P.Solberg (Subaru)	-	1	2	2	-	5
Wilson (Ford)	-	1	-	1	3	3
Atkinson (Subaru)	-	-	2	-	3	-
Aava (Citroën)	-	-	-	2	1	2
Duval (Ford)	-	-	-	1	3	4
Andersson (Suzuki)	-	-	-	-	2	-
Villagra (Ford)	-	-	-	-	-	1

TYRES
Tyres: Pirelli Scorpion
Compound: soft
Number of tyres available per car: 42

WORLD CHAMPIONSHIP POINTS
Drivers
1 Loeb 86; 2 Hirvonen 78; 3 Sordo 51; 4 Atkinson 40; 5 Latvala 34; 6 P.Solberg 32; 7 H.Solberg 22; 8 Galli 17; 9 Wilson 12; 10= Duval, Aava 11 etc
Manufacturers
1 Citroën Total WRT 141; 2 BP Ford Abu Dhabi WRT 121; 3 Subaru WRT 74; 4 Stobart VK M-Sport Ford RT 51; 5 Munchi's Ford WRT 22; 6 Suzuki WRT 20
Junior World Rally Championship
1 Ogier 34; 2 Gallagher 25; 3 Burkart 24; 4 Kosciuszko 22; 5= Sandell, Bettega 14; 7 Prokop 12; 8= Mölder, Schammel 8; 10= Albertini, Bertolotti 7 etc
Production Car World Rally Championship
1 Aigner 30; 2 Hänninen 26; 3 Ketomaa 23; 4 Sandell 22; 5 Prokop 17; 6 Rauam 15; 7 Nutahara 14; 8= Aráujo, Sousa 12; 10= Beltrán, Välimäki 8 etc

ROUTE DETAILS
Total route of 1218.20km of which 353.04km were competitive on 18 stages
Leg 1 Friday 29 August, 7 special stages totalling 138.00km
Leg 2 Saturday 30 August, 6 special stages totalling 130.00km
Leg 3 Sunday 31 August, 5 special stages totalling 85.04km

RESULTS
1	Sébastien Loeb/	Citroën C4 WRC
	Daniel Elena	3h58m48.9s A8
2	Dani Sordo/	Citroën C4 WRC
	Marc Martí	3h59m36.4s A8
3	Mikko Hirvonen/	Ford Focus RS WRC 08
	Jarmo Lehtinen	4h00m00.4s A8
4	Petter Solberg/	Subaru Impreza WRC2008
	Phil Mills	4h02m07.8s A8
5	Urmo Aava/	Citroën C4 WRC
	Kuldar Sikk	4h02m49.6s A8
6	P-G Andersson/	Suzuki SX4 WRC
	Jonas Andersson	4h06m56.3s A8
7	Toni Gardemeister/	Suzuki SX4 WRC
	Tomi Tuominen	4h07m13.8s A8
8	Federico Villagra/	Ford Focus RS WRC 07
	Jorge Pérez Companc	4h07m53.9s A8
9	Henning Solberg/	Ford Focus RS WRC 07
	Cato Menkerud	4h07m34.1s A8
10	Martin Prokop/	Mitsubishi Lancer Evo IX
	Jan Tománek	4h13m07.9s N4

57 starters, 35 finishers

PREVIOUS WINNERS

*Non-championship event

Main and Inset: François Duval replaced Jari-Matti Latvala in the factory Ford squad but was forced to cede third place to team-mate and title aspirant Mikko Hirvonen on the final morning.
Photographs: PHOTO4

DANI SORDO considered the question, grinned and then started to laugh. He shook his head, smiled and departed. He hadn't said a word. He didn't need to. In all honesty, the rest of the world already knew that he couldn't beat his team-mate Sébastien Loeb, not even if they were in the Spaniard's back yard. And, even if Sordo's number two Citroën had threatened the sister machine of Loeb, team principal Olivier Quesnel had made it quite clear that such a situation would only be a temporary one. In Quesnel's eyes, there would only be one rally winner in Catalunya.

Loeb needed no such stage management. He went out and drove faster than everybody else, and by some considerable margin. This was an ultra-dominant event for the C4 WRC. Fastest and second fastest on every one of the Friday stages, the Loeb-Sordo-C4 combo had Ford men Mikko Hirvonen and François Duval well and truly stumped by lunchtime on leg one.

On the eve of the event the Ford camp had been buzzing with confidence. Don't forget, we were told, Marcus Grönholm led this event last year. And, on top of that, there was definitely more performance coming from the Focus RS WRC 08 now. No, this one wouldn't be a whitewash. No way.

No, it was a 'redwash', from the first stage to the last. Hirvonen had talked of trying to contain Loeb's lead to 10 seconds through the opening day. He lost virtually all of that in the first stage. By midday, he was 25 seconds down, and by the end of the day he was in excess of 40 seconds off the top. With Sordo safe in second, Hirvonen wasn't even third – Duval, who had returned to the BP team at Jari-Matti Latvala's expense in an effort to put his asphalt expertise to good use, held that place. Mikko was fourth, and a deeply disgruntled fourth at that.

Duval and Hirvonen traded places on the final day, but not even the extra point for the Finn came as much consolation in view of Citroën's dominance.

At the head of the field, Loeb's mood was understandably brighter. He could now win the title – although it remained an outside bet – on his home round of the WRC in Corsica a week later. Loeb never has been the best at describing what he's just done in a rally car, so he was more than happy for Quesnel to step in and do it for him.

"He's just incredible," said the team boss. "You know, he can do just what he wants and nobody can stop him."

And that included Sordo, who finished a comfortable second. Dani's only consolation was that, unlike his opposite number at Ford, he hadn't had to relinquish a position in the way Duval had. The Belgian understood the game, however.

"It makes sense, eh..." was all Duval offered.

Petter Solberg guided his Subaru home in fifth, albeit two minutes off the back of Duval's Focus. The Norwegian had been embroiled in a scrap with Urmo Aava, but when the Citroën driver bounced his C4 off a barrier in the penultimate stage, the position went to Solberg. The suspension damage incurred by Aava left him trailing another close fight between Latvala's Stobart Ford and the second Subaru of Chris Atkinson. After struggling to find any form through the first two days, Latvala got himself into gear on the Sunday and beat Atkinson to sixth by just 1.1 seconds. Norwegian privateer Andreas Mikkelsen collected the final point in his RAMSport-run Ford.

Above: Second and third-place co drivers Marc Martí (foreground) and Jarmo Lehtinen celebrate.

Left: Citroën team boss Olivier Quesnel was delighted with Dani Sordo's second place – crucial to its manufacturers' title bid.

Bottom left: Sordo was on home soil but could only manage one fastest stage time as team-mate Sébastien Loeb dominated.

Middle Left: Lacking a pre-event test on asphalt, Petter Solberg had to make do with fifth place.

Far left: Andreas Mikkelsen impressed with eighth place in his privateer Focus.
Photographs: PHOTO4

Leg 1 — Port Aventura / Mediterranean Sea

Position	1	2	3	4	5	6	7	8	9	10	11	12	13	14	15	16	17	18
Loeb	1	1	1	1	1	1	1	1	1	1	1	1	1	1	1	1	1	1
Sordo	2	2	2	2	2	2	2	2	2	2	2	2	2	2	2	2	2	2
Hirvonen	4	3	4	4	3	4	4	4	4	4	4	4	4	4	4	4	3	3
Duval	3	4	3	3	3	3	3	3	3	3	3	3	3	3	3	3	4	4
P.Solberg	8	7	5	5	5	5	5	5	5	5	5	5	5	5	5	6	5	5
Latvala	7	8	8	8	7	7	8	8	8	8	8	8	8	8	8	7	6	6
Atkinson	9	9	9	9	9	9	7	7	7	7	7	7	7	7	7	7	8	7
Mikkelsen	5	5	7	7	8	9	9	9	9	9	9	9	9	9	9	9	9	8
Wilson	15	11	11	11	10	10	10	10	10	10	10	10	10	10	10	10	9	9
Tirabassi	14	12	13	12	12	12	12	11	12	12	12	12	11	11	11	11	10	10
H.Solberg	12	15	15	14	14	13	14	14	14	13	13	13	12	12	12	12	11	11
Villagra	13	16	14	15	14	13	13	13	13	14	14	14	13	13	13	13	12	12
Gardemeister	11	10	10	10	18	17	15	15	15	15	15	15	14	14	14	14	13	13
Østberg	22	21	19	18	17	16	16	16	16	16	15	15	15	15	15	14	14	14
Boland	23	22	21	21	21	20	19	19	20	20	20	19	17	17	17	17	15	15
Jones	20	20	20	20	20	18	28	28	26	26	25	23	22	22	22	20	18	18
Al-Qassimi	16	14	16	16	15	42	38	38	35	29	28	26	24	24	24	23	21	21
Andersson	10	56	62	62	65	61	56	56	56	48	48	43	40	37	37	37	32	32
Aava	6	6	6	6	6	6	6	6	6	6	6	6	6	6	6	5	35	R
Van Merksteijn	19	17	17	17	16	15	17	17	17	17	17	17	16	16	16	16	R	
Rautenbach	17	13	12	13	11	11	11	11	12	11	11	11	11	R				
Van Merksteijn Jr	18	18	44	57	60	59	R											

Leg 2 — Port Aventura / Mediterranean Sea

Leg 3 — Port Aventura

- ▶ Stage start
- Stage finish
- 7 Special stages
- → Rally direction

SPAIN

Top: Thousands of fans flocked to the stages to cheer on local hero Sordo.

Above right: The event marked Brice Tirabassi's debut for Subaru. He finished 10th.
Photographs: PHOTO4

FINISH LINES...

Stobart driver Matthew Wilson scored another top 10 finish with ninth place, while Subaru new boy Brice Tirabassi was 10th in the Impreza WRC2008. This was the first time the Banbury-based team had run three of its new-shape Imprezas and, it's fair to say, the former Junior World Rally Champion wasn't overly impressed. Not the best of English-speakers, at service after service Tirabassi got out of the car, crossed his arms on an imaginary steering wheel and widened his eyes. Understeer was the prolonged problem for him... The partnership between Subaru and Prodrive came under intense scrutiny on this event but Matsatsugu Nagato, executive VP of Fuji Heavy Industries (Subaru's parent company), made a rare visit to a rally to support the partnership... Citroën revealed its potential plans for the future with the C4 WRC Hymotion4 – the world's first dual-fuel World Rally Car... Not everything went Citroën's way in Catalunya: this should have been the event where Sébastien Ogier claimed his first Junior World Rally Championship title. All was going to plan until the Frenchman clouted a bank on Saturday afternoon. Retirement beckoned and the Junior title would have to wait another week... Martin Prokop took full advantage of his fellow Citroën C2 Super 1600 driver's slip-up to steam in and claim his first JWRC success of the season.

RUNNING ORDER

1	Sébastien Loeb/	Citroën C4 WRC
	Daniel Elena	A8
3	Mikko Hirvonen/	Ford Focus RS WRC 08
	Jarmo Lehtinen	A8
2	Dani Sordo/	Citroën C4 WRC
	Marc Martí	A8
6	Chris Atkinson/	Subaru Impreza WRC2008
	Stéphane Prévot	A8
8	Jari-Matti Latvala/	Ford Focus RS WRC 07
	Miikka Anttila	A8
5	Petter Solberg/	Subaru Impreza WRC2008
	Phil Mills	A8
10	Henning Solberg/	Ford Focus RS WRC 07
	Cato Menkerud	A8
7	Matthew Wilson/	Ford Focus RS WRC 07
	Scott Martin	A8
4	François Duval/	Ford Focus RS WRC 08
	Patrick Pivato	A8
16	Urmo Aava/	Citroen C4 WRC
	Kuldar Sikk	A8
9	Federico Villagra/	Ford Focus RS WRC 07
	Jorge Pérez Companc	A8
17	Conrad Rautenbach/	Citroën C4 WRC
	David Senior	A8
11	Toni Gardemeister/	Suzuki SX4 WRC
	Tomi Tuominen	A8
18	Andreas Mikkelsen/	Ford Focus RS WRC 07
	Ola Fløene	A8
12	P-G Andersson/	Suzuki SX4 WRC
	Jonas Andersson	A8
19	Mads Østberg/	Subaru Impreza WRC2007
	Ole Kristian Unnerud	A8
14	Khalid Al-Qassimi/	Ford Focus RS WRC 07
	Michael Orr	A8
15	Brice Tirabassi/	Subaru Impreza WRC2008
	Fabrice Gordon	A8
21	Eamonn Boland/	Subaru Impreza WRC2007
	MJ Morrissey	A8
22	Peter van Merksteijn Jr/	Ford Focus RS WRC 06
	Eddy Chevaillier	A8
23	Gareth Jones/	Subaru Impreza WRC2007
	Clive Jenkins	A8
24	Peter van Merksteijn/	Ford Focus RS WRC 07
	Erwin Berkhof	A8

SPECIAL STAGE TIMES

SS1 La Mussara 1 (20.48km)

1 S.Loeb/D.Elena (Citroën C4 WRC) 11m17.3s; 2 D.Sordo/M.Martí (Citroën C4 WRC) 11m18.8s; 3 F.Duval/P.Pivato (Ford Focus RS WRC 08) 11m24.3s; 4 M.Hirvonen/J.Lehtinen (Ford Focus RS WRC 08) 11m24.5s; 5 A.Mikkelsen/O.Fløene (Ford Focus RS WRC 07) 11m30.9s; 6 U.Aava/K.Sikk (Citroën C4 WRC) 11m34.9s; JC S.Ogier/J.Ingrassia (Citroën C2 S1600) 12m13.7s

SS2 Querol 1 (21.26km)

1 Loeb/Elena (Citroën) 11m13.2s; 2 Sordo/Martí (Citroën) 11m19.1s; 3 Hirvonen/Lehtinen (Ford) 11m20.4s; 4 Duval/Pivato (Ford) 11m22.4s; 5 P.Solberg/P.Mills (Subaru Impreza WRC2008) 11m31.2s; 6 Aava/Sikk (Citroën) 11m36.6s; JC Ogier/Ingrassia (Citroën) 12m18.9s

SS3 El Montmell 1 (24.14km)

1 Loeb/Elena (Citroën) 12m39.0s; 2 Sordo/Martí (Citroën) 12m39.1s; 3 Duval/Pivato (Ford) 12m46.4s; 4 Hirvonen/Lehtinen (Ford) 12m50.4s; 5 P.Solberg/Mills (Subaru) 12m53.8s; 6 Aava/Sikk (Citroën) 13m00.1s; JC Ogier/Ingrassia (Citroën) 13m48.4s

SS4 La Mussara 2 (20.48km)

1 Loeb/Elena (Citroën) 12m39.0s; 2 Sordo/Martí (Citroën) 12m39.1s; 3 Hirvonen/Lehtinen (Ford) 12m50.4s; 4 Duval/Pivato (Ford) 12m46.4s; 5 C.Atkinson/S.Prévot (Subaru Impreza WRC2008) 11m25.1s; 6 J-M Latvala/M.Anttila (Ford Focus RS WRC 08) 11m29.2s; JC Ogier/Ingrassia (Citroën) 12m09.1s

SS5 Querol 2 (21.26km)

1 Loeb/Elena (Citroën) 11m15.0s; 2 Sordo/Martí (Citroën) 11m18.5s; 3 Hirvonen/Lehtinen (Ford) 11m20.5s; 4 Duval/Pivato (Ford) 11m21.7s; 5 Atkinson/Prévot (Subaru) 11m30.3s; 6 P.Solberg/Mills (Subaru) 11m31.4s; JC M.Prokop/J.Tománek (Citroën C2 S1600) 12m15.6s

SS6 El Montmell 2 (24.14km)

1 Loeb/Elena (Citroën) 12m33.0s; 2 Sordo/Martí (Citroën) 12m36.5s; 3 Duval/Pivato (Ford) 12m39.7s; 4 Hirvonen/Lehtinen (Ford) 12m42.5s; 5 Atkinson/Prévot (Subaru) 12m50.7s; 6 P.Solberg/Mills (Subaru) 12m51.7s; JC Ogier/Ingrassia (Citroën) 13m42.1s

SS7 El Priorat / La Ribera d'Ebre 1 (38.27km)

1 Loeb/Elena (Citroën) 21m30.9s; 2 Duval/Pivato (Ford) 21m32.3s; 3 Sordo/Martí (Citroën) 21m33.3s; 4 Hirvonen/Lehtinen (Ford) 21m37.4s; 5 Atkinson/Prévot (Subaru) 21m52.3s; 6 P.Solberg/Mills (Subaru) 21m55.7s; JC Ogier/Ingrassia (Citroën) 23m06.0s

SS8 Les Garrigues 1 (8.60km)

1 Loeb/Elena (Citroën) 5m02.7s; 2 Sordo/Martí (Citroën) 5m05.3s; 3 Duval/Pivato (Ford) 5m06.2s; 4 Hirvonen/Lehtinen (Ford) 5m07.8s; 5 Aava/Sikk (Citroën) 5m08.8s; 6 Atkinson/Prévot (Subaru) 5m09.1s; JC Ogier/Ingrassia (Citroën) 5m32.0s

SS9 La Llena 1 (17.12km)

1 Loeb/Elena (Citroën) 9m35.6s; 2 Sordo/Martí (Citroën) 9m38.5s; 3 Duval/Pivato (Ford) 9m39.8s; 4 Hirvonen/Lehtinen (Ford) 9m41.5s; 5 Aava/Sikk (Citroën) 9m47.3s; 6 P.Solberg/Mills (Subaru) 9m50.3s; JC Ogier/Ingrassia (Citroën) 10m38.3s

SS10 El Priorat / La Ribera d'Ebre 2 (38.27km)

1 Hirvonen/Lehtinen (Ford) 21m39.3s; 2 Loeb/Elena (Citroën) 21m39.5s; 3 Sordo/Martí (Citroën) 21m40.8s; 4 Duval/Pivato (Ford) 21m42.2s; 5 Atkinson/Prévot (Subaru) 21m54.2s; 6 P.Solberg/Mills (Subaru) 21m55.4s; JC Prokop/Tománek (Citroën) 23m07.6s

SS11 Les Garrigues 2 (8.60km)

1 Loeb/Elena (Citroën) 5m04.8s; 2 Duval/Pivato (Ford) 5m05.7s; 3 Hirvonen/Lehtinen (Ford) 5m05.9s; 4 Sordo/Martí (Citroën) 5m07.4s; 5 Aava/Sikk (Citroën) 5m08.8s; 6 P.Solberg/Mills (Subaru) 5m09.0s; JC Ogier/Ingrassia (Citroën) 5m31.7s

SS12 La Llena 2 (17.12km)

1 Duval/Pivato (Ford) 9m49.6s; 2 Loeb/Elena (Citroën) 9m52.2s; 3 Sordo/Martí (Citroën) 9m52.3s; 4 Hirvonen/Lehtinen (Ford) 9m54.3s; 5 Aava/Sikk (Citroën) 9m56.4s; 6 P.Solberg/Mills (Subaru) 10m04.8s; JC Prokop/Tománek (Citroën) 10m45.6s

SS13 Riudecanyes 1 (16.32km)

1 Duval/Pivato (Ford) 10m32.8s; 2 Sordo/Martí (Citroën) 10m35.1s; 3 Loeb/Elena (Citroën) 10m36.5s; 4= Mikkelsen/Fløene (Ford), Latvala/Anttila (Ford) 10m38.3s; 6 Atkinson/Prévot (Subaru) 10m39.2s; JC A.Burkart/M.Kölbach (Citroën C2 S1600) 11m24.8s

SS14 Santa Marina 1 (26.51km)

1 Loeb/Elena (Citroën) 15m49.1s; 2 Sordo/Martí (Citroën) 15m50.3s; 3 Duval/Pivato (Ford) 15m52.3s; 4 Hirvonen/Lehtinen (Ford) 15m54.1s; 5 P.Solberg/Mills (Subaru) 15m59.5s; 6 Aava/Sikk (Citroën) 16m01.3s; JC Burkart/Koelbach (Citroën) 17m11.7s

SS15 La Serra d'Almos 1 (4.11km)

1 Sordo/Martí (Citroën) 2m37.3s; 2 Hirvonen/Lehtinen (Ford) 2m37.8s; 3 Aava/Sikk (Citroën) 2m38.5s; 4 Loeb/Elena (Citroën) 2m39.2s; 5 Duval/Pivato (Ford) 2m39.6s; 6 Atkinson/Prévot (Subaru) 2m39.9s; JC M.Kosciuszko/M.Szczepaniak (Suzuki Swift S1600) 2m54.8s

SS16 Riudecanyes 2 (16.32km)

1 Hirvonen/Lehtinen (Ford) 10m32.7s; 2 Latvala/Anttila (Ford) 10m34.1s; 3 Sordo/Martí (Citroën) 10m34.9s; 4 Loeb/Elena (Citroën) 10m37.8s; 5 Aava/Sikk (Citroën) 10m38.2s; 6 Mikkelsen/Fløene (Ford) 10m38.4s; JC Burkart/Koelbach (Citroën) 11m21.6s

SS17 Santa Marina 2 (26.51km)

1 Hirvonen/Lehtinen (Ford) 15m53.9s; 2 Loeb/Elena (Citroën) 15m55.7s; 3 P.Solberg/Mills (Subaru) 15m57.0s; 4 Sordo/Martí (Citroën) 15m58.2s; 5 Latvala/Anttila (Ford) 15m59.5s; 6 Atkinson/Prévot (Subaru) 16m02.3s; JC Kosciuszko/Szczepaniak (Suzuki Swift S1600) 17m17.6s

SS18 La Serra d'Almos 2 (4.11km)

1 Hirvonen/Lehtinen (Ford) 2m39.9s; 2 Duval/Pivato (Ford) 2m40.0s; 3 Atkinson/Prévot (Subaru) 2m40.4s; 4 P.Solberg/Mills (Subaru) 2m41.2s; 5 Sordo/Martí (Citroën) 2m41.6s; 6 Loeb/Elena (Citroën) 2m41.9s; JC J.Mölder/F.Miclotte (Suzuki Swift S1600) 2m54.0s

Cars that retired and subsequently restarted and were classified under SupeRally regs:

12	Andersson/Andersson	Suzuki SX4 WRC		
	Off road	SS2	A8
14	Al-Qassimi/Orr	Ford Focus RS WRC 07	
	Mechancal	SS6	A8

MAJOR RETIREMENTS

22	Van Merksteijn Jr/Chevaillier	Ford Focus RS WRC 06	
	Off road	SS7	A8
17	Rautenbach/Senior	Citroën C4 WRC	
	Mechanical	SS13	A8
24	Van Merksteijn/Berkhof	Ford Focus RS WRC 07	
	Mechanical	SS17	A8
16	Aava/Sikk	Citroën C4 WRC	
	Mechanical	SS18A	A8

FIA CLASS WINNERS

A8	Over 2000cc	Loeb/Elena
		Citroën C4 WRC
A7	1600-2000cc	Bettega/Scattolin
		Renault Clio R3
A6	1400-1600cc	Prokop/Tománek
		Citroën C2 S1600
N4	Over 2000cc	Van den Heuvel/Kolman
		Mitsubishi Lancer Evo IX
N3	1600-2000cc	Gibert/Codina
		Renault Clio RS

RALLY LEADERS

Overall: SS1-18 Loeb
JWRC: SS1-11 Ogier; SS12-18 Prokop

SPECIAL STAGE ANALYSIS

	1st	2nd	3rd	4th	5th	6th
Loeb (Citroën)	11	3	1	2	-	1
Hirvonen (Ford)	4	1	4	8	-	-
Duval (Ford)	2	3	6	4	1	-
Sordo (Citroën)	1	10	4	2	1	-
Latvala (Ford)	-	1	-	1	1	1
P.Solberg (Subaru)	-	-	1	1	3	7
Aava (Citroën)	-	-	1	-	5	4
Atkinson (Subaru)	-	-	1	-	5	4
Mikkelsen (Ford)	-	-	-	1	1	1

TYRES

Tyres: Pirelli Pzero
Compound: hard/soft
Number of tyres available per car: 54

WORLD CHAMPIONSHIP POINTS

Drivers

1 Loeb 96; 2 Hirvonen 84; 3 Sordo 59; 4 Atkinson 42; 5 Latvala 37; 6 P.Solberg 36; 7 H.Solberg 22; 8 Galli 17; 9 Duval 16; 10 Wilson 12 etc

Manufacturers

1 Citroën Total WRT 159; 2 BP Ford Abu Dhabi WRT 132; 3 Subaru WRT 80; 4 Stobart VK M-Sport Ford RT 55; 5 Munchi's Ford WRT 22; 6 Suzuki WRT 20

Junior World Rally Championship

1 Ogier 34; 2= Burkart, Gallagher 30; 4= Kosciuszko, Prokop, Bettega 22; 7 Sandell 18; 8 Mölder 11; 9 Albertini 9; 10= Schammel, Bertolotti 8 etc

Production Car World Rally Championship

1 Aigner 30; 2 Hänninen 26; 3 Ketomaa 23; 4 Sandell 22; 5 Prokop 17; 6 Rauam 15; 7 Nutahara 14; 8= Aráujo, Sousa 12; 10= Beltrán, Välimäki 8 etc

Route Details

Total route of 1313.99km of which 353.62km were competitive on 18 stages

Leg 1 Friday 3 October, 6 Special Stages totalling 131.76km
Leg 2 Saturday 4 October, 6 Special Stages totalling 127.98km
Leg 3 Sunday 5 October, 6 Special Stages totalling 93.88km

RESULTS

1	Sébastien Loeb/	Citroën C4 WRC	
	Daniel Elena	3h21m17.4s	A8
2	Dani Sordo/	Citroën C4 WRC	
	Marc Martí	3h21m42.3s	A8
3	Mikko Hirvonen/	Ford Focus RS WRC 08	
	Jarmo Lehtinen	3h22m19.9s	A8
4	François Duval/	Ford Focus RS WRC 08	
	Patrick Pivato	3h22m28.2s	A8
5	Petter Solberg/	Subaru Impreza WRC2008	
	Phil Mills	3h24m44.8s	A8
6	Jari-Matti Latvala/	Ford Focus RS WRC 07	
	Miikka Anttila	3h25m21.2s	A8
7	Chris Atkinson/	Subaru Impreza WRC2008	
	Stéphane Prévot	3h25m22.3s	A8
8	Andreas Mikkelsen/	Ford Focus RS WRC	
	Ola Fløene	3h26m37.0s	A8
9	Matthew Wilson/	Ford Focus RS WRC 07	
	Scott Martin	3h29m00.6s	A8
10	Brice Tirabassi/	Subaru Impreza WRC2008	
	Fabrice Gordon	3h30m22.4s	A8

69 starters, 48 finishers

RECENT WINNERS

1980*	Antonio Zanini/Jordi Sabater	Porsche 911SC
1981*	Eugenio Ortiz/Guillermo Barreras	Renault 5 Turbo
1982*	Antonio Zanini/Victor Sabater	Talbot Sunbeam Lotus
1983*	Adartico Vudafieri/Tiziano Siviero	Lancia 037 Rally
1984*	Salvador Servia/Jordi Sabater	Opel Manta 400
1985*	Fabrizio Tabaton/Luciano Tedeschini	Lancia 037 Rally
1986*	Fabrizio Tabaton/Luciano Tedeschini	Lancia Delta S4
1987*	Dario Cerrato/Giuseppe Cerri	Lancia Delta HF 4x4
1988*	Bruno Saby/Jean-François Fauchille	Lancia Delta HF 4x4
1989*	Yves Loubet/Jean-Marc Andrié	Lancia Delta Integrale
1990*	Dario Cerrato/Giuseppe Cerri	Lancia Delta Integrale 16v
1991	Armin Schwarz/Arne Hertz	Toyota Celica GT4
1992	Carlos Sainz/Luis Moya	Toyota Celica Turbo 4wd
1993	François Delecour/Daniel Grataloup	Ford Escort RS Cosworth
1994	Enrico Bertone/Massimo Chiapponi	Toyota Celica Turbo 4wd
1995	Carlos Sainz/Luis Moya	Subaru Impreza 555
1996	Colin McRae/Derek Ringer	Subaru Impreza 555
1997	Tommi Mäkinen/Seppo Harjanne	Mitsubishi Lancer E4
1998	Didier Auriol/Denis Giraudet	Toyota Corolla WRC
1999	Philippe Bugalski/Jean-Paul Chiaroni	Citroën Xsara Kit
2000	Colin McRae/Nicky Grist	Ford Focus RS WRC
2001	Didier Auriol/Denis Giraudet	Peugeot 206 WRC
2002	Gilles Panizzi/Hervé Panizzi	Peugeot 206 WRC
2003	Gilles Panizzi/Hervé Panizzi	Peugeot 206 WRC
2004	Markko Märtin/Michael Park	Ford Focus RS WRC 04
2005	Sébastien Loeb/Daniel Elena	Citroën Xsara WRC
2006	Sébastien Loeb/Daniel Elena	Citroën Xsara WRC
2007	Sébastien Loeb/Daniel Elena	Citroën C4 WRC

*Non-championship event

Rally de France Tour de Corse

Main: Mikko Hirvonen had to rely on fellow Ford drivers François Duval and Jari-Matti Latvala picking up time penalties to reclaim second place following a puncture on the final morning.
Photograph: Race&motion

Above left and right: Despite a late puncture Petter Solberg was fifth for the second event in a row.
Photographs: PHOTO4

SÉBASTIEN LOEB was torn. The Japanese Grand Prix was reaching a fascinating stage in the restaurant of the Best Western hotel in Ajaccio. But he had to go. That 10th World Rally Championship victory of the season wasn't going to win itself. So helmet on, off he went. The helmet wasn't a WRC regulation version, however – it was to go with the scooter he was riding to the service park. Using the scooter bought him an extra 10 minutes in bed and the opportunity to quicken his pulse through the early-morning Ajaccio traffic.

Some might say the cut and thrust of the bike offered more of an adrenalin rush than driving his Citroën C4 WRC on some of the toughest asphalt roads on the planet. And that was no reflection on Loeb, his driving, his car, or indeed the Corsican roads. It was simply that he had the Tour de Corse won on Friday and the weekend drive was, well, just that. By Sunday lunchtime, even the self-effacing four-time world champion admitted he was surprised at the competition.

"I'm in a slow rhythm," he pondered, "but I'm still fastest. It hasn't been the most exciting rally. Usually it's nice to have a fight, this can keep the rally interesting, but at the same time it's nice to win again."

There hadn't been much danger of Loeb forgetting how to win, given that his last success had come just seven days earlier on the other side of the Mediterranean in Salou, Spain.

After Citroën's one-two in Catalunya, much had been made of Ford posing a stronger threat in Corsica. It was said that the more abrasive and twistier roads of the French island would suit the Focus better than the super-smooth and circuit-like lines of the Spanish roads. Even Loeb was talking up the fight: Mikko Hirvonen and François Duval were, he reckoned, a threat.

And they were, at least until lunchtime on day one. Maybe we should make that until the end of stage one. Or maybe they weren't very threatening at all... Then again, who can threaten Loeb, particularly on his favoured surface? And the Fords were undoubtedly quicker than they were in Spain. Second fastest on

stage one, Hirvonen had Sordo worried enough for the Spaniard to push even harder in SS2, allowing him to take the place back from his rival.

Stage three, however, laid bare Sordo's inconsistency. Braking for a right-hander not far into the test, he dropped the C4, clouted a bank, ripped a wheel off and bent the roll cage. Team principal Olivier Quesnel was far from impressed. "I think he forgot about the manufacturers' championship," he lamented. "Rally drivers are like this. They put on their crash helmet and forget. This won't happen again."

Not to Dani in Corsica it wouldn't. Having damaged the roll cage, he was out for the rest of the event. With one Citroën gone, Ford was obviously desperate for both works cars to score as many points as possible. Hirvonen demonstrated just how much speed he's found this season by holding Duval at bay for much of the event. Disaster struck for the Finn, however, on the first Sunday stage when he damaged a wheel rim bouncing his car through a pothole. The tyre went down immediately and he dropped from second to fifth place, doing little for his title tilt. With Duval and Stobart Ford driver Jari-Matti Latvala ahead of him there was immediate talk of team orders being implemented, with the only fly in the ointment being Petter Solberg's fourth-placed Subaru. That problem was solved on the very next stage when the 2003 world champion also suffered a puncture, dropping him behind Hirvonen. Ford's mathematicians went to work and devised the cunning plan that unfolded at the start of the final stage, the upshot being that Hirvonen's title chances remained alive, just, while Duval scored his a second podium finish in a week. Fourth for Latvala was a major improvement for a driver who had been all at sea in Spain seven days earlier. "Maybe," suggested the Finn, "I'd had the handbrake on in Spain and I only realised this morning."

Solberg's fifth place was backed up by team-mate Chris Atkinson, who collected sixth. Neither Subaru set the world alight but, like Latvala, there had been an improvement from the week before.

Right: Latvala impressed his Ford bosses with fourth place.

Above: Winner Sébastien Loeb moved to within six points of a fifth world title.

Top: This was Loeb's fourth consecutive win in Corsica.

Opposite: Hirvonen's second place kept his championship hopes alive – but only just.
Photographs: PHOTO4

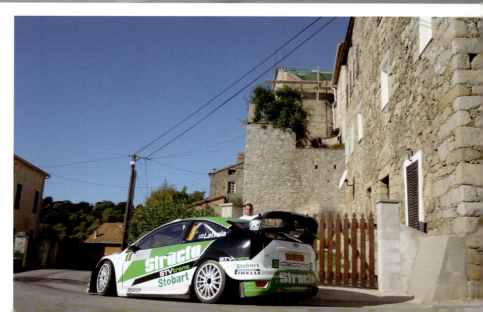

Rallye de France - Tour de Corse Results

10-12 OCTOBER 2008 | FIA WORLD RALLY CHAMPIONSHIP ROUND 13

Race&motion

Position	Stage Numbers	1	2	3	4	5	6	7	8	9	10	11	12	13	14	15	16
	Loeb	1	1	1	1	1	1	1	1	1	1	1	1	1	1	1	1
	Hirvonen	2	3	2	2	2	2	2	2	2	2	2	2	1	5	4	2
	Duval	4	4	3	3	3	3	3	3	3	3	3	3	2	2	2	3
	Latvala	5	5	5	4	4	5	5	5	4	4	4	3	3	3	3	4
	P.Solberg	7	7	4	6	6	4	4	4	5	5	5	5	4	5	5	5
	Atkinson	6	6	6	5	5	6	6	6	6	6	6	6	6	6	6	6
	Aava	8	17	15	15	14	10	7	7	7	7	7	7	7	7	7	7
	Wilson	9	8	13	13	13	14	11	11	10	9	9	9	8	8	8	8
	Ostberg	14	13	11	11	12	13	12	13	12	12	9	10	10	9	9	9
	Clark	18	16	17	17	17	16	15	16	15	16	12	12	11	10	10	10
	Mikkelsen	45	20	14	14	13	8	16	15	13	13	16	15	15	13	12	11
	Al-Qassimi	16	15	16	16	16	15	14	14	14	14	11	11	12	11	11	12
	Gardemeister	13	11	7	7	7	7	9	8	8	8	13	13	13	12	13	13
	Rautenbach	11	10	10	10	9	9	11	10	16	15	15	14	14	14	14	14
	H.Solberg	15	14	12	12	11	25	20	18	17	17	19	17	16	15	15	15
	Jones	19	19	18	18	17	17	17	18	18	17	16	16	17	16	16	16
	Andersson	12	9	8	8	10	12	10	11	10	10	14	23	19	17	17	17
	Tirabassi	10	12	9	8	8	9	8	9	9	9	9	8	8	8	8	R
	Sordo	3	2	R													

Leg 1

Ajaccio

1 4 · 3 6 · 2 5

Mediterranean Sea

Leg 2

9 12 · 8 11 · 7 10

Ajaccio

7 Special stages
→ Rally direction
▶ Stage start
▦ Stage finish

Leg 3

CORSICA

Ajaccio

13 15 · 14 16

Above: Sébastien Ogier had to settle for second in the Junior class but it was enough to claim the prestigious young driver title.

FINISH LINES...

Good things come to those who wait, and while Sébastien Ogier's week-long wait was self-inflicted following his Catalan shunt, that only made the moment when he was crowned Junior World Rally Champion all the sweeter – especially as it happened on his native French soil. Ogier only needed to finish ahead of fellow Citroën C2 driver Aaron Burkart to take the crown, which is something he's hardly struggled to do since he arrived in the sport in Mexico earlier this season. Despite sometimes only driving "at 50 per cent" in Corsica, Ogier still managed to collect second place in the Junior category. He was a world champion, and a deserving one at that following a dominant season... After a barren start to the year, Martin Prokop won his second JWRC round in seven days. The Czech Republic driver had been untroubled throughout the event and was left to rue a lack of results earlier in the year, which had ruled him out of the title chase... Back at the front of the field, Estonian privateer Urmo Aava grabbed two more points after another impressive run in the PH Sport Citroën C4 WRC, while Matthew Wilson survived an off-road moment on the opening day to bring his Stobart Ford home in the final points-paying position.

RUNNING ORDER

1	Sébastien Loeb	Citroën C4 WRC
	Daniel Elena	A8
3	Mikko Hirvonen/	Ford Focus RS WRC 08
	Jarmo Lehtinen	A8
2	Dani Sordo/	Citroën C4 WRC
	Marc Martí	A8
6	Chris Atkinson/	Subaru Impreza WRC2008
	Stéphane Prévot	A8
8	Jari-Matti Latvala/	Ford Focus RS WRC 07
	Miikka Anttila	A8
5	Petter Solberg/	Subaru Impreza WRC2008
	Phil Mills	A8
16	Henning Solberg/	Ford Focus RS WRC 07
	Cato Menkerud	A8
4	François Duval/	Ford Focus RS WRC 07
	Patrick Pivato	A8
7	Matthew Wilson/	Ford Focus RS WRC 07
	Scott Martin	A8
25	Urmo Aava/	Citroen C4 WRC
	Kuldar Sikk	A8
24	Conrad Rautenbach/	Citroen C4 WRC
	David Senior	A8
23	Andreas Mikkelsen	Ford Focus RS WRC 07
	Ola Fløene	A8
11	Toni Gardemeister/	Suzuki SX4 WRC
	Tomi Tuominen	A8
12	P-G Andersson/	Suzuki SX4 WRC
	Jonas Andersson	A8
21	Mads Østberg/	Subaru Impreza WRC2007
	Ole Kristian Unnerud	A8
17	Khalid Al-Qassimi/	Ford Focus RS WRC 07
	Michael Orr	A8
15	Barry Clark/	Ford Focus RS WRC 07
	Paul Nagle	A8
14	Brice Tirabassi/	Subaru Impreza WRC2008
	Fabrice Gordon	A8
22	Gareth Jones/	Subaru Impreza WRC2007
	Clive Jenkins	A8
61	Alain Vauthier	Peugeot 206 WRC
	Gaetan Houssin	A8

SPECIAL STAGE TIMES

SS1 Acqua Doria – Serra di Ferro 1 (15.92km)
1 S.Loeb/D.Elena (Citroën C4 WRC) 9m27.4s; 2 M.Hirvonen/J.Lehtinen (Ford Focus RS WRC 08) 9m31.4s; 3 D.Sordo/M.Martí (Citroën C4 WRC) 9m31.9s; 4 F.Duval/P.Pivato (Ford Focus RS WRC 08) 9m34.7s; 5 J-M.Latvala/M.Anttila (Ford Focus RS WRC 07) 9m38.0s; 6 C.Atkinson/S.Prévot (Subaru Impreza WRC2008) 9m40.0s; JC M.Prokop/J.Tománek (Citroën C2 S1600) 10m29.2s

SS2 Portigliolo – Bocca Albitrina 1 (16.62km)
1 Loeb/Elena (Citroën) 9m21.9s; 2 Sordo/Martí (Citroën) 9m24.6s; 3 Duval/Pivato (Ford) 9m27.3s; 4 Hirvonen/Lehtinen (Ford) 9m28.3s; 5 Latvala/Anttila (Ford) 9m31.9s; 6 P.Solberg/P.Mills (Subaru Impreza WRC2008) 9m32.9s; JC Prokop/Tománek (Citroën) 10m22.4s

SS3 Arbellara – Aullene 1 (27.42km)
1 Loeb/Elena (Citroën) 15m51.4s; 2 Duval/Pivato (Ford) 15m55.3s;

3 Hirvonen/Lehtinen (Ford) 15m55.4s; 4 P.Solberg/Mills (Subaru) 16m02.3s; 5 Atkinson/Prévot (Subaru) 16m05.6s; 6 Latvala/Anttila (Ford) 16m07.2s; JC Prokop/Tománek (Citroën) 7m18.3s

SS4 Acqua Doria – Serra di Ferro 2 (15.92km)

1 Loeb/Elena (Citroën) 9m32.2s; 2 Hirvonen/Lehtinen (Ford) 9m38.3s; 3 Duval/Pivato (Ford) 9m39.0s; 4 Atkinson/Prévot (Subaru) 9m43.5s; 5 Latvala/Anttila (Ford) 9m45.0s; 6 A.Mikkelsen/O.Fløene (Ford Focus RS WRC) 9m48.8s; JC P.Campana/S.Teissier (Renault Clio R3) 10m30.3s

SS5 Portigliolo – Bocca Albitrina 2 (16.62km)

1 Loeb/Elena (Citroën) 9m22.5s; 2 Hirvonen/Lehtinen (Ford) 9m27.7s; 3 Duval/Pivato (Ford) 9m27.8s; 4 P.Solberg/Mills (Subaru) 9m32.9s; 5 Atkinson/Prévot (Subaru) 9m33.9s; 6 Latvala/Anttila (Ford) 9m34.5s; JC A.Bettega/S.Scattolin (Renault Clio R3) 10m21.6s

SS6 Arbellara – Aullene 2 (7.42km)

1 Loeb/Elena (Citroën) 15m48.9s; 2 Duval/Pivato (Ford) 15m54.2s; 3 Hirvonen/Lehtinen (Ford) 15m55.5s; 4 P.Solberg/Mills (Subaru) 15m56.5s; 5 Latvala/Anttila (Ford) 16m00.4s; 6 Atkinson/Prévot (Subaru) 16m03.0s; JC Campana/Teissier (Renault) 17m12.1s

SS7 Carbuccia – Scalella 1 (21.88km)

1 Loeb/Elena (Citroën) 14m26.3s; 2 Duval/Pivato (Ford) 14m29.2s; 3 Hirvonen/Lehtinen (Ford) 14m31.3s; 4 P.Solberg/Mills (Subaru) 14m36.9s; 5 Atkinson/Prévot (Subaru) 14m39.4s; 6 Latvala/Anttila (Ford) 14m40.6s; JC Prokop/Tománek (Citroën) 15m50.8s

SS8 Calcatoggio – Plage du Liamone 1 (25.17km)

1 Loeb/Elena (Citroën) 17m09.2s; 2 Hirvonen/Lehtinen (Ford) 17m10.4s; 3 Duval/Pivato (Ford) 17m14.8s; 4 Latvala/Anttila (Ford) 17m17.7s; 5 P.Solberg/Mills (Subaru) 17m21.9s; 6 Atkinson/Prévot (Subaru) 17m22.5s; JC Prokop/Tománek (Citroën) 18m30.8s

SS9 Appricciani – Coggia 1 (14.37km)

1 Loeb/Elena (Citroën) 9m23.9s; 2 Duval/Pivato (Ford) 9m25.7s; 3 Hirvonen/Lehtinen (Ford) 9m27.1s; 4 Latvala/Anttila (Ford) 9m29.2s; 5 P.Solberg/Mills (Subaru) 9m32.5s; 6 Mikkelsen/Fløene (Ford) 9m33.1s; JC Prokop/Tománek (Citroën) 10m20.4s

SS10 Carbuccia – Scalella 2 (21.88km)

1 Loeb/Elena (Citroën) 14m33.6s; 2 Hirvonen/Lehtinen (Ford) 14m36.9s; 3 Latvala/Anttila (Ford) 14m37.3s; 4 Duval/Pivato (Ford) 14m38.6s; 5 P.Solberg/Mills (Subaru) 14m40.8s; 6 U.Aava/K.Sikk (Citroën C4 WRC) 14m48.8s; JC Prokop/Tománek (Citroën) 15m53.8s

SS11 Calcatoggio – Plage du Liamone 2 (25.17km)

1 Loeb/Elena (Citroën) 17m08.0s; 2 Latvala/Anttila (Ford) 17m13.8s; 3 Hirvonen/Lehtinen (Ford) 17m15.4s; 4 Duval/Pivato (Ford) 17m16.7s; 5 P.Solberg/Mills (Subaru) 17m23.7s; 6 Atkinson/Prévot (Subaru) 17m29.9s; JC Prokop/Tománek (Citroën) 18m21.9s

SS12 Appricciani – Coggia 2 (14.37km)

1 Duval/Pivato (Ford) 9m21.3s; 2= Loeb/Elena (Citroën), Hirvonen/Lehtinen (Ford) 9m22.6s; 4 Latvala/Anttila (Ford) 9m22.9s; 5 P.Solberg/Mills (Subaru) 9m29.3s; 6 Mikkelsen/Fløene (Ford) 9m37.5s; JC S.Ogier/J.Ingrassia (Citroën C2 S1600) 10m20.3s

SS13 Agosta – Pont de Calzola 1 (31.81km)

1 Loeb/Elena (Citroën) 19m10.2s; 2 Latvala/Anttila (Ford) 19m16.3s; 3 Duval/Pivato (Ford) 19m20.4s; 4 P.Solberg/Mills (Subaru) 19m25.0s; 5 M.Wilson/S.Martin (Ford Focus RS WRC 07) 19m38.6s; 6 Aava/Sikk (Citroën) 19m39.6s; JC Bettega/Scattolin (Renault) 20m46.1s

SS14 Pietra Rossa – Verghia 1 (26.32km)

1 Loeb/Elena (Citroën) 16m25.6s; 2 Hirvonen/Lehtinen (Ford) 16m26.2s; 3 Latvala/Anttila (Ford) 16m27.0s; 4 Mikkelsen/Fløene (Ford) 16m40.3s; 5 Aava/Sikk (Citroën) 16m42.0s; 6 Duval/Pivato (Ford) 16m42.7s; JC Ogier/Ingrassia (Citroën) 17m58.2s

SS15 Agosta – Pont de Calzola 2 (31.81km)

1= Latvala/Anttila (Ford), Loeb/Elena (Citroën) 19m22.0s; 3 Duval/Pivato (Ford) 19m23.4s; 4 Hirvonen/Lehtinen (Ford) 19m24.3s; 5 P.Solberg/Mills (Subaru) 19m24.9s; 6 Mikkelsen/Fløene (Ford) 19m33.0s; JC P.Marché/J.Giroux (Suzuki Swift S1600) 20m57.5s

SS16 Pietra Rossa – Verghia 2 (26.32km)

1 Hirvonen/Lehtinen (Ford) 16m27.4s; 2 Loeb/Elena (Citroën) 16m32.3s; 3 Duval/Pivato (Ford) 16m38.5s; 4 Mikkelsen/Fløene (Ford) 16m38.6s; 5 Latvala/Anttila (Ford) 16m41.7s; 6 H.Solberg/C.Menkerud (Ford Focus RS WRC 07) 16m50.5s; JC Ogier/Ingrassia (Citroën) 18m02.0s

Cars that retired and subsequently re-started and were classified under SupeRally regs:

| 12 | Andersson/Andersson | Suzuki SX4 WRC | | |
| | Off road | SS11 | A8 | |

MAJOR RETIREMENTS

2	Sordo/Martí	Citroën C4 WRC		
	Accident	SS3	A8	
14	Tirabassi/Gordon	Subaru Impreza WRC2008		
	Mechanical	SS14	A8	

FIA CLASS WINNERS

A8	Over 2000 cc	Loeb/Elena
		Citroën C4 WRC
A7	1600-2000cc	Campana/Teissier
		Renault Clio R3
A6	1400-1600cc	Prokop/Tománek
		Citroën C2 S1600
N4	Over 2000cc	Hänninen/Markkula
		Mitsubishi Lancer Evo IX
N3	1600-2000cc	Giovanni/Nanni
		Renault Clio Ragnotti
N1	Upto 1400cc	Maestracci/Poggi
		Skoda Fabia

RALLY LEADERS

Overall: SS1-16 Loeb

JWRC: SS1-5 Prokop; SS6-8 Campana; SS9-16 Prokop

SPECIAL STAGE ANALYSIS

	1st	2nd	3rd	4th	5th	6th
Loeb (Citroën)	14	2	-	-	-	-
Hirvonen (Ford)	1	7	5	2	-	-
Duval (Ford)	1	4	7	3	-	1
Latvala (Ford)	1	2	2	3	5	3
Sordo (Citroën)	-	1	1	-	-	-
P.Solberg (Subaru)	-	-	-	5	6	1
Mikkelsen (Ford)	-	-	-	2	-	3
Atkinson (Subaru)	-	-	-	1	3	4
Aava (Citroen)	-	-	-	-	1	3
Wilson (Ford)	-	-	-	-	1	-
H.Solberg (Ford)	-	-	-	-	-	1

TYRES

Tyres: Pirelli Pzero

Compound: hard/soft

Number of tyres available per car: 54

WORLD CHAMPIONSHIP POINTS

Drivers

1 Loeb 106; 2 Hirvonen 92; 3 Sordo 59; 4 Atkinson 45; 5 Latvala 42; 6 P.Solberg 40; 7= H.Solberg, Duval 22; 9 Galli 17; 10= Wilson, Aava 13 etc

Manufacturers

1 Citroën Total WRT 169; 2 BP Ford Abu Dhabi WRT 146; 3 Subaru WRT 87; 4 Stobart VK M-Sport Ford RT 62; 5 Munchi's Ford WRT 22; 6 Suzuki WRT 21

Junior World Rally Championship

1 Ogier 42; 2 Burkart 34; 3 Prokop 32; 4 Gallagher 30; 5= Kosciuszko, Bettega 22; 7 Sandell 21; 8 Mölder 11; 9 Albertini 9; 10= Schammel, Bertolotti, Niegel 8 etc

Production Car World Rally Championship

1 Aigner 30; 2 Hänninen 26; 3 Ketomaa 23; 4 Sandell 22; 5 Prokop 17; 6 Rauam 15; 7 Nutahara 14; 8= Aráujo, Sousa 12; 10= Beltrán, Välimäki 8 etc

ROUTE DETAILS

Total route of 1094.36km of which 359.02km were competitive on 16 stages

Leg 1 Friday 10 October, 6 Special Stages totalling 119.92km
Leg 2 Saturday 11 October, 6 Special Stages totalling 122.84km
Leg 3 Sunday 12 October, 4 Special Stages totalling 116.26km

RESULTS

1	Sébastien Loeb/	Citroën C4 WRC	
	Daniel Elena	3h42m58.0s	A8
2	Mikko Hirvonen/	Ford Focus RS WRC 08	
	Jarmo Lehtinen	3h46m22.7s	A8
3	François Duval/	Ford Focus RS WRC 08	
	Patrick Pivato	3h46m29.6s	A8
4	Jari-Matti Latvala/	Ford Focus RS WRC 07	
	Miikka Anttila	3h45m05.5s	A8
5	Petter Solberg/	Subaru Impreza WRC2008	
	Phil Mills	3h48m33.4s	A8
6	Chris Atkinson/	Subaru Impreza WRC2008	
	Stéphane Prévot	3h49m08.4s	A8
7	Urmo Aava/	Citroen C4 WRC	
	Kuldar Sikk	3h49m23.2s	A8
8	Matthew Wilson/	Ford Focus RS WRC 07	
	Scott Martin	3h52m00.2s	A8
9	Mads Østberg/	Subaru Impreza WRC 2007	
	Ole Kristian Unnerud	3h52m11.3s	A8
10	Barry Clark/	Ford Focus RS WRC 07	
	Paul Nagle	3h56m36.3s	A8

71 starters, 54 finishers

RECENT WINNERS

1970	Bernard Darniche/Guy Demange	Alpine Renault A110
1972	Jean-Claude Andruet/'Biche'	Alpine Renault A110
1973	Jean-Pierre Nicolas/Michel Vial	Alpine Renault A110
1974	Jean-Claude Andruet/'Biche'	Lancia Stratos
1975	Bernard Darniche/Alain Mahé	Lancia Stratos
1976	Sandro Munari/Silvio Maiga	Lancia Stratos
1977	Bernard Darniche/Alain Mahé	Fiat Abarth 131
1978	Bernard Darniche/Alain Mahé	Fiat Abarth 131
1979	Bernard Darniche/Alain Mahé	Lancia Stratos
1980	Jean-Luc Thérier/Michel Vial	Porsche 911SC
1981	Bernard Darniche/Alain Mahé	Lancia Stratos
1982	Jean Ragnotti/Jean-Marc Andrié	Renault 5 Turbo
1983	Markku Alén/Ilkka Kivimäki	Lancia 037 Rally
1984	Markku Alén/Ilkka Kivimäki	Lancia 037 Rally
1985	Jean Ragnotti/Jean-Marc Andrié	Renault 5 Maxi Turbo
1986	Bruno Saby/Jean-Francois Fauchille	Peugeot 205 Turbo 16 E2
1987	Bernard Béguin/Jean-Jacques Lenne	BMW M3
1988	Didier Auriol/Bernard Occelli	Ford Sierra RS Cosworth
1989	Didier Auriol/Bernard Occelli	Lancia Delta Integrale
1990	Didier Auriol/Bernard Occelli	Lancia Delta Integrale 16v
1991	Carlos Sainz/Luis Moya	Toyota Celica GT4
1992	Didier Auriol/Bernard Occelli	Lancia Delta HF Integrale
1993	François Delecour/Daniel Grataloup	Ford Escort RS Cosworth
1994	Didier Auriol/Bernard Occelli	Toyota Celica Turbo 4wd
1995	Didier Auriol/Denis Giraudet	Toyota Celica GT-Four
1996	Philippe Bugalski/Jean-Paul Chiaroni	Renault Maxi Mégane
1997	Colin McRae/Nicky Grist	Subaru Impreza WRC97
1998	Colin McRae/Nicky Grist	Subaru Impreza WRC98
1999	Philippe Bugalski/Jean-Paul Chiaroni	Citroën Xsara Kit
2000	Gilles Panizzi/Hervé Panizzi	Peugeot 206 WRC
2001	Jesús Puras/Marc Martí	Citroën Xsara WRC
2002	Gilles Panizzi/Hervé Panizzi	Peugeot 206 WRC
2003	Petter Solberg/Phil Mills	Subaru Impreza WRC2003
2004	Markko Märtin/Michael Park	Ford Focus RS WRC 04
2005	Sébastien Loeb/Daniel Elena	Citroën Xsara WRC
2006	Sébastien Loeb/Daniel Elena	Citroën Xsara WRC
2007	Sébastien Loeb/Daniel Elena	Citroën C4 WRC

Pioneer Carrozzeria Rally Japan

Sébastien Loeb drove
cautiously to take third
place but with it his fifth
consecutive world
championship.
Photograph: Race&motion

Above: Japanese fans have a reputation for their passionate (and interesting) support of the WRC....

Right: P-G Andersson pictured in the Sapporo Dome superspecial stage took his best result of the season with fifth on Suzuki's home soil.

Below right: Jari-Matti Latvala's second place finish was vital to Ford's manufacturers' title challenge.

Far right: Mikko Hirvonen's victory wasn't enough to win the championship, but was richly deserved.

Photographs: PHOTO4

THIS YEAR'S Rally Japan will be remembered for three reasons: the near-fatal accident of popular co-driver Patrick Pivato, Sébastien Loeb winning his fifth consecutive drivers' title, and Mikko Hirvonen winning the rally.

For days before the rally, Loeb had talked of simply doing enough and no more on this event in order to clinch the championship. He needed third place, and that was what he would be aiming for. Heavy snowfall in the run up to the event merely served to strengthen his resolve to take no risks. Anybody who doubted that policy need only to look at the number one Citroën's time through the opening stage. He was 13.3 seconds slower than Hirvonen's benchmark.

"I could find no rhythm," he grumbled at the stage finish. "It was very difficult. I was not driving like usual."

But Loeb's problems were put into perspective on stage six, when François Duval slid wide at a left-hand corner and clouted a metal post. The impact tore the right-hand side of his Ford wide open, seriously injuring his co-driver Pivato. The stage was stopped and Pivato was airlifted to hospital. The initial prognosis of a broken leg and pelvis was serious, but not life-threatening. Unfortunately that changed when the Frenchman suffered internal bleeding overnight on Friday, and only a series of operations and blood transfusions saved his life.

Through that major drama, Hirvonen kept his head down and kept on putting the times in. He built and maintained his lead over team-mate Jari-Matti Latvala until the finish. If he was to stand any chance of stopping Loeb's title charge, he knew he had to win. And win he did. Now, it was down to Loeb.

After his early wobble, Loeb moved into that all-important third place following's Duval's crash. He then found his rhythm and a sensible pace, and drove at it for the next two days. His only moment, and it sounded like a big one, came in torrential rain on the final day, when he spun the Citroën on a badly rutted straight in the re-run Sikot test. Loeb was quick to point out that he was fortunate not to have hit anything, but that incident was soon forgotten once he was handed a bottle of champagne at the finish. Having won the world title four times previously, the Frenchman knew how to celebrate a fifth one.

Hirvonen's rally-winning celebrations were more mooted. But he was satisfied that the one-two he and Latvala had scored, allied to Loeb's third place and Dani Sordo's retirement through a turbo problem, had ensured the manufacturers' championship would go down to the wire in Wales.

Subaru driver Chris Atkinson was a distant fourth, collecting the spot after team-mate Petter Solberg ditched his Impreza WRC2008 in SS18. But over the balance of the rally the Norwegian had been the quicker of the two Subaru drivers, as Solberg's four fastest times gave the Japanese fans something to cheer.

There was even more for local fans to cheer as Suzuki saved its best performance of the season for its home event. With P-G Andersson finishing fifth and Toni Gardemeister in sixth it was smiles all round at Suzuki, particularly as Gardemeister had also scored the SX4 WRC's first ever fastest time on a world championship round.

Above: Toni Gardemeister recorded Suzuki's first special stage win, albeit within the confines of the Sapporo Dome.

Left: Mechanical problems restricted Federico Villagra to ninth overall on his final outing of the season.

Bottom left: Chris Atkinson upheld Subaru honour with a fourth-place finish.

Middle left: The cars weren't the only attraction on Rally Japan.

Far left: Patrick Pivato suffered serious injuries when he and driver François Duval crashed.
Photographs: PHOTO4 unless specified

Pioneer Carrozzeria Rally Japan Results

31 OCTOBER – 02 NOVEMBER 2008 | FIA WORLD RALLY CHAMPIONSHIP ROUND 14

Leg 1 · Sapporo
Leg 2 · Sapporo
Leg 3 · Sapporo · JAPAN

- ▶ Stage start
- ▦ Stage finish
- ❼ Special stages
- → Rally direction

Position	Stage Numbers	1	2	4	5	6	9	10	11	12	13	14	15	16	17	18	19	20	21	22	23	24	25	26	27	28	29
	Hirvonen	1	1	1	1	1	1	1	1	1	1	1	1	1	1	1	1	1	1	1	1	1	1	1	1	1	1
	Latvala	2	2	2	3	2	2	2	2	2	2	2	2	2	2	2	2	2	2	2	2	2	2	2	2	2	2
	Loeb	6	4	4	4	3	3	3	3	3	3	3	3	3	3	3	2	3	3	3	3	3	3	3	3	3	3
	Atkinson	9	9	9	8	7	5	4	4	5	5	5	5	5	4	4	4	4	4	4	4	4	4	4	4	4	4
	Andersson	8	8	8	9	5	7	7	5	6	6	6	6	9	8	7	7	7	7	7	6	6	5	5	5		
	Gardemeister	10	10	10	10	8	8	8	8	9	9	9	9	8	7	6	6	6	6	5	5	5	5	5	6	6	6
	Wilson	5	6	6	7	4	5	6	5	7	7	8	7	7	6	5	5	5	5	6	7	7	7	7	7	7	7
	P.Solberg	6	7	7	6	6	4	5	7	4	4	4	4	4	5	8	13	12	9	9	9	9	8	8	9	9	9
	Villagra	12	25	25	20	18	17	15	15	11	10	10	10	10	10	9	10	9	8	8	8	8	9	9	9		
	Hänninen	30	26	24	24	22	22	21	20	15	14	13	13	13	14	12	11	11	12	11	11	11	11	12	12	10	
	Sordo	4	5	5	5	31	54	63	63	46	29	27	27	24	19	19	19	16	16	15	13	13	13	13	11	10	R
	H.Solberg	11	11	11	11	9	9	9	9	9	8	8	7	7	6	6	9	15	20	20	19	R					
	Rautenbach	78	78	80	76	76	77	78	77	72	69	63	63	58	45	39	38	35	35	34	R						
	Duval	3	3	3	2	R																					

Above right: Juho Hänninen moved into the Production championship lead by moving into the class lead on the final stage.
Photographs: PHOTO4

FINISH LINES...

After running as high as fourth overall, Matthew Wilson had slipped back down to seventh by the finish of Rally Japan. The Briton admitted being first on the scene of his friend and Stobart team-mate Patrick Pivato's accident, and seeing his injuries, hadn't helped his focus... Petter Solberg returned to the event under SuperRally rules to take eighth place and the final drivers' point... Federico Villagra was ninth in the Munchi's Ford, while Juho Hänninen rounded out the top 10 in his Group N Mitsubishi Lancer... Hänninen's third Production Car World Rally Championship win of the season had looked a distant possibility on Friday. The Finn wasn't happy on the twisty, tight stages and had predicted that his rally "would start on Saturday". It certainly did: Hänninen reeled off fastest time after fastest time to move back up the P-WRC leaderboard, eventually settling in second place. Second became first when Evgeny Novikov suffered a heart-breaking final-stage puncture. Novikov had demonstrated pace, maturity and self-assurance way beyond his 18 years to dominate the P-WRC round for the majority of the three days in his Lancer... Former P-WRC champion Toshi Arai was a welcome visitor to the podium, collecting third in class in his Subaru Impreza WRX... The event also marked the world championship debut of the Mitsubishi Lancer Evo X. Three of the cars started the rally, and drivers Katsuhiko Taguchi and Fumio Nutahara both scored P-WRC points.

RUNNING ORDER

1	Sébastien Loeb / Daniel Elena	Citroën C4 WRC	A8
3	Mikko Hirvonen / Jarmo Lehtinen	Ford Focus RS WRC 08	A8
2	Dani Sordo / Marc Martí	Citroën C4 WRC	A8
6	Chris Atkinson / Stéphane Prévot	Subaru Impreza WRC2008	A8
4	Jari-Matti Latvala / Miikka Anttila	Ford Focus RS WRC 08	A8
5	Petter Solberg / Phil Mills	Subaru Impreza WRC2008	A8
10	Henning Solberg /	Ford Focus RS WRC 07	
	Cato Menkerud	A8	
7	François Duval / Patrick Pivato	Ford Focus RS WRC 07	A8
8	Matthew Wilson / Scott Martin	Ford Focus RS WRC 07	A8
9	Federico Villagra / Jorge Pérez Companc	Ford Focus RS WRC 07	A8
14	Conrad Rautenbach / David Senior	Citroën C4 WRC	A8
11	Toni Gardemeister / Tomi Tuominen	Suzuki SX4 WRC	A8
12	P-G Andersson / Jonas Andersson	Suzuki SX4 WRC	A8
52	Juho Hänninen / Mikko Markkula	Mitsubishi Lancer Evo IX	N4
57	Martin Rauam / Silver Kutt	Mitsubishi Lancer Evo IX	N4
56	Fumio Nutahara / Hakaru Ichino	Mitsubishi Lancer Evo X	N4
50	Armindo Aráujo / Miguel Ramalho	Mitsubishi Lancer Evo IX	N4
32	Mirco Baldacci / Giovanni Agnese	Mitsubishi Lancer Evo IX	N4
31	Toshi Arai / Glenn Macneall	Subaru Impreza	N4
43	Evgeniy Vertunov / Georgy Troshkin	Subaru Impreza	N4

SPECIAL STAGE TIMES

SS1 Heper 1 (13.24km)
1 M.Hirvonen/J.Lehtinen (Ford Focus RS WRC 08) 9m57.9s; 2 J-M Latvala/M.Anttila (Ford Focus RS WRC 08) 10m01.7s; 3 F.Duval/P.Pivato (Ford Focus RS WRC 07) 10m04.9s; 4 D.Sordo/M.Martí (Citroën C4 WRC) 10m09.0s; 5 M.Wilson/S.Martin (Ford Focus RS WRC 07) 10m10.9s; 6 P.Solberg/P.Mills (Subaru Impreza WRC2008) 10m 11.2s; PC E.Brynildsen/D.Giraudet (Mitsubishi Lancer Evo IX) 10m43.1s

SS2 Yuparo 1 (11.10km)
1 Hirvonen/Lehtinen (Ford) 8m24.2s; 2 S.Loeb/D.Elena (Citroën C4 WRC) 8m26.3s; 3 Duval/Pivato (Ford) 8m27.5s; 4 Latvala/Anttila (Ford) 8m28.3s; 5 Sordo/Martí (Citroën) 8m28.9s; 6 Wilson/Martin (Ford) 8m32.2s; PC E.Novikov/D.Moscatt (Mitsubishi Lancer IX)

8m56.6s

SS3 Isepo 1 (13.67km)
Cancelled due to abnormal weather and resulting deterioration of the road

SS4 Pipaoi 1 (5.74km)
1 Loeb/Elena (Citroën) 3m17.3s; 2 Latvala/Anttila (Ford) 3m18.6s; 3 Hirvonen/Lehtinen (Ford) 3m19.6s; 4 Duval/Pivato (Ford) 3m19.9s; 5 C.Atkinson/S.Prévot (Subaru Impreza WRC2008) 3m20.9s; 6 P.Solberg/Mills (Subaru) 3m21.0s; PC T.Arai/G.Macneall (Subaru Impreza) 3m36.5s

SS5 Heper 2 (13.24km)
1 Hirvonen/Lehtinen (Ford) 9m35.6s; 2 Duval/Pivato (Ford) 9m36.9s; 3 Loeb/Elena (Citroën) 9m42.9s; 4 Latvala/Anttila (Ford) 9m44.2s; 5 Atkinson/Prévot (Subaru) 9m48.9s; 6 Sordo/Martí (Citroën) 9m51.6s; PC Novikov/Moscatt (Mitsubishi) 10m31.2s

SS6 Yuparo 2 (11.10km)
1 Hirvonen/Lehtinen (Ford) 8m02.5s; 2 Latvala/Anttila (Ford) 8m09.1s; 3 Loeb/Elena (Citroën) 8m09.4s; 4 Wilson/Martin (Ford) 8m11.2s; 5 P-G.Andersson/J.Andersson (Suzuki SX4 WRC) 8m11.2s; 6 Atkinson/Prévot (Subaru) 8m13.7s; PC S.Marrini/T.Sandroni (Mitsubishi Lancer Evo IX) 8m19.2s

SS7 Isepo 2 (13.67km)
Cancelled due to abnormal weather and resulting deterioration of the road

SS8 Pipaoi 2 (5.74km)
Cancelled as a result of the delays caused after François Duval's accident

SS9 Sapporo 1 (1.49km)
1 Hirvonen/Lehtinen (Ford) 1m39.4s; 2 Loeb/Elena (Citroën) 1m39.5s; 3 Latvala/Anttila (Ford) 1m41.4s; 4 Atkinson/Prévot (Subaru) 1m42.3s; 5 H.Solberg/C.Menkerud (Ford Focus RS WRC 07) 1m42.7s; 6 P.Solberg/Mills (Subaru) 1m42.8s; PC J.Hänninen/M.Markkula (Mitsubishi Lancer Evo IX) 1m46.6s

SS10 Sapporo 2 (1.49km)
1 Hirvonen/Lehtinen (Ford) 1m41.6s; 2 Atkinson/Prévot (Subaru) 1m42.9s; 3 Latvala/Anttila (Ford) 1m43.7s; 4

T.Gardemeister/T.Tuominen (Suzuki SX4 WRC) 1m44.5s; 5 Loeb/Elena (Citroën) 1m44.8s; 6= F.Villagra/J.P.Companc (Ford Focus RS WRC 07), P.Solberg/Mills (Subaru), Wilson/Martin (Ford) 1m45.8s; PC Hänninen/Markkula (Mitsubishi) 1m45.9s

SS11 Imeru 1 (2.57km)
1 Sordo/Martí (Citroën) 1m42.5s; 2 Andersson/Andersson (Suzuki) 1m44.0s; 3 H.Solberg/Menkerud (Ford) 1m44.1s; 4= Wilson/Martin (Ford), Atkinson/Prévot (Subaru) 1m44.4s; 6 Loeb/Elena (Citroën) 1m45.0s; PC Hänninen/Markkula (Mitsubishi) 1m50.8s

SS12 Nikara 1 (31.12km)
1 P.Solberg/Mills (Subaru) 18m37.0s; 2= Hirvonen/Lehtinen (Ford), Sordo/Martí (Citroën) 18m38.8s; 4 Latvala/Anttila (Ford) 18m41.4s; 5 Loeb/Elena (Citroën) 18m44.7s; 6 H.Solberg/Menkerud (Ford) 18m50.1s; PC Hänninen/Markkula (Mitsubishi) 19m51.1s

SS13 Kamuycep 1 (33.66km)
1 Latvala/Anttila (Ford) 21m58.1s; 2 Sordo/Martí (Citroën) 22m02.8s; 3 Loeb/Elena (Citroën) 22m06.6s; 4 Hirvonen/Lehtinen (Ford) 22m09.0s; 5 P.Solberg/Mills (Subaru) 22m14.6s; 6 Atkinson/Prévot (Subaru) 22m21.6s; PC Hänninen/Markkula (Mitsubishi) 23m37.2s

SS14 Kina 1 (9.55km)
1 H.Solberg/Menkerud (Ford) 5m54.6s; 2 Sordo/Martí (Citroën) 5m55.3s; 3 Latvala/Anttila (Ford) 5m55.8s; 4 Hirvonen/Lehtinen (Ford) 5m56.2s; 5 Loeb/Elena (Citroën) 5m56.4s; 6 P.Solberg/Mills (Subaru) 6m00.0s; PC Hänninen/Markkula (Mitsubishi) 6m22.8s

SS15 Imeru 2 (2.57km)
1 Loeb/Elena (Citroën) 1m42.5s; 2= H.Solberg/Menkerud (Ford), Sordo/Martí (Citroën) 1m42.8s; 4 Hirvonen/Lehtinen (Ford) 1m43.2s; 5 P.Solberg/Mills (Subaru) 1m43.3s; 6 Wilson/Martin (Ford) 1m43.5s; PC A.Araújo/M.Ramalho (Mitsubishi Lancer Evo IX) 1m51.4s

SS16 Nikara 2 (31.12km)
1 Latvala/Anttila (Ford) 18m22.8s; 2 Hirvonen/Lehtinen (Ford) 18m24.0s; 3 Loeb/Elena (Citroën) 18m24.1s; 4 P.Solberg/Mills (Subaru) 18m24.8s; 5 Atkinson/Prévot (Subaru) 18m27.7s; 6 Sordo/Martí (Citroën) 18m41.3s; PC Novikov/Moscatt (Mitsubishi) 20m16.3s

SS17 Kamuycep 2 (33.66km)
1 Hirvonen/Lehtinen (Ford) 21m22.7s; 2 Latvala/Anttila (Ford) 21m25.9s; 3 P.Solberg/Mills (Subaru) 21m30.2s; 4 Sordo/Martí (Citroën) 21m38.8s; 5 Atkinson/Prévot (Subaru) 21m43.8s; 6 Loeb/Elena (Citroën) 21m44.3s; PC Arai/Macneall (Subaru) 23m33.1s

SS18 Kina 2 (9.55km)
1 Hirvonen/Lehtinen (Ford) 5m54.3s; 2 Sordo/Martí (Citroën) 5m55.1s; 3 Latvala/Anttila (Ford) 5m55.4s; 4 Loeb/Elena (Citroën) 5m56.6s; 5 Andersson/Andersson (Suzuki) 6m02.0s; 6 Wilson/Martin (Ford) 6m07.6s; PC Arai/Macneall (Subaru) 6m33.7s

SS19 Sapporo 3 (1.49km)
1= Gardemeister/Tuominen (Suzuki), Sordo/Martí (Citroën) 1m25.4s; 3 Latvala/Anttila (Ford) 1m27.4s; 4 Andersson/Andersson (Suzuki) 1m27.8s; 5 Villagra/Companc (Ford); 6 Hänninen/Markkula (Mitsubishi) 1m28.6s; PC Hänninen/Markkula (Mitsubishi) 1m28.6s

SS20 Sapporo 4 (1.49km)
1 Sordo/Martí (Citroën) 1m23.2s; 2 Gardemeister/Tuominen (Suzuki) 1m23.6s; 3 Latvala/Anttila (Ford) 1m24.2s; 4= Hirvonen/Lehtinen (Ford), Loeb/Elena (Citroën) 1m24.7s; 6 Wilson/Martin (Ford) 1m24.9s; PC Hänninen/Markkula (Mitsubishi) 1m28.3s

SS21 Koyka 1 (3.57km)
1 P.Solberg/Mills (Subaru) 2m00.2s; 2 Hirvonen/Lehtinen (Ford) 2m00.6s; 3 Andersson/Andersson (Suzuki) 2m01.4s; 4 H.Solberg/Menkerud (Ford) 2m02.1s; 5 Loeb/Elena (Citroën) 2m02.7s; 6 Sordo/Martí (Citroën) 2m03.1s; PC Novikov/Moscatt (Mitsubishi) 2m12.1s

SS22 Iwanke 1 (13.57km)
1 Hirvonen/Lehtinen (Ford) 8m13.0s; 2 Latvala/Anttila (Ford) 8m14.8s; 3 P.Solberg/Mills (Subaru) 8m19.2s; 4 Andersson/Andersson (Suzuki) 8m20.5s; 5 Gardemeister/Tuominen (Suzuki) 8m24.2s; 6 Wilson/Martin (Ford) 8m25.1s; PC Hänninen/Markkula (Mitsubishi) 9m10.7s

SS23 Sikot 1 (27.76km)
1 Latvala/Anttila (Ford) 17m49.5s; 2 Andersson/Andersson (Suzuki) 18m01.8s; 3 Hirvonen/Lehtinen (Ford) 18m03.3s; 4 P.Solberg/Mills (Subaru) 18m16.0s; 5 Gardemeister/Tuominen (Suzuki) 18m23.2s; 6 Wilson/Martin (Ford) 18m32.5s; PC Novikov/Moscatt (Mitsubishi) 19m29.2s

SS24 Imeru 3 (2.57km)
1 Latvala/Anttila (Ford) 1m57.3s; 2 Hirvonen/Lehtinen (Ford) 1m57.5s; 3 P.Solberg/Mills (Subaru) 1m57.9s; 4 Atkinson/Prévot (Subaru) 1m59.3s; 5 Loeb/Elena (Citroën) 2m01.9s; 6 Andersson/Andersson (Suzuki) 2m02.7s; PC Arai/Macneall (Subaru) 2m10.9s

SS25 Sapporo 5 (1.49km)
1 A.Kim/M.Nakasato (Mitsubishi Lancer Evo VIII) 1m45.7s; 2 Atkinson/Prévot (Subaru) 1m45.8s; 3 K.Kitamura/N.Takeshita (Subaru Impreza) 1m46.5s; 4 Gardemeister/Tuominen (Suzuki) 1m46.7s; 5= K.Taguchi/M.Stacey (Mitsubishi Lancer Evo X), Brynildsen/Giraudet (Mitsubishi) 1m46.9s; PC= K.Taguchi/M.Stacey (Mitsubishi Lancer Evo X), Brynildsen/Giraudet (Mitsubishi) 1m46.9s

SS26 Koyka 2 (3.57km)
1 Hirvonen/Lehtinen (Ford) 2m08.6s; 2 P.Solberg/Mills (Subaru) 2m09.5s; 3 Latvala/Anttila (Ford) 2m13.0s; 4 Andersson/Andersson (Suzuki) 2m13.2s; 5 Sordo/Martí (Citroën) 2m13.4s; 6 Atkinson/Prévot (Subaru) 2m14.5s; PC Arai/Macneall (Subaru) 2m28.0s

SS27 Iwanke 2 (13.57km)
1 Hirvonen/Lehtinen (Ford) 8m39.9s; 2 Andersson/Andersson (Suzuki) 8m40.6s; 3 P.Solberg/Mills (Subaru) 8m42.5s; 4 Latvala/Anttila (Ford) 8m54.0s; 5 Sordo/Martí (Citroën) 8m55.2s; 6 Loeb/Elena (Citroën) 8m55.4s; PC Arai/Macneall (Subaru) 9m24.9s

SS28 Sikot 2 (27.76km)
1 P.Solberg/Mills (Subaru) 18m00.2s; 2 Andersson/Andersson (Suzuki) 18m16.5s; 3 Sordo/Martí (Citroën) 18m17.1s; 4 Atkinson/Prévot (Subaru) 18m24.3s; 5 Hirvonen/Lehtinen (Ford) 18m30.8s; 6 Loeb/Elena (Citroën) 18m41.6s; PC Hänninen/Markkula (Mitsubishi) 19m22.1s

SS29 Imeru 4 (2.57km)
1 P.Solberg/Mills (Subaru) 2m03.8s; 2 Sordo/Martí (Citroën) 2m04.3s; 3 Latvala/Anttila (Ford) 2m05.9s; 4 Atkinson/Prévot (Subaru) 2m06.2s; 5 Andersson/Andersson (Suzuki) 2m07.8s; 6 Gardemeister/Tuominen (Suzuki) 2m08.5s; PC T.Kamada/N.Kase (Subaru Impreza) 2m16.4s

Cars that retired and subsequently restarted and were classified under SuperRally regs:

5	P.Solberg/Mills	Subaru Impreza WRC2008		
	Accident	SS18	A8	

MAJOR RETIREMENTS
7	Duval/Pivato	Ford Focus RS WRC 07		
	Accident	SS6	A8	
10	H.Solberg/Menkerud	Ford Focus RS WRC 07		
	Accident	SS23	A8	
14	Rautenbach/Senior	Citroën C4 WRC		
	Accident	SS23	A8	
2	Sordo/Martí	Citroën C4 WRC		
	Withdrew	SS29C	A8	

FIA CLASS WINNERS
A8	Over 2000cc	Hirvonen/Lehtinen
		Ford Focus RS WRC 08
A7	1600-2000cc	Kagawa/Adachi
		Honda Integra Type-R
A6	1400-1600cc	Irinatsu/Haenuki
		Honda Civic
A5	Upto 1400cc	Amano/Inoue
		Toyota Yaris
N4	Over 2000cc	Hänninen/Markkula
		Mitsubishi Lancer Evo IX
N3	1600-2000cc	Aikawa/Ando
		Ford Fiesta ST
N1	Upto 1400cc	Y.Harah/S.Hara
		Daihatsu Boon

RALLY LEADERS
Overall: SS1-29 Hirvonen

PC: SS1-8 Brynildsen; SS9-29 Novikov E; SS29 Hänninen

SPECIAL STAGE ANALYSIS
	1st	2nd	3rd	4th	5th	6th
Hirvonen (Ford)	11	4	2	4	1	-
Latvala (Ford)	4	5	8	4	-	-
P.Solberg (Subaru)	4	1	4	2	2	5
Sordo (Citroën)	3	6	1	2	3	3
Loeb (Citroën)	2	2	4	2	5	4
H.Solberg (Ford)	1	1	1	1	1	1
Gardmeister (Suzuki)	1	1	-	2	2	1
Kim (Mitsubishi)	1	-	-	-	-	-
Andersson (Suzuki)	-	4	1	3	3	1
Atkinson (Subaru)	-	2	-	5	4	3
Duval (Ford)	-	1	2	1	-	-
Kitamura (Subaru)	-	-	1	-	-	-
Wilson (Ford)	-	-	-	2	1	7
Villagra (Ford)	-	-	-	-	1	1
Taguchi (Mitsubishi)	-	-	-	-	1	-
Brynildsen (Mitsubishi)	-	-	-	-	1	-
Hänninen (Mitsubishi)	-	-	-	-	-	1

TYRES
Tyres: Pirelli Scorpion
Compound: soft
Number of tyres available per car: 42

WORLD CHAMPIONSHIP POINTS
Drivers
1 Loeb 112; 2 Hirvonen 102; 3 Sordo 59; 4= Latvala, Atkinson 50; 6 P.Solberg 41; 7= H.Solberg, Duval 22; 9 Galli 17; Wilson 15 etc

Manufacturers
1 Citroën Total WRT 175; 2 BP Ford Abu Dhabi WRT 164; 3 Subaru WRT 93; 4 Stobart VK M-Sport Ford RT 64; 5 Suzuki WRT 28; 6 Munchi's Ford WRT 22

Junior World Rally Championship
1 Ogier 42; 2 Burkart 34; 3 Prokop 32; 4 Gallagher 30; 5= Kosciuszko, Bettega 22; 7 Sandell 21; 8 Mölder 11; 9 Albertini 9; 10= Schammel, Bertolotti, Niegel 8 etc

Production Car World Rally Championship
1 Hänninen 36; 2 Aigner 30; 3 Ketomaa 23; 4 Sandell 22; 5 Prokop 17; 6= Rauam, Nutahara 15; 8= Araújo, Sousa 12; 10= Arai, Baldacci 9 etc

Route Details
Total Route of 1316.28 km of which 343.69 km were competitive on 27 stages
Leg 1 Friday 31st October, 10 special stages totalling 90.48 km
Leg 2 Saturday 1st November, 10 special stages totalling 156.78 km
Leg 3 Sunday 2nd November, 7 special stages totalling 96.43 km

RESULTS
1	Mikko Hirvonen/ Jarmo Lehtinen	Ford Focus RS WRC 08 3h25m03.0s A8	
2	Jari-Matti Latvala/ Miikka Anttila	Ford Focus RS WRC 08 3h25m34.1s A8	
3	Sébastien Loeb/ Daniel Elena	Citroën C4 WRC 3h27m33.6s A8	
4	Chris Atkinson/ Stéphane Prévot	Subaru Impreza WRC2008 3h28m45.4s A8	
5	P-G Andersson/ Jonas Andersson	Suzuki SX4 WRC 3m30.15.9s A8	
6	Toni Gardemeister/ Tomi Tuominen	Suzuki SX4 WRC 3h31m12.4s A8	
7	Matthew Wilson/ Scott Martin	Ford Focus RS WRC 07 3h32m08.3s A8	
8	Petter Solberg/ Phil Mills	Subaru Impreza WRC2008 3h37m52.9s A8	
9	Federico Villagra/ Jorge Pérez Companc	Ford Focus RS WRC 07 3h40m43.8s A8	
10	Juho Hänninen/ Mikko Markkula	Mitsubishi Lancer Evo IX 3h43m30.4s N4	

86 starters, 57 finishers

PREVIOUS WINNERS
2001*	Ishida/Ishida	Mitsubishi Lancer Evo
2002*	Possum Bourne/Mark Stacey	Subaru Impreza WRX
2003*	Toshihiro Arai/Tony Sircombe	Subaru Impreza WRX
2004	Petter Solberg/Phil Mills	Subaru Impreza WRC2004
2005	Marcus Grönholm/Timo Rautiainen	Peugeot 307 WRC
2006	Sébastien Loeb/Daniel Elena	Citroën Xsara WRC
2007	Mikko Hirvonen/Jarmo Lehtinen	Ford Focus RS WRC 07

*Non-championship event

Dani Sordo battled through icy stages to claim third and help Citroen to its first manufacturers' crown since 2005.
Photograph: PHOT04

Above and below right: Sébastien Loeb broke his own record of 10 wins in a season with his first victory on Rally GB

Middle and Far right: MotoGP legend Valentino Rossi created a wave of publicity on his way to 12th overall

Photographs: PHOTO4

PLEASED AS he was to see his old friend and fierce rival Marcus Grönholm, Sébastien Loeb's smile turned to a grimace almost as quickly as the perfunctory handshakes were done.

"I don't like, I don't like it at all," said Loeb. Grönholm smiled. The Finn had known Rally GB in all its moods; he knew about icy roads in Wales. To remind him, Loeb ventured: "You are straight, straight, straight; good grip, good grip, good grip. Then you brake for the corner. Bam!"

The final word from Loeb was onomatopoeic for many. The Frenchman underlined his feelings by twirling his arms and spinning himself on the spot, eyes wide. "I don't like..." he added, somewhat superfluously.

Loeb's feelings were understandable. The final round of this year's World Rally Championship did indeed turn into an ice-fed crash-fest, and the five-time world champion was first off the road. He rolled his Lancer recce car on the liaison section after the Myherin test. Standing in a freezing forest waiting for a replacement car, hail bouncing off his back and no chance of seeking shelter in the single-seat tractor which had been deployed to rescue his inverted Mitsubishi, it's fair to say Loeb wasn't looking forward to the next few days.

For the first two days, he moaned solidly about the road, his sentiments echoed – somewhat predictably – by Citroën team principal Olivier Quesnel. On the third and final day, a similarly icy encounter in the Neath Valley stages, Loeb finally channelled his energies into his driving. And then he kicked ass.

Ford's Jari-Matti Latvala had led the event into Sunday morning, but once Loeb engaged himself in the battle, he was at his unstoppable best. He blitzed the Port Talbot and Rheola stages first time through to close the gap to Latvala. Then Loeb was hit with a 10-second jump start penalty in the penultimate test, meaning he went into the finale 2.8 seconds down instead of 7.8 up.

The Frenchman protested his innocence. "I know

when I've done a jump start," he said. "Not this time."

This sequence of events would have rattled a lesser driver, but not Loeb. He put the penalty, along with the ice, at the back of his mind in a compartment marked 'insignificant' and got on with the job in hand. He won the event by 2.7 seconds, which became 12.7 when organisers admitted their mistake at the SS18 startline.

Rally GB was classic Loeb. His genius delivered an 11th season win and sealed his success on every rally he's ever wanted to win.

For Latvala, the disappointment was double – not only did he lose out on a second win of the year, but Ford also missed out on a third consecutive manufacturers' championship. This time, however, the blame couldn't be laid at his door. J-ML had done his bit, after all. No, this time it was his team-mate Mikko Hirvonen who'd failed to deliver the goods after rolling his Focus on the second run through Sweet Lamb. Some consolation for the championship runner-up was that he set his own record this season, becoming the first driver ever to score points on every one of the 15 rounds of the championship.

Loeb's team-mate Dani Sordo capped a solid second half to the season with a sure-footed, trouble-free and oft pacy run to third place in the number two C4 WRC. The Spaniard's mature approach was precisely what was called for following a limelight-stealing drive on the opening day from Citroën's latest blue-eyed boy, Sébastien Ogier. Ogier, on his debut in a C4 WRC, had stunned the WRC pack by leading for the lion's share of the leg. Undoubtedly the recently-crowned Junior World Rally Champion was enjoying favourable conditions – not to mention advance warning of the trickiest and slipperiest corners – further down the field, but he was still there in P1. That was until he suffered gearbox problems late in the day and then rolled on Saturday's first test. Sordo, whose seat hasn't been the safest all season, must have been a touch relieved to bring his car home without a mark on it.

Above: Ford's hopes ended when Mikko Hirvonen suffered this roll on the opening day.

Left: Jari-Matti Latvala led until the final stage after a fine drive but couldn't hold Loeb back.

Far left: On what has since proved to be Subaru's final WRC outing for now, Petter Solberg was fourth.

Top left: P-G Andersson starred again, holding third at the end of day one. He fell to fifth as Suzuki also prepared to bow out of the top level.

Photographs: PHOTO4

Wales Rally GB Results

04-07 DECEMBER 2008 | FIA WORLD RALLY CHAMPIONSHIP ROUND 15

Position / Stage Numbers	2	3	5	6	7	8	9	10	11	12	13	14	15	16	17	18	19
Loeb	8	5	3	2	2	2	3	2	2	2	2	2	2	2	2	2	1
Latvala	9	3	4	1	1	1	1	1	1	1	1	1	1	1	1	1	2
Sordo	12	9	10	7	6	6	2	3	3	3	3	3	3	3	3	3	3
P.Solberg	3	7	5	5	5	5	4	4	4	4	4	4	4	4	4	4	4
Andersson	4	4	6	3	4	3	6	6	6	6	6	5	5	5	5	5	5
Duval	2	10	7	9	8	7	7	7	7	8	7	7	7	7	7	6	6
Gardemeister	7	8	9	12	11	11	9	9	9	9	9	8	8	8	8	7	7
Hirvonen	10	11	44	33	30	29	20	15	13	12	11	9	9	9	9	8	8
Wilson	11	12	12	11	10	10	11	11	10	10	10	10	10	10	10	9	9
Clark	14	14	13	13	12	12	10	10	11	12	11	11	11	11	11	10	10
Flodin	18	16	16	15	14	14	12	12	13	13	12	12	12	12	11	11	
Rossi	45	34	30	26	24	24	19	17	16	16	17	15	15	14	13	12	
Rautenbach	13	17	15	16	16	15	27	23	23	22	23	20	20	17	19	18	17	15
Al-Qassimi	23	28	26	25	21	21	18	19	18	18	18	17	16	17	17	16	16
Perez	37	29	27	23	22	23	21	22	22	22	21	21	21	20	20	20	19
Ogier	1	1	1	8	7	9	24	30	33	31	32	35	36	34	30	27	26
Weston Jr	40	31	32	30	37	47	43	41	37	36	38	38	38	38	37	36	33
Boland	50	65	68	58	56	53	48	47	47	46	45	40	40	37	36	35	34
Atkinson	6	6	8	6	R												
Ostberg	5	2	2	4	3	4	5	5	5	5	5	12	20	R			
Jones	26	27	23	24	23	22	22	21	19	19	27	25	25	24	R		
H.Solberg	20	13	11	10	9	8	8	8	8	7	7	6	6	6	6	R	

Leg 1 — GREAT BRITAIN — Swansea

Leg 2 — Swansea — Cardiff — Bristol Channel

Leg 3 — Swansea — Cardiff (finish)

- ▶ Stage start
- ⌗ Stage finish
- ⬤7 Special stages
- → Rally direction

Top: Andreas Aigner won the Production championship after title rival Juho Hänninen (above right) retired on the opening day.

Above middle: Muddy stages meant cars arrived at service needing a good clean.
Photographs: PHOTO4

FINISH LINES...

Petter Solberg ended a tricky season with fourth place. The Norwegian was pleased with the way his Impreza was working in the mud, but the further into the long stages the car got the more errant its handling became. It was a familiar story. At least Solberg brought his car home – team-mate Chris Atkinson's car went home in a box after the Australian suffered a huge high-speed accident in Walters' Arena on Friday night. Atkinson was briefly hospitalised for a check-up, but released later the same evening... P-G Andersson had ended the opening day in third place after his – and the SX4 WRC's – strongest day in the championship. He eventually finished fifth behind Solberg, with team-mate Toni Gardemeister also in the points in seventh... One place ahead of the Finn was François Duval, who completed his first event with Denis Giraudet as co-driver in the Stobart Ford in place of the injured Patrik Pivato... Patrik Flodin celebrated his maiden Production Car WRC win. The Subaru Impreza driver picked up the lead when British Rally Champion aspirant Guy Wilks hit trouble in his Mitsubishi. Wilks recovered his pace to finish third in class, securing a second British title in the process. Ahead of him Austria's Andreas Aigner also had reason to celebrate. The Red Bull-backed driver made the most of Juho Hänninen's day-one retirement to take second in class and the Production world title... Away from the WRC regulars, it was car number 46 which received the most attention as MotoGP superstar Valentino Rossi braved the icy conditions to guide his Stobart Ford home in 12th place.

RUNNING ORDER

1 Sébastien Loeb / Daniel Elena — Citroën C4 WRC / A8

3 Mikko Hirvonen / Jarmo Lehtinen — Ford Focus RS WRC 08 / A8

2 Dani Sordo / Marc Martí — Citroën C4 WRC / A8

4 Jari-Matti Latvala / Miikka Anttila — Ford Focus RS WRC 08 / A8

6 Chris Atkinson / Stéphane Prévot — Subaru Impreza WRC2008 / A8

5 Petter Solberg / Phil Mills — Subaru Impreza WRC2008 / A8

7 François Duval / Denis Giraudet — Ford Focus RS WRC 07 / A8

14 Henning Solberg / Cato Menkerud — Ford Focus RS WRC 07 / A8

8 Matthew Wilson / Scott Martin — Ford Focus RS WRC 07 / A8

12 P-G Andersson / Jonas Andersson — Suzuki SX4 WRC / A8

11 Toni Gardemeister / Tomi Tuominen — Suzuki SX4 WRC / A8

16 Conrad Rautenbach / David Senior — Citroën C4 WRC / A8

17 Sébastien Ogier / Julien Ingrassia — Citroën C4 WRC / A8

18 Mads Ostberg / Ole Kristian Unnerud — Subaru Impreza WRC2007 / A8

19 Khalid Al-Qassimi / Michael Orr — Ford Focus RS WRC 07 / A8

20 Barry Clark / Paul Nagle — Ford Focus RS WRC 07 / A8

21 Eamonn Boland / Damien Morrissey — Subaru Impreza WRC2007 / A8

46 Valentino Rossi / Carlo Cassina — Ford Focus RS WRC 07 / A8

22 Gareth Jones / Clive Jenkins — Subaru Impreza WRC2007 / A8

23 Steve Perez — Ford Focus RS WRC 05

Paul Spooner — A8

24 Dave Weston Jr / Aled Davies — Ford Focus RS WRC 03 / A8

SPECIAL STAGE TIMES

SS1 Hafren 1 (19.10km)*
Cancelled due to safety concerns - too much ice on the road
* Stage length had already been cut to 3.67km due to adverse weather conditions

SS2 Sweet Lamb 1 (5.11km)*
1 S.Ogier/J.Ingrassia (Citroën C4 WRC) 2m48.6s; 2 F.Duval/D.Giraudet (Ford Focus RS WRC 07) 2m53.7s; 3 P.Solberg/P.Mills (Subaru Impreza WRC2008) 2m54.0s; 4 P.Andersson/J.Andersson (Suzuki SX4 WRC) 2m54.5s; 5 M.Ostberg/O.Unnerud (Subaru Impreza WRC2007) 2m56.1s; 6 C.Atkinson/S.Prévot (Subaru Impreza WRC2008) 2m56.9s; PC M.Higgins/R.Kennedy (Subaru Impreza) 3m06.6s
* Stage length was cut to 4.28km due to adverse weather conditions

SS3 Myherin 1 (35.34km)*
1 J-M.Latvala/M.Anttila (Ford Focus RS WRC 08) 10m59.2s; 2 Ostberg/Unnerud (Subaru) 11m01.2s; 3 S.Loeb/D.Elena (Citroën C4 WRC) 11m04.0s; 4 D.Sordo/M.Martí (Citroën C4 WRC) 11m05.9s; 5 Ogier/Ingrassia (Citroën) 11m06.4s; 6 Andersson/Andersson (Suzuki) 11m07.2s; PC G.Wilks/P.Pugh (Mitsubishi Lancer Evo IX) 11m41.5s
* Stage length was cut to 18.28km due to adverse weather conditions

SS4 Hafren 2 (19.10km)*
Cancelled due to safety concerns - too much ice on the road
* Stage length had already been cut to 3.67km due to adverse weather conditions

SS5 Sweet Lamb 2 (5.11km)*
1 Loeb/Elena (Citroën) 2m52.2s; 2 Duval/Giraudet (Ford) 2m52.2s;

3 Ostberg/Unnerud (Subaru) 2m52.4s; 4 P.Solberg/Mills (Subaru) 2m52.4s; 5 H.Solberg/C.Menkerud (Ford Focus RS WRC 07) 2m52.8s; 6 Ogier/Ingrassia (Citroën) 2m54.4s; PC Wilks/Pugh (Mitsubishi) 3m01.9s
* Stage length was cut to 4.28km due to adverse weather conditions

SS6 Myherin 2 (35.34km)*
1 Latvala/Anttila (Ford) 10m56.5s; 2 Loeb/Elena (Citroën) 11m08.0s; 3 Andersson/Andersson (Suzuki) 11m09.3s; 4 Sordo/Martí (Citroën) 11m09.8s; 5 Atkinson/Prévot (Subaru) 11m13.4s; 6 H.Solberg/Menkerud (Ford) 11m14.6s; PC Wilks/Pugh (Mitsubishi) 11m56.0s
* Stage length was cut to 18.28km due to adverse weather conditions

SS7 Walters Arena 1 (2.29km)
1 Latvala/Anttila (Ford) 1m44.5s; 2 Loeb/Elena (Citroën) 1m46.9s; 3 P.Solberg/Mills (Subaru) 1m47.1s; 4 Sordo/Martí (Citroën) 1m47.3s; 5 Ostberg/Unnerud (Subaru) 1m47.6s; 6 Andersson/Andersson (Suzuki) 1m48.5s; PC Wilks/Pugh (Mitsubishi) 1m51.1s

SS8 Walters Arena 2 (2.29km)
1 Loeb/Elena (Citroën) 1m45.0s; 2 Andersson/Andersson (Suzuki) 1m45.7s; 3= Sordo/Martí (Citroën), P.Solberg/Mills (Subaru) 1m45.8s; 5 Latvala/Anttila (Ford) 1m45.9s; 6 Duval/Giraudet (Ford) 1m46.9s; PC N.Al-Attiyah/C.Patterson (Subaru Impreza) 1m49.1s

SS9 Resolfen 1 (30.68km)
1 Sordo/Martí (Citroën) 17m12.5s; 2 M.Hirvonen/J.Lehtinen (Ford Focus RS WRC 08) 17m30.5; 3 Loeb/Elena (Citroën) 17m36.0s; 4 P.Solberg/Mills (Subaru) 17m38.6s; 5 T.Gardemeister/T.Tuominen (Suzuki SX4 WRC) 17m41.4s; 6 Latvala/Anttila (Ford) 17m43.9s; PC P.Flodin/G.Bergsten (Subaru Impreza) 18m19.1s

SS10 Halfway 1 (18.57km)
1 Latvala/Anttila (Ford) 11m24.3s; 2 Loeb/Elena (Citroën) 11m29.3s; 3 Hirvonen/Lehtinen (Ford) 11m40.5; 4 Sordo/Martí (Citroën) 11m45.3s; 5 P.Solberg/Mills (Subaru) 11m45.6s; 6 Andersson/Andersson (Suzuki) 11m48.4s; PC P.Sandell/E.Axelsson (Peugeot 207 S2000) 12m17.1s

SS11 Crychan 1 (14.86km)
1 Sordo/Martí (Citroën) 9m25.1s; 2 Hirvonen/Lehtinen (Ford) 9m26.9s; 3 Loeb/Elena (Citroën) 9m28.2s; 4 Latvala/Anttila (Ford) 9m29.3s; 5 H.Solberg/Menkerud (Ford) 9m29.7s; 6 P.Solberg/Mills (Subaru) 9m32.2s; PC Sandell/Axelsson (Peugeot) 9m50.6s

SS12 Resolfen 2 (30.68km)
1 Hirvonen/Lehtinen (Ford) 16m19.9s; 2 Loeb/Elena (Citroën) 16m35.4s; 3 P.Solberg/Mills (Subaru) 16m35.6s; 4 Latvala/Anttila (Ford) 16m35.9s; 5 H.Solberg/Menkerud (Ford) 16m39.0s; 6 Sordo/Martí (Citroën) 16m39.7s; PC Flodin/Bergsten (Subaru) 17m44.2s

SS13 Halfway 2 (18.57km)
1 Loeb/Elena (Citroën) 11m11.9s; 2 Hirvonen/Lehtinen (Ford) 11m16.9s; 3 Latvala/Anttila (Ford) 11m17.9s; 4 Sordo/Martí (Citroën) 11m19.1s; 5 P.Solberg/Mills (Subaru) 11m20.8s; 6 H.Solberg/Menkerud (Ford) 11m25.3s; PC Sandell/Axelsson (Peugeot) 12m08.8s

SS14 Crychan 2 (14.86km)
1 Latvala/Anttila (Ford) 9m00.6s; 2 Hirvonen/Lehtinen (Ford) 9m03.7s; 3 P.Solberg/Mills (Subaru) 9m07.3s; 4 Sordo/Martí (Citroën) 9m08.0s; 5 Loeb/Elena (Citroën) 9m09.0s; 6 H.Solberg/Menkerud (Ford) 9m11.5s; PC Sandell/Axelsson (Peugeot) 9m48.5s

SS15 Cardiff (0.99km)
1 Loeb/Elena (Citroën) 56.5s; 2 P.Solberg/Mills (Subaru) 56.9s; 3 Duval/Giraudet (Ford Focus) 57.1s; 4 Hirvonen/Lehtinen (Ford) 57.8s; 5 Sordo/Martí (Citroën) 57.9s; 6= H.Solberg/Menkerud, Gardemeister/Tuominen (Suzuki) 58.5s; PC A.Aráujo/M.Ramalho (Mitsubishi Lancer Evo IX) 58.9s

SS16 Rheola 1 (27.96km)
1 Loeb/Elena (Citroën) 16m15.0s; 2 Latvala/Anttila (Ford) 16m20.1s; 3 Sordo/Martí (Citroën) 16m25.3s; 4 P.Solberg/Mills (Subaru) 16m34.2s; 5 Hirvonen/Lehtinen (Ford) 16m42.7s; 6 Andersson/Andersson (Suzuki) 16m48.1s; PC Flodin/Bergsten (Subaru) 17m50.0s

SS17 Port Talbot 1 (20.09km)
1 Loeb/Elena (Citroën) 11m17.9s; 2 Latvala/Anttila (Ford) 11m18.7s; 3 Sordo/Martí (Citroën) 11m28.5s; 4 Hirvonen/Lehtinen (Ford) 11m32.8s; 5 H.Solberg/Menkerud (Ford) 11m35.9s; 6 P.Solberg/Mills (Subaru) 11m41.4s; PC Sandell/Axelsson (Peugeot) 12m17.5s

SS18 Rheola 2 (27.96km)
1 Loeb/Elena (Citroën) 16m25.0s; 2 Hirvonen/Lehtinen (Ford) 16m33.7s; 3 Latvala/Anttila (Ford) 16m34.2s; 4 P.Solberg/Mills (Subaru) 16m40.7s; 5 Sordo/Martí (Citroën) 16m49.5s; 6 Ogier/Ingrassia (Citroën) 16m50.5s; PC Flodin/Bergsten (Subaru) 17m27.5s

SS19 Port Talbot 2 (20.09km)
1 Loeb/Elena (Citroën) 11m12.0s; 2 Latvala/Anttila (Ford) 11m16.9s; 3 Hirvonen/Lehtinen (Ford) 11m22.3s; 4 Sordo/Martí (Citroën) 11m26.6s; 5 P.Solberg/Mills (Subaru) 11m28.0s; 6 Gardemeister/Tuominen (Suzuki) 11m36.1s; PC Flodin/Bergsten (Subaru) 12m10.8s

Cars that retired and subsequently restarted and were classified under SuperRally regs:

| 17 | Ogier/Ingrassia | Citroën C4 WRC | | |
| | Off road | SS9 | A8 | |

MAJOR RETIREMENTS
6	Atkinson/Prévot	Subaru Impreza WRC2008		
	Accident	SS7	A8	
18	Ostberg/Unnerud	Subaru Impreza WRC2007		
	Withdrawn	SS15E	A8	
22	Jones/Jenkins	Subaru Impreza WRC2007		
	Mechanical	SS17	A8	
14	H.Solberg/Menkerud	Ford Focus RS WRC 07		
	Mechanical	SS18	A8	

FIA CLASS WINNERS
A8	Over 2000cc	Loeb/Elena
		Citroën C4 WRC
A7	1600-2000cc	Griotti/Bonato
		Renault Clio R3
A6	1400-1600cc	Pritchard/Gwynn
		Citroën C2-R2
A5	Up to 1400cc	Jones/Burley
		Skoda Felicia
N4	Over 2000cc	Flodin/Bergsten
		Subaru Impreza
N3	1600-2000cc	Cave/Price
		Ford Fiesta ST
N2	1400-1600cc	Nichol/Morrison
		Suzuki Swift
N1	Up to 1400cc	Harrison/Thomas
		MG ZR 105

RALLY LEADERS
Overall: SS2-5 Ogier; SS6-18 Latvala; SS19 Loeb
PC: SS2 M.Higgins; SS3-8 Wilks; SS9-19 Flodin

SPECIAL STAGE ANALYSIS
	1st	2nd	3rd	4th	5th	6th
Loeb (Citroën)	8	4	3	-	1	-
Latvala (Ford)	5	3	2	2	1	1
Sordo (Citroën)	2	-	3	7	2	1
Hirvonen (Ford)	1	5	2	2	1	-
Ogier (Citroën)	1	-	-	-	1	2
Duval (Ford)	-	2	1	-	-	1
P.Solberg (Subaru)	-	1	5	4	3	2
Andersson (Suzuki)	-	1	1	1	-	4
Ostberg (Subaru)	-	1	1	-	2	-
H.Solberg (Ford)	-	-	-	-	4	4
Gardemeister (Suzuki)	-	-	-	-	1	2
Atkinson (Subaru)	-	-	-	-	1	1

TYRES
Tyres: Pirelli Scorpion
Compound: soft
Number of tyres available per car: 42

WORLD CHAMPIONSHIP POINTS
Drivers
1 Loeb 122; 2 Hirvonen 103; 3 Sordo 65; 4 Latvala 58; 5 Atkinson 50; 6 P.Solberg 46; 7 Duval 25; 8 H.Solberg 22; 9 Galli 17; 10 Wilson 15 etc

Manufacturers
1 Citroën Total WRT 191; 2 BP Ford Abu Dhabi WRT 173; 3 Subaru WRT 98; 4 Stobart VK M-Sport Ford RT 67; 5 Suzuki WRT 34; 6 Munchi's Ford WRT 22.

Junior World Rally Championship
1 Ogier 42; 2 Burkart 34; 3 Prokop 32; 4 Gallagher 30; 5= Kosciuszko, Bettega 22; 7 Sandell 21; 8 Mölder 11; 9 Albertini 9; 10= Schammel, Bertolotti, Niegel 8 etc

Production Car World Rally Championship
1 Aigner 38; 2 Hänninen 36; 3 Ketomaa 28; 4 Sandell 22; 5 Prokop 17; 6= Rauam, Nutahara 15; 8 Aráujo 14; 9 Sousa 12; 10 Flodin 10 etc

Route Details
Total route of 1428.44km of which 348.99km were competitive on 19 special stages*
Leg 1 Friday 5 December, 8 special stages totalling 123.68km*
Leg 2 Saturday 6 December, 7 special stages totalling 129.21km
Leg 3 Sunday 7 December, 4 special stages totalling 96.10km
* Leg 1 route reduced to 49.70km due to adverse weather conditions.

RESULTS
1	Sébastien Loeb	Citroën C4 WRC	
	Daniel Elena	2h43m09.6s A8	
2	Jari-Matti Latvala/	Ford Focus RS WRC 08	
	Miikka Anttila	2h43m22.3s A8	
3	Dani Sordo/	Citroën C4 WRC	
	Marc Martí	2h44m30.2s A8	
4	Petter Solberg/	Subaru Impreza WRC2008	
	Phil Mills	2h45m09.2s A8	
5	P-G Andersson/	Suzuki SX4 WRC	
	Jonas Andersson	2h47m13.7s A8	
6	François Duval/	Ford Focus RS WRC 07	
	Denis Giraudet	2h48m17.4s A8	
7	Toni Gardemeister/	Suzuki SX4 WRC	
	Tomi Tuominen	2h48m34.6s A8	
8	Mikko Hirvonen/	Ford Focus RS WRC 08	
	Jarmo Lehtinen	2h48m48.4s A8	
9	Matthew Wilson/	Ford Focus RS WRC 07	
	Scott Martin	2h51m23.5s A8	
10	Barry Clark/	Ford Focus RS WRC 07	
	Paul Nagle	2h53m02.7s A8	

79 starters, 47 finishers

PREVIOUS WINNERS SINCE 1971
1971	Stig Blomqvist/Arne Hertz	Saab 96 V4
1972	Roger Clark/Tony Mason	Ford Escort RS1600
1973	Timo Mäkinen/Henry Liddon	Ford Escort RS1600
1974	Timo Mäkinen/Henry Liddon	Ford Escort RS1600
1975	Timo Mäkinen/Henry Liddon	Ford Escort RS1800
1976	Roger Clark/Stuart Pegg	Ford Escort RS1800
1977	Björn Waldegård/Hans Thorszelius	Ford Escort RS1800
1978	Hannu Mikkola/Arne Hertz	Ford Escort RS1800
1979	Hannu Mikkola/Arne Hertz	Ford Escort RS1800
1980	Henri Toivonen/Paul White	Talbot Sunbeam Lotus
1981	Hannu Mikkola/Arne Hertz	Audi Quattro A1
1982	Hannu Mikkola/Arne Hertz	Audi Quattro A1
1983	Stig Blomqvist/Björn Cederberg	Audi Quattro A2
1984	Ari Vatanen/Terry Harryman	Peugeot 205 Turbo 16
1985	Henri Toivonen/Neil Wilson	Lancia Delta S4
1986	Timo Salonen/Seppo Harjanne	Peugeot 205 Turbo 16 E2
1987	Juha Kankkunen/Juha Piironen	Lancia Delta HF Turbo
1988	Markku Alén/Ilkka Kivimäki	Lancia Delta Integrale
1989	Pentti Airikkala/Ronan McNamee	Mitsubishi Galant VR-4
1990	Carlos Sainz/Luis Moya	Toyota Celica GT4
1991	Juha Kankkunen/Juha Piironen	Lancia Delta Integrale 16v
1992	Carlos Sainz/Luis Moya	Toyota Celica Turbo 4WD
1993	Juha Kankkunen/Juha Piironen	Toyota Celica Turbo 4WD
1994	Colin McRae/Derek Ringer	Subaru Impreza 555
1995	Colin McRae/Derek Ringer	Subaru Impreza 555
1996	Armin Schwarz/Denis Giraudet	Toyota Celica GT-Four
1997	Colin McRae/Nicky Grist	Subaru Impreza WRC97
1998	Richard Burns/Robert Reid	Mitsubishi Carisma GT
1999	Richard Burns/Robert Reid	Subaru Impreza WRC99
2000	Richard Burns/Robert Reid	Subaru Impreza WRC2000
2001	Marcus Grönholm/Timo Rautiainen	Peugeot 206 WRC
2002	Petter Solberg/Phil Mills	Subaru Impreza WRC2002
2003	Petter Solberg/Phil Mills	Subaru Impreza WRC2003
2004	Petter Solberg/Phil Mills	Subaru Impreza WRC2004
2005	Petter Solberg/Phil Mills	Subaru Impreza WRC2005
2006	Marcus Grönholm/Timo Rautiainen	Ford Focus RS WRC 06
2007	Mikko Hirvonen/Jarmo Lehtinen	Ford Focus RS WRC 07

FIA WORLD RALLY CHAMPIONSHIP FOR DRIVERS

ROUND		1	2	3	4	5	6	7	8	9	10	11	12	13	14	15	TOTAL
1	SÉBASTIEN LOEB	10	R	10	10	0	10	10	6	10	10	10	10	10	6	10	122
2	MIKKO HIRVONEN	8	8	5	4	10	8	6	10	8	5	6	6	8	10	1	103
3	DANIEL SORDO	11th	3	16th	6	8	4	4	5	5	8	8	8	R	R	6	65
4	JARI-MATTI LATVALA	12th	10	6	12th	2	6	2	8	38th	9th	R	3	5	8	8	58
5	CHRIS ATKINSON	6	21st	8	8	6	3	R	13th	6	3	R	2	3	5	R	50
6	PETTER SOLBERG	4	5	11th	R	R	10th	8	3	3	4	5	4	4	1	5	46
7	FRANÇOIS DUVAL	5	-	-	-	-	-	-	-	-	6	R	5	6	R	3	25
8	HENNING SOLBERG	9th	13th	4	R	5	2	1	4	4	2	9th	11th	15th	R	R	22
9	GIGI GALLI	3	6	R	2	1	5	R	R	R	R	-	-	-	-	-	17
10	MATTHEW WILSON	10th	R	3	R	4	12th	3	2	9th	12th	17th	9th	1	2	9th	15
11	URMO AAVA	-	18th	-	-	R	1	5	R	15th	1	4	35th	2	-	-	13
12	P-G ANDERSSON	1	R	R	24th	R	9th	11th	R	R	15th	3	32nd	17th	4	4	12
13	TONI GARDEMEISTER	R	2	R	R	R	R	9th	R	1	10th	2	13th	13th	3	2	10
14	FEDERICO VILLAGRA	-	-	2	3	3	14th	13th	9th	R	-	1	12th	-	9th	-	9
15	CONRAD RAUTENBACH	R	16th	15th	5	15th	13th	10th	1	10th	13th	R	R	14th	R	15th	6
16	ANDREAS MIKKELSEN	-	4	-	-	-	R	-	19th	12th	11th	-	1	11th	-	-	5
17	MATTI RANTANEN	-	-	-	-	-	-	-	2	-	-	-	-	-	-	-	2
=	JEAN-MARIE CUOQ	2	-	-	-	-	-	-	-	-	-	-	-	-	-	-	2
19	ANDREAS AIGNER	-	31st	-	1	-	-	14th	11th	R	-	R	-	-	-	13th	1
=	SEBASTIEN OGIER	-	-	1	-	11th	22nd	-	-	35th	19th	-	R	20th	-	26th	1
=	JUHO HÄNNINEN	-	1	-	-	-	-	21st	-	13th	-	14th	29th	-	10th	R	1

FIA WORLD RALLY CHAMPIONSHIP FOR MANUFACTURERS

ROUND		1	2	3	4	5	6	7	8	9	10	11	12	13	14	15	TOTAL
1	CITROËN TOTAL WRT	11	4	10	16	9	14	15	11	15	18	18	18	10	6	16	191
2	BP FORD ABU DHABI WRT	8	18	11	7	13	14	10	18	9	7	6	11	14	18	9	173
3	SUBARU WRT	10	6	9	8	6	3	8	3	9	7	5	6	7	6	5	98
4	STOBART VK M-SPORT FORD	8	8	3	3	7	5	3	4	4	6	0	4	7	2	3	67
5	SUZUKI WRT	2	3	0	1	0	1	3	0	2	1	7	0	1	7	6	34
6	MUNCHI'S FORD WRT	-	-	6	4	4	2	0	3	0	-	3	0	-	0	-	22

KEY TO ROUNDS: 1-MONTE CARLO; 2-SWEDEN; 3-MEXICO; 4-ARGENTINA; 5-JORDAN; 6-ITALY; 7-GREECE; 8-TURKEY; 9-FINLAND; 10-GERMANY; 11-NEW ZEALAND; 12-SPAIN; 13-CORSICA; 14-JAPAN; 15-GREAT BRITAIN

Photograph: Race&motion

JUNIOR WORLD RALLY CHAMPIONSHIP

ROUND		1	2	3	4	5	6	7	TOTAL
1	SÉBASTIEN OGIER	10	10	4	pass	10	R	8	42
2	AARON BURKART	5	pass	6	5	8	6	4	34
3	MARTIN PROKOP	2	pass	10th	10	R	10	10	32
4	SHAUN GALLAGHER	3	8	5	4	5	5	pass	30
5	MICHAL KOSCIUSZKO	6	R	10	6	pass	9th	R	22
6	ALESSANDRO BETTEGA	pass	R	8	R	6	8	R	22
7	PATRIK SANDELL	4	R	2	8	pass	4	3	21
8	JAAN MÖLDER	8	R	9th	R	pass	3	0	11
9	STEFANO ALBERTINI	pass	4	3	13th	10th	2	0	9
10	GILLES SCHAMMEL	pass	6	12th	2	R	R	0	8
=	FLORIAN NIEGEL	pass	5	R	9th	1	10th	2	8
=	SIMONE BERTOLOTTI	pass	3	R	10th	4	1	R	8

KEY TO ROUNDS: 1-MEXICO; 2-JORDAN; 3-ITALY; 4-FINLAND; 5-GERMANY; 6-SPAIN; 7-CORSICA

PASS – ROUNDS THAT THE DRIVER HAS ELECTED NOT TO SCORE POINTS ON

PRODUCTION WORLD RALLY CHAMPIONSHIP

ROUND		1	2	3	4	5	6	7	8	TOTAL
1	ANDREAS AIGNER	14th	10	10	10	pass	R	pass	8	38
2	JUHO HÄNNINEN	10	pass	2	pass	10	4	10	R	36
3	JARI KETOMAA	8	6	R	pass	6	3	pass	5	28
4	PATRIK SANDELL	6	R	R	8	pass	8	pass	R	22
5	MARTIN PROKOP	5	2	14th	exc	pass	10	pass	R	17
6	MARTIN RAUAM	pass	4	exc	5	pass	6	R	-	15
=	FUMIO NUTAHARA	pass	5	5	pass	4	R	1	R	15
8	ARMINDO ARAÚJO	2	pass	6	4	pass	12th	9th	2	14
9	BERNARDO SOUSA	1	1	8	11th	pass	2	pass	9th	12
10	PATRIK FLODIN	16th	-	-	-	exc	-	-	10	10

KEY TO ROUNDS: 1-SWEDEN; 2-ARGENTINA; 3-GREECE; 4-TURKEY; 5-FINLAND; 6-NEW ZEALAND; 7-JAPAN; 8-GREAT BRITAIN

PASS – ROUNDS THAT THE DRIVER HAS ELECTED NOT TO SCORE POINTS ON

Technically Speaking

FORD FOCUS RS WRC 08

ENGINE

Designation	Duratec WRC
Cylinders	Four in-line
Mounts	Transverse/front
Capacity	1998cc
Bore & stroke	85x88mm
Valves/camshaft	16/DOHC
Fuel system	Ford/PI Research
Turbocharger	Garrett
Max power	300bhp@6000rpm
Max torque	550NM@4000rpm
Oil supplier	Castrol

TRANSMISSION

Gearbox	M-Sport/Ricardo 5-speed sequential
Drive type	4WD
Clutch /differentials	M-Sport/Sachs multi-disc carbon clutch, M-Sport active centre diff. Pi electronic control units

Photograph: Race&motion

DIMENSIONS

Overall length	4362mm
Overall width	1800mm
Wheelbase	2640mm
Weight	1230kg
Front track	-
Rear track	-
Body	Three-door steel

CHASSIS

Steering	Rack and pinion (power-assisted)
Front suspension	MacPherson struts, Reiger damping
Rear suspension	Trailing arm, Reiger damping
Wheel sizes	7x15in (gravel) 8x18in (asphalt)
Tyres	Pirelli
Front brakes	300/370mm Brembo discs, 4-8 piston callipers
Rear brakes	300/370mm Brembo discs, 4-8 piston callipers

Team Principal: Malcolm Wilson

Technical Director: Christian Loriaux

Sponsors: BP, Castrol, Pirelli, Abu Dhabi, OZ, Brembo, Sparco

CITROËN C4 WRC

ENGINE

Designation	XU7JP4
Cylinders	Four in-line
Mounts	Transverse/front
Capacity	1998cc
Bore & stroke	-
Valves/camshaft	16-valve/DOHC
Fuel system	Magneti Marelli MR3
Turbocharger	Garrett
Max power	315bhp@5500rpm
Max torque	580Nm@2750rpm
Oil supplier	Total

TRANSMISSION

Gearbox	X-trac 6-speed, sequential
Drive type	4WD
Clutch /differentials	Triple-plate carbon, electronic control centre diff, mechanical front and rear

Photograph: Race&motion

DIMENSIONS

Overall length	4274mm
Overall width	1800mm
Wheelbase	2608mm
Weight	1230kg
Front track	1598mm
Rear track	1598mm
Body	Three-door steel

CHASSIS

Steering	Rack and pinion (hydraulic power-assisted)
Front suspension	MacPherson strut with coil spring Citroën/Exe-TC damping
Rear suspension	MacPherson strut with coil spring Citroën/Exe-TC damping
Wheel sizes	7x15/8x15in
Tyres	Pirelli
Front brakes	376x28mm Alcon discs, 6-8 piston callipers
Rear brakes	278x20mm Alcon discs, 6-8 piston callipers

Team Principal: Olivier Quesnel

Technical Director: Xavier Mestelan-Pinon

Sponsors: Total, Red Bull, Meteo France, Eurodatacar, Pirelli

SUBARU IMPREZA WRC2008

ENGINE

Designation	H-4
Cylinders	Horizontally opposed four
Mounts	Longitudinal
Capacity	1994cc
Bore & stroke	92/75mm
Valves/camshaft	16/4 DOHC
Fuel system	STi sequential injection
Turbocharger	IHI
Max power	300bhp@5500rpm
Max torque	650NM@3000rpm
Oil supplier	Motul

TRANSMISSION

Gearbox	Six-speed electro-hydraulic
Drive type	4WD
Clutch /differentials	AP Carbon, electro-hydraulic centre diff; mechanical front and rear diff

Photograph: Race&motion

DIMENSIONS

Overall length	4415mm
Overall width	1800mm
Wheelbase	2635mm
Weight	1230kg
Front track	1550mm
Rear track	1560mm
Body	Four-door steel

CHASSIS

Steering	Rack and pinion (power-assisted)
Front suspension	MacPherson strut, SWRT dampers
Rear suspension	MacPherson strut, SWRT dampers
Wheel sizes	7x15in (gravel) 8x18in (asphalt)
Tyres	Pirelli
Front brakes	AP 378/310x32mm 6-8 piston callipers
Rear brakes	AP 310x28mm 6-8 piston callipers

Team Principal: David Richards

Technical Director: David Lapworth

Sponsors: STi, BBS, Denso, Motul, PIAA, Snap-on, Sparco

SUZUKI SX4 WRC

ENGINE

Designation	J20
Cylinders	Four in-line
Mounts	Transverse
Capacity	1997cc
Bore & stroke	-
Valves/camshaft	16/4 DOHC
Fuel system	Suzuki
Turbocharger	Garrett
Max power	320bhp@4500rpm
Max torque	590NM@3500rpm
Oil supplier	Shell

TRANSMISSION

Gearbox	Five-speed sequential
Drive type	4WD
Clutch /differentials	Carbon, electronic centre diff; mechanical front and rear diff

Photograph: Race&motion

DIMENSIONS

Overall length	4135mm
Overall width	1770mm
Wheelbase	2500mm
Weight	1230kg
Front track	-
Rear track	-
Body	Four-door steel

CHASSIS

Steering	Rack and pinion (power assisted)
Front suspension	MacPherson strut, Reiger dampers
Rear suspension	MacPherson strut, Reiger dampers
Wheel sizes	7x15in (gravel) 8x18in (asphalt)
Tyres	Pirelli
Front brakes	370/300x32mm 8/4-piston callipers
Rear brakes	300x28mm 4-piston callipers

Team Principal and Technical Director: Shusuke Inagaki

Sponsors: Shell, NTN, Sanden, OMP

ENGINE

Cylinders	Four in-line
Mounts Front	Transverse
Capacity	1587cc
Bore & stroke	78.5x82mm
Compression ratio	-
Valves/camshaft	16/DOHC
Fuel system	Magneti Marelli MF-4M
Max power	255bhp@8500rpm
Max torque	205Nm@7000rpm

DIMENSIONS

Overall length	3660mm
Overall width	1795mm
Wheelbase	2326mm
Weight	1000kg
Front track	1600mm
Rear track	1600mm
Body	Three-door steel

CITROËN C2 S1600

TRANSMISSION

Gearbox	Sadev 6-speed sequential
Drive type	FWD
Clutch/differentials	184mm dia.plate/pas mechanical

CHASSIS

Steering	Rack and pinion (power-assisted)
Front suspension	MacPherson struts, Ohlins damping
Rear suspension	Trailing arms, Ohlins damping
Wheel sizes	6x15in (gravel) 7x17in (asphalt)
Tyres	Pirelli
Front brakes	300-355mm discs, 4 piston callipers
Rear brakes	280mm discs, 2 piston callipers

ENGINE

Cylinders	Four in-line
Mounts Front	Transverse
Capacity	1598cc
Bore & stroke	81x77.5mm
Compression ratio	12.9:1
Valves/camshaft	16/DOHC
Fuel system	Suzuki injection
Max power	218bhp@8750bhp
Max torque	186NM@7250rpm

DIMENSIONS

Overall length	3695mm
Overall width	1805mm
Wheelbase	2390mm
Weight	1000kg
Front track	-
Rear track	-
Body	Three-door steel

SUZUKI SWIFT SPORT

TRANSMISSION

Gearbox	Suzuki 5-speed
Drive type	FWD
Clutch/differentials	Single-plate, 184mm dia./passive mechanical

CHASSIS

Steering	Rack and pinion (power-assisted)
Front suspension	MacPherson struts, Kayaba/Reiger damping
Rear suspension	Trailing arms, coil springs, Reiger damping
Wheel sizes	6x15in (gravel) 7x17in (asphalt)
Tyres	Pirelli
Front brakes	Brembo 300/355mm discs, 4 piston callipers
Rear brakes	Brembo 278mm discs, 2 piston callipers

ENGINE

Designation	4G63
Cylinders	Four in-line
Mounts	Front, Transverse
Capacity	1997cc
Bore & stroke	85x88mm
Valves/camshaft	16/DOHC
Fuel system	ATL/Bosch
Turbocharger	Mitsubishi
Max power	270bhp@4300rpm
Max torque	550Nm@3200rpm

DIMENSIONS

Overall length	4490mm
Overall width	1770mm
Wheelbase	2625mm
Weight	1330kg
Front track	-
Rear track	-
Body	Four-door steel

MITSUBISHI LANCER EVO IX

TRANSMISSION

Gearbox	Ricardo 5-speed H-pattern dog gearbox
Drive type	4WD
Clutch/differentials	Front and rear mechanical Ralliart; active centre GEMS

CHASSIS

Steering	Rack and pinion (power-assisted)
Front suspension	Reiger adjustable/ MacPherson struts
Rear suspension	Multi-link with Reiger adjustable
Wheel sizes	8x17in (asphalt) 7x15in (gravel)
Front brakes	300mm-355mm 4 piston callipers
Rear brakes	295mm 4 piston callipers

SUBARU IMPREZA N14

ENGINE

Designation	H-4
Cylinders	Horizontally opposed four
Mounts	Longitudinal
Capacity	1994cc
Bore & stroke	92/75mm
Valves/camshaft	16/4 OHC
Fuel system	FT3-99
Turbocharger	IHI
Max power	257bhp@5500rpm
Max torque	547NM@3000rpm

DIMENSIONS

Overall length	4415mm
Overall width	1795mm
Wheelbase	2625mm
Weight	1365kg
Front track	1550mm
Rear track	1560mm
Body	Four-door steel

TRANSMISSION

Gearbox	Prodrive 5-speed manual 'dog box
Drive type	4WD
Clutch/differentials	STi 6-paddle clutch, electro-mechanical locking centre diff, plated LSD front and rear diffs

CHASSIS

Steering	Rack and pinion (power-assisted)
Front suspension	MacPherson strut, Prodrive-Ohlins dampers
Rear suspension	MacPherson strut, Prodrive-Ohlins dampers

Wheel sizes	7x15in (gravel) 8x18in (asphalt)
Tyres	Not restricted
Front brakes	355/295mm 4-piston callipers
Rear brakes	285mm 4-piston callipers

ABARTH GRANDE PUNTO

ENGINE

Designation	FTP
Cylinders	Four in-line
Mounts	Front, transverse
Capacity	1997cc
Bore & stroke	85mmx88mm
Valves/camshaft	16/DOHC
Fuel system	Magneti Marelli MF-4M
Max power	270bhp@8250bhp
Max torque	225Nm@6500bhp

DIMENSIONS

Overall length	4030mm
Overall width	1800mm
Wheelbase	2536mm
Weight	-
Body	Three-door steel

TRANSMISSION

Gearbox	Sadev 6-speed sequential
Drive type	4WD
Clutch/differentials	Sadev plated clutch, mechanical front, centre and rear differentials

CHASSIS

Steering	Rack and pinion (power-assisted)
Front suspension	Ohlins shock absorber MacPherson strut
Rear suspension	Ohlins shock absorber MacPherson strut

Wheel sizes	8x18in (asphalt) 6.5x15in (gravel)
Front brakes	300/355mm 4 piston callipers
Rear brakes	300 discs, 4 piston callipers

PEUGEOT 207 S2000

ENGINE

Designation	EW10J4s
Cylinders	Four in-line
Mounts	Front, transverse
Capacity	1998cc
Bore & stroke	86mmx86mm
Valves/camshaft	16/DOHC
Fuel system	Magneti Marelli
Max power	280bhp@8250rpm
Max torque	250Nm@6500rpm

DIMENSIONS

Overall length	4030mm
Overall width	1800mm
Wheelbase	2560mm
Weight	-
Body	Three-door steel

TRANSMISSION

Gearbox	Sadev 6-speed sequential
Drive type	4WD
Clutch/differentials	Twin disc Peugeot clutch, mechanical front, centre and rear differentials

CHASSIS

Steering	Rack and pinion (power-assisted)
Front suspension	Pseudo MacPherson/Peugeot damper
Rear suspension	Pseudo MacPherson/Peugeot damper

Wheel sizes	8x18in (asphalt) 6.5x15in (gravel)
Front brakes	300/355mm, 4 piston callipers
Rear brakes	300mm discs, 4 piston callipers

Production Car World Rally Championship

Andreas Aigner and Juho Hänninen led a new generation of Production drivers in 2008, with the former claiming the title by a slender two points. By Richard Rodgers

Main: Andreas Aigner scored his third Production win on the trot in Turkey.

Inset: The Austrian finally fulfilled his potential, defeating rival Juho Hänninen in a last-round title decider.

Right: Hänninen began his campaign with victory in Sweden

Photographs: PHOTO4

WHEN ANDREAS Aigner trailed home 14th of the 19 Production Car World Rally Championship runners in Sweden last February there was little to suggest the 24-year-old would end the 2008 season atop of the final points table.

After completing the opening leg in fifth place, a mistake on the second stage of day two sent him careering off the road. Eighteen minutes were lost before he was able to resume his charge after a group of spectators helped to haul his car out of a ditch.

But, according to his then-team boss Raimund Baumschlager, the error provided the perfect impetus for the young Austrian.

"He was under pressure after Sweden, so when he got to Argentina for the next round he had to get a result," says Baumschlager. "He drives the best when he is under pressure so I was expecting something good from him."

'Something good' translated into Aigner's maiden victory in the Group N class and the first real evidence that he was worthy of the hype that had surrounded his success in a Red Bull-funded search to find a new rallying star back in 2004.

With a mere four starts at world championship level under his belt, Aigner was thrust into a Skoda Fabia World Rally Car for a 10-event programme in 2006. The opportunity amounted to the tallest of tall orders. He lacked experience and there were not the funds for Baumschlager's team to rectify the Fabia's inherent handling problems and shortage of power. The fact that Aigner claimed sixth place on Rallye Deutschland was testament to his undoubted talent, although it took until the victory in Argentina in '08 for it to be truly recognised.

Much had been expected of him in 2007 when he stepped down to the PWRC to drive a Mitsubishi Lancer Evo IX. Sticking with Baumschlager's team provided useful continuity, but there wasn't the flurry of victories some expected as Aigner took time to adapt to the new discipline.

But Red Bull and Baumschlager stuck by their man and their loyalty was rewarded when he romped home to victory in South America by more than a minute, despite heavy rain turning most of the first day's stages into a quagmire. It wasn't that Aigner was the quickest driver in Argentina – he was fastest on only three of the event's 21 stages – but he was able to avoid the pitfalls that savaged many of his 24 rivals. Well almost.

Amid thick fog on the penultimate stage, Aigner failed to spot a large rock. Despite bashing it with his front-left wheel, bending his Lancer's steering arm in the process, the tyre remained inflated and Aigner was able to hold on for a richly-deserved victory, having led from stage two onwards.

It got better for Aigner when he won again on the next round in Greece, although he was more reliant on two of his chief adversaries slipping up after he hit trouble on the very first stage. He'd barely covered a mile of the run when he spun into a ditch and damaged his car's intercooler. The resulting loss of power meant he haemorrhaged more than 90 seconds to Juho Hänninen, the man he would ultimately go on to fight for the title on the final round in Great Britain.

When Hänninen, who won the opening encounter in Sweden, and former champion Nasser Al-Attiyah were both delayed Aigner was able to build up a healthy advantage. But just like on the previous round in Argentina there was late drama. Aigner started the final day with a lead of more than two minutes, but a broken rear differential cut that gap to less than 30 seconds. However, repairs at mid-morning service enabled him to resume at full speed to secure victory ahead of team-mate Bernardo Sousa, who was promoted to second when it was discovered during post-event technical checks that the front brake discs of Martin Rauam's Lancer hadn't been homologated.

The trip to Turkey two weeks later produced a record-equalling third successive win for Aigner and handed him a 16-point lead at the season's halfway mark, despite an engine overheating problem hampering his outright speed on the gruelling event.

Although Aigner was competing on the next rally in Finland, he hadn't nominated it as one of his scoring rounds, which was somewhat fortuitous after he crashed into a lake on the opening morning. With Aigner not chasing points it was therefore vital that Hänninen took full advantage.

After overcoming the threat posed by guest driver Juha Salo, Hänninen duly delivered his first victory since the championship's last visit to Scandinavia back in February. In doing so he cut Aigner's advantage to eight points heading to New Zealand at the end of August.

There, neither driver enjoyed trouble-free runs. Aigner crashed out after being slowed by a double puncture on the first stage. Hänninen cut the deficit to Aigner to four points, although he was frustrated he didn't make greater inroads into his rival's title lead. It hadn't helped that he'd dropped to 19th on day one when he got stuck in a ditch.

He need not have worried too much though. With two rounds remaining, Aigner had one scoring opportunity left while Hänninen had two. If he won in Japan, Hänninen would head to the Rally GB finale six points clear of Aigner, putting the title pretty much beyond the reach of the Austrian.

With that in mind, and with snow lining part of the route, the 27-year-old adopted a cautious approach in Japan to ensure he didn't slip up. But he was too cautious, reaching the overnight halt on day one in ninth in class. It prompted a heroic fight back, which culminated in victory on the very last stage when the impressive Evgeniy Novikov was slowed by a faulty differential.

Tricky weather again greeted the crews on Rally GB where the stage was set for a title showdown between Aigner and Hänninen. In the event the expected squabble proved to be short-lived when a faulty centre differential slowed Hänninen on the first stage to be run in the icy conditions. To make matters worse for Hänninen, there was only a remote service halt during the day and scant opportunity for effective repairs to be carried out. It meant Juho had to soldier through the day's remaining stages on two-wheel-

drive in the hope that a thorough overhaul of his car when he returned to the main service in Swansea could reignite his faltering title challenge.

But he never made it that far after his Lancer's engine was drowned out in the ford on the second run through the Myherin stage, which resulted in his early retirement. There were no such problems for Aigner, who was occupying the third place he needed to take the title. It was a nervy run over the next two days but he was error-free and inherited second place when the engine in Patrik Sandell's Peugeot 207 broke on the last test.

While Aigner claimed the title – albeit by a slender two-point margin – there was little to separate him from Hänninen during the season. Both drivers were victorious on three occasions although Hänninen was undoubtedly the faster driver, setting the quickest time on 49 stages compared to the 11 Aigner managed. "I definitely improved so much as a driver this year," says Aigner, "but I still can't believe I won. On Rally GB so many of us had problems but I was lucky that I didn't."

Hänninen's recovery drive in Japan alone was worthy of the title. Privately he was shattered to come up short in his title quest after having gone to great lengths to secure the budget to compete in Wales. Publicly he was his usual calm and philosophical self, and even telephoned Aigner while he was heading to the finish to offer his congratulations.

It seems ironic but, at the time of writing, Aigner was facing up to a season of uncertainty. Lacking the sponsorship required to secure a seat in a World Rally Car, he could end up without a drive at all, while Hänninen will form part of Skoda's two-car team in the Intercontinental Rally Challenge. While the drive signals a move away from the WRC, it could help to secure a very bright future for the talented Finn, given the Czech make's investment.

Should Hänninen have joined Skoda with the title in the bag? Apart from his mistake in New Zealand, he drove impeccably throughout the season and would have claimed a fourth win in Greece but for two mechanical failures that held him back.

The fact the title race was dominated by two relatively young drivers is testament to the appeal the Production series has for emerging talents. Martin Prokop and Patrik Flodin, the only other winners last season, are 26 and 24 respectively, while the established old guard – drivers like Nasser Al-Attiyah, Toshi Arai and Fumio Nutahara – failed to offer a sustained threat.

With World Rally Car seats financially out of the question for so many, the PWRC provides an opportunity to gain experience of four-wheel-drive on six events for around £300,000 – roughly the cost of one event in a WR Car. And more and more young drivers are taking up the challenge, with eight of the top 10 in the 2008 standings aged under 30.

Jari Ketomaa was on that list and impressed from the outset in his maiden season in the showroom class. He will be a favourite for the crown this year providing he can put together a programme. He actually led the standings after Argentina in April but lost vital points in Greece (his first outing in the new Subaru Impreza N14 after he upgraded from the older-specification N12) when he retired with a broken fuel pump on the final day of the event.

The 29-year-old fought back on home soil in Finland, taking third despite inflicting extensive damage to his car when he rolled. He rolled again in New Zealand but still managed to land a points finish. Ketomaa rounded out his season with fourth place on Rally GB after battling a down-on-power engine for much of the event.

Patrik Sandell bucked the trend by opting against running a standard Group N production model and entering a Super 2000-specification machine instead. The hugely capable Swede showed well and could have claimed wins in Sweden – he slid into a ditch on the final stage and got stuck for two minutes – and again in Great Britain, where engine failure forced him to retire with the finish in sight. Sandell enjoyed success in Turkey, where he finished second, and in New Zealand, where he repeated the feat albeit in a Mitsubishi Lancer, which he hired locally because he couldn't afford to freight the 207 to the southern hemisphere and back.

Sandell was the only driver to run an S2000 model regularly. Despite a few reliability issues, the 26-year-old insists it was a gamble worth taking. "I wanted to get as much experience driving Super 2000s for when they adopt them for the new [championship]

regulations," he says. "I can see people not wanting to do the same because the car is underdeveloped for the WRC and the rallies are longer than in the Intercontinental Rally Challenge, where they are used a lot. Although we had some problems it was the right decision to take this car and I can see more Super 2000s competing this year."

As well executed as it was, Martin Prokop admitted he had little reason to celebrate his maiden PWRC victory in New Zealand. His campaign had been obliterated by a brace of non-scores mid-season and the 10 points he accrued in the southern hemisphere did little to cheer the Czech, who should have offered more of a threat to the frontrunners.

Martin Rauam would have figured higher up in the final standings had he not been stripped of second place in Greece for a technical infringement. Budget woes kept him out of Rally GB and it's unclear whether he will have the finance to build on the experience he has gained – and the impressive speed he has shown – during the last two seasons.

Veteran Fumio Nutahara made an encouraging start to his campaign with a succession of fourth-place finishes in Argentina and Greece, but his challenge gradually tailed off, although he led in New Zealand before crashing. A switch to the latest-generation Mitsubishi Lancer Evolution X in November on his home event, Rally Japan, made little difference to his fortunes, although the car is still in its early stages of development.

Armindo Aráujo failed to make the progress many had expected from his second stint in the PWRC, although it was never for want of trying.

Bernardo Sousa was another young driver to shine in 2008. The Portuguese's best result came in Greece when he profited from Rauam's exclusion to bag second place. He also scored points on three other events but his true form was masked by the recurrence of an old shoulder injury, which required surgery following Rally New Zealand in August. With insufficient funds to secure a full programme, Patrik Flodin restricted his efforts to three events. He was stripped of second place in Finland for a turbocharger irregularity but rounded out his truncated campaign with victory on Rally GB after a rousing drive.

A solitary third-place finish in Turkey was a rare highlight during what was otherwise yet another frustrating season for Mirco Baldacci. The San Marino driver's pace was never in doubt but time and again he hit trouble, most notably in New Zealand when he left the road while leading on the penultimate afternoon.

Toshi Arai's title defence offered little potency, largely due to the failings of his latest-specification Subaru Impreza. Third place on Rally Japan was a case of too little, too late.

Eighteen-year-old Evgeniy Novikov showed flashes of speed – he was second in New Zealand until his Lancer's gearbox broke – but nothing in the way of points until the penultimate round in Japan, where he would have won had he not hit trouble on the final stage. His eight-event programme in a Citroën C4 WRC in 2009 will represent a steep learning curve.

Eyvind Brynildsen was another promising youngster who had also failed to convert his pace into solid results until the trip to Japan. He led for much of the opening day but lost time on the first superspecial stage when he spun. After broken rear suspension slowed him on day two, he claimed fourth overall.

And what of Nasser Al-Attiyah? The 2006 champion failed to score a solitary point as a spate of accidents and mechanical failures took hold. Although the Qatari was quick when everything gelled, his burgeoning cross-country career diverted some of the focus that made him such a force a few seasons ago.

MITSUBISHI EDGES JAPANESE POWER STRUGGLE

Race&motion

NEVER HAS the rivalry between Mitsubishi and Subaru been more apparent than in the Production Car World Rally Championship.

The Japanese makes have fought for bragging rights in the Group N-based competition for almost two decades. Since 1995 only one other manufacturer – Proton – has captured the crown. Otherwise honours have been shared between Mitsubishi, which has recorded eight title triumphs including Andreas Aigner's success last year, and Subaru, which secured the honours between 2003 and '07.

For both firms winning the PWRC is a massive accomplishment, not just because of the prestige attached to being successful but also because the market for sales of rally cars and spares is huge: Subaru sold 200 vehicles last year alone.

With both manufacturers launching new cars in 2008 the season took on added significance. Unlike Mitsubishi, which didn't debut its Lancer Evolution X until Rally Japan in November, Subaru unleashed its new N14 on the championship-opening Swedish Rally in February. Although the car had claimed a debut victory on the Middle East championship round in Qatar the month before and showed well in the hands of Swiss privateer Olivier Burri on Rally Monte Carlo until he was sidelined by engine woes, it was still untried at PWRC level and still in need of development.

With the bulk of the front-running drivers opting for Mitsubishi's proven Lancer Evo IX, Subaru's hopes in Sweden rested with marque stalwarts Nasser Al-Attiyah and Toshi Arai, and emerging Russian driver Evgeniy Vertunov. Jari Ketomaa was also Subaru mounted, albeit in the older N12, and it wasn't until the third round in Greece that he got his hands on the hatchback version.

While Ketomaa excelled in Sweden, claiming second in class, Arai, who admitted he was struggling to adapt to the new machine's lack of stability, could do no better than sixth after he was delayed by a puncture and a spin. Al-Attiyah, meanwhile, crashed on the final stage, but not before he had been dogged by an intermittent power glitch caused by a suspected faulty electronic control unit.

Fortunes failed to improve in Argentina, venue for the next round of the championship in April.

Arai led until a broken steering arm forced him out, while Al-Attiyah had set a succession of fastest stage times but was ultimately foiled by an overheating engine while running second on the final stage. There was more woe after the event when Evgeniy Novikov announced he was ditching his N14.

As the season wore on, Subaru's fortunes gradually improved. Special dispensation was obtained from motorsport's world governing body, the FIA, to strengthen the otherwise flimsy front suspension – which had been adapted from the N12 and proved too weak – while the ECU glitches that dogged the cars during the early events had also been cured.

The tweaks culminated in podium finishes for Ketomaa in Finland and for Arai in Japan. But the biggest cheer was reserved for the final round in Great Britain when Patrik Flodin claimed the car's maiden PWRC victory.

Above: Patrik Flodin's part-season came good with a win on the final round in Wales.

Below: Fumio Nutahara gave the Mitsubishi Lancer Evo X its Production debut on home soil in Japan.
Photograph: PHOTO4

Junior World Rally Championship

In 2008 Sébastien Ogier showed the sort of promise another young Frenchman displayed en route to winning the inaugural Junior title. And we all know what Mr Loeb has achieved since then...

By Anthony Peacock

WHEN – if it ever does – all the excitement about Sébastien Ogier dies down, spare a thought for the man who nearly beat him to the 2008 Junior World Rally Championship. Aaron Nicolai Burkart came within a couple of places of depriving the 'Second Coming of Loeb' of his title, after a strong showing on the final round in Corsica. Surely that achievement alone earns Burkart a place among the pantheon of world rally greats? Err, no.

Burkart is a very likeable person and a far more talented driver than 95 per cent of the world's population. But the German is realistic enough to know that he is no Loeb (or even Ogier). The fact remains that he finished the Junior world championship year in second place, just eight points behind the man who is touted as the future of the sport, thanks to an impressively consistent run towards the end of the season.

The Junior World Rally Championship was born as a much-needed concept and delivered instant results in the shape of Sébastien Loeb, the inaugural 2001 title holder. Granted, none of his successors ever achieved quite the same meteoric success, but there were still some genuine stars: people like P-G Andersson, Dani Sordo, Kris Meeke (who guested this year in Germany), Guy Wilks and now Sébastien Ogier. Drivers whose raw speed occasionally had the ability

to make spectators gasp and journalists to double-check the timing screens. Think back to what Colin McRae used to be capable of doing in an old Vauxhall Nova and you get the picture.

This year, Ogier was on his own when it came to exploring the edge. The rest were just waiting for him to make a mistake at some point – as all fast, young drivers inevitably do – and sure enough, they were not disappointed. But there was about as much chance of somebody deservedly beating Ogier to the Junior title as there was of somebody beating Loeb to the overall honours.

As is the case with most problems affecting the world at the moment, the root cause of this situation was money, but this time it had nothing to do with someone called Bobby-Jo over-reaching himself to buy a new trailer in Alabama. Instead, the rising costs of the Junior formula have forced teams to look for drivers with ever more prosperous backers – and this often comes down to family or business connections rather than just talent. Had it not been for some judicious help from the French Motorsport Federation (the FFSA) and Citroën Sport this year, Ogier would have been on the sidelines. "If I'm here now, it's down to them," said the young Frenchman. "Without them I would be at home looking for a job." Instead of which,

Above: Three wins for Sébastien Ogier gave him the Junior crown at his first attempt.

Right: Ogier and Aaron Burkart fought for the JWRC title on the final round in Corsica.

Far right: Michal Kosciuszko impressed in the early rounds, but his challenge fell away.

Above right: Martin Prokop could have won the title but for a spate of mechanical glitches.

Top right: Burkart's third season in the JWRC was his best so far, finishing second overall.
Photographs: PHOTO4 unless specified

Race&motion

he has netted himself a neat factory contract: the lesson for national federations worldwide could not be made clearer.

Not only did the drivers behind Ogier have money, but they also had experience. Burkart had been competing in the Junior world championship in a Citroën C2 Super 1600 since 2006 – and he also had a solid supplementary programme of extra European events in the car. Martin Prokop, who was third, first competed in the Juniors back in '05. In fact, the highest-placed rookie after Ogier was the Italian Stefano Albertini, who finished ninth overall.

Before the start of the year though, Ogier was very much an enigma – so it was expected to be another Suzuki versus Citroën battle, as it had been in 2007. That year was a classic, with the title decided in a tense fight between Suzuki team-mates P-G Andersson and Urmo Aava on the final round in Corsica. With both of them graduating to the WRC ranks, Suzuki Sport Europe came up with Jaan Molder and Michal Kosciuszko to drive the 'factory' Swifts. Molder, although a previous rally winner in the JWRC, was unlikely to spring any surprises but Kosciuszko had shown flashes of brilliance with various ageing Suzukis and Renault Clios in the past.

In the red corner there was Ogier – about whom the jury was out – and the known quantities of Burkart and Prokop. Of the two Prokop was the more interesting prospect. Having proved himself to be the most improved driver of the year in 2007, the question was whether or not he could continue to climb the learning curve to the next level.

Other names to watch included Shaun Gallagher, stepping up to a Citroën C2 S1600 having won the Junior rookie title in 2007, and former JWRC champion Patrik Sandell, at the wheel of a Renault Clio R3. Driving a similar car was the Italian Alessandro Bettega: the son of the late great Attilio.

Then Ogier came along and blew his opposition away at the first round in Mexico. Not only that but he scored overall points by finishing eighth; the first time a Junior driver has ever been on the general leaderboard. More worrying for the Suzuki drivers, separated by just a handful of seconds in second and third, was the fact that Ogier had beaten them by a minute and half. As for Burkart in fourth, he was more than five minutes down

SUZUKI'S LATEST JUNIOR BATTLE IS ITS TOUGHEST

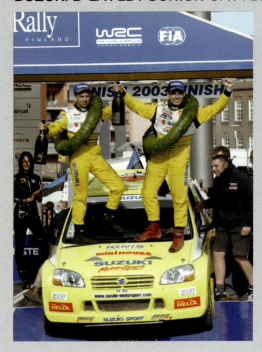

SUZUKI'S JUNIOR WRC adventure started back in 2002 on the Monte Carlo Rally, and while it is by no means necessarily over, the withdrawal of the factory WRC team means that it will now just run on a strictly commercial basis via Suzuki Sport Europe in Hungary.

It's easy to forget that Suzuki is one of the most successful manufacturers in the Junior world championship, and the only one to have claimed the title twice with the same driver: P-G Andersson. The first podium came on Rallye Deutschland thanks to Niki Schelle with the original Ignis in 2002, while Daniel Carlsson claimed the first JWRC win for Suzuki on Rally Finland in '03. The following year heralded the introduction of the four-door Ignis; a car that had been on the receiving end of a sound beating with the ugly stick but actually won its first event, the 2004 Acropolis, with Guy Wilks. As one team member put it at the time: "If we don't win rallies with this car, at least we can use it to deliver pizzas in the evening."

Win rallies it did though. After the success of Wilks in Greece, Andersson took his first win by leading home a Suzuki one-two-three on the 2004 Rally of Turkey. By the end of the year the JWRC title was his, and Suzuki then decided to gain experience by entering all of the '05 events, with mixed fortunes. The new Swift – a car that the average person might actually find aesthetically appealing – made its debut in Finland that year, and took its first win in Britain. With Andersson missing out on the title in 2006 thanks to a stewards' exclusion in Turkey, he finally got revenge in '07 after a season-long battle with Aava.

Now it looks like the glory days might be over for one of the Junior world championship's staunchest supporters. Following Andersson's 2007 title he was promoted to the main SX4 WRC squad, prompting Suzuki's inimitable former team principal Nobuhiro 'Monster' Tajima to say: "This proves how much the Junior world championship works for Suzuki. We have a young driver like P-G, who we have taken from the beginning, and now he has grown up in the Suzuki family to drive the World Rally Car."

Regrettably for P-G, the Suzuki family – along with 'Monster' himself – is no longer a nuclear one. While Suzuki has probably done enough to make P-G a valued commodity on the current driver market, not every driver the team has unearthed made it to stardom. Chief of those was home-grown hero Kazuhiko Niwa, an avowed exponent of the ancient Japanese art of bending competition car metal. In fact a veritable plethora of drivers have passed through Suzuki's doors over the years, including blasts from the past such as Daniel Carlsson, Salvador Canellas and Mirco Baldacci, all of whom were lured by the prospect of an eventual World Rally Car drive...

Above: Suzuki's JWRC team launched several driver's careers including Swede Daniel Carlsson, who became a factory Peugeot pilot two years later.

Below: P-G Andersson secured a second Junior title in 2007 before graduating to the firm's new WRC team in '08
Photographs: PHOTO4

the road: the time to cook and eat a burrito.

It was clear that a rapid reassessment of the situation would be required. Ogier won round two in Jordan by another whopping five minutes to cement a growing reputation, but his rivals were quick to point out that the opening pair of long-haul events had not attracted a full field of Junior entrants. The real test would be found on the rocky roads of Sardinia. And there, for the first time, the wunderkind was found wanting.

While trying to pass another car on stage four, he picked up a puncture and went off the road. He recovered to finish fifth, but it gave Kosciuszko – who claimed his debut Junior win in Sardinia – a glimmer of hope heading into Rally Finland, which Ogier was not officially contesting. That event was eventually won by Prokop, but the young Czech's title chances had already been terminally compromised by a high-speed roll in Mexico and an engine failure in Sardinia. The bad luck continued with a broken alternator in Germany, and not even two wins on the final two rounds – in Spain and France – could give him any chance of title success. He nonetheless finished third at the final reckoning: an impressive achievement given that he was trailing Ogier by 22 points midway through the year. With a bit more luck on his side, the Czech would have been a convincing title challenger to the Frenchman – and he may well have edged it.

Kosciuszko's season went the opposite way. After his third place in Finland, a throttle cable snapped in Spain, losing him 13 minutes and all hope of staying in the title race. On the final round in Corsica, he went off. By then all Ogier had to do was creep round and keep it on the island – quite literally – while making sure that Burkart did not climb too high up the order.

The young Frenchman described Corsica as "the worst three days of my life", having learnt the hard way to pay for his mistakes. Just a week earlier, on the Catalunya Rally, he had a high-speed spin while leading, which damaged his C2's radiator to the extent that it would not reach service back in the Port Aventura theme park. Game over – but not for Burkart, whose fine second place behind Ogier in Germany, plus third in Spain, had kept him in the hunt for the title at the final round.

As always in the Junior World Rally Championship consistency was key, a butt of constant criticism from those who do not benefit from it. Burkart and Gallagher (who finished fourth at the end of the year after a solid run) did; many others did not.

In particular, one of the stars of the season – who largely passed unnoticed – was Bettega. He only posted three results but all of them were on the podium, in Italy, Germany and Spain. He was challenging for another podium in Corsica when he went off the road on the final loop of stages, due to a problem with a wheel. The Italian was driving a Renault Clio R3, which he generally used to better effect than the 2006 Junior world champion Sandell – although the Swede finished two more rallies than Bettega, with a best result of second in Finland. Having ended up sixth overall in the standings, Bettega was the best finisher in the heavier R3 class – which is still not quite the equivalent in performance of a Super 1600, despite the best intentions of the FIA.

Nonetheless, there's little doubt that Super 1600 is a dying breed. Just Citroën and Suzuki still make the top category car in the Junior World Rally Championship, and there will now be doubts over the commitment of the latter. With the popularity of R3 on the increase – thanks to exciting new cars from the likes of Honda – and an increased emphasis on genuinely junior machinery, such as the affordable Citroën C2-R2 MAX, the JWRC is steadily getting back to what it should be: the ultimate cradle of rallying talent.